STORM AND CONQUEST

The Clash of Empires in the Eastern Seas, 1809

STEPHEN TAYLOR

W. W. Norton & Company
New York London

For information about permission to reproduce selections from this book,
write to Permissions, W. W. Norton & Company, Inc., 500 Fifth Avenue,
New York, NY 10110   ·

For information about special discounts for bulk purchases, please contact
W. W. Norton Special Sales at specialsales@wwnorton.com or 800-233-4830

Manufacturing by Courier Westford
Production manager: Anna Oler

Library of Congress Cataloging-in-Publication Data

Taylor, Stephen, 1948–
Storm and conquest : the clash of empires in the eastern seas, 1809 /
Stephen Taylor.—1st American ed.
p. cm.
Includes bibliographical references and index.
ISBN 978-0-393-06047-8 (hardcover)
1. Napoleonic Wars, 1800–1815—Naval operations. 2. Indian Ocean Region—
History, Naval—19th century. 3. Mauritius—History—19th century. 4. Réunion—
History—19th century. I. Title.
DC202.3.T39 2008
940.2'745091824—dc22   2007037327

W. W. Norton & Company, Inc.
500 Fifth Avenue, New York, N.Y. 10110
www.wwnorton.com

W. W. Norton & Company Ltd.
Castle House, 75/76 Wells Street, London W1T 3QT

1 2 3 4 5 6 7 8 9 0

To Wil, my son and shipmate

Contents

CONTENTS

Illustrations

Text Illustrations

Plate Illustrations

The author and publishers would like to thank the following institutions and individuals for their permission to reproduce illustrations:

Text illustrations: Duncan Stewart, pp 3, 191, 237; Royal Albert Museum, Exeter, p5; National Maritime Museum, Greenwich, pp 49, 79, 277, 315; Mary Evans Picture Library, p263; Private collections, pp 19, 35, 67, 91, 105, 125, 141, 161, 175, 193, 209, 221, 249, 301

Plate section: Royal Albert Memorial Museum, Exeter, 1; National Maritime Museum, Greenwich, 2, 4, 5, 9, 10, 11, 12, 13, 14; Sir Abe Bailey Bequest, Iziko South African National Gallery, Cape Town, 3; The Lord Middleton, 6; Bibliothèque centrale du Département Marine à Vincennes, 7; Cecil Higgins Art Gallery, Bedford, 8

Preface

Over the first weeks of 1808, a grand and powerful fleet mustered in the south of England. For weeks Portsmouth harbour resounded by day with the hammering of carpenters, the cries of men from ships at anchor, and echoed by night with song and the stamp of hornpipes from the seamen's taverns. To all outward appearances, the ships preparing to set sail for the Indian Ocean that season might have been men-of-war, for each was pierced for at least a dozen cannon and some of the larger vessels resembled the new frigates moored at the nearby Royal Navy station of Spithead. In fact, they were East Indiamen, vessels of the self-styled 'Grandest Company of Merchants in the World'; but, although their purpose was trade, the underlying military nature of the voyage could not have been clearer.

General Arthur Wellesley was soon to open up a front in Portugal against Bonaparte's seemingly unstoppable march across Europe, and saltpetre, the principal ingredient of gunpowder, had become a strategic resource of the utmost importance. The East India Company fleet, bound for the Coromandel Coast, was contracted to supply the Government with 6,000 tons of Bengali saltpetre, the purest known form of the substance, and the Indiamen were to sail with a Navy escort. This was no idle precaution: while Nelson's victory at Trafalgar had left England supreme in home waters, the Indian Ocean had never been more perilous. On top of the perennial hazard of storms in the so-called 'hurricane season', French frigates and privateers had removed from the Mediterranean in order to prey on English shipping in the Bay of Bengal, and had done so with spectacular success. Ile de France, or Mauritius, a speck of an island in the southern latitudes of that immense ocean, was the minuscule bastion from which these raiders ventured forth; and to such effect that a dozen English merchant ships had been taken in just three months.

On the eve of 3 March, the fleet was ready. Captain Henry Sturrock of the *Preston* called at The George to tell his most distinguished passenger, Lady Barlow, wife of the Governor of Madras, that the wind had come about and she and her daughters might board in the morning. Well before dawn, shrouded figures gathered at the Sally Port before crunching across shingle to rowing boats. At eight o'clock the first of the Indiamen weighed anchor.

Even as the land slipped away, so did the first life. John Joice, one of a hundred men of His Majesty's 69th Regiment of Foot, bound for Madras, died before sunset among his comrades on the *Canton*. At daylight the next day his body was dropped over the side. There was no pause then, or a few days later when Eliza Gamble died on the *Hugh Inglis*; Eliza was aged four, the daughter of Sergeant William Gamble of the 17th Light Dragoons. But as one young life ended, another began. On the *Preston* it was recorded: 'Mrs Brooke, passenger for Madras, was safely delivered of a daughter.'

Three days out they hit bad weather. The *Canton*'s log for 8 March reads

> An amazing high sea running which causes the ship to labour much and take in a great deal of water. Find great difficulty in steering. At 11pm in reefing the foretopsail, James Wilton, ordinary seaman, fell from the yard upon deck and fractured his skull, which caused his death at 4am.

As rapidly as it had come the gale departed and now, with a steady following breeze, the Indiamen rounded Lizard Point, the southernmost tip of mainland Britain, passing out into the Atlantic with the furl and snap of canvas overhead, a bawling in the rigging and the buoyant cheer of men assured that they were the boldest, finest seafarers in the world.

Over the coming months, three more fleets of Indiamen would follow in their wake. By the time an unusually balmy spring had turned to summer, a total of twenty-eight ships had set out for India to collect saltpetre for the Peninsular War. It was to be more than a year before the first came in sight of England again and the ships that anchored in the Downs the following summer were a battered remnant, the sailors a reduced and chastened band. Even the oldest hands confessed that they had never seen anything like it.

Quite what had occurred that season in the Indian Ocean took the

Company months to piece together, and even then many mysteries remained. In plain terms, however, the India House had suffered the worst calamity in its shipping history. No fewer than fifteen ships had come to grief: seven simply disappeared, never to be seen again; two went aground and were lost; and six were captured by French frigates – one of them twice. Thousands of tons of saltpetre for the war were at the bottom of the sea. In human terms, more than 1,000 people were dead, many of them 'personages'.

The Directors of Leadenhall Street, whose usual demeanour was that of Elizabethan pirates, paled. These disasters were linked with that ocean speck, a place so insignificant in size that it was not represented on maps other than as a dot at Lat 20° 15'S, Long 57° 15'E – a volcanic creation that jutted out of the sea like a row of green fangs. Then they recalled William Pitt's grimly prophetic words twenty years earlier: 'As long as the French hold the Ile de France, the British will never be masters of India.' And they resolved on action.

The story of that year is partly told in a remarkable collection of books: a series of vast slab-like volumes in gold-lettered maroon board, each the size of a medieval Bible, which cover hundreds of feet of shelf space below the British Library. These are the Indiamen captains' logbooks, flaking with age, the ink fading, each bearing the hand of the keeper, each strangely opaque and yet revelatory. Each is a diary, set down 200 years ago, of life on a floating island 140 feet in length, on which around 250 souls were confined for half a year. Sometimes they are illegible. Often they make dull reading: endless entries of weather conditions, wind direction, ship routine. Then they will spring to life with incident – with deaths, beatings, storms, and battles. The reader finds himself scanning pages for the tell-tale signs, dense passages of script, often scrawled hastily and in crisis, from which drama at sea emerges in all its terrifying unpredictability.

The East Indiamen were unique. They were merchant ships, they were fighting ships, and they were troopships. Yet they were also the first ships systematically to move civilian passengers around the globe – a forerunner, in a sense, of the great P&O liners of a more cosseted age of travel. Every Company servant in India had this one experience in common, of a great voyage traversing two of the world's oceans. I became intrigued by the Indiaman as a social cocoon, with life on what one writer (of fiction) called 'a creaking, leaking incompetent concoction of oak and pitch and nails and faith', and by images of the great cabin (which was actually quite small) where the rich and privileged, the nabobs, dandies, and military officers (an unhappy species at sea) along with their ladies and children, loved, hated, gamed, drank, feuded, celebrated, sometimes died but usually endured a confinement that lasted anything from four to eight months and which would today be found insupportable.

A second great collection, the logbooks and dispatches of the Admiralty, relate the upshot of the disasters, the Mauritius campaign. This was one of the darker chapters in the Navy's history and, unsurprisingly, it rarely features in the chronicles of that glowing age, although Patrick O'Brian did exploit its dramatic potential in one of the stories of the fictional Aubrey/Maturin series. Unvarnished, it is a tale of cruelty, mutiny and defeat of a kind that Trafalgar had appeared to make unthinkable.

Among the navy commanders who bestrode the quarterdeck during that time, two in particular stand out: Sir Edward Pellew was a legendary figure, the most spectacularly successful frigate captain of the age, now Commander-in-Chief of the East Indies squadron; and the brutal, tormented Robert Corbet who created a legend of a different kind, as the most hated captain of his day.

Indiamen and navy ships – both were dependent on the crucial figure in all English maritime endeavour, the men who were plucked, frequently against their will, from the lowest rung of early nineteenth-century society, and sentenced to a form of servitude in which they were flogged and abused, and yet who came to occupy a heroic place in popular culture and took the fiercest pride in themselves and their duty.

The hands who sailed in the Indiamen fleets of 1808 were, in a sense, explorers – men of the shires who took leave of families and communities, bound for what they knew by reputation to be places of fabulous strangeness, the Coromandel Coast, the Spice Islands, Cathay. There was no certainty of return but they would have expected that, should they be spared, they would come back with yarns of curious folk and weird creatures. In the event, those who did return, to make their way to the taverns, offering thanks for their survival and raising a tankard to the shipmates they would never see again, had another story to tell. Of storms, mutinies and battles, and all the other dramas of war in the Eastern Seas.

Dramatis Personae

In India

Rear-Admiral Sir Edward Pellew: commander of the East Indies squadron, aged fifty-one. One of the outstanding figures of naval history, a brilliant frigate captain, fighting commander and all-round man of action, but frustrated in his efforts to bring the French to battle in the Indian Ocean.

Captain Pownoll Bastard Pellew: his elder son, aged twenty-one, a dreamy, romantic fellow and a severe disappointment to his father.

Captain Fleetwood Pellew: the younger of Pellew's boys, now nineteen, dashing, handsome and showing promise of following in his father's footsteps.

Sir George Barlow: aged forty-six. Newly arrived and unpopular Governor of Madras. He had briefly been Governor-General in Calcutta, the most powerful official in India, but his background was thought too lowly for so exalted a post and he was replaced by Lord Minto.

Lady Barlow: the Governor's vivacious wife, now aged thirty-seven. Like her husband, of humble origins, the daughter of a soldier, she had created a vibrant social circle in Calcutta. She was rejoining her husband in Madras after a year in England.

Eliza Barlow: aged nineteen and the eldest of the Barlows' children (of whom there were thirteen at this stage) she was accompanying her mother to India in the hope of making a good marriage.

Captain Pratt Barlow: a distant relative of the Governor and his aide-de-camp. Aged twenty-three, he had accompanied Lady Barlow to England.

Lieutenant-General Hay Macdowall: hard-living and aristocratic Commander-in-Chief of the Madras Army, and a bitter foe of the Governor. In his early fifties, he was a heavy drinking and intemperate man.

Sir Henry Gwillim: Judge of the Madras Supreme Court. Another turbulent figure – a radical egalitarian who sympathised with native interests and had fallen foul of the Madras authorities.

Mary Symonds: his sister-in-law, aged about thirty. A strong-minded and spirited woman, she had remained single, but not for lack of suitors.

Lord Minto: recently arrived in Calcutta as Governor-General, aged fifty-seven, born into a line of Scottish aristocrats. Bold, ambitious and able.

William Hope: the tough old 'nabob' of Madras, formerly a private in the East India Company's Army who had gone into trade and made an immense fortune. Had four children by his Indian wife, Kezia.

Emilia Scott: wife of William Scott, a rising star in the Company. She was renowned for having survived a famous wreck, of the East Indiaman *Earl of Abergavenny* in 1805.

At the Cape

Rear-Admiral Albemarle Bertie: Commander of the Cape squadron, aged fifty-three, he had risen through no act of any particular distinction. Cantankerous yet loyal to his captains

Captain Robert Corbet: shadowy and notoriously brutal commander of the frigate *Nereide*. Served under Nelson and won his praise but had a record of cruelty long before his arrival at the Cape. His undoubted seafaring abilities had saved him from being disciplined thus far.

Captain Josias Rowley: Commodore, or senior captain, at the Cape, aged forty-three. One of the unsung heroes of navy history, humane, cool-headed and brilliant in an unfashionably self-effacing way, he was on the verge of the defining campaign of his life.

Captain Nesbit Willoughby: an aristocratic firebrand – disputatious, ferociously combative and seemingly indestructible. Aged thirty-one, had survived twice being convicted by courts martial for insolence towards senior officers and now commanded the sloop *Otter*.

Lord Caledon: young and inexperienced, he had been appointed Governor of Britain's newest colony while not yet thirty.

At Ile de France

Charles Decaen: Governor of French territories in the East, one of Bonaparte's youngest generals and an instinctive authoritarian. Now aged thirty-nine, he dreamt of reclaiming France's lost colonies in the East, but had been repeatedly let down by the Emperor.

Captain Matthew Flinders: a Royal Navy officer held captive by Decaen since 1803. He made the first circumnavigation of Terra Australis where he met Commodore Hamelin (below) and was sailing home when he called at Ile de France and, suspected of spying, was taken prisoner.

Thomas Pitot: a Port Louis trader and close friend of Flinders, whom he joined in musical evenings and accompanied on walks among the island's natural beauties.

Captain Jacques Felix Hamelin: Commodore of a formidable new frigate squadron in the Indian Ocean, aged forty. He had engaged in a number of actions in European waters, but his most signal achievement so far had been a voyage of exploration to the South Seas.

Captain Pierre Bouvet: colourful corsair and frigate captain. Born on Bourbon of a seafaring family and grew up in the era of the great Indian Ocean corsair, Robert Surcouf. Repeatedly captured but escaped. An outstanding fighting captain.

Indiaman captains

John Ramsden of the *Phoenix*: one of the once-notable breed of Indiamen captains who left no mark on history, but who represented the essence of Britain's seafaring past, an able man in a crisis, and a reassuring presence among his passengers.

Henry Sturrock of the *Preston*: well-connected among the Company elite, he had made a specialisation of transporting rich and important civilians around the world in the closest that the quarters of an early nineteenth-century Indiaman could come to luxury.

John Dale of the *Streatham*: famed for an exploit when, as a young third officer, he single-handedly saved more than a hundred survivors of the *Winterton* wreck off Madagascar in 1792. Now aged thirty-nine, he was one of the Company's most respected captains.

Henry Meriton of the *Ceylon*: another renowned officer – one of the few survivors of the loss of the *Halsewell* and the only Indiaman captain to have taken a French man-of-war.

John Stewart of the *Windham*: a tough, pugnacious Scot, aged thirty-four. A typical Indiaman captain in that he had been at sea for the greater part of his life. He was commanding his ship on their third voyage to India.

Navy ships, British

Culloden: a 74-gun ship of the line and one of the famous ships of Nelson's Navy, the scene of a mutiny in 1794 and a veteran of the Battle of the Nile. Since 1804 she had been the flagship of Sir Edward Pellew in India.

Victor: an 18-gun sloop in Pellew's squadron. Formerly the *Revenant*, captured from the French, she had been purpose-built for the legendary corsair, Robert Surcouf, and was one of the fastest ships in the Eastern Seas.

Raisonnable: a 64, the first ship in which Nelson served, aged twelve. She was now worn out and attached to the Cape squadron where she was the flagship of Commodore Josias Rowley. He would move from her into the *Boadicea*, a 38-gun frigate.

Nereide: the 36-gun frigate of Robert Corbet, captured from the French in 1797. Quite possibly one of the unhappiest ships in navy history.

Iphigenia: a new 38-gun frigate at the Cape, commissioned at Chatham in 1808 and commanded by Henry Lambert, an officer who had served under Pellew in India.

Sirius: another 38, with recent service in the Mediterranean, she had been given in 1808 to Captain Samuel Pym and sent to the Cape.

Navy ships, French

Venus: of 44 guns, one of the heaviest and most powerful new French frigates afloat. The flagship of Commodore Jacques Hamelin, she had the capacity to wreak havoc among the East India Company's ships.

Minerve: an exceptionally large but elderly frigate of 52 guns, captured from the Portuguese; nearing the end of her useful life, she nevertheless added significantly to the squadron at Ile de France.

Bellone: like the Venus, a 44 mounting 18-pounder guns, compared with the usual 12-pounders of British frigates. Commanded by Victor Duperré.

PART I: STORM

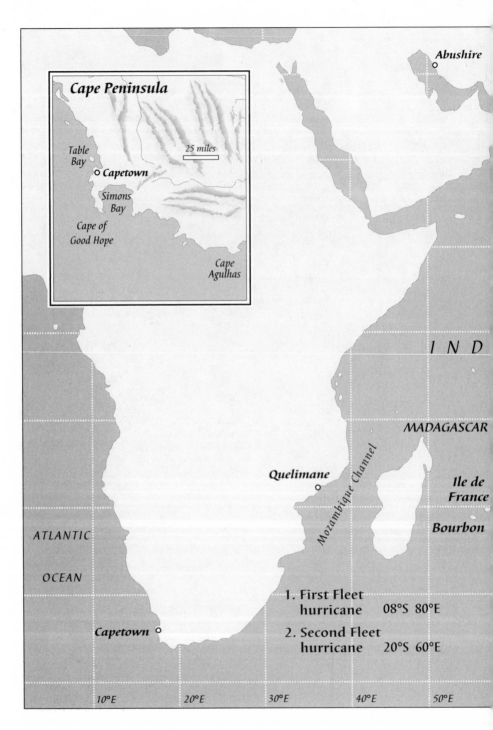

The Indian Ocean in 1809

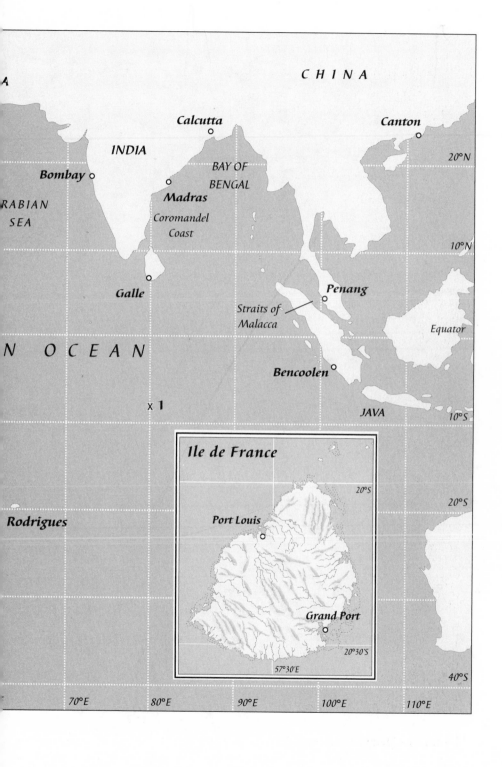

CHINA

INDIA

Calcutta

Canton

20°N

Bombay

BAY OF
BENGAL

Madras

Coromandel
Coast

ARABIAN
SEA

10°N

Galle

Penang

Straits of
Malacca

Equator

N OCEAN

x 1

Bencoolen

JAVA

10°S

Ile de France

20°S

20°S

Rodrigues

Port Louis

Grand Port

20°30'S

57°30'E

40°S

70°E   80°E   90°E   100°E   110°E

1

Admiral Pellew's strategy

Madras, 3–26 August 1808

The first sail tips were sighted across an empty sea just before noon. A lookout's call of raucous excitement brought men racing to the battlements of Fort St George. Slowly, from a fiercely shimmering distance, the shapes came into focus until there could be no mistaking their identity: the season's first Indiaman fleet and their navy escort were approaching Madras. This news was quickly taken to Sir George Barlow and, despite the Governor's reputation for icy reserve, the return to India of his wife after an absence of almost two years brought him to the ramparts as well. With a thunder of saluting cannons from sea and shore, the ships came to anchor a few hundred yards off where they swayed on that lustrous sea, a thicket of bristling masts – ten Indiamen in all, bearing passengers and cargo for the East India Company's southern presidency.

On board the *Preston*, Lady Barlow and her two daughters Eliza and Charlotte sat down to dinner in the great cabin for the last time that afternoon with heartfelt relief. Despite the comparative splendour of their apartment in the roundhouse, Lady Barlow and her girls had found five months quite sufficient for the company of Arthur Brooke, a minor official, his family, and the Misses Dodson.[1] A little after half-past four they came on deck where, with a last flourish of gallantry, Captain Henry Sturrock saw the ladies into the ship's chair before they were lifted clear and lowered into a *masoolah*, the buoyant palm-tree craft of the local boatmen, for the fraught dash through the surf for which Madras was notorious. They came ashore breathless, more than a little wet and, after so many weeks at sea, decidedly dizzy.

That same day – 3 August 1808 – the *Madras Courier* brought out an extraordinary edition to announce the arrival of the Indiamen fleet with

7

the Governor's wife. Trumpeting the first dispatches to be received from Europe in months, the paper was also delighted to report that, contrary to reports of his demise, His Majesty, George III, was in good health.

For weeks the temperature had held at around 40°C, reducing Madras to the state of torpid semi-consciousness that always preceded the monsoon. Now residents emerged from behind shutters and the fort came alive. Indiamen brought the thrill of letters from home as well as the latest news of political and military affairs, not to mention the so-called 'fishing fleet', a collection of unattached young women in search of rich husbands.

Another infusion of new blood had been anticipated no less keenly by a tall figure who observed the Indiamen that day from the rear gallery window of HMS *Culloden*. He was Rear-Admiral Sir Edward Pellew, commander of the East Indies Squadron. She was his flagship, a 74-gun ship of the line, and the floating headquarters of naval operations against Bonaparte in the Indian Ocean.* She had a noble record, was a veteran of Nelson's triumphant campaigns, including the Battle of the Nile, and it was no fault of Pellew's that she had seen scant action since he brought her out at the head of the squadron in 1804.

As the Indiamen came to anchor, a lieutenant put off from *Culloden* in a cutter. He went from ship to ship, ordering the hands to be turned out, inspecting them, the lines of men in their straw hats, loose duck trousers and light blouses, marking the strong in limb and noting those whose skin wore a pallor despite weeks of sun in the yardarms, pausing to ask a man's rank and taking a particular interest in any whose experience had raised them to the status of perhaps gunner's mate or foretopman. It was then that he took his pick of them.

There was no question of dissent; the men had time only to go below to bundle up a few possessions and say farewell to their messmates before being rowed across to *Culloden*. Having signed on for an Indiaman voyage, a round trip of about a year, those pressed into the Navy that day would now stay in the Indies as long as the squadron remained, or their health lasted, or – more likely than either – death intervened. In all, no fewer than 137 men were taken from the ten Indiamen, roughly a tenth of their crews, all prime hands.[2]

---

* A ship of the line was one of between 64 and 100 guns, powerful enough to be in a line of battle during major fleet actions. In general, most Navy ships in the East Indies at the time were frigates of 36 or 38 guns.

For the Indiamen's captains there could be no open opposition either. Although they fumed – they were, after all, superior in rank to the lieutenant and finely got up in their gold-braided blue coats, cocked hats, white breeches and silk stockings – an icy reserve towards *Culloden*'s officer was as much as the situation would bear. Later in their cabins, however, the captains of the *Lord Nelson* and the *Calcutta* wrote letters of protest to Pellew, stating that they had been left so short-handed they could not proceed safely. On the strength of their plea, twenty-four men were returned.[3]

A few days later, Pellew could not but have noted the departure for Bengal of four Indiamen and how clumsily they manoeuvred, now that their best hands had stowed their hammocks on *Culloden*. He took no pleasure in the fact. He was a seaman first and last, reluctant to interfere in the smooth running of any ship. At the same time he was a true son of the Navy, ruthless in pursuing the needs of the Service, and with resources strained as never before by French resurgence in the Eastern Seas, Pellew had opened what amounted to a campaign against the Company for the bodies of British sailors.

Sir Edward Pellew, Rear-Admiral of the White, was a Navy man in the grand tradition, a Cornish seaman's son who followed his father to sea as a boy of thirteen, scaled the ratlines of promotion through his fighting qualities and ability rather than patronage, and won renown as the most dashing frigate commander of his day. He did not, by his own claim, look the heroic type, being 'pock Marked, Ugly, Uninteresting and Un-educated'.[4] (There was a strong element of hyperbole in this; although the scars of childhood smallpox had blemished his handsome features, Pellew was tall with an air of natural command and splendidly set up, and his letters must be as eloquent as any other great seaman's.) He also stood out for exceptional courage, or rather utter disdain for danger, in a service in which mere bravery was a prerequisite. His seamanship was outstanding and – that rare and most indefinable quality in a warrior – he was lucky.*

* There are echoes here of Patrick O'Brian's hero 'Lucky' Jack Aubrey, but Pellew is perhaps best remembered today as a character in another navy fiction series, C.S. Forester's Hornblower stories.

A year older than Nelson, his reputation as a fighting sea officer actually glowed the more brightly until the genius of his illustrious contemporary revealed itself in fleet command. Pellew won his laurels as captain of the *Nymphe*, a 36-gun frigate, in a bloody engagement off Portland that saw the capture of the superior *Le Cléopatre*. This was the first sea battle against revolutionary France in 1793 and it turned Pellew overnight into a naval hero, the subject of popular ballads and a knight of the realm. But it was only the beginning. Four years later he fought an action in *Indefatigable* against a French 74 that entered navy legend: in the only instance of a frigate destroying an enemy ship of the line, he drove the *Droits de l'Homme* ashore in an all-night battle near Brest.

For a big man his agility was astonishing and even aged forty he could beat any of his hands in a race to the topmast. On his way to lunch in Plymouth on a winter's day in 1796, Pellew heard that the *Dutton* Indiaman had gone aground near by with 500 troops, women and children. He raced to the scene, pulled himself out to the ship on a rope, and, finding panic, took charge by threatening to run through any man who did not obey him. As boats came alongside, he supervised the evacuation of women and children, then the troops. All but fifteen lives were saved, and Pellew was cheered to the skies on coming ashore. This single-handed rescue caused another sensation and earned him a baronetcy.

Among his most attractive qualities was a love of chivalry. A French officer recorded how, on receiving a captain's sword in surrender, Pellew drew his own with the words, 'Pray take this and keep it as a souvenir of the profound admiration with which your bravery has inspired me', before offering his wounded foe an arm and conducting him to a cabin beside his own. More than once he provided for the dependants of those he had defeated.

If he was the beau ideal of the navy commander, he also had a human side that included a strong streak of cupidity. He never forgot his humble origins and never missed an opportunity to enhance his fortune, pursuing prize money almost as avidly as he did glory. Nor was he politically innocent. He obtained a seat in Parliament and used his preferment to secure promotion for, as he wrote to a friend, 'I am older than I was and can't get to the Mast Head as well as I used. I want to be an Admiral.'[5] Duly promoted, he was rewarded with the Indies command. That was in 1804, the year before Trafalgar, when he turned forty-seven.

Four years on, he might have reflected sardonically on the transience of glory. While Nelson had won immortality in death, Pellew had been left to fume in his tropical exile – constrained from prosecuting war at sea and undermined by political enemies at home. True, his piratical eye had brought him a phenomenal amount of prize money. India had made his fortune, to the tune of some £80,000 (about £5 million today). However, Pellew was above all a fighter who had accepted his command 'in the hope of giving a blow to the inveterate and restless Enemies of Mankind'.[6] He had succeeded insofar as destroying a small Dutch squadron in Java. But as for the most inveterate of those foes, he had failed to strike at the French. Worse, they had tarnished the reputation of which he was properly proud.

The trouble was the so-called 'Gibraltar of the East', the twin islands of Ile de France and Bourbon, or, as they are now known, Mauritius and Réunion.

It is hard today, looking at a map of the Indian Ocean and locating those tiny specks – they lie due east of the vastness of Madagascar like pebbles in the shadow of a mountain – to imagine that at the time they appeared to threaten the East India Company's control of India, and consequently Britain's survival as a great power. Quite simply, the benefits of Trafalgar had not been felt in the Eastern Seas. 'Here alone in the whole world', the naval historian N.A.M. Rodger has written, 'there were still French warships at sea in a good state of efficiency.'[7] Here alone the French retained a capacity to strike at Britain's commercial lifeline, and in the past year they had done so from Ile de France with spectacular success – under Pellew's nose.

Lying off Fort St George – in Madras roads, as the anchorage was known – the East Indies squadron presented a formidable aspect. It comprised four 74s, *Culloden*, *Albion*, *Powerful* and *Russel*, ten frigates, among them *Cornwallis*, *Terpsichore*, *Phaeton*, *Drake*, *Psyche*, *Pitt* and *Fox*, and the 18-gun sloops *Rattlesnake* and *Dasher*. In reality, they were never in one place, being generally dispersed in escorting merchant fleets. Most were elderly and in need of repairs. And even when they were healthy, their crews most certainly were not. To the usual high attrition rate of life at sea – from action, desertion and accident – had to be added the particular circumstance of service in India, where the virulence of a fever could send a hearty man to his grave in forty-eight hours.

In 1805, Pellew had pressed 818 hands out of the total 6,155 crew from arriving Indiamen. The following year the figure was 694 out of 4,215.[8] After furious protests from the East India Company to the Admiralty, an agreement was reached that pressing would be limited 'so that only such men may be taken out as will not distress the [Company's] ships'.[9] Pellew took note of this stricture when he could but ultimately here was a circle that could not be squared. However many Indiamen hands were pressed, they did not make up the numbers dying on navy ships or who had to be sent home as invalids.

On top of his manning problems, Pellew had a devilishly elusive foe. Bonaparte now lacked the resources for fleet actions; instead, Ile de France and Bourbon provided havens for navy captains and privateers who had no intention of giving battle but proved infuriatingly adept at picking off isolated merchantmen. Captain Jacques Epron's 44-gun frigate *Piemontaise* had been especially troublesome until, five months earlier, she was intercepted by the *San Fiorenzo*, an English 36, and fought to a standstill in an epic three-day action that left Captain George Hardinge among sixty-two dead and reduced both ships to splintered hulks.

An even greater threat – more effective than any frigate captain – was posed by one of the great corsairs. Robert Surcouf had made his name and fortune years before Pellew's arrival in the East, capturing the 1,200-ton Indiaman *Kent* in 1800 and retiring to St Malo. At the Emperor's urging, he returned to Ile de France in 1807 in *Revenant*, an 18-gun sloop built to Surcouf's design, her hull completely sheathed in copper, one of the fastest ships afloat. Over the past year, *Revenant* had become the bane of shipping in the Bay of Bengal, where she had taken more than thirty prizes. In one two-month spell alone, nineteen British vessels were captured by *Revenant* and two French frigates.

The losses produced squeals of outrage from the merchants of Calcutta who drafted a memorial to the Admiralty, pointing out that 'the two small islands of Mauritias [sic] and Bourbon' were the source of their 'unprecedented suffering', and laying responsibility directly at Pellew's door. Surcouf's activity had been conducted 'within one hundred leagues of Madras roads, the principal Station of His Majesty's ships, where at the same time the Flag of a British Rear-Admiral [was] displayed.'[10]

There was much more – pages of indignation: Pellew had launched an expedition against the Dutch 'a prostrate foe . . . when our trade was menaced on all sides with imminent danger'; moreover, 'notwithstanding the Enemy dispatched their prizes to the Isle of France distant nearly three thousand miles, not a single instance of recapture has occurred'.

Pellew was bitter, and with reason. Finding a handful of French raiders in the vastness of the Indian Ocean was an impossible task. Moreover, although the merchants' losses were indeed severe, they failed to mention that he had offered to convoy their ships and been declined. It suited the nature of Calcutta's trade to engage small local vessels, or country ships, for individual voyages rather than wait for convoys to be assembled – even though this exposed them to predators. The Bombay merchants, who accepted Pellew's offer, had not lost a ship. Nor had any Indiamen been taken, thanks to the convoy system. 'The merchants of Bengal', he wrote angrily, 'have made individual interest their study, and not the general good.'[11]

The most galling aspect of all, however, was that Pellew had been denied the chance to deal with this evil at source. The merchants rounded off their memorial with a plea that the threat from the islands be removed.

Nothing would have pleased Pellew more. Two years earlier he had presented a plan for a joint Navy and Army invasion, starting with the seizure of Bourbon and followed by a landing on the southern shore of Ile de France. It was the one blow that he could deal to the enemy. Logistically, it was ambitious but, with the Company's forces in India, feasible. Strategically, it was common sense. The French had lost their last foothold in India with the capture of Pondicherry five years earlier. Seizing Ile de France and Bourbon would drive them from the Indian Ocean once and for all. It was not simply a matter of securing British shipping. Bonaparte, it was known, still nurtured ambitions to supplant Britain in India. As recently as April, Pellew had sailed to Bombay to investigate intelligence that the Emperor was planning an invasion. Though it proved a false alarm, the threat would exist as long as the islands remained in his possession.

In the meantime, Pellew's plan had been left to gather dust. Whatever the strategic logic, it would require vast resources; and the Company, under pressure from shareholders at a time when its long decline had already begun, was reluctant to commit itself when there seemed a chance that the Government might shoulder the burden. Not for nothing had the India House been called 'a corporation of men with long heads and deep purposes'.

One small step had been taken. In 1806 British forces recaptured the Cape from the Dutch and based a squadron there under Rear-Admiral Albemarle Bertie to secure the route to India. But its impact had been limited. A blockade of the islands, instituted recently in the hope of starving them into submission, had had little discernible impact; and it had not prevented ships slipping out on raiding expeditions.

Not that Pellew would be concerned with Ile de France for much longer. After four years in Madras, he was to sail home in a few months. Now aged fifty-one, he had suffered in health and, like an old ship, he was starting to wear. 'My floor timbers are very shaky,' he wrote to his friend, Alex Broughton, in England. 'Grey as a badger, fat as a pig and running to belly.'[12]

Two hopes sustained him. The first was for a last crack at the French. 'I shall be glad to have one kick at Bonaparte's flag before I die. I would freely give back the whole for such a day as Trafalgar – how sweetly could I give up Life in such a cause.'[13] The other was for the advancement of his two eldest sons. Both had followed him into the Navy, both had accompanied him to India, and for both he had intrigued shamelessly. For if Pellew had one weakness besides money, it was his boys.

The eldest was Captain Pownoll Bastard Pellew. He had joined the squadron two years earlier as a nineteen-year-old lieutenant, thanks to Pellew's intervention with Lord St Vincent, the First Sea Lord. Almost immediately Pellew appointed the boy an Acting Captain and then, after an indecently brief pause, given him the *Terpsichore*, a 32-gun frigate, by way of promotion to Post Captain. It was to be expected that admirals would take certain liberties in their positions, but even so there must have been dark mutterings among the senior captains of the squadron when, shortly before the Indiamen fleet anchored off Madras, Pellew made Pownoll commander of his flagship, HMS *Culloden*. The lad was aged just twenty-one.

If he, too, had been a fighting man this nepotism might have passed unnoticed, but Pownoll had none of the fire that burned in his father's belly. He was a romantic, good-looking boy of sensitive disposition who dreamt not of glory, but of a pretty wife and a cottage in Devon. Pellew, who loved both his sons to distraction, had been slow to recognise this: Pownoll, he protested, was 'a fine boy' and 'a steady good officer', albeit susceptible to the wiles of the Madras ladies. 'He is always in love and I have hard work to keep him from the noose,' Pellew had written recently to Broughton.

In the meantime Fleetwood Pellew, the admiral's second son, had also joined the squadron. 'A prodigious fine boy' in his father's view, Fleetwood at least showed a real relish for battle, so that when he was given command of a sloop at the age of seventeen it seemed less scandalous. He cut a dashing figure as well, being brave and even more handsome than his brother, and when he won his spurs in the expedition against the Dutch at Java, his father's pride in writing to Broughton was unrestrained:

> He led the squadron with the greatest judgment . . . He placed his ship ag't the Dutch frigate and batteries with equal skill and led in the boats to Boarding . . . I assure you, a prettier exploit I never saw. You will say Aye, Aye, here is the Father. I have done – but I assure you I say not half of what others say of him. My heart swelled when I heard a general shout on board *Culloden* – Well done, Fleetwood well done, bravo – was the cry all around me. What Father could have kept his Eyes dry? I was obliged to wipe them before I could again look thro' the glass.[14]

More and more it was his younger son who won his favour. Fleetwood was 'beyond comparison the finest youth of the Squadron, universally beloved', 'a real treasure', and 'the flower of my flock and the flower of my fleet'. In May, when he was nineteen, Pellew gave him command of the frigate *San Fiorenzo* – replacing the gallant Hardinge who had been killed in the action with *Piemontaise* – and sent him off in search of further glory.*

Meanwhile, though his affection for the elder was not diminished, the admiral had belatedly realised that Pownoll was no warrior. He had

---

* Pellew's great rival Sir Thomas Troubridge was at least as blatant in providing for his son. But whereas Pellew was endlessly tolerant, Troubridge was stern. On hearing that his son had acquitted himself well, Troubridge remarked: 'Had he done otherwise I would with great composure put a pistol ball through his nob.'

recently written to Broughton: 'Can you find a nice Wife for him? He is a good fellow and is extremely anxious to be married and settled as he calls it.' The young ladies of Madras were not to be trusted for 'they really push them[selves] upon the boys in so bare faced a manner they can hardly get off without saying soft things.' Pownoll's last hope, he thought, was to find 'a good Girl with either Money or Connections'.[15]

Thus were matters poised when the Indiaman fleet bearing Lady Barlow and her two daughters anchored off Madras on 3 August. Pellew was on cordial terms with Sir George Barlow and, during the public revels that followed the return of the Governor's wife, it was not lost on the admiral that Eliza, the Barlows' charming and accomplished elder daughter, was a good girl with money *and* connections. The old fox may, therefore, have had more in mind than simply a warm gesture when the *Madras Courier* announced on 17 August: 'Cards of invitation have been issued by His Excellency Sir Edward Pellew for a Ball on the 26th inst, at which time the Company will be invited to meet Lady Barlow.'

Palanquins and carriages came bobbing along the Mount Road that evening, proceeding up a drive lit by torches to the Admiral's House, where they were met by Pellew and his elder son, tall men both, sweating furiously in their blue-and-gold uniforms and breeches. Guests remarked on the dazzling decor of Pellew's residence and, a charmingly gracious touch, that the ballroom floor had been freshly painted with Sir George Barlow's arms, in honour of his wife.[16]

All the nabobs were in attendance. There was William Hope, the very incarnation of the Company's entrepreneurial spirit, once a lowly army private and now the richest man in Madras, with ethics as rough as his business methods. Some way off, no doubt, for they were bitter antagonists, stood Sir Henry Gwillim, judge of the Supreme Court and a radical – some said revolutionary – Whig of incandescent temper. In the corner was William Petrie, a leathery old hand who, as Second in Council, was the Governor's deputy; he was also an embittered man who loathed his superior and intrigued constantly against him.

The only notable absentee was Lieutenant-General Hay Macdowall, Commander-in-Chief of the Army. As he was Petrie's sole rival in his detestation of Sir George Barlow, the general might not have attended anyway, but on this occasion he was away from Madras.

Lady Barlow made a convincing belle, being led off in the first set by Pownoll Pellew, then through a cotillion. The Governor evidently did not dance but his aide-de-camp, a distant relative named Captain Pratt Barlow, cut an elegant figure on the floor. The Madras gentry were proud of their dress – 'costume was as gay as, nay, gayer than that of England', one visitor wrote – and ladies in velvet or silk, in crimson, green and scarlet, swirled across the floor with partners in gold-brocade coats and buckskin breeches. Their stamina was astonishing for, as was pointed out, 'no one went to church without losing some ounces by perspiration; how much more then under the exercise of the dance?'[17]

Supper was announced at midnight, when Lady Barlow was led by the admiral through a path of blue lights to tents pitched in the garden, 'followed by all the gay circle' while a band played 'The Roast Beef of Old England'. Pellew was a highly sociable creature as well as a fighting man; he kept a good table and had not stinted on drink.

> The Supper was a display of every delicacy which was procurable and the wines were of the first quality. Champagne was most liberally supplied and by its exhilarating powers caused the Dancing to be resumed with, if possible, additional spirit. It was not until 4 in the morning that the Country Dances were given up. In this finale his Excellency the Admiral danced with Lady Barlow with a spirit and activity equal to the youngest man present. Her Ladyship, altho she had danced the whole evening, entered equally into the spirit of the scene and thus the party finished with the same éclat as it had commenced. Afterwards a few thirsty souls sat down to a second supper at which some appropriate patriotic songs were sung until daylight.[18]

Lady Barlow had brought a breath of new life to Madras, and its inhabitants were grateful. They noted her outgoing informality, her energy on the dance floor, especially when partnered by the Governor's dashing young aide, and contrasted her manner with the cold, reserved demeanour of her unpopular husband.

All in all, the evening was such a triumph that it came as no surprise when the admiral's son announced that he would stage a second ball two weeks later. This too was ostensibly in Lady Barlow's honour, but to anyone present the true purpose soon became apparent as Captain Pellew danced with nineteen-year-old Eliza Barlow until the early hours of the morning. Whatever intimacies they exchanged that night were sufficient to prompt the delivery of an envelope a day later at the Governor's House. It contained the lines from *Romeo and Juliet* beginning 'O! She doth teach the torches to burn', followed by a poem – one of unusual eloquence considering that it came from the hand of a callow if romantic young sea officer and was in that most awkward form, the acrostic:

Mark! Midst the boasted beauties, rare
In this gay scene of peace and joy
Say – who so shines, supremely fair,
So graceful moves to melody?

By all the sylphs that hover here
And guard the maidens of the plain
Robb'd from some higher, happier sphere
Love sure has brought her *Here* to reign!
O'er each fond, conscious youth, to hand control,
With angel face and form, to charm the soul.[19]

Miss Barlow could have little imagined that her fortunes would take so swift a turn. But it was not unusual for fresh 'fishing fleet' arrivals to be snapped up on Madras's marriage market and the particular circumstances made a prolonged courtship impossible. When the admiral sailed home in *Culloden* in just a few weeks, so would Captain Pellew.

2

A Petition from Bombay

Madras and Bombay, 15 September–20 October 1808

Through those searing weeks of the approaching monsoon HMS *Culloden* lay at anchor off Fort St George. Pellew, drafting his final orders from Madras, could anticipate sailing home with satisfaction. He had made his fortune and provided liberally for his sons. News had just arrived of his promotion to Vice-Admiral of the Blue. And now those perfidious wretches, the Calcutta merchants, had come to him as petitioners: they desired that their next sailing to Penang should be in convoy; would Sir Edward be so good as to provide them with an escort? It was a small victory, but one to savour.

Midway through September, Pellew received intelligence that was to bear significantly on his plans. It came in a letter from HMS *Nereide*, a frigate of Admiral Bertie's squadron, now come to anchor in Bombay. Her commander, Captain Robert Corbet, wrote that while lately engaged in blockading Ile de France he had captured an enemy brig and learnt that the island had just been reinforced 'by two very fine Frigates, *Manche* and *Caroline*'.[1]

Corbet's news was disturbing but not entirely bad. The corsair Surcouf was about to quit the Eastern Seas as a result of a quarrel with Charles Decaen, the dictatorial Governor of Ile de France; Decaen had requisitioned the *Revenant*, claiming it was needed for the island's defence, and, when Surcouf objected, seized his possessions. The new French ships, both of 40 guns, would join the *Canonnière*, a similarly large but elderly frigate. They were faster and more powerful than any British frigate in these seas and, in the hands of a man like Surcouf, could have spelled disaster. Much would depend on their commanders. For now Pellew was simply glad to know of their presence, having been ill-served in the past with information on French ships. 'For the most part,' he complained, 'the first intelligence of their appearance in the Bay of Bengal is announced by their success.'[2]

Captain Corbet's dispatch was followed a few days later by a second letter from the *Nereide* – but one of a quite different character. It was in a rough hand, dated 28 August, and came through an unofficial channel. Its contents were clear enough, however, and as Pellew read curiosity turned to concern. It was a petition, from the crew:

> Your petitioners [have] never before experienced such oppressive usage as we now labour under, under the command of Capt Robert Corbet, whose capricious temper on the least occasion will cause us to be beaten with large sticks which he has given directions to be made. There are a number of men who have been beaten to such a degree (some three or four times a day) they have been incapable of doing their duty. He also at other times punished men with a Thief's Cat* and when the skin was broke has put salt pickle on their backs.[3]

There was more: shore liberty had been denied and sentries were posted around the ship to prevent desertions. 'We are more like a prison ship than a man of war. From gunfire in the morning until sunset the gangway is attended by the master of arms to prevent more than two men at a time going to the privy . . . so some discommode their trowsers.'

It ended with a plea: 'We humbly beg that you will take it into your most serious consideration and grant us some redress, either give us another captain or draft us into some other ship under your command . . . This is the second letter we have written, fearing the first had miscarried.'

Pellew was in an awkward position. He knew Robert Corbet by reputation – as a zealous and well-regarded captain (he liked to remind colleagues that he had won praise while a young officer from no less than Lord Nelson) – and the *Nereide* was engaged on vital blockade duty. In his younger days Pellew had been a strict disciplinarian himself and knew about troublesome crews. These forces had collided to produce a mutiny

---

* The cat-o'-nine-tails, the standard instrument of navy punishment, consisted of nine lengths of cord each of about two feet, attached to a handle and knotted at the end of each strand. The much-detested thief's cat had more and larger knots and was in theory used only on men found guilty of stealing.

while he was captain of HMS *Impetueux* in 1799, for which three men were hanged. But whatever his faults, Pellew was never a cruel or oppressive commander and while the Nereides' petition could not be altogether taken at face value, it had a ring of authenticity that impressed him. These were respectful, experienced hands. Referring to Corbet's habit of abusing them as 'Cowards', they wrote: 'We cannot perceive how we merit [this] as we have never had the pleasure of being in an action with him but a number of us have been in several actions where we always endeavoured to support the British Flag triumphant.'

Pellew's initial concerns may have been allayed by the arrival a day or so later of a letter from Corbet himself. It was dated 31 August, three days after the petition.

> Sir, I lose no time in informing your Excellency that this morning (through the usual means of seamen accusing each other) I discovered that one or more anonymous letters had been sent to your Excellency by part of the crew of this ship against me their captain ... Three good men, one a petty officer, are concerned in it, no more.[4]

Though he was unlikely to have been won over by its contemptuous tone towards the men, Pellew was reassured. Corbet requested a court-martial hearing, as was proper, and advised that three of his accusers had been sent 'out of the dread of punishment' to HMS *Powerful*, pending a hearing. Pellew replied approvingly: 'The measures you have pursued ... are perfectly satisfactory to me and honourable to your character.'[5] He then issued Corbet with two specific orders.

As Pellew pointed out, he was about to quit India and, with the early departure of two other ships, it was unlikely that enough captains could be assembled at Bombay for a court martial. If this proved the case, Corbet was to 'proceed immediately to the Cape of Good Hope and lay the whole of the proceedings before the Commander in Chief of that station in order that he may take such measures as the case shall appear to him to demand'.

Pellew then went on: 'You will be pleased to read this letter to the ship's company and assure them that every attention shall be paid to their complaints.' His concern for *Nereide*'s company was commendable. It was also good sense. Handling men cruelly was not only an affront to decency, it was a wilful squandering of resources. Pellew had established himself in

India as a leading reformer in the trend towards milder navy discipline. He insisted on receiving monthly punishment returns from every ship under his command, a system later adopted by the Admiralty for general use. In fact, had Pellew been able to inspect *Nereide*'s log at this point he could only have been the more deeply disturbed.

Corbet had assured Pellew that 'so far as being in a dangerous state, *Nereide*'s discipline is at this moment surpassed by *no ship*'.[6] However, the nature of his disciplinary regime is revealed by a fairly typical handful of entries on the ship's passage to Bombay.

> 29 July, off St Mary's Island: Patrick Dunn 48 lashes for theft. Thos Christian 72 lashes for attempting to desert. Robt Viner 48 Do for Do [i.e. ditto for ditto]. Thos Brown, Wm Dowling & Michael Sorcedore 36 each for Do, Inigo Gardner 12 for neglect & Inigo Finnamore 36 for sleeping on duty.

> 2 August: Edwd Hurst & Michael Purcell 36 lashes each for straggling. George Less, Michael Keefe & Thos Warstone 48 Do for Do, Inigo Carrim 60 for Do, Wm Jones 24 for Do, Joshua Dodd & Edwd Kirkham 24 for neglect, Wm Wiggins 24 for dirtiness.[7]

There then followed ten days of only intermittent beatings before Corbet again got the bit between his teeth:

> 12 August: George Parkinson 36 lashes for drunkenness, Inigo Gardner 24 Do for dirtiness, Joshua Flynn 24 for disobedience of orders, Thos Christian 48 Do for straggling, Robt Viner 36 Do for Do, Thos Brown 36 for dirtiness, Richard Mason 11 for Do & Thos Barlow 12 for Do.

The crew's petition had not exaggerated. HMS *Nereide* was that rare but terrible thing in the Navy, a hell afloat.

Having declared his desire to face his accusers at a court martial, Corbet proceeded to do everything he could to avoid it. The opportunity was provided by a diplomatic mission.

London and Calcutta were full of fears at the time over Bonaparte's apparent intention to launch a seaborne invasion of India from Ile de

France and Persia. Calcutta, in the person of Lord Minto, the Governor-General, had responded by sending an envoy, General Malcolm, to dissuade the Shah from cooperation with the French. London, in the meantime, sent out its own emissary, Sir Harford Jones, who had just arrived in Bombay on his way to Persia. Even though Jones already had a ship at his disposal, Corbet took it upon himself to offer Jones a passage to the Persian port of Abushire in the *Nereide* and informed Pellew accordingly.

Now the admiral started to smell a rat. On 19 September he wrote to Corbet:

> I trust you will have carried into execution the orders I have already sent you for your return to your station without delay. The Admiralty have provided for [Jones's] conveyance, giving the *Sapphire* for his accommodation . . . Sir Harford Jones must on all such occasions direct his requests and reasons for my consideration and you are not to exercise any discretional power in that reference.[8]

But Corbet had not waited for a reply, having sailed for Persia on 11 September. Pellew was furious and now convinced that something serious was amiss.

Over the following weeks, while the *Nereide* made her way up the Persian Gulf to Abushire, the mood on the quarterdeck was as savage as the heat: two men were tied up and given twenty-four each for fighting; two more received the same for disobedience; the following day one got thirty-six for 'mutinous expression', and three others two dozen for disobedience. Quite what acts of disobedience were required to attract punishment is never spelled out, but this – along with insolence and contempt – became the charge most frequently cited in the pages of *Nereide*'s otherwise chillingly opaque logbook.

She returned to Bombay briefly towards the end of October – around the same time as the *Lord Eldon* and four other Indiamen anchored at the end of a rapid 123-day passage from Portsmouth. Corbet's reputation may have preceded him because when a lieutenant from *Nereide* came on board the *Lord Eldon*, a hand named John de Silva jumped overboard and swam to shore. From the Indiaman's crew of fifty-three, the lieutenant picked out four, including the remarkable figure of Hector McNeil, a sixty-three-year-old sailmaker. Although the *Lord Eldon*'s log makes plain that they were pressed, they were entered in *Nereide*'s book as volunteers.[9]

Also awaiting Corbet at Bombay was Pellew's letter of 19 September. Its icy tone at last precipitated action. Expressing regret at 'Your Excellency's expressions of displeasure', Corbet replied that he had 'determined upon putting to sea immediately in execution of your orders and of submitting everything as it now stands to the Commander of the Cape Station'.[10] The delay had been fatal, however. When *Nereide* sailed again from Bombay she was a fireship, primed and ready to explode.

The monsoon came early that year and it had been raining for some days when carriages came sloshing up the muddy track to St Mary's Church on 1 October for the marriage that united two of the leading families in British India. The pews were packed, on the one side, with the blue-and-gold ranks of the Navy squadron, and on the other by Sir George Barlow, his lady, and the redcoats of the Company establishment. At the altar stood Captain Pownoll Pellew and Eliza Barlow. He was twenty-one, she was nineteen, and just eight weeks had elapsed since their meeting.

Madras had barely recovered its breath when another sensational item of gossip swept like a monsoon wind among the groups gathering on Mount Road in the evening. This was that each of the delighted fathers had contributed equally towards a staggering dowry of £20,000.[11] Youth, beauty, position – and now wealth as well. It seemed hard to imagine any union more blessed by fortune and circumstance.

While the Pellew romance had kept everyone talking through the onset of the rains, a second subject was not far behind it – the Governor's wife. The presidency had never had a first lady like Lady Barlow, certainly not one who mingled with the inhabitants so freely, and the weeks had passed in an unbroken succession of receptions, levees and masquerades. Guests spoke of her 'condescension and affability', and of her sociability, while her energy on the dance floor was the subject of admiration and amazement. Her midday tiffin parties were 'a table of gaiety in which she was fond of indulging'.[12] It was widely said that she took too much wine at such times, but then drinking in India attracted little attention other than from the Directors, who some-times admonished their distant servants for 'incorrigible sottishness'.

Sensuality and flirtation were features of Madras life, as Maria Graham, the wife of a navy captain, made clear in an account of her visit at this time. A Madras lady's day, she wrote, consisted of little more than holding court to young men in the morning, taking liberally of wine at dinner, undressing for an afternoon rest with a novel, then returning to the table before setting off for a night of dancing.[13] All of which sounds typical of Lady Barlow's daily round. She may have raised a few eyebrows by appearing at a masquerade as Mary Queen of Scots, on the arm of the Governor's aide-de-camp as Darnley. But the settlement little suspected as yet that the Governor's wife was in the grips of an intoxication that went well beyond her love of wine and dancing.[14]

Although there would seem to be echoes here of a British India that is familiar, these are deceptive. The Madras of 1808 bore no relation to the Raj era, the world of clubs and hill stations, of pukka sahibs and their sharp-eyed mems, of tight dress, rigorous respectability and unspeakable snobbery.

It was the first English settlement in India, having been established in 1640, fully fifty years before Calcutta, and it was always different. For one thing, the site could scarcely have been less suitable to its purpose as a trading port for, crucially, there was no harbour. Fort St George stood at the edge of a sandy beach that stretched away for miles in either direction, offering ships neither pier for landing nor shelter from the storms that battered the eastern seaboard of India, the Coromandel Coast, during the hurricane season. Now, as they had for the 170-odd years since Madras's founding, ships anchored off the fort, leaving their human and mercantile cargoes to be ferried over a sand bar to the beach.

Nor did that first view of the place, invariably glimpsed from the sea, offer much to charm the new arrival. 'The long flat shore, unrelieved by bay or cove, gave no promise that it would contain behind the fringe of coconut palms anything to fascinate the eye,' wrote one visitor.[15] The next phase of the introduction was uncomfortable, and often dangerous, as the newcomer took the hair-raising ride to shore in a *masoolah*. Only then did Madras start to reveal its capacity to beguile.[16]

Dominating the settlement was Fort St George, a bastioned pentagon.

The town that lay within the fort, however, was a surprisingly tranquil place of gardens and neoclassical structures. What gave each building a distinctive brilliance under that tropical sky was *chunam*, a stucco of ground seashells that polished to a marble-like sheen: there was Government House; there the homes built by two distinguished former residents, Robert Clive and Arthur Wellesley; and there exquisite St Mary's, the oldest Protestant church in the East, a magical creation of artisan design and skills.

Few of the inhabitants stayed in the fort. 'Everybody lives in the country,' wrote one bemused visitor, Maria Graham. Another called it 'a city of magnificent distances'. The European suburbs lay south-west of the fort, where residents were borne in the ubiquitous litter known as the palanquin along Mount Road, an avenue as 'smooth as a bowling green and planted on each side with banyan and yellow tulip trees'. Trees were one of the glories of Madras – palms, tamarinds, blossoming flamboyants, the peepuls, with their feathery leaves trembling lightly in a breath of air, and, towering above them all, the banyans with trunks as thick as oaks, sprouting tendrils that drooped to the ground in plumes, like leafy waterfalls.

The Madras gentry had indeed given themselves space to breathe, building their fine homes amid lush acres at the end of long, tree-lined drives. These houses were of a style characteristic of the English presence throughout the East: double-storeyed, with an elegant portico above a ground level with arches around an area that was used mainly for storage, known as the go-down. A broad staircase led to the upper level with a central hall, high-ceilinged rooms and verandahs. Windows were shuttered or screened with rattan – kept constantly wet during the hot season – to allow airing.

There was of course an earthier side to the settlement – a warren of taverns, punch houses and trading establishments that lay just north of the fort's bastions and was known as Blacktown. Once inhabited entirely by native Indians, it had become a racial and cultural stewpot where many less-affluent English made their homes. James Wathen, a visitor of the time, found 'Hindoos, Portuguese, Chinese, Persians, Arabs and Armenians', as well as sailors on leave and soldiers from the garrison. Here, too, was to be had a flavour of the exotic: jugglers, sadhus and sword-swallowers. The population of Blacktown also bore testimony to a time when whites, notably soldiers, had been encouraged to intermarry with Indian women and so produce a new assimilated generation of Company servants.

Despite this diversity, however, Madras was virtually defined by its isolation. Like the ships at anchor, its contact with the outside world was sporadic. Like the ships, too, it was a small community, looking either in on itself or out to sea, and distant from regulating pressures. If Calcutta was the sophisticated metropolis of Company India – Regency Bath relocated in the Bay of Bengal, according to William Dalrymple – Madras was its wild frontier, a place hostile to authority, representing at its best a spirited individualism, at its worst an undisciplined rapacity. The 'Gentlemen of the Coast', as the merchant class liked to be known, were buccaneers in the full sense of the word. Governors were rarely popular and one who tried to interfere with institutionalised corruption, Lord Pigot, was overthrown by his soldiers in 1776 and died in their custody.

Now, once again, the settlement and its presiding authority were in conflict.

The portrait of Sir George Hilaro Barlow that still hangs within the ramparts of Fort St George shows a slight, angry-looking man. The opulent dress – lace cuffs and gorgeous red cloak, set off with the Order of the Bath – sits awkwardly on this pugnacious, terrier-like figure. It is by no means a distinguished piece of art, but in declining to endow his subject with false dignity, the artist, George Watson, succeeded in depicting a lone Englishman at odds with his stormy domain, and produced something quite unlike the run-of-the-mill imperial portrait.

History has not been kind to Barlow – 'by nature a time-server . . . lacking in breadth of vision', as one historian described him. Certainly, in an age of dazzling proconsuls, he lacked lustre, and he was not helped by an aloof manner, the refuge of many a shy spirit. His background was distinctly common. He came from trade when that was a taint, even in India; the diarist William Hickey sneeringly called him 'the silk mercer of Covent Garden' – for such was his father's business – and avowed that 'nature had intended him for nothing more elevated'. But while Hickey's memoirs are a vivid record of the age, his judgement was, at best, capricious – and his summation of Barlow well wide of the mark. 'I do not believe', he wrote, 'he had one individual person about whom he cared or in whose welfare he felt at all interested.'[17] Sir George was, in fact, devoted to his wife.

He had come to Madras eight months earlier in unfortunate circumstances. His entire service, since 1779, had been in Calcutta where he had been unexpectedly catapulted into the position of Governor-General by the sudden death of Lord Cornwallis. Through no fault of his, it was then decided in London that a more exalted being was required in the post and Barlow was relegated to the southern presidency.*

Unsurprisingly, Madras detested him from the outset, as an outsider as well as a loyal Company man whose orders were to root out corruption in a place where it was rampant. It did not help either that he was displacing a long-serving local official, William Petrie, who, as his deputy, set out to undermine him. Barlow's biggest challenge of all, however, was imposing reforms on the Madras Army, and a new commander with grievances of his own, Lieutenant-General Hay Macdowall.

In the days after his daughter's wedding, Barlow sat at a desk that took in a great sweep of the Indian Ocean and gave thanks for this brief respite from Macdowall. Some weeks earlier the general had left Madras with an entourage borne by a caravan of bullocks. Nominally, he was doing his rounds, bolstering morale in outlying forts. In reality, however, it was plain that Macdowall, far from raising spirits, was fanning the embers of discontent. Reports had started to filter back to Fort St George – of revelry, heavy drinking and wild talk around mess tables at which the general had been present; of toasts to the military brotherhood and, astonishingly, to the coup that had deposed Lord Pigot as Governor.[18]

The well-known public difficulties of Barlow's life were accompanied

---

* The East India Company was founded by a Royal Charter of 1600 by which Queen Elizabeth I granted a small company of London merchants a monopoly of all English trade to the east of the Cape of Good Hope. Having competed initially against European rivals – Portuguese, Dutch and French – the Company had become by this time the most dominant body in the history of world trade. It had also evolved far beyond its initial charter as a mercantile body into an imperial power. The three presidencies of Calcutta, Madras and Bombay provided local administration and imposed taxes as well as conducting trade. Each presidency had its own standing army, consisting mainly of white officers of the Company's Army and local sepoy troops. Each presidency had once been autonomous but, since the creation of the post of Governor-General in the late eighteenth century, Calcutta (or Bengal as it was sometimes known synonymously) had been the senior presidency, the Company's headquarters in India.

by private, not to say secret, concerns. He could only have been gratified by the splendid match so rapidly made by Eliza with the son of his good friend Sir Edward Pellew. His wife was another matter. Lady Barlow had become a cause of profound anxiety to the Governor.

George Barlow and Elizabeth Smith met in Calcutta in 1789 – ten years after his arrival as a writer, or clerk, the lowest office in the Company's administration – and married in haste. Elizabeth was nineteen and George twenty-seven at the time of a union that was undoubtedly highly physical: Eliza, their first child, was born within seven months, and she was followed by further children at almost yearly intervals. Elizabeth appears to have been of humble beginnings; her father was probably an Irish soldier, Burton Smith. There is no record of her appearance, but her rise in Indian society indicates that she was attractive, perhaps a beauty. She was, at any rate, vivacious and uninhibited, as well as being extremely fond of claret and a veritable dervish on the dance floor.[19]

Her husband, by contrast, was shy to the point of diffidence, a modest, conscientious official, conspicuous among the high-living exotics of Company India for his integrity. All of which makes him sound rather a dull dog. But he won the respect of the magnificent Lord Wellesley, one of the most flamboyant of India's Governor-Generals. Wellesley, elder brother of the later Duke of Wellington, made Barlow his deputy and recommended him as his successor, citing his 'eminent talents, knowledge, integrity and discretion'.[20] Remarkably, the aristocrat had a personal liking for the shy plebeian. They were friends and Wellesley spoke of his 'warm and unalterable sentiment of private regard and respect' for Barlow.[21]

Madras and Bombay still had their own governors with local responsibilities but they could be held to account by the Governor-General who, in turn, took his orders from the Directors at the East India House in London. In the meantime, because of its vital contribution to Britain's growing economic prosperity – indeed, to its transition as a global power – the Company had lost its independence from Parliament. Senior positions, both in London and Calcutta, had to be approved by the government and, increasingly, the India House and Whitehall became entwined. As the Company's domains grew, so did imperial and strategic objectives, drawing in the forces of the Crown – the Navy to maintain control over the eastern trade route, and the Army to supplement the Company's forces in Bengal, Madras and Bombay. This was not merely against the possibility of conflicts with local rulers but with France which, while it had abandoned trade interests in India since the loss of its last territory, Pondicherry, still sought opportunities to destroy Britain's economic powerbase.

In 1805 Lord Cornwallis, the new Governor-General, died and the impossible happened. The silk-mercer's son moved to Government House – to the unadulterated delight of his wife. Calcutta had long been without an active first lady and her love of gossip, riding, dancing and music made her a highly visible figure. It was at this time that Sir George (he had been created a baronet two years earlier) took on as his aide-de-camp Captain Pratt Barlow, aged twenty and the son of a cousin. Patronage virtually defined Company India and the young man came out with a reference from Sir George's brother, William, who thought him 'well-informed, persevering, of mild and amiable temper & gentlemanly manners'.[22]

No sooner had Barlow been confirmed as Governor-General than he was being undermined. Lobbying began in London to have him replaced by a man of 'Rank, Weight and Consideration'. At this point Lady Barlow returned to England.

Barlow was too shrewd not to anticipate the likely outcome of the wrangling. It seems that he was considering a dignified withdrawal and that Lady Barlow was to establish a home in anticipation of his return, while at the same time installing the youngest of their still-growing brood of children in school. For this purpose Barlow took the entire passenger section of a fast-sailing brig, the *Mercury*, for his wife, three children and three servants. As a woman of rank she was thought to require an escort. The role fell to the young officer who had become almost part of their household – Captain Pratt Barlow. Whether the choice excited any attention at the time is not clear, but an observer of what followed remarked:

> I have made long voyages and I say that if I had been Sir George
> Barlow I would not have permitted my wife to make such a voyage for
> six months, a woman of such fascinating talents, which made it most
> dangerous to trust her without a female companion.[23]

They landed at Falmouth in April 1807 and proceeded to London. In the many months that followed it would have been remarkable had Barlow not noted a change in the tone and frequency of his wife's letters. At first they were marked by her usual fondness, addressed to her 'dearest, beloved Barlow'.[24] Then they dropped off and finally ceased.

But if Lady Barlow had fallen silent about her doings, Sir George's brother had not. William Barlow was his closest sibling and, while not explicitly critical, hinted that 'my sister', as he called Lady Barlow, spent too much time in society and not enough with her children. Then there was her phenomenal extravagance: in five months after her arrival, she had called on him for a total of £1,400.[25] As the rent of 13 guineas a week for her house in Hollen Street was already paid, she had gone through the fantastic sum of £100 a week. Even for the wife of an Indian nabob, such spending was almost unimaginable.

Over these months William had suffered other doubts. Though he never spelled them out the allusion was clear. A statement of expenditure that he kept, detailing Lady Barlow's demands, gave no details of what the money had been spent on but noted that it had been collected on her behalf 'by Captain Pratt Barlow'. It was also evident that these drawings had ceased at the end of August 1807, just before the young officer sailed back to India.[26] Privately, at least, William had started to entertain doubts about the character of the man he had so heartily recommended, and his earlier breezy confidence that 'he will not disgrace his [family's] name'.

Around this time it was finally resolved that Barlow should indeed be replaced by a nobleman, and Lord Minto was sent out to Calcutta. Barlow was appointed to Madras with the Order of the Bath as a sop. Lady Barlow sailed back to India, with their two eldest girls.

But her return had not relieved his anxieties. It would perhaps have been expecting too much for a renewal of the ardour that had brought them thirteen children in nineteen years of marriage. Still, Lady Barlow was only thirty-seven, while Sir George was an extremely fit forty-six, and he must have hoped for a demonstration of that open affection which had always been so marked on her side. In this he had been disappointed.

Did he now start to have suspicions? That Lady Barlow was spending a good deal of time with his young aide and had taken to riding out with him was public knowledge. But though the signs were there, events were to show that Sir George was almost the last to accept evidence of his wife's infatuation with Captain Pratt Barlow.

3

General Macdowall's grievance

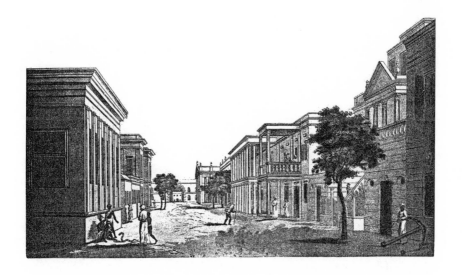

Madras, 10–24 October 1808

At daylight on 10 October, just a week after the Pellew wedding, a seventeen-gun salute echoed out from Fort St George. It announced the return of General Macdowall's caravan, and though the rains had brought a cooling balm to Madras, the temperature rose again.

The only known portrait of General Hay Macdowall is by Sir Henry Raeburn. It is a touchstone of the Scottish artist's work, a bravura portrayal of rugged masculinity that echoes his better-known works of Highland chiefs. The general, in full uniform, is set in heroic mode, a Wellington-like figure with arrogant gaze and disdainful demeanour. Raeburn was the Reynolds of Scotland and it says something for Macdowall's eye to his place in history that he had the portrait executed on one of his rare visits to his native land. What makes the painting of particular interest here, however, is how it contrasts with that of Sir George Barlow by George Watson. The two artists were seen as honourable rivals and it is curiously apt that they should have been chosen to portray the opposing protagonists in a far-off drama: the patrician and the parvenu, the dashing soldier and the besieged bureaucrat. The canvases could scarcely better illustrate the enmity that developed between their subjects.

Macdowall was a member of an old landed Scottish family, the Macdowalls of Castle Sempill, and saw action as a lieutenant with the 42nd Royal Highland Regiment, the Black Watch, at the end of the American War of Independence. Service with another Highland regiment proved more congenial in Bengal, where, as a young major, he fell in with the memoirist William Hickey – then at a self-avowedly dissolute point in his life.

The Bachelors Club, so named because any member who married had to resign, was described by Hickey as a 'very jovial society of young bucks'. Macdowall was evidently never tempted to marry, but he did, like many, take Indian mistresses, or *bibis*. He also engaged in epic drinking bouts, for which he gained a reputation as one of the strongest heads in India, as well as being a heavy gambler at the hazard table.

It was in this society that he met Arthur Wellesley, another handsome young colonel. The two became friends in what was, even by local standards, a hard-drinking school. Hickey, no slouch himself when it came to dealing with a claret bottle, once quailed at the prospect of a night in their company, declaring himself 'wholly unfit to encounter such men as [Colonel] Hay Macdoual [and] Colonel Wellesley'. He was, nevertheless, engaged until two o'clock in the morning when, having drunk twenty-two toasts in large goblets, 'each person staggered to his carriage or palanquin and was conveyed to town.' The next day, Hickey was incapable of leaving his bed. 'Indeed, a more severe debauch I never was engaged in any part of the world,' he wrote.[1]

Wellesley soon recognised the seeds of self-destruction in such excess and resolved to abandon the company of men like Macdowall, and 'drink little or no wine, exercize . . . and, if possible, keep in good humour'. The last, he added, was the most difficult, 'for there is scarcely a good humoured man in India'.[2] His advice was lost on Macdowall. While Wellesley started his ascent to glory, his old comrade remained wedded to intemperance. Events in 1803 epitomised their diverging fortunes: in southern India, Wellesley won what he regarded as the greatest of his victories, over the Marathas at Assaye; in Ceylon, Macdowall commanded an expedition against the King of Kandy, secured the Sinhalese capital with a force of 3,000, and then withdrew prematurely – leaving a garrison of 1,000 that was massacred a few months later.

To say the least, it was with a sense of promise unfulfilled that Macdowall assumed command of the Company's Army in Madras in 1807.* The

---

* The Indian Army was a bafflingly complex organisation. Macdowall, like Wellesley, was a Crown officer, but there was nothing unusual about one of the King's men commanding one of the Company's armies (whether that of Madras, Bengal or Bombay). Company regiments were made up of European or, more commonly, native (sepoy) troops. Crown regiments were fewer in number and, of course, European. Crown officers, who bought their commissions, tended to be held in higher regard – and certainly held themselves in higher regard – than Company officers, although the latter did not purchase their commands, and were, in theory, promoted on merit.

problems began immediately. His predecessor, Sir John Craddock, had left under a cloud after insisting on a new uniform code that provoked a sepoy mutiny at Vellore. The result of this was that the Directors, in far-off Leadenhall Street, resolved that in future the Commander-in-Chief should not sit on the Governor's ruling council. No slight to Macdowall was intended; and Barlow, who took over as Governor three months later, certainly had no part in the decision. The general himself nevertheless took it as an insult, and set himself in opposition to Barlow's administration. A personal animosity soon developed; and looking again at their portraits, the aristocrat and the outsider, it is easy to see how differences of class and character hardened into hatred.

Shortly before setting off on his garrison tour, Macdowall had written a letter to Barlow that is fairly characteristic of his style. 'Almost every individual in the Service is dissatisfied ... The degradation of the military character, from the Commander-in-Chief to the youngest ensign, are among prominent features. I must lament the expediency which occasioned these disgusting measures.'[3]

Among the measures that so disgusted Macdowall was the reform of an allowance to white officers of the Company's sepoy regiments. The allowance, known as the Tent Contract, had once been a legitimate return for campaign expenses but was now a source of corruption and the recommendation for its abolition came from within the Army itself: Lieutenant-Colonel John Munro, the Quartermaster-General, pointed out in a secret report that it offered officers 'strong inducements to neglect their most important duties' to their men.[4] There was clear evidence to this effect, but in the Madras Army as a whole there was more room for bombastic posturing than good sense. The officer corps, according to one of their number, had come to 'look on hectoring manners and strong language as almost the natural accompaniments of bravery, and therefore ingredients in the character of an officer and a gentleman; the man who did not show something bordering on these was liable to insult.'[5]

Days before Macdowall's return to Madras, Colonel Munro's report was leaked – with electrifying effect. Senior officers pronounced that their honour had been impugned, drew up a petition accusing Munro of 'cruel and wanton insult', and demanded that he be court-martialled.[6] It was signed by twenty-eight regimental commanders.

As the leaking of so sensitive a paper was bound to cause mischief, the question arises whether it was done deliberately. The historian of the so-called White Mutiny thought not – that it became public because of 'some indiscretion, the history of which is now obscure'. But according to a senior officer who was closely involved, the author of the leak was Macdowall's friend Colonel Francis Capper, the Adjutant-General, who had long played an influential role at Fort St George.[7]

It may still take a stretch of the imagination to see how the Army's bile came to be poured on Barlow. The officer who pinpointed Capper as the source of the leak, Colonel John Malcolm, put it down to a combination of Macdowall's personality – the Commander-in-Chief, he declared, was 'very sparingly endowed with temper and judgment' – and 'the peculiar nature of the service' in Madras.[8] For peculiar nature of the service one might read isolation. Garrisons were scattered over the thousands of square miles of the southern presidency. With little prospect of honour or glory since the defeat of Tipu Sultan of Mysore, the Madras Army had been largely idle and its officers had many hours to brood on imaginary slights, as one of them wrote:

> The want of amusement, the want of employment, the want of books
> – the practice of passing long hours at the mess and billiard table, the
> little change in the narrow circle, and particularly the want of female
> society. All this created a savage spirit.[9]

Such was the temper – from coastal Masulipatam in the north, to rocky Trichinopoly in the south – of garrisons lately visited by a commander who, 'at his own table expressed in contemptuous language his hostility to the Government of Sir George Barlow'. One observer of the ensuing turmoil wrote witheringly of Macdowall: 'His high situation, his address & ready table eloquence made his words full heavy & eagerly caught by the poor deluded wretches whom he [was] commander of.'[10]

For all that imposing appearance, Macdowall had demonstrated a curious lack of resolve before and did so again now. Presented on his return with the petition for a court martial on Colonel Munro, he prevaricated. The only proper response would have been to dismiss it out of hand. But even after receiving legal advice that Munro had no case to answer the general failed to put his foot down and a source of bitterness was left to fester.

Macdowall's personal grievance was also unresolved. Months earlier he had written to the Directors, threatening to resign unless given a seat on Barlow's council. Although post of the greatest importance might be carried by overland riders in a few months, letters otherwise went by sea, and no reply could be expected within a year. But Macdowall had had enough. At the end of October, he started to speak openly of resigning and returning home. He would seem to have grown tired of the whole business – of India and its pleasures, the drinking sessions, the *bibis* and the hunting. He may already have started to negotiate a passage in one of the Indiamen anchored off Fort St George. He was not to know that the Directors were even then reconsidering. A month later they ruled that it had been a mistake to exclude him from council and that he might take his seat. By the time this news arrived he was long gone and matters had spun out of control.

Barlow would have been untroubled to hear rumours that his most intractable enemy wanted to leave Madras. For the time being though, he was still savouring the impending departure of that other foe of constituted authority, Sir Henry Gwillim, lately of the Madras Supreme Court, accompanied by his sister-in-law, Mary Symonds.

Mary would have followed the courtship and marriage of the governor's daughter with uncommon interest. Like Eliza Barlow, she had come to Madras in search of a husband. Unlike her, she was leaving without one. Not that she indulged in any recriminations on the matter, for she was without a trace of self-pity. Her sense, pride and independent spirit could have placed her within a Jane Austen novel, for, having been wooed by more than one nabob, she would have cherished the observation of the truth universally acknowledged about a man with a fortune being in want of a wife. But she had known shame and tragedy too, and both cast a shadow over her departure.[11]

Of Mary Symonds's appearance there is no record, although the fact that her elder sister Elizabeth was written of as a notable beauty and she was not might suggest that she suffered by comparison. However, it was Mary whose personality stood out in their letters home from Madras, and who was able to rise above disaster when it came; and it was not for lack of suitors or proposals that she had failed to find a husband, but rather because, like Lizzie Bennet, she was unwilling to settle for less than she expected.

It was seven years since the sisters had landed in the *Hindostan* with Elizabeth's husband, Henry Gwillim, a judge taking his place on the Supreme Court bench. They made a lively addition to Madras society – Gwillim, erudite, a brilliant jurist with strong opinions that chimed with the new libertarian spirit abroad in Europe, Elizabeth, or Betsy, aged thirty-seven but still beautiful, keenly interested in all aspects of her new home, its inhabitants and wildlife, and Mary, in her early twenties and almost as sweet-natured as she was spirited.

At first they participated fully in the general round of dinners and balls, marvelling as most newcomers did at the unexpected opulence of their little society. Betsy thought Madras 'like prints one has seen of Grecian cities'. The houses, with their flat roofs and long colonnades, covered in *chunam* stucco and shining like marble, made her feel as if she were living in an Italian palace. At table there were more attendants than diners: 'Ladies have servants who stand behind their chairs and fan them during dinner,' she marvelled. But it was their eye for the native inhabitants that set the sisters' letters apart from other contemporary accounts. A description of a ball is the more vivid for an image of palanquin bearers:

> They set the palankeen under the trees before the doors and lie down to sleep or talk . . . all the house is lighted up, with people dining and dancing in the verandahs while the attendants are lying around the garden. There will be 400 or 500 of these people in their muslin robes scattered under the trees before the house.[12]

They did not long remain at the centre of society. Gwillim might have been a judge but he was also a radical who had drunk deeply from the libertarian well. He hated militarism, admired the campaigning journalist William Cobbett and regarded himself as a man of the people. Lord Minto, the Governor-General, described him dryly as 'a Welshman and a fiery Briton in all senses'. So rigorous a soul was not one to indulge the frivolity and profligacy of the Madras gentry, and within a year the Gwillim household had moved from the Mount Road to San Thomé, the old Portuguese settlement a few miles south, a quiet spot on the Adyar river where the sisters began a study of plants and birdlife. Mary declared India 'a very pleasant country for those who are never tired of balls & dinners', but thought it more agreeable to study 'this extraordinary people, among the oldest nations of the world'. She lusted candidly after the jewellery of the Hindu women, 'worn with great taste and elegance'. She wrote: 'When a set of these women walks from the well with their bright vases on their heads they look more dignified than you can imagine. As to the Moor people, as they are called, the Arabian Nights will give you an almost exact description.'[13]

Their letters convey an impression of an agreeable, self-sufficient home: the sisters passing their days in painting; the judge returning from court at the end of the day, falling asleep in his armchair over a book; and every now and again the palpable excitement of a ship from home bringing letters and little treats – bonnets, bottled preserves, even a joint of bacon.

Not that they were lonely. The house was often visited by a circle of young bachelors. But Mary was not easily won, as a letter from Betsy to their mother in 1805 makes clear: 'You may be disappointed to hear that she has refused another offer which was made her. The gentleman was in so good a situation it was certain he had large means . . . If nothing comes to induce her to change her state you must be content to have an old maid for a daughter.'[14]

Old maid she was not, and even when aged almost thirty had two younger suitors. Richard Clarke was the son of a family friend and had been given a position as Gwillim's clerk. William Biss was from their native Hereford, an army cadet with good looks and charm. Although Mary admitted 'I don't look half so young and blooming as I did ten years ago', these gallants squired her around Madras. She wrote home with a sparkiness again redolent of Austen: 'I took the trouble of going to two of the balls in order to oblige [them] but I am by no means fond of such hurly burly for it is all the same thing over and over & all the same people for the most part [although] just now we have plenty of new faces to stare at and new fashions to laugh at.'[15]

It was in 1806 that controversy started to envelop Henry Gwillim. At this point he was a respected if austere figure and had recently been knighted.

Of his ability and integrity there was no doubt. He was also, however, prickly, quarrelsome and intolerant of those he saw as his intellectual inferiors, notably Sir William Bentinck, Barlow's predecessor as Governor. India had only aggravated his temper, which became especially choleric in the hot season. He was once found by a visitor, 'rolling on his own floor, roaring like a baited bull'.[16] None of this detracts from the courage of his stand on behalf of the settlement's Indian inhabitants.

It was inevitable that Gwillim would find himself at odds with the Company regime – that 'copperplate empire', as one historian called it, where 'men lived by the ledger and ruled with the quill'.[17] He was by now quite as cantankerous as his idol Cobbett, whose campaigns for social and political reform had lately extended to the India House.* Unsurprisingly, his hostility towards the raffish Madras set hardened during a trial that came before him that year. It was an ugly affair, a murder trial involving two army officers who had bullied one of their fellows, a quiet young man, into a duel in which he was killed. According to a witness at the trial, the jury were all for a guilty verdict but were bribed by the foreman, William Hope, the former army private who had become the leading nabob in Madras. An onlooker wrote:

> When they came into court Hope pronounced 'Not guilty.' A dead silence prevailed. It was really awful. I shall never forget Sir Henry Gwillam [sic] saying: 'Not guilty! A most merciful Jury! Prisoners, had you been found guilty, you never would have seen the sun rise again. You have had a most narrow escape of your lives. Let it be a warning to you.'[18]

But the event that brought Gwillim into open conflict with the settlement was the mutiny at Vellore in 1806. In events that anticipated the great Mutiny by more than fifty years, sepoys, provoked by the introduction of a new uniform code that stipulated shaving of beards, turned on their European fellows, shooting about two hundred of them. The sepoys' objection, on religious grounds, had been dismissed by Bentinck and Sir John Craddock, the army commander, and both tried to claim that the

---

* Among other things, Cobbett's pamphlets disclosed that the Company, far from contributing to the Exchequer, had become a drain on it because dividends paid to stockholders had to be raised out of general taxation.

mutiny was part of a wider Muslim plot to expel the English. The flaw in this logic was that the majority of mutineers were Hindus.[19] The traumatised whites of Madras were nevertheless impressed with their peril.

The feeling in the Gwillim household about the mutiny can be gauged from Betsy and Mary's letters. Unlike those Madras ladies who dreaded being murdered in their beds, the sisters blamed 'the obstinacy and arrogance' of the authorities for interfering with indigenous culture – 'the sepoys feared they were going to lose their caste,' Betsy wrote, adding tartly: 'Our government were in no hurry to communicate an affair likely to do them so little credit.'[20]

Gwillim meanwhile declared his opposition to the raising of a militia to protect white inhabitants, describing it as 'offensive to the Natives and injurious to the public interest'. Dispute turned to confrontation when the militia detained a man at a disturbance. Gwillim, finding the fellow was 'a poor wandering sadhu', ordered his release. The militia refused. Gwillim issued an order of habeas corpus. At this point Governor Bentinck, who had accused him of 'promulgating opinions from the bench highly dangerous to the public safety', considered having him arrested but instead fired off a stream of dispatches, urging that he be recalled.[21]

Home life would seem not to have altered much thus far. Betsy and Mary continued to entertain young men: there is mention of play-readings and song evenings, and a dinner, attended by the young Fleetwood Pellew, at which Betsy noted 'I really never saw such a row of beautiful faces as down the table.' Mary had cooled towards William Biss – 'he is a good soul but I believe he will be spoiled, for everybody loves him' – while remaining fond of Richard Clarke. Still, she felt awkward about their age difference:

> I shall wait patiently and remain ever as I am unless I meet a man in whom I find those qualities which I think necessary to my happiness. I know several young men who would be most happy to take me, such as I am, to whom no reasonable woman of eighteen or twenty could object, but as they are men twenty-two to twenty-five, I should think myself guilty of an unpardonable rashness doing them the injury to accept them.[22]

The unfolding drama at the Supreme Court, as well as a hint of apprehension, is conveyed by Mary's last letter home, dated 4 March 1807, citing its bearer as one 'able to tell you some particulars of the situation Sir Henry stands in'. After that there was silence. The torrid season was approaching, however, and with it the political temperature rose.

The militia was still refusing to produce the suspect when, on 10 June, Gwillim again took his seat and addressed a Grand Jury. What followed from the judge was a powerful and moving statement on the rule of law versus military despotism that concluded:

> Why have the natives of India clung to the English in preference to other Europeans? It is because they have felt themselves at liberty with them. We are bound to give the natives the benefit of equal laws – we are bound to do it by the laws of God and the laws of man – they are our equals by nature, our brethren.[23]

Thus far Gwillim had not been entirely without supporters, but from the point that he started to endorse native rights the mood of the settlement turned violently against him.

Four weeks later, at the height of the crisis, Betsy Gwillim died aged forty-four. There is no explanation of the cause, for the family archive dries up with Mary's last letter. It may be fair to suggest, however, that the strain of their recent lives played a part. She and Sir Henry were childless, and as they were ostracised their home must have become a lonely place. Madras would remember her, perhaps with a touch of guilt, as 'a lady possessed of great acquirements and in her youth much admired for her beauty'.[24]

Sir Henry's tribute, typically, was more severe – a black marble slab laid over her body at St Mary's Church, where it remains:

> Elizabetha, Pia Conjux
> Henrici Gwillim Eo. Aur.
> Vixit Ann XLIV. Mens VIII*

The Directors had meanwhile sent off one of their orders couched in terms redolent of an exceptionally censorious and sour-faced parson. As they saw it, 'leaving Judge Gwillim in his place [may] be considered by the [native] people as a triumph'.[25] And so it was that even as the fleet bringing Lady Barlow back to India anchored in Madras, a disgraced

---

* Elizabeth, Pious Wife of Henry Gwillim, Conquered in the forty-fourth year and eighth month.

judge and his sister-in-law were making their preparations to depart on the return voyage to England.

Sir Edward Pellew was also getting ready to sail. Early in October he repaired on board HMS *Culloden* and, as the monsoon rain sluiced down outside the glass panes of the admiral's cabin, dictated dispatches to a clerk scratching away at a desk. Pellew's last duty before leaving Madras was to provide for convoying home the Indiamen and he now issued a series of departing orders.

Three fleets were expected to sail by the end of February, two from India and one from China, and all would require Navy escorts. In the case of the India fleets there was a strategic element, as both would carry Bengal saltpetre for the Peninsular War. Whether this lent urgency to their departures is not clear, but both would undoubtedly be traversing the Indian Ocean between November and March, known as the hurricane season. There was the further risk that they might encounter the new French frigates, *Manche* and *Caroline*. The First Fleet, as it would be known, was to depart from Madras by the end of the month. It would consist of nine Indiamen convoyed by HMS *Albion*, a 74. The spring sailing, or the Second Fleet, would be larger, fifteen ships from all three presidencies, and would muster off Ceylon to be escorted by the frigate HMS *Terpsichore*.

As for Pellew, he wrote to the Admiralty that *Culloden* would proceed via Bengal to Penang, an island off west Malaya, where he would welcome his successor, Rear-Admiral William Drury, arriving from England, and hand over command. Pellew anticipated that the ships from China, carrying tea, that new mainstay of the Company's trade, would reach Penang around the same time and he intended to take them home himself.

Preparations for *Culloden*'s departure gathered pace. On 15 October, amid the thudding of carpenters and clatter of armourers, the sails were loosed and set out to dry. The log records the receipt on board of the admiral's wine – the quantity was not specified but Pellew had a good head for claret – along with '3,000 shirts, 800 cotton trousers, 330 blue jackets, 12 trousers for boys, 150 pairs of shoes'. Also taken to *Culloden*'s hold were the fruits of Pellew's years in the East, a treasury of trade goods, valuable and decorative objects – along with a live leopard, a trophy for the grand estate he intended to acquire in Devon.

All this while the five hundred or so hands filled their bellies with fresh meat while they could, receiving on board between four and six live bullocks a day and eating the lot. Two seamen were apprehended bringing spirits on board, for which they were given eighteen lashes apiece, while an able seaman named William Boxley got thirty-six for indecency, which usually meant sodomy or bestiality; Boxley was evidently a stubborn bugger as he had been found guilty of the same offence in June.[26]

Sir George Barlow must have had regrets about *Culloden*'s departure. She was taking not only his first-born child but, in Pellew, one of the very few men of influence in Madras that he had been able to count an ally. As they took their leave of one another Barlow was reassured by Pellew's declaration that he saw their destinies as intertwined and would represent the Governor to the best of his ability among the powerful at home.[27]

On the eve of *Culloden*'s sailing Pellew hosted a dinner on board for General Macdowall. As Commanders-in-Chief of their respective forces they were bound to exchange ritual courtesies, but their dealings may well have gone beyond the purely formal. Pellew had warmth and charm and perhaps offered Macdowall some friendly advice on dealing with the aloof Barlow.

Also on board *Culloden* were Captain Pownoll Pellew and his new bride. In the captain's spacious quarters, where she had begun her married life, Eliza wrote a final letter to her father, expressing herself 'as happy and as comfortable as I can be living in sight of my friends [but] unable to see them' and vowing 'to prove myself worthy of such good parents'. Her husband also wrote that night, promising his father-in-law that 'all the most amiable and lovely girl deserves shall be her portion from me'. Sir George 'had made me the happiest man in the world by trusting Eliza in me & by having contributed so generously to all our future wants'.[28]

That generosity, and his share of prize money, would enable Pownoll to leave the Navy. When *Culloden* raised her anchor around noon on 24 October to the roar of a 17-gun salute from the fort and set a course for Bengal, the young couple were at last homeward bound to the countryside cottage of which he had dreamt.

4

'Sir Henry Gwillim embarks . . . and the Devil go with him'

Madras and at Sea, 23 October 1808–12 January 1809

Even as the admiral's flagship set her course north for Bengal, a small exodus had begun from the beach beside Fort St George where the *masoolah* boatmen had their craft drawn up. In turbans and loincloths, dark glistening figures had spent weeks in driving monsoon rains, ferrying out cargoes of saltpetre and supplies to the nine ships anchored almost two miles offshore. Now, in the final phase, they carried the baggage of those about to take ship, followed by the passengers themselves.

From the highest to the lowest – from Mount Road nabob to regimental fort scruff – about five hundred Company servants and dependants were homeward bound that October. There were dozens of families, a veritable corps of army officers, a handful of men who had made fortunes and reputations, and a few besides Sir Henry Gwillim departing under a cloud. There were more disappointed maids than just Mary Symonds, quite a few widows and an astonishing number of children being sent home on their own for schooling. And there were the rank-and-file, the soldiers lucky just to have survived their term of duty – as so many of their fellows had failed to do – and the military and naval invalids, whose survival still hung in the balance. In keeping with the age, they would be transported in conditions ranging from the closest to luxury early nineteenth-century sea travel could offer, the roundhouse of an Indiaman, to dank, fetid quarters below decks where there was barely space to sling a hammock.

The nine ships in which they were to travel had come together over recent weeks in the roads off Fort St George. Of these vessels, some stand out for attention.[1]

The *Lord Nelson*, a large vessel of 818 tons, was a product of the renowned Barnards yard on the Thames and, being on her fourth voyage, somewhat elderly for an Indiaman. She had already had an adventurous career, offering gallant resistance when attacked by the 28-gun French privateer *Bellone*, off Ireland in 1803, before being disabled – and almost immediately recaptured.* Appropriately for her name, she was painted in the Nelsonian check pattern that, having been adopted by the Navy, was becoming common in Indiamen; less aptly, she was only a middling sailer, one captain noting sourly that 'from an ill-formed bow she always pitched heavily when sailing by the wind even in moderate weather'.

Her skipper, William Hutton, was the most experienced of the nine captains and was designated their Commodore, next in line after Captain John Ferrier of HMS *Albion*, and would therefore take command if they became separated from the navy ship. Unusually for the senior captain, Hutton still had accommodation available and he took the step of inviting applications for passage through an advertisement in the *Courier*.[2] The only cabin passengers at this stage – a lieutenant-colonel of the 17th Native Infantry, his wife and three children, two Calcutta gentlemen and an army surgeon – were hoping there would be no response so they would be left to spread themselves in comfort around the roundhouse.

So severely had the *Lord Nelson* suffered from the attentions of *Culloden*'s impress gang that Hutton had protested that he could not sail in safety and Pellew returned some of her hands. Hutton had nevertheless to take on lascars, the native Muslim sailors of India, to make up his complement of hands to around 110. There was nothing unusual about this – virtually every Indiaman was in the same position – but most of Hutton's colleagues were in agreement that *Lord Nelson* was 'miserably manned'.[3]

The *Ceylon* was another of the larger ships and Captain Thomas Hudson also had cause to watch *Culloden*'s departure with resentment. On anchoring in Madras a year earlier, twenty-three of his best men had been taken into the flagship. In Bengal, another ten men were pressed by HMS *Russel*. Three more were taken by the sloop *Dasher* and five by other navy ships, so that if Hudson should now have examined the names of his original 114 men and struck out all those taken by the Navy, adding

* In Patrick O'Brian's novel *Post Captain*, in which Jack Aubrey takes passage in the *Lord Nelson* and virtually takes command of her during this action, she is wrongly described as being on her last voyage.

the six dead of disease, the six deserters, the two who drowned in Diamond Harbour, and William Harrison, the carpenter's mate, who decided he had seen quite enough of all this and enrolled in the Light Dragoons, he would have counted a total loss of 56 – fully half his crew. He had been fortunate in recruiting a few Danes in Bengal but had also been obliged to make up the rest with lascars.[4]

The *Glory*, one of the category of smaller 500-ton ships known as 'Extras', stood out for all the wrong reasons. As well as being small, she was notoriously the worst sailer in the fleet – not only slow and ill-handling but 'very crank', in other words built too deep or narrow and so inclined to lean over towards either port or starboard.[5] She was an unhappy ship in general. On an earlier voyage, Captain Thomas Taylor fell out so badly with a passenger that they fought a duel on reaching Madras in which Taylor was killed.[6] The *Glory*'s melancholy reputation had preceded her, for although Horatio Beevor, her new captain, had taken on a small band of passengers in Bengal, she too had spare cabin space. Beevor had therefore subscribed to the advertisement placed by Hutton in the *Courier*.

The *Preston*, Captain Henry Sturrock, and the *Phoenix*, Captain John Ramsden, were both well-run, efficient ships commanded by men who in their different ways could have served as models for an Indiaman captain. Although navy captains tended to look down on them as mere traders, deficient in 'those high and delicate refinements which constitute the distinction between the art of war and the art of gain', a successful Indiaman captain required special qualities.[7] To the ability of a seaman, he had to add the flair of a businessman. Having acquired a ship by a combination of influence, good fortune and investment, he had generally three voyages in which to recoup his outgoings and make enough to retire in something like the manner of the nabobs he transported. The means for this were private trade – and passage money. It followed that he had also to be a diplomat, for an Indiaman captain's reputation mattered a great deal in the gossipy circles of Calcutta and Madras, where the man who had earned his passengers' gratitude through a storm survived, or fostered harmony by the grace of his manners, became known and was sought out. On top of these qualities, he had to be prepared to fight his ship if necessary.[8]

Sturrock and Ramsden had a good deal in common. Both would appear to have come from the kind of modestly genteel background that provided access to the Company's marine service. Sturrock joined as a fourteen-year-old midshipman, Ramsden as a teenage contractor, before each rose through the ranks to command. Both had made eight voyages to India and were commanding a ship for the third time. Where they differed was in the way they utilised their passenger quarters.

The section of an Indiaman occupied by the senior officers and cabin passengers was at the rear, beneath the top deck, or the poop, which extended about thirty feet forward of the stern. Immediately below, at the level of the quarterdeck, were to be found the cuddy, or dining saloon, separated from the captain's cabin by a narrow passage, and beyond that, across the entire width of the stern, the roundhouse. Well-lit, airy and high enough above the sea to keep the occupants dry even in rough weather, this was the most sought-after accommodation and was generally divided into between three and six cabins by means of adjustable canvas or wooden partitions, the proportion of each being determined by the number of passengers and the depth of their pockets. Each cabin was an empty shell, to be furnished by the occupant. As well as the wealthy and distinguished, the roundhouse was occupied by ladies travelling alone, as they were held to be under the captain's protection.

Below the roundhouse, on the gundeck, was the great cabin – more accurately a series of cabins, occupied mainly by male passengers travelling alone, such as army officers. Forward of the great cabin was the steerage area, where the ship's junior officers had their quarters and the lower order of passengers, ensigns and writers, were accommodated. If a ship was carrying a number of children, as many did on the passage home, they too would be housed here. William Hickey, homeward bound in 1808, booked a section of the *Castle Eden*'s great cabin – to his lasting regret, for she was carrying fifteen children and he found that the combination of their shrieks from steerage, the stinks that sank to this lower level, the bulkheads' creaking, and the frequency with which the sea burst in on his quarters and over his bed, made for a miserable voyage.

Sturrock had built a career out of transporting the genteel and rich. The *Preston*'s roundhouse had been turned over to a kind of grand suite, the most recent occupants of which had been Lady Barlow and the Calcutta

54

hostess and beauty, Lady Russell. Homeward bound, it had been taken by James Watts, a senior Company official of handsome fortune, accompanied by his wife, three children and two servants. Furnished in the manner of a small but cosy Georgian room with sea couches which converted into sofas during the daytime, a bureau with bookshelves, a table and chairs, a washstand and foot-tub, this suite would have constituted the most luxurious passenger accommodation available, and would have cost the occupant about £2,000 – the equivalent today of about £120,000.

A similar suite in the great cabin below was occupied by James Lautour, a scion of Madras's most powerful banking family, and his wife Barbara. The space forward of this was divided between a Mr Christopher Teesdale and three lieutenants of the 80th Regiment.

If Sturrock's speciality was providing luxury for wealthy travellers – and charging them rather more than he ought under Company rules – Ramsden offered different virtues: a tight, well-run ship with basic comforts for the less well off. As a result, the *Phoenix*'s quarters were heaving. In all, thirteen adults and eleven children were berthed in the roundhouse, great cabin and steerage. Among them were Sir Henry Gwillim and Mary Symonds.

On 23 October, amid 'hard rain, thunder & lightning', the disgraced judge and the spinster joined a bedraggled band of gentlefolk on the beach to be rowed out by *masoolah* to the waiting Indiamen. Gwillim was by now fixed in the public eye as a revolutionary Jacobin and Madras watched his going without regret; one local resident uttered what sounded very like a curse: 'Sir Henry Gwillim embarks on the *Phoenix* and the Devil go with him.'9

For her part, Mary had not lost all hope. Through the upheavals of recent months, Richard Clarke had remained loyal – both as Gwillim's clerk and her suitor – and, since Betsy's death, had become virtually part of the household. He was returning to England in the same ship and Mary, in one of her last letters, wrote of him with a warmth that suggested she might, after all, marry a man five years her junior: 'He has not much beauty of feature, but a peculiar sweetness of expression. He is never ruffled by trifles but has occasionally shown that he has no want of proper spirit.'10 Mary would have six months in intimate proximity with Richard to decide whether she might spend the rest of her life with him.

An Indiaman voyage, as Lord Macaulay noted, provided the best conceivable test of love and friendship. It also posed an unrivalled opportunity for discord. We can imagine the horror of a voyager coming on board to find in such close proximity a fellow of incompatible manners or opinions, a woman of tyrannical or plaintive disposition. What of a man like Sir Henry Gwillim? A noble defender of principle he might be, but he was intolerant and opinionated too. Discomfort and peril would draw out deeper personal truths.

The rains had blown away when, on 26 October, two days after *Culloden*'s departure, the signal came from HMS *Albion* for the nine Indiamen to weigh. It was mid-afternoon and across the fleet stomachs were full with the last fresh beef this side of the Cape when the hands made their way to capstans and into the rigging. By the time a light breeze filled those acres of canvas and bore them away the sun was dipping behind Fort St George. From the battlements they made a brief, brave show on that curiously pink sea – *Albion*, then the Indiamen in two lines abreast – before being swallowed by night on the Indian Ocean.

The First Fleet was under way.

Ramsden took in the scene from *Phoenix*'s quarterdeck with pleasure. Just nine months had passed since he set forth from Spithead and the way things were going he could look forward to being back in the Downs by March – earlier if the weather helped them. In addition to her cargo of saltpetre, the *Phoenix* was carrying his own private trade. It would not enable him to retire just yet; but one more voyage should do the trick.

Ramsden was aged forty, a Londoner of sufficiently well-to-do background to have been baptised at St Martin-in-the-Fields. The *Phoenix* was his second command and they were likely to end their careers together. She was a contented ship. Although Indiamen were, in theory, run along similar disciplinary lines to navy ships, few Indiamen captains were keen floggers and a dozen lashes was sufficient to meet the requirement for most offences.

Ramsden's regime was more moderate than most. On the outward voyage, while the *Phoenix* was at St Helena, the cutter was taken off in the dark of night by six deserters; the only culprit at hand, a gunner named William Howell who was found drunk and asleep on his watch, was broken to able seaman. A few days later Philip Suring, also rated able, was found guilty of theft and sentenced to thirty-six lashes, but after he had received eighteen he was cut down 'to receive the remainder of his punishment at a future period'. It was never carried out and only one other man was flogged in the entire seven months of the voyage.[11] In the same period, men were being given up to four dozen almost daily on HMS *Nereide*.

Set fares were laid down for each category of passenger, from £50 for a cadet to £250 for a colonel, although some captains would charge far more. Before her death Betsy Gwillim had fulminated against those, 'who are so enormous in their demands for a passage home that many people are mere prisoners in this place'.[12] But Ramsden appears to have been a stickler for regulations. In addition to the three members of the Gwillim party, his passenger quarters contained Thomas Daniell (no relation to the artist), his wife and three children, four gentlemen, a Mrs Rowley and her two children, two officers of the 33rd Regiment, and six children travelling alone. Some must have been accommodated in quarters that resembled those of Mary Sherwood, the children's author, on the *Devonshire*:

> Our cabin was just the width of one gun, with room beside for a small table and single chair. Our cot, slung cross-ways over the gun, could not swing, there not being height sufficient . . . We were also in constant darkness . . . When the pumps were at work, the bilge water ran through this miserable place, this worse than dog kennel, and to finish the horrors of it, it was only separated by a canvas partition from the place in which the soldiers sat, and, I believe, slept and dressed.[13]

Gwillim – even in his reduced circumstances the most distinguished passenger on board – would probably have taken one of the roundhouse cabins with his young aide Clarke. Mary had a small roundhouse cabin of her own. But she enjoyed precedence at dinner where she and Mrs Rowley were seated on either side of Captain Ramsden. This was a formal affair, introduced by the beating of drums, for which the ladies dressed in their finery, and at which the captain presided in uniform. Ramsden was a cultivated as well as well-travelled man and Mary, who had seen a good deal of callow youth, evidently appreciated his company. While her suitor Clarke occupied a place at the lower end of the table, Ramsden was soon treating her with more attention than was usual. And as she was a lady travelling under his protection, he would give her his arm when she appeared on deck, to walk and converse with her.

Another element in this social mix invites speculation. As Macaulay said, no one on an Indiaman was able to escape his fellows except by imprisoning himself in his cabin. How, in such circumstances, did a judge of the rigorous rectitude of Gwillim conduct himself towards a crook like Robert Sherson? A former civil servant in Madras, Sherson was accused of embezzling grain relief for the victims of a drought and was on his way home to face the Directors' inquisition.[14] The judge and the fraudster, united in their disgrace, would have endless opportunities to discuss the merits of their respective cases.

Over the first few days the wind blew lightly and intermittently under a clear sky and even with a full press of sail the fleet made only between one and three knots. Crews were finding their way again at the start of the voyage and, depleted as they were, each ship ran according to her abilities, so that the ordered lines of sailing soon disintegrated and Captain Ferrier on HMS *Albion* felt obliged to signal his nine charges to close up.

On 30 October the wind got up, bringing squalls that sheeted across the decks but also filled sails, and they made between five and six knots. This was not exactly cracking on by navy standards – a frigate might make ten or even eleven knots – but an Indiaman's progress was dictated by safety rather than haste and it was customary to stow staysails and topgallants in the evening watch. Like most navy captains, Ferrier would have been bristling with impatience; but he was not alone. The fleet could move only at the pace of the slowest ship, and it was evident that the sad old *Glory* was going to be a trial for them all. Towards the end of each day they had to shorten sail so she could catch up, and once or twice she had to be taken in tow by the *Lord Nelson*.

To read the logbooks of the First Fleet ships today is to experience at second hand a curious sense of apprehension. The record of daily shipboard life gives no hint of incipient calamity and to freeze a moment on, say, 7 November, one might imagine them, ordered and trim once more, in two lines abreast, each an island domain, each with its little dramas, moving steadily south. Almost two weeks after sailing from Madras, routines had been established – routines for passengers as well as crew, of meals, card games in the cuddy, and turns on the quarterdeck – and as the months of the voyage stretched ahead, the shared experience of the bewildering land that had until recently been their home seemed increasingly strange as it was lost farther and farther behind the horizon.

In the early hours of that morning one of ten French prisoners on the *Preston* died and was dropped over the side after a brief ceremony. At around the same time Philip Jones, who was among the twenty-five navy invalids on the *Phoenix*, also expired and was dealt with in the same way. As it was a Sunday, each ship would normally have held Divine Service, but none of the captains appears to have been particularly devout for it required no more than a light squall of rain for them all to call it off. Soon after the beginning of the afternoon watch a strong breeze came up in the north-east and drove the clouds off, so that by the time the hands were piped to dinner the sky surrounded them as a luminous blue void. It was still fine in the pink of the evening when passengers took an airing and off-duty men danced a hornpipe or two and sang their songs on the forecastle.

They were following the Outer Passage, the route dictated by the north-east monsoon, following an arc out into the Indian Ocean that ran east of Ceylon then due south. This would keep them well to the east of Ile de France and the twin threats that it posed.

First, naturally, was the trio of French frigates based at Port Louis – the elderly *Canonnière*, now bolstered by *Manche* and *Caroline*. With a Navy 74 as escort, most captains would in truth have been fairly sanguine about this danger. Indiamen mounted their own guns and nine of them together could put up a stout resistance, even if parted from the *Albion*. The real concern was that they might become separated from one another. A big Indiaman might superficially resemble a frigate but, once isolated, the 18-gun *Phoenix*, for example, would be no match for the 40-gun *Manche*.

The second threat in the vicinity of Ile de France was the weather. A monsoon wind that blew hereabouts from December to March was notoriously productive of storms, to the extent that this was known as the hurricane season. Not that the captains believed they had anything particular to fear from the weather on 10 November, as they crossed the line of the Equator, still more than 2,000 miles north-east of the island.

The first mishap occurred four days later, as Ramsden recorded in the log:

> At a quarter before 2am saw a ship right ahead on a contrary tack. Hove all aback but did not clear her & she fell athwart our hawse on the starboard bow. Found it was the *Ann*. She carried away jib boom, spritsail yard, flying jib boom & bumpkin. Sprung the headrails and damaged the figure[head]. At 3am got clear of her.[15]

The collision, though spectacular and terrifying for passengers on both ships, damaged only spars in the bows. Running repairs were made over the next two days. Now, however, the fleet spread itself and for the next week ships came in and out of view of one another. Visibility was also reduced as repeated squalls blew up in the north-east, sweeping across the sea in wicked black clouds. For a few hours on 19 November the sky cleared under a moderate breeze, so that parasols and dresses appeared on deck amid bright sunshine. But as Ramsden sat down to his log that evening a heavy swell was moving in the south. He noted their position: Latitude 08° 27'S, Longitude 87° 75'E.

The next morning the swell continued to rise and for the first time a real blow came on. Ramsden had little hesitation in cancelling Divine Service before the wind turned to a gale and orders were issued to close reef sails. Now the crews were really put to the test. Surrounded by swirling blocks of sea and, as the log put it, 'the ship pitching dreadfully, burying her forecastle and at times the bowsprit', topmen hauled themselves up ratlines through sheeting rain and clambered out on yardarms. Here, a hundred feet or so above the plunging deck, braced against the yards, feet planted on ropes slung below and swaying with a mast that might be moving through sixty degrees, they handed in sails – topgallants and tops on the foremast, main and mizzen (the hindmost) – and furled them, reducing the amount of canvas exposed to the wind.

Supper that night, 20 November, would have been a sober affair, with diners holding fast to chairs cleated to decks and bolsters placed on tables to confine the dishes that were sliding about. *Phoenix* was still pitching fearfully and Ramsden, while presenting a confident demeanour, was not the sort of captain to raise false expectations. A blow like this might last for days. But among those at table, Gwillim and Mary at least were impressed by the calmness of the captain and his officers, and relieved to be in such hands.[16]

In the morning, however, it was as much as any passenger could do to get down from their cots and dress without being hurled across the cabin. Those venturing up on deck found a scene like that which greeted William Hickey during a similar storm:

> Never to the last day of my existence shall I forget the shock at what I beheld. The horizon all round was of a blackish purple, above which rolled great masses of cloud of a deep copper colour; vivid lightning in every quarter, thunder awfully roaring at a distance; a short irregular sea breaking with a tremendous surf, the wind whistling shrill as a boatswain's pipe through the blocks and rigging. The scene was such as to appal the bravest man on board.[17]

The gale was turning into a hurricane. Through the howl, Ramsden ordered the men back into the tops. His priority was to take all the sails in and let her run off under bare poles. But while the men wrestled with the furious canvas, the main topsail was shredded. Then, with a crack of explosive force, both fore and mizzen staysails blew away into infinity. There was nothing else out there but black skies and white seas. The fleet had disintegrated.

Around dusk Ramsden was told about the water building up below. An inspection found that in her lurching motion *Phoenix* was taking sea through a section of the starboard bow damaged in the collision with the *Ann*. In such weather she was bound to ship water through the ports and from waves across the gundeck; the ship's pumps could deal with that. But this new source was another matter. Lascars had been working the hand pumps since the storm's onset. Now they were starting to lose ground and Ramsden ordered all hands to the forward gundeck, where a human chain was set up to bail out water as it came in.

There is only the one record of events on *Phoenix*. Ramsden's log is a typical slab of Indiaman record. What makes it dramatic is the way that neat mundane daily details of wind direction, course and positional observations suddenly give way to a scrawl of disjointed notes: 'Ship making much water and lurching heavily to leeward. Attempted to take main topsail in to ease her, split it. Fore and mizzen staysails blew away' . . . 'At noon still continuing to blow a heavy gale, pumping going on as before.'[18] For all the taut drama of such entries, it is left to our imagination to fill the silences from around the ship – not just the roundhouse but, for example, the space forward of steerage occupied by the invalids.

In this low, dark, stinking part of the ship, no fewer than eighty-nine invalids messed in quarters similar to those of the crew, between the great guns where they slung their hammocks and took their meals. Their names are not recorded, but we know that sixty-four were soldiers, light dragoons and infantrymen, and twenty-five navy sailors. They were ailing and in some cases dying.

A handful were accompanied by women. Take Mrs Pridie, the wife of a trooper in the 59th Regiment. She was not mentioned in the passenger list and we know of her existence only because she died at 4 a.m. on 16 November, four days before the storm began, and was 'committed to the deep with the usual ceremony' the following day. One of the few wives allowed to go with her man to India – usually after a quayside lottery just before departure – she had survived about three years at the Madras garrison, only to die in a black maelstrom in mid-ocean. Her passing was barely noticed. United in terror and misery, hurled from side to side with water swirling around their feet in flickering candlelight, the invalids resembled a vision of the damned.

For most of the following day, 22 November, the wind blew as furiously as it had for the past two days – 'a perfect hurricane', Ramsden thought. Then, late in the afternoon, it dropped. The sense of relief that flooded through the ship is almost palpable as one reads:

> At 4pm the weather moderating fast & clearing up. Nothing in sight.
> At 5pm almost calm, set the close reefed mizzen topsail & loosened the foresail.

There may have been time for a proper meal, the first in two days, and grog for the hands. But celebration was premature. So, it proved, was Ramsden's order to set the sails. They had merely passed through the eye of the hurricane. Two hours later, the wind came tearing up again, pulling chains of black cloud and sending the men hastily back to the yards. In handing in the mizzen topsail, Thomas Pain, rated able, lost his footing and plunged into the sea, never to be seen again.

As the storm closed in, they had a brief, ghastly vision. Out of the dark another Indiaman appeared like a flailing phantom, her mizzenmast and main topmast blown away, scudding along out of control. She passed within a few feet of *Phoenix*'s stern and then was gone again into the night – so quickly that no one could be sure which ship had come so close to causing their mutual destruction; she was, in fact, the *Diana*.

Soon afterwards, at 11 p.m., the hurricane returned with all its former fury and now, bent by the wind, the *Phoenix* was 'laying over a good deal & shipping very heavy seas, making much water at the ports and scuttles & also at the rudder head and quarter gallery'.

Up to this point, the intake of water had been stabilised by having all four pumps going and keeping a bailing party on the gundeck. By midnight, however, the water level in the hold had risen to three feet. At this point a new crisis occurred. 'At 1am one of the pumps choaked and could not be cleared. Continued to work the three pumps and bailing on the gundeck, the scuppers not venting all the water she took in there.'

By 2 a.m. there was five feet of water in the hold and it was rising about one foot every hour. At this rate it was inevitable that the *Phoenix* would founder, possibly before dawn. When a sufficient volume of water built up in the hold, she would simply be dragged down. Ramsden later admitted that at this point he believed they were doomed.[19] As it was, only the fact that *Phoenix* was relatively well manned had preserved her thus far.

Those in the roundhouse were certain of their fate. On this third night of terror they may even have reached a point of exhaustion where the prospect of death was losing its dread. Gwillim had been resigned to it these past twenty-four hours. Mary recalled the loss of an old friend, Captain Price of the *Prince of Wales*, who had drowned when the ship foundered off the Cape in 1804. 'We all admired him very much,' she wrote. 'He had such a character that nobody chose to credit the loss of his ship.' Their own loss would doubtless follow a similar pattern: anxiety over their failure to arrive at the Cape; a prolonged silence pending reports from parts like Madagascar, where they might have put in for repairs; and finally an exchange of letters between London and Madras, confirming that the *Phoenix* must have foundered. A year could be expected to pass before anxiety became certainty.

At 3 a.m. a glimpse of hope appeared when the main pump was cleared. By then the water was almost eight feet deep and everything depended on whether the additional pump, combined with a huge human effort, could start to reduce the water level. Ramsden went about the ship, from passengers to invalids, urging that if they valued their lives, every man able to rise should put his hands to the pumps or join in bailing water from the gundeck. Although the response to this appeal was never spelt out, it would seem that even judge and fraudster, Gwillim and Sherson, were to have a hand in their own salvation.

After an hour the water level had stabilised. Ramsden noted tersely: 'Just held our own.' By 5 a.m. they had started to gain. At 6 a.m. the level was down to six feet.

The storm had not yet loosed its hold on the ship, however. With a final furious burst of energy, it tore away the foretopmast along with the best bower anchor. Midway through the morning they shipped a heavy sea which

> stove in the upper gallery windows and partly filled the cuddy and roundhouse with water.

For the rest of that day, 23 November, survival hung in the balance. The wind was more variable but continued to buffet them in great gusts, while the sea rose and fell in thudding blows. A giant wave swept the quarterdeck clear of an able seaman named Hammond Garbo, along with the binnacles containing navigation instruments and a ladder to the poop.

But by evening the wind had moderated and the water in the hold was reduced to three feet. Some of the hands were stood down from the pumps and, wet and exhausted though they were, the company slept easily for the first time in four nights. Not until morning was it noticed that another of the invalids of the 59th Regiment had died.

The *Phoenix* had been left in a shocking state. Most of the rigging was gone, along with the tops of all three masts, parts of the bulwark and all hammock netting. Sails had been reduced to shreds. What had become of the rest of the fleet was anyone's guess, but it was clear that *Phoenix* would have to cope on her own. Ramsden called his senior officers to a conclave: the question was, should they return to Madras or proceed as best they could to the Cape? The unanimous opinion was that they should go on.

Over the next four days, under a sunny sky and on a calm sea, they remained almost motionless as the ship underwent basic repairs. Reprieved from death, men fell to their tasks with willing hands and singing hearts as new topmasts were swayed up and sails stitched. Ramsden did not even pause for Divine Service on the first Sunday after their escape. On 30 November he could record that, with a pleasant trade wind behind, they were slipping along at seven knots.

Only thirty-one days later a lookout in the foretop called down that he could see land in the west. An observation showed that they were at Latitude 34° 05'S, Longitude 25° 44'E. The land was Cape St Francis and they were within a few days of Table Bay and sanctuary.

A spartan time they had had of it. The poultry coops had blown off the poop deck in the hurricane and, apart from three pigs preserved on the gundeck that were served up on Christmas Day, a diet of salt beef and salt pork with seamen's biscuits had to serve for the entire company. Still, they had endured and, as so often, there were those who had been brought closer by crisis. A woman named Maria Graham who experienced something similar wrote of the bond that developed between seamen and passengers in extremis:

> Those who spend their life on shore can have no idea of the activity, courage and presence of mind every day displayed on board ship: there is no moment in which the seriousness of business relaxes because there is no moment in which self-preservation does not require exertion. When bad weather comes on, when gales are blowing and seas running which threaten destruction, the skilful mariner forgets the danger and only sees the way to secure his ship; his word seems like fate, the slightest alteration in the setting of a sail, a single turn of the wheel, seems to baffle the storm and to lay all quiet around.

The curse on the *Phoenix* – 'Sir Henry Gwillim embarks ... and the Devil go with him' – had lifted. And at the end, her voyage had touched with tenderness the lives of at least two of those on board, Captain Ramsden and the lady passenger who had been beside him in the cuddy through that time of dread and elation.

Mary Symonds had once vowed to remain a spinster, 'unless I meet a man in whom I find those qualities which I think necessary to my happiness'. She would not, after all, marry young Richard Clarke, but her long quest for a suitable partner was over. In the strong figure of a phlegmatic forty-year-old Indiaman captain, Mary had found her mate.[20]

On 12 January, *Phoenix* anchored in Table Bay where she found a handful of ships from the navy squadron. Of the rest of the First Fleet there was no sign.

5

'Not heard of again'

At Sea and Table Bay, 22 November 1808–12 January 1809

In the hours after the fleet disintegrated each ship became an isolated speck, careering along atop the crest of doom. Among those at its very edge was the *Diana*.

The *Diana* had last been sighted on 22 November from the *Phoenix*, looming out of a shrieking night like some ghost ship and coming within a few feet of a collision that must have destroyed both. Like the *Phoenix*, she had just come through the calm at the centre of the storm and like her was about to enter its most ferocious phase. Like *Phoenix*, too, she was fighting for her life.

Diana had suffered less from the impress than some others in the First Fleet, having lost just seven men, but that figure does not reveal the extent of her difficulties for she had a mere fifty-seven hands in all, about twenty fewer than an Extra ship of her 600 tons required. Her mizzen mast and main topmast were already gone and she had five feet of water in the hold as the hurricane came on in all its black elemental force.

At midnight the drenched figure of Captain John Marshall entered the roundhouse and told his passengers the gravity of their position: they were shipping more water than the pumps could deal with; the seamen were exhausted and unless they received help with pumping and bailing the ship would undoubtedly founder. All the male passengers came forward – two lieutenant-colonels, Burrows and Huddlestone, two captains, Latter and Campbell, three lieutenants, Scott, Ker and Williams, an assistant surgeon named Thomas Morgan and the sole civilian, W.C. Ord, a Company official, with his servant Richard Parks. 'Every passenger [was] employed in this business,' Marshall wrote.[1] And though exhausting, the exertion of handling the pumps and bailing was preferable to the passivity of the women, children and invalids – the interminable hours of anxiety, broken by moments of heart-clutching terror as another demon seized the ship and shook her from bowsprit to stern.

They battled the tide rising inside the ship all night. Daylight brought no relief from the storm and at 7 a.m., amid one especially terrible buffeting, the foretopmast was carried away. At such moments – 'every person very much fatigued with constant hard labour' – their efforts seemed futile. Nevertheless, they had started to reduce the water level and with 'all hands pumping & bailing & with the greatest exertions' it was down to two feet by midday. That was on 23 November, and *Diana* had been in the storm's grip for almost forty-eight hours. But the worst was yet to come. Captain Marshall's log tells the story from noon:

> Still continuing to blow a hurricane with every gust apparently more violent than the last, the ship labouring in a most dreadful manner, the water in the hold gradually increasing in spite of every exertion until it reached to six feet. The gundeck forward of the main hatchway four feet deep*.[2]

At five in the evening the gundeck was still taking water on, with the effect of pulling the *Diana* further down by the head in the towering white seas. Those confined below could see nothing of the oncoming blows, were unable to brace themselves as yet another shock ran through the ship, casting bodies aside into the porridge of flotsam, bedding, clothing and other possessions, that swirled round them. Many nursed fractures and contusions.

All hope seemed to be gone. Marshall had ceased to scan the blizzard of sea, spray and rain for a hint of light. He could see nothing anyway and by now, as he put it, 'expected to sink every minute'. It was only out of instinct that he sent the women and children to the highest internal section of the ship, the roundhouse, to await the inevitable. They included his own heavily pregnant wife, three army officers' wives, Mrs Latter, Mrs Campbell and Mrs Mason, a maid, Ellen Hare, and three children. They remained in a state of abject terror for several hours as winds shattered the

---

* This seeming discrepancy between the depths of water on different decks is not explained. The level of four feet on the gundeck may have been the high point reached by the water as the ship pitched forward. What is clear is that the sea inundated the crews' quarters on the gundeck, an extraordinarily high and perilous level.

exposed stern galleries around them and blew away furniture into the night. In the midst of these horrors, a Mrs Radcliffe, a recent widow whose fourteen-month-old son had died at sea two weeks earlier, found that she did, after all, want to live.

After consulting his chief mate, Marshall decided that 'the last effort which could be made to save the ship' was cutting down the foremast. With the mizzen and maintop gone, this was the only thing that might ease the forward drag and prevent the ship being pulled down by the head.

Felling a mast would normally have been no job at all, but for men fighting exhaustion and barely able to stay upright in the furies, it was as much as they could manage. When finally the mast went, it came down on the bowsprit, adding to the drag – until a couple of men, with one last desperate effort, managed to chop away the bowsprit, and the whole mass of wreckage was swept off on the wind, clear of the ship.

In that moment the head was released, and came up like a drowning man bursting to the surface.

> Everyone's hopes were revived of saving the ship & fresh efforts were made at the pumps & bailing. In a short time the water in the hold was reduced to five feet at which depth it was kept until midnight when the wind moderated considerably & enabled us to open two of the scuppers which carried off a great deal of water.[3]

The scene in the morning was a shambles. Quarterdeck and forecastle were piled with the ruins of rigging, shattered timber and shreds of dirty canvas. Of the three masts only about twenty feet of the lower main was still standing. The lower decks were similarly devastated. Inspecting the crew's quarters on the gundeck, Marshall found 'everything destroyed, not a man having a chest with anything to put on and all completely worn out with fatigue'. So done in were the hands that it was as much as they could manage over the next twenty-four hours to clear the gundeck.

Their livestock had been wiped out. The ship's cow, three calves and four goats died below decks; thirty dozen fowls and eight dozen ducks had been swept away in their coops. The entire company would be on bare rations from now on, for four casks of salt meat and large quantities of biscuit and rice had also been destroyed, along with nearly all the little luxuries for the passengers' table in the cuddy. Indeed, there would be no more set meals of any sort, all the cuddy furniture having been lost out of the shattered gallery.

But this was no time for self-pity. At 9 a.m., Marshall called a conference of his officers and the senior male passengers when he pointed out that the hands, to whom they owed their lives, had lost everything they possessed and were left with just what they stood up in. He went on to propose that 'a subscription should be immediately started for their relief . . . and that it should be done not only out of humanity & consideration for the unparalleled exertions which they had made towards saving the ship but also as an act of policy to stimulate further exertions towards putting her in a state to enable us to proceed.'

Such pragmatic compassion was much to Marshall's credit. So was the response of the officers and passengers who immediately subscribed £675.

The *Diana* remained vulnerable to further storms but now the Indian Ocean showed a benign aspect. For five days they lay under a topaz sky, moving on a gentle swell from the east as the ship was brought back into rudimentary sailing order. Their ordeal had passed, but there was still no lack of human drama as the voyage resumed.

> 24 Nov: Thomas Needham, invalid, put in irons for having been accused by Lt-Col Burrows of stealing 21 guineas from one of his trunks.
> 28 Nov: Released from confinement Thos Needham, Lt-Col Burrows having found the money which he was accused of having stolen.
>
> 13 Dec: Confined Solomon Mears [seaman] in irons for mutinous conduct.
> 16 Dec: Released Solomon Mears from confinement on a promise of his future good behaviour.

Marshall's simple decency shines throughout the pages of his log. He was no flogger – indeed, he positively disliked the Cat. Another man found guilty of insolence and drunkenness was also released on a promise of better conduct.

Then there was the case of Mrs Redmond, one of the army women, who got her hands on a knife and stabbed a seaman. The widow of an infantryman, proceeding home with a three-year-old daughter, Mrs Redmond was berthed forward among the invalids and seamen and like them had lost all her meagre possessions. No explanation for her actions is given by the log; she was put in irons for three days, then released.4

On a warm, sultry Christmas Day, the company and passengers sheltered under tarpaulins on deck as Captain Marshall conducted Divine Service with a rare fervour. They gave thanks for their deliverance, and as it was Christmas an extra ration of salt pork and weevilled biscuit was distributed.

Three days later the captain's wife gave birth in the roundhouse to a son.

The drama played out in the *Ceylon*'s roundhouse also had strands of birth and death, and of awakening love. Once again we start with glimpses through the log – of a table dominated by military figures, a colonel and a major as well as William Black, an army surgeon, and Captain William Parker of the Bengal Artillery. Parker's wife Sophie, heavily pregnant, had assisted another passenger, Grace Cowell, when she gave birth to a daughter on 11 November. Now she was near her own time.

When the hurricane came, *Ceylon* was the ship least equipped to deal with it. She, it may be recalled, had suffered more than any other from the press, having lost fifty-six men, more than half her crew. And her captain, Thomas Hudson, sick with a Bengal fever, was a dying man. He was still able to rouse himself from his cot at dawn on 21 November when she was laid on her beam end, sideways to the wind with the beam actually touching the sea, and in peril of capsizing.

> At 7am, her gunwale frequently lying under and the water within being up to the gundeck, judged it necessary to get the ship before the wind if possible. Saw a ship on the quarter with her main topmasts and mizzen masts gone which appeared to be the *Diana*. Got the pilot's anchor aft and over the lee quarter to abt 20 fathoms to make the ship wear.* She went off at one point only & the main topsail broke loose & blew away & the boat was washed from the lee quarter . . .
>
> Abt 9 the wind suddenly moderated & the ship suddenly went off before it which enabled us to get the water off the gundeck. It

---

* In the case of the *Ceylon*, the sea had risen internally to the level of the gundeck because she was laid over on her or side, or beam end. The manoeuvre described, 'to make the ship wear', was intended to bring her about so that the wind was behind, rather than side-on, to diminish the danger of capsizing.

continued moderate till about 11 when the storm came on again with equal violence in the NW. At noon blowing a perfect hurricane with a very heavy sea & the spray so thick we could scarcely see the length of the ship.[5]

When Hudson visited his passengers it was to find a scene similar to that described by another captain, of a dishevelled group assembled in a cuddy 'half full of water, where chests and bedding were washed about'. After two days, dread was mingled with confusion, exhaustion, and even in some cases a curious exhilaration.

> Some were praying and lamenting, others moody and silent, and others again wildly excited and delirious in their talk.[6]

Hudson had averted the immediate danger of capsizing. Now a new threat emerged. The water, which had been reduced by pumping, was rising again as the blow hardened. Twenty-four hours later it was still battering the *Ceylon* when 'the foretopmast went away abt 4ft above the Cap. It being impossible to send anyone aloft, could not cut away the wreck.'[7]

Dragged down, she was again shipping water at a fatal rate . . . up to four feet . . . then five feet. Hudson returned to the cuddy, reporting that the lascars and Danes who had replaced the pressed hands had been paralysed by fear, or fatalism, and were refusing to man the pumps.

Once more it would be the Indiaman's passengers who would be the agents of their own salvation. Army officers and invalid soldiers bailed for all they were worth while the hands, glistening and streaming, grappled *Ceylon*'s guns to the ports and heaved them overboard. In the next three hours it made little difference. 'We were not able to gain on the water anywhere,' Hudson noted grimly.

Well to the fore at this time was the captain of artillery, William Parker. Seized with a fierce strength, he was fighting to save not only himself but his wife and their unborn child. In the cuddy, Sophie Parker had gone into labour. Which came first is not clear. But at around six in the evening of 23 November, when hope had all but passed, the wind began to moderate.

> At half past six the pumps gained. Cont'd bailing as before. At 7 the wind was considerably abated. The ship righted.

74

And at some point that same evening, Sophie Parker gave birth to a son.

Another human cycle had also begun. William Black, the army surgeon, and Miss Sarah Parkinson were falling in love. He was a veteran of some years' service, unmarried. Of her nothing is known, although it might be speculated that she was returning from a failed 'fishing fleet' venture. What can be said is that love came upon them with an intensity born of their shared experience; and they were in such haste to consummate it that they would not wait to reach England, but married directly upon landing in Capetown.[8]

Death had not quite finished with the *Ceylon*. As she limped towards Africa, some undisclosed pestilence moved through the ship. Among the first to be dropped over the side, two weeks after the storm, was Grace Cowell's baby, whom Mrs Parker had helped to deliver on 11 November. Three seamen died in as many days and were followed by five invalids of the 80th Regiment. Captain Hudson, whose hand and abilities were shown in his log throughout the storm, returned to his cot. He would live to see the Cape, but not his native shore.

On 12 January, as the *Ceylon* approached Cape Agulhas, the southernmost tip of Africa and the point at which the Indian Ocean merges into the Atlantic, a lookout called down that he could see three strangers. There was no alarm. They were too far south to be French. On approaching, one became instantly recognisable by her double-streaked hull as the *Preston*, with two other Indiamen of the fleet, the *Tigris* and *Ann*.

The captains were experienced men who had seen a great deal over the years but nothing, they were agreed, like the conditions they had met in 08° 30'S, 80°E. What made it more remarkable was how conditions had varied from ship to ship once the fleet disintegrated. 'The violence was very different within a few miles,' Ramsden of the *Phoenix* recalled.[9]

Captain Dougald Macdougall's *Tigris* had also come within an ace of foundering. He was in a similar position to *Ceylon* in that out of a small crew of sixty-three, a third had been lost to the press and desertion. Moreover, she was a nursery ship carrying eighteen unaccompanied small children who were in no position to help during the crisis. But by great fortune she had on board nine French prisoners of war, probably seamen from the *Piemontaise* frigate captured in May. Macdougall called on them to assist with pumping and bailing, and for the next two days old foes stood shoulder to shoulder in the cause of self-preservation.[10] He said later that without the Frenchmen *Tigris* would undoubtedly have foundered.

The hindmost ships, on the other hand, escaped the worst. Among them was the *Preston*. Captain Sturrock was usually a step ahead of his peers and had somehow contrived to acquire a full, able-bodied crew. When she ran into trouble, Sturrock was able to shorten sail smartly and, in hoving to for two days, *Preston* dropped behind the eye of the storm.[11] The praise lavished on her captain by *Preston*'s richest passenger, James Lautour of the Madras banking dynasty, would add to Sturrock's growing reputation.

That the *Ann* should also be let off lightly was more due to good fortune than anything else. Captain James Masson later claimed that she was the worst-manned ship in the fleet. He exaggerated, but she would still have had a terrible time had she not just happened to fall behind and hence outside the hurricane, so that on 22 November, while others were in dire peril, *Ann* experienced no more than a gale. Her sole casualty was Mrs Dalrymple, wife of Major Samuel Dalrymple of the Madras Artillery, who died four weeks later of an unexplained malaise. A bereft Dalrymple and their three children, aged between one and four, would leave the ship at the Cape.[12]

They tacked into Table Bay in dribs and drabs . . . the *Phoenix* on 12 January, followed a week later by *Ceylon*, *Preston*, *Tigris* and *Ann*. Behind came their erstwhile escort, HMS *Albion*. She caused a particular stir. Vice-Admiral Albemarle Bertie, commander of the Cape Squadron, took a phlegmatic view of the damaged Indiamen but was aghast to see a 74-gun ship of the line come in 'a perfect wreck'.

She has lost her mizzen mast and topmast; nineteen of her main deck guns are thrown overboard also; and the ship so leaky and opening so much that she required to be frapped together in three places. Captain Ferrier's verbal information was that if the gale continued a few hours longer, *Albion* must have foundered.[13]

Four days then passed before the ruined *Diana* was blown in under a south-easter. She had suffered more than any and it was agreed that her survival had been miraculous. At this point, mounting concern turned to grim foreboding. Where were the three missing ships? What had become of *Lord Nelson*, the *Glory* and the *Experiment*? At first it was speculated that they might have put in at Madagascar, or even tacked eastwards to Penang for repairs. In the weeks and months ahead there would be no shortage of theories.

Ramsden in the *Phoenix* had been closest to them when the first phase of the hurricane descended on 21 November and the last he saw of the *Lord Nelson*, she was about two miles to the south-east, flying along with sails set as if to outrun the storm. He recalled that she had been much by the head, her bows buried in the waves, a sign that she was too heavily laden forward. As for manning, he observed grimly: 'She was miserably serviced as to quality of men and her officers were sickly.'[14]

The *Glory* had been astern of *Lord Nelson*, also with plenty of sail out. Everyone agreed that she was a handful even in good weather, being of a crank condition that rendered her more liable to capsize. Ramsden had also heard that she was 'leaky in the wooden ends forward and her head was loose'.[15] As for the *Experiment* – like the *Glory* an Extra ship – it was recalled that she too was poorly manned and by the head.

But ultimately here were theories that could never be confirmed, questions that would never be fully answered. As weeks and months went by without news, even anxious letters from Leadenhall Street to outlying parts of the Company's domain dried up.

Mysteries concerned not only the ships' fate but the identities of those who had been on board them. The *Lord Nelson* and the *Glory* had both solicited for more passengers in Madras; the names of those who responded, including last-minute groups of invalids or soldiers, would never be known.

The toll was grim enough: on the *Lord Nelson*, Captain William Hutton, 110 officers and crew, and among the passengers Lieutenant-Colonel T.D. Richardson, his wife and three children, James Lorimer, a surgeon, and two male civilians; in the *Glory*, Captain Horatio Beevor, another sixty seamen along with Mr and Mrs Henry Johnstone, Mrs Phoebe Leister and Colonel Burrows of the 14th Regiment; and in the *Experiment*, Captain John Logan, about sixty hands and Thomas Bainbridge, superintendent of surgeons, and his wife, George Ellice Esq. of the Company's service, two army officers and three children.[16]

At the subsequent inquiry it was assumed that all three foundered after being simply overwhelmed by the seas. But all that could be said with certainty was the epitaph entered against the name of each ship in the Company's marine records: 'Parted Company from the fleet in a gale in 08° 30'S, 80°E and not heard of again.'

6

'A cabal in the maintop'

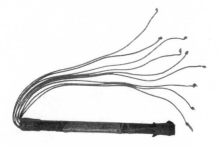

Off Madagascar, 6–8 January 1809

On 6 January, as the devastated Indiamen neared the Cape, one of His Majesty's frigates rode at anchor off eastern Madagascar. It was a sight to gladden the eye of any mariner – a fine ship like *Nereide* at rest on a golden evening, the Indian Ocean stretching away like a flame to the east as the sun was lost behind the lush mass of that vast island. After weeks at sea, here was an idyll: men might cast lines for the prodigious sea life lurking below on coral reefs, or gaze on that landscape and exchange tales of curious folk and queerer creatures. But whatever the setting, there would be no such complacence on HMS *Nereide*.

Captain Robert Corbet watched with a gaze like an awl as provisions were hoisted on board his ship. Here was more to hearten a seaman, for the foodstuffs were of a quality not often enjoyed by navy crews: fresh beef and pork, as well as casks of the preserved variety, vast quantities of sugar, rice, bread, flour and suet and – the sure sign of a captain who cared about his people's health – 160 bottles of lime juice.[1] There were 505 gallons of spirits for the men's grog, and 2,699 gallons of wine, which would be enough to keep the ship's officers in humour for as long as their cruise might last.

But of cheer there was not a sign. Her sails were furled as tight as drums, her rigging was taut, her decks were scoured with holystones to an oily smoothness and the hammocks were folded as neatly as linen in a basket, but beneath that spick-and-span surface the *Nereide* was awash with hatred. To the men, the appearance of these provisions, these fresh foodstuffs that would replace their unloved burgoo and hard-tack, was no more welcome than a lee shore for it could only mean that they were set for another extended spell at sea.

That night the sullen mutterings among the hands at mess tables took on a new vehemence. That night some of the senior men formulated a plan of action.

It was two months since *Nereide* had sailed from Bombay, two months since Corbet's high-handed manner provoked Pellew's wrath, bringing an order to proceed directly to the Cape and there lay his crew's cruelty petition before Admiral Bertie for a court martial. While promising obedience ('I am determined upon putting to sea immediately in execution of your orders') and outwardly chastened ('I regret leaving the station under your disapprobation') Corbet had betrayed disrespect for Pellew.[2] He was Bertie's man, and confident of his support. Had not Bertie singled out his prowess in blockading Ile de France?

If Corbet had obeyed Pellew's orders naval history might have been rewritten. Instead of sailing for the Cape, however, he set a course for Ile de France. As *Nereide* neared the island on 11 December a strange sail came in sight that proved to be the *Leopard*, a lumbering old 50-gun fourth-rate of ill repute.* But no ship could have been more welcomed by Corbet, for she carried dispatches from Bertie dated 2 November – four days before *Nereide* left India. Headed 'Most Secret', they ordered him to establish a rendezvous near the Seychelles islands during the hurricane season – from December to March – and resume the blockade of Ile de France. The island was reportedly on the verge of famine and Bertie was concerned that it should obtain no relief. The order continued:

> And whereas the French are endeavouring to organise an army in Persia whose object it will be to overthrow our Government in India you are to be most attentive to procuring every intelligence related thereto.[3]

Corbet did not hesitate. Here was a commission that promised action and which he saw as releasing him from Pellew's order. The court martial could wait.

Days later, as *Nereide* approached Bourbon on 17 December, a lookout sighted another strange sail on a north-easterly course towards Ile de France. A chase began, extending through the rest of the day, all that night

* In the Aubrey/Maturin novels of Patrick O'Brian she is usually referred to as 'the horrible old *Leopard* '.

and into the morning. She was a fast-sailing French imperial corvette, the *Mouche*, and but for the fact that her normal complement of eighty was reduced to thirty men, she would have escaped. As it was, even after most of her 12 guns had been cast overboard to lighten her, she was caught at 11 a.m. and, following a volley from *Nereide*, hauled down her colours. [4]

Either through this encounter, or in taking a second prize, a merchant lugger, off Ile de France some days later, Corbet came upon precious intelligence. In August he had been the first to discover that the 40-gun frigates *Manche* and *Caroline* had arrived at Port Louis. Now he learnt that two more even heavier frigates, *Venus* and *Bellone*, both of 44 guns, were on their way from France to the island.

Something, clearly, was up. Whether the French squadron was to join the long-feared invasion of India, or its purpose was to disrupt merchant shipping – and hence the flow of saltpetre to Britain – its arrival marked a bold challenge. The commander, Commodore Jacques Felix Hamelin, was a celebrated navigator of the Eastern Seas, having led an expedition to chart the coastlines of Terra Australis and New Guinea between 1801 and 1803. His fighting qualities were unknown but he had Bonaparte's confidence and his four frigates were the latest products of French shipyards, hence the finest of their class afloat.

All the while the Nereides' resentment deepened. To what extent they were aware of these new factors is not clear, but Corbet was not the kind of captain to take the men into his confidence. So far as they were concerned, more than four months had passed since their protest and Pellew's sympathetic response, when Corbet had been obliged to read out to them the admiral's assurance that 'every attention' would be paid to their complaint. In the event, no attention had been paid, and now it was obvious that there was no prospect of an early proceeding to the Cape.

True, in one respect, conditions had improved. After sailing from Bombay, Corbet had handed out floggings with his customary ferocity: in the space of a few days a man named William Wiggins, the gunroom cook, an American all of fifty-three years, received five dozen for a combination of disobedience, theft and dirtiness. Since receiving his orders, however, Corbet had been so caught up by events, exhilarated perhaps by a spell of action, that in the past three weeks just two men had been beaten.

But the divide between captain and crew now went deeper than the lash. Even the godlike power of a British man-of-war commander had limits. And the Nereides were determined on relief from the saturnine zealot who glowered at them from the quarterdeck.

They had been together for two years of unrelieved pain and misery. HMS *Nereide* was an elderly 36-gun frigate, captured from the French in 1797 and under Corbet's command since 1806. He decided at the outset that 'the foundation of her company were about one hundred men who had served under discipline very contrary to what my ideas have pointed out to me as most beneficial to HM service'.[5]

From this ill-omened beginning the ship joined an unofficial attempt by Captain Home Popham to seize Buenos Aires. The *Nereide*'s part in what became a disastrous campaign consisted of spending several months at anchor in the Plata river, awaiting orders that never arrived. Desertions to Buenos Aires began; Corbet saw this as 'a strenuous opposition to discipline'. More men fled the ship, some of whom went over to the enemy. Matters reached a point that, by Corbet's own account, 'no opportunity [of deserting] offered that was not embraced'. So far as *Nereide*'s captain was concerned, however, even those who remained loyal were recalcitrants who required 'the most rigid discipline'.[6]

In February 1808 *Nereide* was assigned to Bertie's squadron at the Cape. There one Joseph Wilkinson, a Lincoln man aged twenty-three, joined the ship. He was described in the ship's paybook as a volunteer, but so were others who had undoubtedly been pressed, such as Hector McNeil, the sixty-three-year-old from the *Lord Eldon*. Whatever the case, it was a fateful event. Wilkinson was a good seaman and, despite his youth, a bold, forthright individual.

Corbet, seemingly in the belief that *Nereide* had been a happy ship before, would later maintain: 'From this time I date the seeds of disaffection.'[7]

As another captain of the time observed: 'No absolute monarch can be more despotic than the captain of a man-of-war, if he so pleases . . . No creature existing has it so much in his power to render the lives of those under his command either miserable or happy.' At the same time, as the historian N.A.M. Rodger has written, attitudes to naval discipline had begun to evolve since the great Spithead mutinies of 1797. It was increasingly the mark of a good officer to keep flogging to a minimum. The once-common practice of 'starting' – beating men to their stations with ropes or sticks – was now officially frowned upon. A change had taken place in seamen's attitudes as well. If they were skilled, they knew their worth and expected officers to treat them with respect. In Rodger's words 'when they had occasion to complain of ill-treatment, it was often the shame . . . as much as the brutality they dwelt on. They resented casual insults, especially to their professional abilities.'[8]

Nereide had been a deeply unhappy vessel on the Plata, but it was the start of her service in the Indian Ocean that marked her descent into an island of suffering.

Blockade sailing was an awkward combination – tedious but demanding. To isolate the Ile de France and Bourbon, ships like *Nereide* see-sawed their way between the two, passing off Port Louis and St Paul, a circuit of around 130 miles that could take anything from a day to a week, depending on the direction of wind and current. It required constant attention to both and imposed a demanding regime in the tops. The French refusal to come out and fight only added to the frustration.

Corbet had been at sea for twenty years and his shining hopes were fading. What chance now another Trafalgar? He was a solitary figure who rarely socialised with his officers and in the isolation of his command – the months remote from the fellowship and influence of other captains – he became consumed by a kind of mania. Corbet excelled at presenting a ship which, to all appearances, was taut and smart. Appearances were, in fact, his obsession. Sails and rigging received his most particular attention, and well might the seaman shudder who did not do likewise. When his telescope scoured the sea fruitlessly, as it did all too often, his eye would return to his own ship – and his men.

One hand, George Scargil, who was beaten 'to that degree that I have been stupid and not known what I was about', recalled that 'it was for my cringles not being close to the yard'.[9] It was not only in the matter of the ship that Corbet demanded neatness, but also in those who manned her: one of the offences for which they were most frequently flogged was 'dirtiness'. (This should not be confused with sodomy, or 'indecency' as it was usually termed in punishment logs.) An ill-turned-out man would be given two dozen as soon as the captain's eye fell on him.

Corbet became convinced that there existed what he called 'a cabal in the maintop'.[10] The topmen were the ship's most able and respected hands, responsible for working the topsails and among those of the *Nereide* was Joseph Wilkinson. As the captain saw it, this elite group was out to provoke him. He said later:

> I am not easily got the better of but the main topmen on some occasions have exhausted my patience and carried their point by doing the worse the last time than the first. If evil-minded and dissatisfied men get together, what will they not do? I persisted in my duty and they treated it with indifference and contempt.[11]

A month before her arrival at Bombay, *Nereide* had called at Madagascar. A dozen men deserted, only to be seized by natives and returned to the ship for bounty. 'Strong examples were absolutely necessary,' Corbet related. 'A knot was taken on each tail of the Cat *in terrorem*.'[12]

His main enforcer was a bosun's mate with the aptly theatrical name of Moses Veale. As well as knotting his Cat into a so-called Thief's Cat – detested by men for the implication of dishonesty as well as the additional pain it inflicted – Veale made sticks of whalebone, filed to thin points at the end and carved into a Turk's head at the handle. The Admiralty might no longer approve of 'starting' but it was daily practice on *Nereide*. Veale strode the deck, beating men to their posts. One hand, Robert Viner, who was often picked out, once received thirty-six lashes for 'straggling' and was then started so severely that the stick broke.[13] Thicker ones were made, which Corbet explained thus: 'The bosun's mates may have been led to increase them in size when continually obliged to make new ones from their being so frequently stole.'[14]

What he saw as this persistent rebellious streak, represented by 'the maintop cabal formed of individuals courting punishment', now persuaded Corbet on a new way to inflict pain – rubbing salt into the wounds of those who had been flogged. This became a regular occurrence in the space of two weeks prior to *Nereide*'s arrival in India when, in a burst of demented fury, twenty-eight men were given between them no less than 904 lashes.[15]

Such was the state of affairs when the frigate anchored in Bombay and the hands drafted their petition to Pellew. It may be thought that their complaint of Corbet's 'capricious temper on the least occasion' was, if anything, understated. What is striking about the protest, however, is its dignity. As much as their captain's cruelty, they were offended by his insults. He would rail at them, crying: 'You Animal'; or 'You Blackguard Vagabond'; or 'You Rascally Cowardly Set'.[16] The imputation of cowardice was particularly detested.

They also blamed Corbet for the fate of the twenty-three hands who had deserted at the Plata and gone over to the enemy, 'never more to see their fathers or mothers, wives, children, friends and to forfeit the first character in the world, that of a British seaman, and to become the lowest, a Spanish soldier.'[17]

Those identified in Bombay as Corbet's accusers included two main topmen, Joseph Wilkinson, who had joined at the Cape, and John Robinson. We know this because both were sent into HMS *Powerful* 'out of dread' pending Corbet's court martial. When this could not be convened, they were returned to *Nereide*.

Since sailing from Bombay, Wilkinson had been moved to second gunner. Robinson remained captain of the maintop. Both were senior men. More significantly, both were highly respected by their shipmates. Allowing for a tendency to romanticise him, the British seaman was a doughty fellow. Superstitious and improvident he might be, but he was also brave and dependable, a man who would look out for his mates. Drunks and desperadoes there were too, along with the odd croaker and mystic. But they respected the best among their own kind and almost invariably looked to them for leadership in a crisis.

Just such a point had been reached on the *Nereide*. So far as the hands were concerned, Corbet had contrived to wriggle out of a court martial. How could they obtain relief from tyranny and bring him to justice? It was to men like Wilkinson and Robinson that they had turned for an answer.

Soon after dawn on 8 January, Francis Noble, one of *Nereide*'s three lieutenants, came on the quarterdeck with orders to weigh anchor and sheet the topsails; they were leaving Madagascar and setting a course for Ile de France. By 7 a.m. the sails had been sheeted home when an agitated-looking Moses Veale reported to Noble 'that the ship's company were assembling on the forecastle and said they would only weigh anchor for the Cape'.[18]

Lieutenant Noble went forward to the end of the quarterdeck. Men were gathered on the forecastle about fifty feet away, across the waist of the open gundeck – 'in tumult', as he put it later. Noble shouted across, demanding to know 'who was the man that dared say he would not weigh anchor'. He was answered, first by Joseph Wilkinson, who replied, 'All, all', and then by a chorus from the company shouting, 'Only for the Cape.'

By this action, Wilkinson identified himself as the ringleader in what followed.

Marines, who helped to man the guns of a man-of-war but were also used to enforce discipline, were ordered up on the quarterdeck by Noble, who also sent down to the officers to come on deck with their arms immediately. When Corbet appeared, Noble was hailing across to Wilkinson, who had been deputed by the men to speak for them. As Noble related:

> I asked Wilkinson if he was the leading man. He replied [that] the company would only weigh anchor for the Cape. Captain Corbet then ordered Lieutenant Blight to put Wilkinson in irons and ordered the hands, 'Up anchor.' [There was] a general cry, 'No, no'.[19]

William Blight, another of *Nereide*'s lieutenants, proceeded across the gundeck and up on to the forecastle where Wilkinson was in the midst of a crowd. This was clearly a flashpoint for violence but Blight went unmolested and when he called out to Wilkinson, 'he came with me immediately'. Together they went below.

> On perceiving him to look anxiously about him and supposing he was going to speak, I remarked it was a very awful time and warned him to hold his tongue. He instantly answered me in a very independent sort of way, 'No Sir, but we have written for redress and we will have it'.[20]

Back on the quarterdeck meanwhile, Corbet ordered the Marines to load their rifles and line up, facing the forecastle like a firing squad. He then took up a trumpet to address the men: 'Humanity induced me to separate if possible the misled from the guilty,' he related. As each man's name was read out from the Open List he was ordered to join the officer of his watch or stay and be considered a mutineer.

During the long minutes that followed, Noble noted three men 'walking about amongst the company and appearing to have a good deal to say', as if urging them to stand firm. They were Robinson, John Mastick, who as captain of the foretop was another senior man, and James Connell of the carpenter's crew. Only a handful of men – 'chiefly foreigners', Blight thought – obediently joined their officers. About a hundred and fifty men had declared themselves mutineers. Corbet took up the trumpet and gave them five minutes to reconsider or 'I will fire on you.'

Low-voiced talk took place on the forecastle before a delegation led by Robinson and Mastick crossed the gundeck to the gangway. Corbet loomed over them on the quarterdeck. Mastick, whose manner was described by one officer as 'forward but not contemptuous', said the men were fearful of doing their duty on account of being flogged so often.

Corbet replied tersely: 'Two thirds of the ships in the Navy do more duty than you are accustomed to in this ship.' While he was in command, he went on, they would receive no better treatment. Briefly emollient, he added: 'I will not go to the Cape as the ship's services are required elsewhere. I wish to go home but I can't have my wish, neither can you.'

The delegates returned to the forecastle where a realisation was growing that what had begun as a demonstration had got dreadfully out of hand. An angry but anxious voice was heard saying: 'You hear we can't go to the Cape. What do you say? Why don't some of you speak?'

Sensing their indecision, Corbet called out: 'I have but two words, Obey or Not Obey.' And after a brief pause: 'What the Devil do you take me for, a Coward or what?'

Four minutes had passed when Robinson came forward to meet Corbet again at the gangway. He had been chosen by the men to tell the captain that

> if he would leave off beating them with the great sticks and take the knots out of the Cats they would go anywhere with him. If not they wished [for] another commander.[21]

Corbet replied briskly that what they wanted was impossible and sent him back. The Marines were ordered to raise their rifles. Voices from the forecastle could now be heard calling, 'Obey! Obey!' When the order came to Up Anchor there were a few half-hearted cries of 'for the Cape', but that was the last sign of opposition. Without further bidding the hands started to take up their stations. The mutiny on HMS *Nereide* was over.

* * *

As a mutiny, at least, it would always be known. Undoubtedly the men had confronted their commander and disobeyed orders, although what had occurred was more a protest that had miscarried. No violence had been offered and the lieutenants, Noble and Blight, were in agreement that the men had been respectful throughout. It could not be remotely compared with a real mutiny, such as the events on the frigate *Hermione* ten years earlier.

Then, too, a brutal captain, Hugh Pigot, 'whose measure of his own competence was the smartness of his ship', had terrified his crew by unpredictable beatings;[22] but when his men rose up, it was to kill Pigot and several of his officers before handing the ship over to the Spaniards. On *Hermione*, as in most mutinies, the leaders were those who had been regarded as the best men. The naval historian Rodger writes: 'Only those who were really admired by their shipmates would be followed ... Almost without exception, mutinies were led by petty officers or long-serving leading hands, the natural aristocracy of the lower deck.'[23]

So too on *Nereide*. Order restored, Corbet consulted Noble and Blight before nine men were seized to join Wilkinson in irons. They included Robinson and Mastick, who had also spoken on the crew's behalf, and were highly regarded by the whole ship including the lieutenants. How the other seven were picked out was never explained. Andrew Redding, captain of the afterguard, James Connell and James Smart, appear to have been seen speaking 'during the tumult'. However, four other men were ordinary hands who were notable only for the fact that they were detested by Corbet for one reason or another. They were William Williams, William McCoy, Robert Viner and Thomas Christian.[24]

In one respect their protest had worked. When *Nereide* sailed later that day it was not for Ile de France but the Cape. (Corbet explained in a letter to Bertie: 'Altho they were compelled into obedience, I thought it prudent to lose no time [in proceeding to the Cape] that the law might take its course.'[25])

Nevertheless, the effect was disastrous to the seamen's cause. Their complaints had been overtaken by events and although they would finally have a chance to put their case to a court martial, Corbet's conduct would now be seen in a quite different light. Whether or not they realised this, he certainly did. For the captain, the mutiny had come as a blessing.

7

Justice at the Cape

Capetown, 12 January–13 February 1809

Capetown was in the midst of its hot, dry summer, when the wind blows in gusts from the south-east and a thin layer of cloud furls over the edge of Table Mountain like a white cape. Below, the streets of neat gabled houses that ran in tiers down to the seafront were unusually busy, and among heavily dressed Dutch burghers could be seen ladies in the newer Calcutta fashions and English sailors in white duck.

The taverns were heaving. Seamen drinking at Het Blauwe Anker (the Blue Anchor) swore that they had never seen anything like it before, either for the wind's fury or the size of those terrible seas. Every man had a story: of shipmates torn from the yards and carried off into oblivion; of those three days and nights when death danced like a spectre in the waves beside them; and of unearthly wailings in the tops, as if from the spirits of the departed. Awe was blended with euphoria because none had expected to come through such a tempest. It was as if the various names given to this place – the Cape of Storms and the Cape of Good Hope, even the Tavern of the Seas – had all come together to define their experience.

Passengers had also gone ashore, giving thanks for survival and a welcome respite from life at sea. News that their battered ships out in the bay would take weeks to repair had been less happily received. The Dutch innkeepers, much gratified by an influx of well-heeled voyagers, were making the most of the opportunity. That unbending soul Sir Henry Gwillim passed lightly over his brush with death – 'it lasted three days and nights and for 24 hours we had little expectation that we should weather it,' he wrote home phlegmatically – but was reduced to real distress by the cost of sustaining his little entourage.

Everything is most extravagantly dear and should we be detained here long I must be ruined. I pay for each of us 16/- a day board and

93

lodging. Would to God I were safe in England though I have much of a disagreeable nature to encounter when I get there.[1]

Gwillim hinted at the attachment that Mary had formed for Captain Ramsden – 'we like him much' – as the courtship that had begun on the *Phoenix* continued. The other couple brought together by crisis, William Black and Sarah Parkinson, duly took their vows at the little Lutheran church, attended by their fellow passengers from the *Ceylon*.

Despite the neatness of the town and the natural beauty all around them, the visitors soon tired of the settlement. Dazzled by India, they found the Cape large, empty and somehow arid, its inhabitants dull, its potential barren. The Cape had been prised from a feeble Dutch grasp just three years earlier in order to secure the route to India and it had nothing as yet of Calcutta's grace or the swagger of Madras. The grandest building was the Castle, a Dutch fort which looked handsome enough against the backdrop of Table Mountain, and for form's sake an aristocrat, the Earl of Caledon, presided here with the title of Governor. But Whitehall's priorities indicated that the Cape was considered a very inferior sort of place. A Calcutta newspaper sneered about a colony 'that boasts the anomalies of a College without professors, a Theatre without actors, an Exchange without commerce and a Bishop without a church'.[2] There were no settlers and, the Army and Navy establishments aside, British residents tended to be refugees from India's climate, invalids on rest cures. The Cape's weather, at least, was found agreeable.

On 26 January, while the Indiamen were still undergoing repairs, a sail was sighted in the west. Hopes rose briefly that she might be one of the missing ships until she was identified as a frigate of Admiral Bertie's squadron – HMS *Nereide*, commanded by Captain Corbet. By nightfall news of the mutiny was all over town.

They came up to a roll of Marines' drums, ten prisoners turned out in their best outfits – clean white duck trousers and jerkins, waistcoats, their pigtails freshly braided. They stood at one end of the captain's cabin, upright, self-respecting. Only the shackles betrayed their peril.

Beyond *Nereide*'s gallery windows a dozen sail lay at anchor, and beyond them the flat-topped mountain and its twin sentinels, Devil's Peak and Lion's Head. Five navy captains in full uniform came in silently and took their seats at the long table, with Captain Josias Rowley of HMS *Raisonnable* in the centre. The senior captain in the Cape squadron, Rowley was a fine seaman destined to play a key role in the battle for the Indian Ocean, and a fair, much-respected commander of men. He was not the presiding officer, however, Captain John Ferrier of the recently arrived *Albion* being his senior.

As prosecutor, Corbet opened by reading his own report of the mutiny. He then called *Nereide*'s three lieutenants, Noble, Blight and Allen, each of whom related what he had seen.

The essential facts were not open to dispute: *Nereide*'s crew had refused to obey an order to weigh until they were confronted with a firing party. Corbet's approach was directed at proving that his foe from 'the cabal in the maintop', Joseph Wilkinson, was the ringleader – even though it quickly became apparent that, because he had been clapped in irons as soon as Corbet came on deck, he was the prisoner least prominent in what followed. At one point Rowley became curious as to why Wilkinson had been singled out and asked Lieutenant Blight.

Q by the court: Why was Wilkinson in particular ordered into irons?
A: I did not know.3

Corbet tried to prove that some of the other men had been disrespectful towards him. Lieutenant Blight did testify that Robinson, Mastick and Connell were 'forward in the tumult' but when Corbet sought to draw him into giving more damaging evidence he declined.

Q: When the prisoner Robinson made the offer to me of going to sea with another captain, was his manner contemptuous?
A: I think not.
Q: When Mastick came and spoke to me, was his manner contemptuous?
A: He appeared very forward but when speaking to you I think not contemptuous.

That, in effect, concluded the prosecution's case. The following day the prisoners' written defence was read out, relating their attempt to obtain relief from Corbet's oppression 'in a regular, respectful and official manner', the failure to convene a court martial in Bombay, and the ship's return to cruising off Ile de France where they again experienced treatment 'such as it was next to impossible for men to bear'.

> On the most trifling occasions and often when we did not know a fault had been committed we have suffered the most unmerciful starting . . . with sticks of a severer kind than is ever used in the British Navy . . . We appeal to the feelings of the Court whether this was treatment for British sailors fighting the battle of their country.
>
> We call God to witness for us that we had no intention of mutiny or any other offence. We only wished to be acquainted when the ship could proceed to the Cape that we might make application for redress of our grievances.

It is hard not to be moved by their plight. The hearing was little more than a ritual. The men were bound to be found guilty, and they knew it. But they would also have known that there was a trend for courts martial to punish one or two ringleaders (sometimes they were chosen by lot) and pardon the rest. Testimony to good character was part of that process, one recognised by the men who proceeded to seek it – even, after all that had passed between them, from Corbet and his officers.

Robinson and Mastick, outstanding hands, were described by the lieutenants as 'particularly good seamen . . . characters deserving the greatest trust'. Even Corbet paid them a grudging tribute: 'I am sorry to have had to bring them forward, having considered them generally good men.' More typical were his statements on the less prominent figures: 'McCoy should not call upon me for a character as he must know if he considers. Of Viner I had better be silent. Christian I do not speak about.'

As he had been since his arrest, one man was singled out. Although the evidence showed his involvement to have been marginal, Wilkinson had been picked out by Corbet as the mutineers' spokesman and it was his opinion that counted with the court. Asked for his character, Corbet replied: 'I decline speaking.' Unsurprisingly, the lieutenants closed ranks behind their captain. Wilkinson was said to be 'very forward and likely to be troublesome'.

One small voice offered dissent. Robert Lesby, Master of the *Nereide*, said: 'I have no fault to find with any of them.'

Proceedings adjourned at midnight on the second day, reconvening the next morning at 10.30. Captain Rowley and his fellows filed in and the court stood as he read their findings.

All ten men were found guilty of mutiny. They were sentenced to death by hanging at the yardarm. But taking into account circumstances 'of a particular and favourable nature', nine of them were recommended for mercy. The exception was Wilkinson.

He was given a day's grace to contemplate eternity. On 2 February he was brought up, his eyes narrowed against the fierce blue brilliance of a Cape summer morning, feeling the comforting smoothness of *Nereide*'s deck under his bare feet for the last time as the noose was slipped around his neck. He looked up at the flat-topped mountain, reflecting perhaps on the circumstances that had brought him here, to join the ship exactly a year ago. The company was drawn up while Admiral Bertie stood at attention beside Corbet and his officers on the quarterdeck, a row of dazzling blue-and-gold figures.

There is no record of how Wilkinson met death, but there were few seamen who had not confronted it before and he had seen many of his mates die. In the nature of their existence, tars lived carelessly from day to day, reckless, forgetful of the past and oblivious to the future. He may even have been helped on his way with rum that morning. As drums rolled and Marines stood with rifles ready, the order was given by Bertie.

Down in the waist, hands jerked and hauled on the rope and a few minutes after 9 a.m. Joseph Wilkinson, a twenty-three-year-old from Lincoln, was dangling from the foremast yardarm.4

A second court martial assembled the following day, in the same great cabin and with the same officers presiding. The accused on this occasion was Robert Corbet. His main accuser was dead, the remainder were still under sentence of death, but the *Nereide*'s crew had at last the chance to state their grievances against their captain. Perhaps understandably, they rather overplayed their hand.

A seaman named John Slade was delegated to act as prosecutor. On top of cruelty he accused Corbet of breaching seven Articles of War, in ways from the trivial – washing clothes on the Sabbath – to the treasonable – selling captured ships to the enemy while they were at the Plata. These charges had no chance of success and Corbet had no difficulty in rebutting them. He still managed to strike a tone both jarring and self-pitying. 'If my prosecutor had had a little more encouragement the whole 36 articles would have been filled up with equal propriety. By the third article my prosecutor has attempted my life. Will he talk of cruelty after this?'5

The case against him came down to the 33rd Article of War, of conduct by an officer 'scandalous, infamous, cruel, oppressive or fraudulent'. Slade's first witness was a topman named John Smith who related a number of occasions when he had been beaten for failing to meet the captain's standards of smartness, including once when he left an edge of topsail showing after it had been hauled in, or reefed. Corbet, he related:

> . . . sent for Moses Veale, bosun's mate, to beat me. After he had beat me Captain Corbet sent the topsail men up on the yard again to shake the reef out. Then he told us to go aloft to take the reef in again. My arm being so sore, I could not tie my points as tight as other men. He asked whose points was that. They told him it was mine. I was then in the top. He called me down and asked me why I did not tie the points tight. I told him my arm was so sore from the beating I had got. He sent for Veale and told him to give me a damn'd good licking which he did.

[The whole process was then repeated. Once again Smith was unable to tie his points.]

> The captain asked me the reason I did not tie the points tauter. I told him my flesh was so sore I could not bear to move, I could not bear my frock to touch [me]. He said *he* would make it sore & called for a bosun's mate and told him to lick me which he did. We went up and shook the reefs out and took them in several times. And after we had done, my flesh being so sore, I was forced to go to the doctor and he put me in his list.

Seven other hands gave similar testimony. William Wiggins, the gunroom cook and one of a number of American seamen on *Nereide*, was among those whose backs had been rubbed with salt after a beating. He also related that he had once passed blood in his urine after being flogged about his loins.

The evidence of Thomas Cumberlidge was enough to turn a strong stomach. He recalled the time when Corbet found excrement on a cable near the head; Cumberlidge was beaten, then ordered to wipe the cable clean with his waistcoat. Afterwards Corbet told him that 'if he ever caught the cable in that state again he'd make me lick it off with my tongue. I then went up to the head and threw my waistcoat overboard.'

George Scargil told of receiving beatings for not being first off the yardarm. John Martin had been beaten and then, because he was unable to stand, hung up from a Jacob's ladder, a rope ladder to the rigging. Augustus Dundas passed over his various beatings with a Cat that had been dipped in pickle but his voice quivered with rage as he related how Corbet abused him as a cowardly rascal. 'He told me to run away and go to the Spaniards as others had done.'

Slade completed the prosecution's case by calling James Campbell, the ship's surgeon. Asked whether he always attended punishments, the surgeon answered somewhat opaquely: 'Always when in health or not suspended from duty.' He testified nevertheless that he had been forced to put ten men on the sick list for a week after floggings. A great many more had received treatment without actually being laid off sick. Frequently men reported to him with severe contusions on their arms and shoulders from starting.

A naval historian of the old school, J.K. Laughton, wrote of Corbet's court martial: 'No charges of diabolical cruelty were ever more simply put, or more clearly proved, even if they were not admitted.'[6]

Corbet, however, appeared blithely oblivious to the ugliness of the evidence. Rising on the second day, he read a statement of defence. Again he cast himself as the plaintiff.

No person looks upon the charge of cruelty with more detestation than myself. It must proceed from a *Bad Heart* and God knows I am unconscious of possessing one ... This court I trust will not suffer an unblemished character to be pulled to pieces because a few dissatisfied persons have set their hearts upon it and have courted punishments for [that] express purpose.[7]

He took comfort from the fact that none of his men had been beaten to death. 'Where no accident has happened from punishment in eight years, I think the supposition may be formed that I am not the odious character described in the 33rd Article of War.' And he invoked to good effect his past touch with naval magic. 'I have stood high in favour. That I was posted by my Lord Nelson will not argue that I commanded my sloop with tyranny.'

The logic of his defence was less impressive. The problems on *Nereide*, he said, had stemmed from a 'strenuous opposition to discipline' among more than half the crew. He then went on to contradict himself by blaming the arrival of Wilkinson for planting 'the seeds of disaffection' among 'the cabal in the maintop'. This group of miscreants had, he averred, actually incited him to beat them.

> This hon court will see through the probability when once the cabal has formed of individuals courting punishment and then appealing to the surgeon to attain the name of having been on his list . . . A sulky indifference to punishment superseded all endeavours to avoid it . . . When necessary to inflict punishment of a lighter nature, some men stood as if seeking an increase of it, some turned their face to it and seemed to wish an unlucky blow on the face or head . . .

Where Corbet really betrayed himself was over the matter of starting. The presiding captains must have been disconcerted by some of what they had heard because they called Moses Veale as a witness. A number of sticks were produced and Veale admitted that they were those with which he had started the men, that he had made others from whalebone and that, yes, he had broken one in beating Robert Viner. Although Corbet did not immediately challenge this, he then claimed lamely that the sticks on show had been 'made for the prosecutor's purpose' or were 'come from some other ship', before trying to recover himself.

> The bosun's mates carry sticks. This I trust is no innovation and shocking as represented to this hon court . . . An idea has crept in and is gaining head that the punishment they call starting is not legal. I combat this opinion strongly. It has been one of the customs used at sea since I have known it. That it is illegal cannot I think be proved, that it is customary requires no proof.

This was a blunder. Whatever his own view, the Admiralty had shown a dislike of starting that had been gathering momentum for a decade. Perhaps sensing his mistake, Corbet became more conciliatory, concluding his defence with a pious expression of hope that 'the weeds of dissatisfaction will be now rooted out and the soil bear more gentle tillage.'

On the evening of 8 February, the five captains filed back into the cabin with their verdict. One by one, the charges were dismissed (two were deemed vexatious, that of treason malicious) before they came to the last. 'The Court was of opinion that the 8th charge of cruelty and oppression had been partly proved, by punishments having been inflicted with sticks of an improper size and such as are not usual in His Majesty's Service and did therefore adjudge the prisoner to be reprimanded.' Some of his accusers were allowed into the great cabin to hear sentence passed on the guilty man.

As an example of navy justice, it was a disgrace. Notions of discipline had shifted to the point that had the court martial been held in a British port the seamen's testimony would have caused an outcry. Things would have gone very much harder with Corbet and he might have been lucky to retain his command.

As to why he was shown leniency, the evidence points to Admiral Bertie's influence. Corbet was nothing if not zealous. He was the most active captain in the blockade and his efforts as a source of intelligence alone made him invaluable to his admiral. Thanks to him, Bertie was able to send home an early report of the threat from four new frigates at Ile de France. Bertie was prepared to overlook Corbet's brutality for his results.* He also wrote to the Admiralty, blaming the whole affair on the 'ignorance of seamen' who suspected Corbet was evading his court martial when actually he was 'exerting his utmost for the public service'. Bertie recommended his 'spirit' and 'zeal' in dealing with 'a most serious mutiny'.[8]

But the travesty of the court martial would not be neglected by Pellew. Although Corbet had escaped for the time being he had made a bad enemy who would pursue him at the Admiralty, to far-reaching effect.

The clamour at the Blue Anchor had no sooner subsided over the *Nereide* affair than a new topic presented itself. The *Ann* Indiaman had been visited by a lieutenant from one of Bertie's ships who pressed eleven of her sixty remaining men. Captain Masson of the *Ann* was furious. It was expected

---

* There has been a historical view that Pellew was dilatory in prosecuting Corbet and that he was only pursued with vigour by Bertie when the reverse was the case.

that hands would be pressed in India, but not at the Cape. He fired off a letter to Bertie, stating that he had been left 'so much reduced as to be wholly unequal to carry on the duty of the ship or prepare her for sea'.[9]

Bertie sent an officer to inspect the *Ann*'s crew, giving rise to another row. The Indiaman's chief mate, a man named Weir, did not bestir himself, and when he was rebuked for not offering the officer a rope, replied sarcastically 'that he had not a man to spare for that purpose'. Instead of taking a well-made point, the officer protested about Weir's 'impertinent and unofficerlike' manner.[10] One other man staged a resistance to this bullying. John Pringle was the Company's agent at the Cape and on being told by Bertie to discipline Weir 'for the disrespect shown to His Majesty's Naval Uniform' he responded coolly:

> Sir, The state of the East India Fleet just arrived is such as requires no comment and with every exertion it is evident how unequal the crews are to work those ships home in safety. I therefore hope, Sir, that when you consider the state of these ships, their value and the importance of their safe arrival to the nation at large, that you will give directions that those who have already entered may be returned and that no others be taken from them on any account whatever.[11]

Bertie continued to bluster. Since Corbet's discovery of the new frigates at Ile de France it had become vital 'that my squadron should be refitted without a moment's delay'; but Pringle's invocation of national interest forced him to relent. After one last, noisy but ineffective broadside – 'I shall not fail to represent to the Admiralty the marked hostility against rendering any assistance to HM Service and the insults offered to its officers' – Bertie ordered the impressed men to be returned.[12]

Pringle replied with quiet dignity: 'I know of no hostility or insult, unless a respectful representation of what duty imposed be termed such.' It was a rare victory for the Company's shipping interest over the Navy – and an immense relief for the eleven hands who, having been spared the possibility of service under Corbet, would be home in a couple of months.

After a month ashore passengers made their way back to the waterfront. Bertie had provided a new escort, and HMS *Thais* sailed on 13 February, taking the *Phoenix*, *Preston*, *Tigris* and *Ann* as far as St Helena. The two most severely damaged Indiamen, *Diana* and *Ceylon*, along with HMS *Albion*, would not be ready to depart until 21 February, when the navy ship took on the nine other mutineers from *Nereide* sailing home to await His Majesty's pleasure. (The court's plea that they be pardoned was duly accepted.)

There was still no further intelligence of the three missing Indiamen. Ramsden was pessimistic although other captains continued to believe that they might yet turn up. That three ships out of a fleet of nine should founder seemed almost inconceivable.

What Sir Henry Gwillim, as a libertarian jurist, had made of the *Nereide* trials was, sadly, not recorded. He, Mary, and her disappointed suitor Richard Clarke returned to the *Phoenix*, landing at Falmouth three months later. Gwillim was summoned to the India House where his scandalous conduct in Madras, his defence of 'the rights of the Natives', was duly censored. He never returned to India but took some comfort from the fact that his last petition from the Bench was upheld: in the case of a man sentenced to death for rape, Gwillim's plea to the King for mercy, on the grounds that the crime was not considered of so heinous a nature by Indians as it was by Europeans, was granted.[13]

Mary Symonds and Captain Ramsden were married, making a home in London and having many years together. Ramsden was not yet finished with the sea, however. He would return in the *Phoenix* the following year to participate in one more drama.

HMS *Nereide* also sailed in February. Corbet and his crew were bound again for Ile de France and, although he knew it not, a rendezvous with the Second Fleet.

8

'One of the most wicked places in the Universe'

Calcutta and Penang, 14 November 1808–23 January 1809

Since departing from Madras, Vice-Admiral Pellew's flagship HMS *Culloden* had been on a farewell voyage around the Bay of Bengal, a progress of pomp and circumstance to the Company's grand eastern capital, Calcutta, and its farthest territory, Penang. After four years as commander of the eastern squadron, Pellew was taking his leave with a succession of salutes, balls, receptions, and feasts which – taken together with the fact that his son was showing off a new wife – turned their departure into something of a viceregal procession.

At that time of year, with the prevailing wind in the south-west, the voyage to Calcutta normally took a few days. But *Culloden* spent three weeks prevailing against a north-easterly. Eliza Pellew had a companion, a Mrs Cotton, the widow of an army officer, which was just as well because with a husband on the quarterdeck and a tradition that required a lady to be virtually invisible on a navy ship, she had many hours to while away in the captain's cabin where she and Pownoll had begun their married life, hours spent reading or playing Clementi sonatinas at the pianoforte that had been his gift to her. More appropriate to a honeymoon voyage were evenings at the admiral's table. Pellew held court in spacious quarters where the claret circulated and the Indian Ocean glowed pinkly beyond the gallery windows.

On 14 November, as *Culloden* approached the treacherous sand bars at the Hooghly's mouth, a pilot came on board and over two days worked her up to windward, tacking and pausing, before dropping the best bower anchor in Saugor roads. As all arrivals to Bengal discovered, the Company's most magnificent possession was a hidden treasure. To cover the last fifty miles, the Pellew party boarded a brig which, flying the admiral's flag, proceeded by twists and turns up the Hooghly, beside the jungle of emerald that clung to its banks, until the muddy brown water took one last turn and there, before them, lay Calcutta.

Eliza, her head still spinning from everything that had befallen her, was overwhelmed. Less than a year had passed since she had left the cloistered school for young ladies in Twickenham where, under the care of a pair of amiable spinsters, she had learnt all she knew of the world and human relations, and been removed across the sea – not only to an ardent courtship and hasty consummation, but to an other-worldly place of gaudy brilliance and impossible riches.[1] Madras was grand; but here, from the river, Eliza stepped straight into the most sumptuous place in the English-speaking world.

Life in Calcutta was defined by the proximity of wealth and death. Its climate was far more deadly than that of Madras, with an average lifespan for a newcomer of two monsoons, so that the end of the fever season in October signalled a wave of thanksgiving parties for another year survived. For those who did endure, the rewards were fantastic. Merchants and officials lived in regal state among the colonnaded palaces along Garden Reach. As a mere lawyer, William Hickey kept a country mansion with sixty-three servants.

If it was a grand spot to make a fortune, it was an even better one to lose or spend it. Clive called the Calcutta of his day 'one of the most wicked places in the Universe . . . Rapacious and luxurious beyond conception.'[2] All the appetites were given free rein. Somewhat perversely, it was also authoritarian. No one went to India but with the Company's permission, and no one stayed but with its approval. Most of the Europeans to be seen in Bengal were in uniform and military methods infected civil life. The Governor-General could send anyone back to England by a stroke of the pen and, however rumbustious their conduct at the dinner table or in the bedchamber, his officers were submissive to regulation.

The Pellews were installed at Government House – Lord Wellesley's extravagant legacy to the Company. Modelled on Kedleston Hall in Derbyshire, this neoclassical palace was ideally suited to a proconsul 'with the ideas of a Prince, not those of a trader in muslin and indigo'. Despite the Directors' efforts to rein in their servants, Calcutta had continued its evolution into the City of Palaces. 'Imagine everything that is glorious in nature combined with everything that is beautiful in architecture and you can faintly picture to yourself what Calcutta is,' wrote one dazzled visitor.3

It was also an insular, self-regarding society, highly conscious of status – as Eliza found on being whirled away by the Calcutta ladies eager for gossip of her mother and Madras. Eliza wrote to Sir George Barlow in terms that reflect the rivalry between the two presidencies and the prominence in both of the redoubtable Lady Barlow.

> Everybody has made particular enquiries after you and my mother and all wish she were here to enliven the place which has been very dull since she left it. They have envied the gaiety at Madras since her residence there. I can assure you every person was much disappointed that she did not come with the Admiral and are glad to find she gives the preference to Calcutta.4

Lord Minto, the Governor-General, having removed himself from Government House to put up the Pellew party, then invited them to Barrackpore, his country estate. It had been Wellesley's intention to link the two residences by a tree-lined avenue of fourteen miles, and although the Directors managed to quash this particular piece of extravagance, Barrackpore was another English *folie de grandeur* in the Bengal jungle, the grounds decorated with ponds, statuary and ornamental bridges. An open-mouthed Eliza wrote to her father that it was the most beautiful place she had ever seen, and was delighted when Minto staged a ball in her honour, which turned out 'very elegant and well attended . . . the dancing continued until half past two when the ladies had supper'. In his letter, Pownoll managed a snide reference to the aristocratic potentate who had supplanted Barlow as Governor-General: 'Lord Minto is, I believe, as polite to us as he is to anybody.'5

For the admiral, the social round had a more serious backdrop. Pellew would dictate the sailing of the Second Fleet, and everyone involved in that enterprise, from the Indiamen captains to their passengers, was now awaiting his orders.

* * *

Among those preparing to sail home that season, none did so with more dread than Emilia Scott. All the usual anxiety of anyone about to embark on six months of discomfort and fear was in her case aggravated by harrowing reality. In Calcutta she was spoken of with a certain awe. Emilia, it was widely known, had been on the *Earl of Abergavenny*.

Emilia and her husband, William, were among Calcutta's brightest young couples and he was one of the Company's rising stars. Like so many before him, like Clive and Hastings no less, William Scott came to Bengal as a writer, the humblest rank in the Civil Service, and worked among the rows of clerks, scratching into slab-like ledgers records of transaction and shipment, profit and loss, crime and punishment, all for the attention of the Directors, who would respond with dispatches noting their approbation of a course of action or – and here the recipient might inwardly quail – their disapprobation. Scott was diligent and, just as important, healthy, so that whereas half of those who began as writers with him died within a few years, he endured; and, because he was also able, he was noted with approbation.

Emilia was the daughter of Thomas Evans, one of the few licensed free merchants and a man of immense wealth. In one record it is said that Emilia was his 'natural daughter', which is to indicate that she was Anglo-Indian.[6] Unions across racial lines had been encouraged by the Company as a source of a loyal secondary population, and it is estimated that one in three British men in India lived with an Indian woman. One of the most memorable images of Company India is Zoffany's portrait of General William Palmer, his wife, Fyze, and their children in an intimate domestic setting. Like the Palmer children, Emilia Evans was much loved by her father who sent her to England to be educated, then went himself to bring her home. In 1805 they sailed for Bengal with Emilia's cousin Rebecca Jackson and a chaperone, Margaret Blair, in the *Abergavenny*.

The *Abergavenny*'s captain was John Wordsworth, a brother of the poet, William, who had invested heavily in the voyage. At 1,200 tons, she was among the largest Indiamen of her day with a crew of 200, and was carrying 160 soldiers and 40 civilian passengers. Late on a dark February afternoon, soon after leaving Portsmouth, she went aground off Portland Bill. There was no panic at first and Captain Wordsworth was confident that he could get her off, but an hour later it was found that she had a leak. One of the ship's officers later related:

> At 6pm the inevitable loss of the ship became more and more apparent; other leaks were discovered, the wind had increased to a gale and the severe beating of the vessel upon the rocks threatened immediate destruction. As the night advanced, the situation on board became the more terrible. The Misses Evans and several other passengers entreated to be sent on shore; but this was impossible.7

At first the hands were kept at the pumps with rations of rum, but once they saw the ship was doomed they attempted to break into the spirit room to drink themselves into oblivion. An officer stationed at the door with a pair of pistols stayed there 'even as the ship was sinking'.

Thomas Evans and Emilia were saved by a skiff that came to their rescue. As the ship settled lower, and the little boat bobbed in a sea swirling blackly around them, it was an open question as to which was the more perilous place to be. An officer wrote: 'There seemed little hope of the boat contending successfully against the high sea in so dark a night.' As it pulled away, Captain Wordsworth leaned out and cried: 'God bless you.' He was among about 260 men and women who died as the *Abergavenny* went down.

Despite this terrifying experience, Evans and his daughter sailed on another Indiaman some months later – and endured a dreadful voyage. By the time Emilia reached Calcutta she would have wished never to sail again. She had, however, acquired a certain celebrity as a survivor of the most famous sea disaster of recent times.

Indiamen wrecks might be compared in their outcomes with a modern airliner crash. When a ship was lost at sea so, almost invariably, was everyone on board. Every European in India, from the grandest nabob to the humblest writer, had this one experience of an Indiaman voyage in common, and it gave birth to a kind of shared lore, of discomforts, disputes and above all of dangers. The fact that many ships were simply swallowed up as if they had never existed, added mystery and a nightmarish fascination to their final hours. Then, every now and again, a handful of survivors would emerge to give substance to these horrible imaginings. Disasters such as those that had befallen the *Grosvenor* and *Halsewell* Indiamen had become the stuff of legend.*

The loss of the *Abergavenny* generated a new wave of dramatic narratives, sixpenny pamphlets, art and verse, including a tribute to her captain by his poet brother, William. The subject naturally exercised Calcutta in a most intimate way, for Thomas Evans was not the only well-known local personality on board and William Hickey, who contributed in no small measure himself to Indiaman lore and used to dine out on his shipboard experiences, wrote about Evans's ordeal in his diary. And he related Emilia's lucky escapes.

Soon after arriving safely in Calcutta in 1806, she met William Scott. Her father was delighted when they married a few months later because Scott was recognised as 'a young man of superior talents and great promise . . . rapidly rising to eminence in the civil service'.[8] The couple, in their early twenties, might have served as a model for what the India House expected of its servants, being diligent, intrepid and loyal. By way of advance, William was posted with his new bride to a remote upcountry station where those who did not die of fever, drink or loneliness, would earn promotion.

Emilia had her second escape from drowning when their pinnace sailing up the Hooghly sprang a leak in the night. They awoke to find the cabin deep in water and were just able to wriggle out of a window, to be rescued by a boat minutes before the pinnace sank.

William duly persevered to be recalled to Calcutta as Deputy Collector of Customs, and the Scotts took their place among the city's smart set, living in a fine house on Garden Reach and joining other couples in evening strolls on the Maidan or driving a phaeton to the racecourse south of Fort William. The future was thus bright when William fell severely ill. His doctor's opinion was that only removal from Bengal's climate could save him. Once again, Emilia found herself facing the terrifying ordeal of an Indiaman voyage.

---

* In 1782, the homeward-bound *Grosvenor* was wrecked in the wilderness of south-east Africa, and although almost all the 140 people on board came ashore safely they suffered persecution, privation and starvation and only 13 eventually reached home. Three years later the *Halsewell* was driven on to the Devon coast. Thirty-three sailors managed to save themselves but more than 160 people, including all the passengers and a dozen women, were lost. Paintings of the *Halsewell*'s captain, Richard Pierce, comforting his two daughters as the ship went down, were celebrated for representing ideals of self-sacrifice and family unity.

The Scotts took pains over their choice of ship. At 819 tons, the *Calcutta* was a spacious vessel, renowned for her sailing qualities, and her captain, William Maxwell, had a high reputation. She was, moreover, the only Indiaman that would be sailing from Bengal that season with a full complement of British hands.[9] *Calcutta*, it would be agreed later, was the best-manned ship in the Second Fleet, and appeared to offer a fearful passenger such as Emilia the best hope of a safe and comfortable passage.

Eight of the fleet were beginning their voyage from Calcutta and while their first officers stayed downriver with the ship, to supervise maintenance and loading, captains had some weeks for the more pleasant aspect of business, conducting their private trade and mixing in the milieu from which they drew patronage and in which they enjoyed prestige.

A navy captain wielded supreme authority over his crew. His Indiaman counterpart did so over a wider spectrum. A tremendous figure in blue coat, black velvet cape, cocked hat, buff breeches and a sword worn on dress occasions, he could be quite as autocratic with his passengers as his crew, greeting them 'with the affable condescension of a rich relative welcoming his cousins at his country house'.[10] In England, one historian has noted, he maintained the status of a gentleman; 'but in India, he was treated as a personage'.[11]

For the months in Calcutta, he would rent a suitably fine house from which to conduct business. By day he disposed of his private trade brought from England and invested in goods that would turn a profit at home. By night he attended social events that brought him into contact with prospective passengers; and because he was included on the guest-list for Government House receptions, he would mix widely while vying with other captains in what amounted to a marketplace. Passengers collected gossip on departing ships while captains studied those who were seeking passage for their standing and ability to pay.

In the fraternity of Indiaman captains, William Maxwell of the *Calcutta* had distinction. The son of a Dundee merchant, he went to sea as a boy, spent five years in the Navy as a midshipman and made five voyages to India as an officer before being appointed commander of the *Calcutta* in 1797. He had since completed four round trips in her, and as the senior captain in the Second Fleet had been designated Commodore. However, it was not simply for his seniority that Maxwell was respected by his peers; *Calcutta* was singled out as a particularly well-managed ship, which is to say that Maxwell was seen as a capable mariner with competent officers.[12]

Maxwell's reputation and the comforts of his ship had attracted, in addition to the Scotts, an unusual number of prominent gentlemen. Five were entitled to use the term 'Esquire' after their names at a time when this indicated gentle birth – Thomas Browne, Bryant Mason, E.A. Cuthbert, William Logan and Francis Fulton, the first four of whom had been among Hickey's high-living circle up to his departure earlier that year. They were to be joined by India's senior clergyman, the Rev. Paul Limerick, a pastor in Bengal for twenty years and garrison chaplain at Fort William. Now in his fifties, Limerick had been appointed Bishop of Calcutta, the first holder of that new office, and was on his way home to be consecrated.[13]

Of more interest to Calcutta were the two widows whose recent experiences had stunned and horrified society. At a time when Europeans tended to be treated with deference if not submissiveness in the East, the husbands of Harriett Arnott and Frances Parr had been murdered in separate but equally shocking incidents.

The Company liked to see Frances Parr's husband, Thomas, as one of its martyrs. In truth, however, he was more of a sacrificial lamb. In 1805 he had been sent as Resident to Bencoolen, the settlement in southern Sumatra that was the source of Britain's pepper, with orders to start coffee cultivation, despite opposition from the local populace. His predecessor had been recalled for shirking that duty and came to Bengal stating plainly that if Parr insisted on carrying it through 'he would to a certainty lose his life, as the Malays would not hesitate about putting him to death, probably by openly and publicly murdering him'.[14]

So it proved. Parr was assassinated by a Buginese knife gang, and his wife, who was reported to have tried to shield him, severely wounded. Bengal's Council, which had sent the couple to Bencoolen, concealed its culpability with panegyrics as to his character – 'an affectionate husband and parent, he united all the social virtues . . . He would have adorned the high and distinguished office to which he had been appointed' – but that gave no details of 'this melancholy catastrophe'.[15] Minto arranged for a marble monument to be erected to the martyr, which still stands in modern Bengkulu. His wife, Frances, at least, had recovered and having seen enough of the East was homeward bound with their two children.

Even the Company would make no claim that Frederick Arnott was a martyr and it was more than happy to emphasise that he had brought his fate on himself. Arnott was an old crony of Hickey's, a former army captain who had set himself up as an indigo planter at Kishnagar, about sixty miles up the Ganges from Calcutta. He settled here with his wife, Harriett, the daughter of an Indiaman officer and a renowned beauty, in a jungle inhabited by tigers, elephants and cobras, and a day's journey from another European. The Arnotts, in short, were the Bengal equivalent of pioneering frontier types, and Frederick's dealings with the natives were correspondingly robust. Having advanced money to *ryots*, local cultivators, for growing indigo, only to find that they had sold it elsewhere, he, in the words of his friend Hickey, 'resolved to execute summary justice'. Arnott tried to take one of the *ryots* hostage but was attacked by the man's fellows and beaten to death. Although Hickey was outraged that his killers were not brought to justice, it was whispered that Arnott had already killed two *ryots* and the general view was that he had acted, at the very least, unwisely.[16]

Harriett Arnott and Frances Parr had been brought together and, united in grief, were sailing home in the same ship. While the Company made some provision for ladies in their position, they were not affluent and it may have taken charity from local society to secure their cabins in the *Calcutta*'s roundhouse.

If the *Calcutta* was the Indiaman of choice that season in Bengal, the *Hugh Inglis* was the very opposite, the ship that no one with a strong instinct for self-preservation, a healthy wallet or any other options in the Second Fleet would have had anything to do with. In a place where word of such matters spread fast, the *Hugh Inglis* was known to be a troubled ship.

No blame for this could attach to Captain William Fairfax. Nor was the Navy very culpable because although the *Hugh Inglis* had lost eight men to impressment, she had been visited by other misfortunes beyond anyone's control. A few days after she reached Saugor roads, and while manoeuvring up to Diamond Harbour, a storm blew up in the north-west with fierce tropical suddenness, carrying away the fore and main topmasts and casting six topmen into the water. Fairfax quickly 'lowered the Boat down and used every exertion to save them'; but sailors were notoriously recalcitrant swimmers and these efforts were in vain.[17]

Since coming to Diamond Harbour, Fairfax had watched helplessly as one by one his crew succumbed to a mystery malaise. The first to die was John Johnson, a quartermaster who had thieved from the ship's stores, received twenty-four lashes for his trouble and was broken to able seaman. His death on 25 October announced the outbreak. Men fit in the morning fell ill in the afternoon and died the next day. By the time the outbreak passed, with the death of the cook, thirteen more men had died. Out of a crew of 110, the *Hugh Inglis* was down to 70 hands.

This was bad enough, but all the more serious for the fact that the *Hugh Inglis* was not seaworthy. On the outward voyage she leaked badly and unless the pumps were manned continually took on eight to twelve inches of water an hour. Although her hull had been caulked since coming into the roads, Fairfax could not be certain how effective this would be until his ship was tested in the open sea. In the meantime he had to consider the real and disturbing possibility that he was taking home an unseaworthy ship with an inadequate crew.

Most fleets included one ship that had been picked as a kind of nursery by parents sending children home. In the First Fleet she was *Tigris*, with eighteen children. In the Second Fleet, the nursery was the *Hugh Inglis*. For reasons that can only be a matter of speculation – the cost may have had something to do with it – the ship that seemed the least safe would be carrying no fewer than twenty-nine children aged seven and under. Three women, the Mesdames Humfrays, Littlejohn and Proctor, formed a matriarchal circle whose offspring accounted for eight of the little passengers. The other twenty-one included three Sherwoods and Taylors, and sundry Carpenters, Morrisons and Colebrookes.

This sad, curiously impersonal list is a reminder of that uniquely British custom, of sending children away alone to a dark, alien land across the world for schooling. A parent's conflict of emotions at such a moment is captured by a visitor to India, Maria Graham, who watched ships departing 'and many an anxious wish went with them. Many a mother had trusted her darling child to the waves, nay, to the care of strangers, in the conviction that depriving herself of watching over it was to secure its permanent advantage.'[18]

At least some children, however, were being sent to England because of a shift in Calcutta's moral climate. The Company's old custom of encouraging unions between its servants and the natives had served its purpose of producing an educated secondary population. But the recently arrived memsahib and missionary had different standards. One mem wrote sniffily of 'English gentlemen hampered by Hindoo women and by crowds of olive-coloured children'.[19] Wellesley had passed laws barring Anglo-Indians from the civil or military service, with the result that white men were sending their offspring to England – not just to be educated, but permanently, to assimilate there as they could no longer do in their native land.

Of the twenty-nine children on the *Hugh Inglis*, the three Sherwoods attract attention. Named in the log as 'Violet 5, Sarah 4, and Louisa 3', they were not the blood children of Mary Martha Butt, also known as the children's author Mrs Sherwood, then living in India. This redoubtable lady had, however, recently embarked on her personal mission to rescue sickly or destitute children of British soldiers and as the three little girls on the *Hugh Inglis* had ages spanning a mere eighteen months, it seems that they were among her earliest evacuees.

For all the Indiamen captains, the arrival in Saugor roads of Admiral Pellew had been a cause for consternation. All had lost men and were desperate to avoid further impressment. In the end, their fears proved groundless. Pellew was in an indulgent frame of mind and, on the point of relinquishing his command, could afford to be generous. Far from pressing more men, he issued three especially short-handed ships with letters of protection, stating that because they had given up as many men as could be spared, 'the captains under my command are therefore forbidden from impress'g any further number'.[20]

In fact, the Bengal captains, recalling what they had seen of manning in the First Fleet when it sailed in October, counted their blessings. Most would later grudgingly acknowledge that they were 'tolerably well manned'.[21] Captain John Franklin of the *Northumberland* was happy to take on a party of Danish prisoners, all experienced seamen, as working hands. All – besides Maxwell whose *Calcutta* had a complete European crew – had taken on lascars.

Opinion of these Muslim sailors was not high. The prevailing view was that lascars, 'from their feeble habits of body . . . are utterly incapable of vigorous exertion and rapid movements, necessary in the boisterous seas of Europe, and not to be depended upon for defending a ship against an enemy'.[22] The Company's treatment of lascars, it must be said, gave them little cause to move rapidly, let alone to defend their ship against an enemy. However, Captain Fairfax, of the hard-pressed *Hugh Inglis*, thought 'a good Lascar better than a poor European', and if this sounds faint praise it was still unusual – which is as well because he had taken on no fewer than forty-five lascars to make up numbers on a leaky ship that, whatever else, would certainly require vigorous exertion from them at the pumps.

Pellew's time in India was drawing to a close. Before starting back down the Hooghly to *Culloden*, however, he issued final orders for the Second Fleet. On sailing, the nine Bengal Indiamen were to proceed to Point de Galle at the southern tip of Ceylon, where they would rendezvous with the three coming from Bombay and three more from Madras. Here, too, they would meet HMS *Terpsichore*, a 32-gun frigate, their escort for the voyage home.

Pellew had no expectation of further dealings with the Second Fleet. When *Culloden* weighed on 6 December and stood out before working down the Sandheads in cool, squally conditions, she was bound for Penang. There was no reason to suppose that this was not just the end of another ordinary season.

Neither Pellew nor the captains about to sail yet had an inkling of the calamity that had just befallen the First Fleet.

The captains returned to their ships at Diamond Harbour to find that the officers left in charge had been under constant pressure during the loading of their cargoes. Each bag of saltpetre taken out to the ships represented another fusillade or salvo for Sir John Moore's beleaguered forces in Portugal and the Master Attendant in charge of dispatching homeward-bound vessels had plainly been under orders to fill each ship to the last ounce of this strategic item. That policy, as a report put it, 'originated from a desire to send to England as large a portion of saltpetre as possible to comply with the demands of government for that article'.[23]

Some captains objected. George Hooper of the *Sir William Bensley*, one of the smaller ships of 600 tons, known as Extras, came on board to find that her hold was filled with 350 tons of saltpetre in deadweight. While such an amount of cargo did not in itself constitute a problem, its nature did because – unlike lighter, more conventional cargoes such as textiles and indigo – it could not readily be moved once they sailed. Hooper's objection, to the Board of Trade in Calcutta, that this proportion of deadweight would affect his ship's handling, was over-ruled, 'being in opposition to [that of] the Master Attendant, which was declared to be decisive'.[24]

Another objection was made by Captain George Weltden of the *Indus* who told the Master Attendant that his ship was quite simply overloaded. He too was ignored.[25]

Even more than manning, this issue of loading and deadweight was to loom large over the Second Fleet. In order to satisfy the Master Attendant, four ships had each to offload 50 tons of kentledge – permanent pig-iron ballast. They were the *Calcutta*, the *Hugh Inglis*, the *Lady Jane Dundas* and the *William Pitt*. All four, being larger ships of about 800 tons, then took on 700 tons of saltpetre on top of other cargoes and the private trade goods of the captains and their officers. Officials, anxious to avoid blame, would later point out that 'such an allotment of saltpetre to ships of 800 tons has at different periods before been made'.[26] But the loading was crucial. Such deadweight cargo had to be evenly distributed about a ship's hold.

Passengers started coming down river in the third week of January, apprehensive of the voyage ahead, confused by their sadness at the moment of departure. They had said farewells to friends and servants, closed their homes for the last time, auctioned most household possessions, set a few remaining items on to a pinnace and seen Garden Reach disappear as they started down the Hooghly, dozens of river craft on choppy waters, all bound to the Indiaman anchorage at Diamond Harbour. Hickey, who had sailed a few months earlier, captured a departing Calcutta resident's sense of loss:

> The thought of leaving a place I had resided in for so many years, the
> number of persons I was sincerely attached to, added to the

melancholy and desponding countenances of my favourite servants, who now for the first time began seriously to apprehend I should quit Bengal, all contributed to increase my dejection and gloom ... I frequently regretted that I had ever thought of returning to Europe. I likewise felt the dreadful change I was about to undergo, from a house wherein not only every comfort but every luxury prevailed, to a dirty little hole of a cabin on a ship.[27]

They were at least escaping the fate of the Dutchman whose tombstone inscription, also recorded by Hickey, ran:

> Mynheer Gludenstack lies interred here,
> Who intended to have gone home next year.

On 26 January they were ready – all nine ships and their navy escort. At the break of a hazy morning, the signal came from HMS *Terpsichore* to weigh and, in the lightest of airs, each was guided by a pilot from Diamond Harbour through the deadly sand bars to Saugor roads. From here they were to set a course down the coast to Ceylon.

As they came out of the roads, it was noted that the two finest ships were not moving with their customary grace. *Calcutta* and *Bengal* were the best sailers, classic 800-ton ships from the Wells yard, yet both their bows were very low in the water – or 'much by the head' – and *Calcutta* was drawing fully twenty-four feet. Here was further evidence of overloading, or at least of deadweight badly distributed. Other ships had similar 700-ton loads of saltpetre. The trouble was that both *Calcutta* and *Bengal* appeared to be carrying too much for'ard. Captain John Samson of the *Earl St Vincent* was heard to remark that if they ran into trouble, *Calcutta* was 'one of the most likely to suffer'. He said much the same of the *Bengal* – 'far too deeply laden'.[28]

The *Indus*, a sluggish sailer at the best of times, was in difficulty already. Captain Weltden had objected that she was too heavily laden. Now the pilot confirmed this, adding 'the ship was not seaworthy. But the whole fleet being at the time under way & the *Indus* being the last ship despatched, it was then too late for any alteration.'[29]

As if that was not bad enough, HMS *Victor*, a sloop, sighted *Indus* just then, limping in the fleet's wake like a wounded animal.* Their captains

---

* The *Victor* was formerly Robert Surcouf's *Revenant*, captured four months earlier.

had had previous dealings, on Christmas Day when four men were pressed into the sloop, and it may be that Weltden's attitude had displeased his navy counterpart. In any event, an officer from HMS *Victor* again came on board, announcing briskly that he needed more men. Weltden went below and returned with his protection from Pellew, forbidding 'captains under my command . . . from impress'g any further number'. After a cursory glance at it, the officer pointed out that the admiral, having departed, was no longer in charge of the squadron; and he picked out six of the *Indus*'s last few English hands.[30] This act of wanton recklessness was all the worse for occurring not at the end of a voyage but the start, when the ship was carrying fourteen passengers including women and children, and when it was too late for Weltden to turn back and replace the men.

Once out into the Bay of Bengal the fleet caught a steady breeze and moved along comfortably under topsails at eight knots. It was a fine Sunday, and although Indiamen captains were a pragmatic lot who needed little encouragement to cancel Divine Service when the weather got up, the start of a voyage brought out what reverential instincts they possessed and voices were raised that day in the seafarers' prayer

> O eternal Lord God who alone spreadest out the heavens, and rulest
>   the raging of the sea;
> Who hast compassed the waters with bounds until day and night
>   come to an end:
> Be pleased to receive into thy Almighty and most gracious protection
> The persons of us thy servants, and the Fleet in which we serve.

Passengers bowed their heads on all nine ships – from the fearful Emilia Scott on *Calcutta*, to the matriarchs with their young charges on the *Hugh Inglis* and the occupants of the *Indus* – and said a heartfelt Amen.

That evening it emerged that all the caulking of the *Hugh Inglis* had not staunched her leaks and at 8 p.m. Fairfax had to order men to the pumps.

HMS *Culloden* came into Penang harbour with her yards manned and her guns thundering, receiving a 13-gun salute from Fort Cornwallis and another from HMS *Russel*, flagship of Rear-Admiral William Drury,

Pellew's successor. Also at anchor was HMS *Phaeton*, a frigate commanded by Captain Fleetwood Pellew.

The departing admiral had a few days to enjoy the reunion with his favourite son, 'the flower of my flock and the flower of my fleet', before Fleetwood joined Pownoll and his wife on sightseeing tours around the island. In their brief time together, Eliza was much taken with her gallant brother-in-law. Still basking in the glory of his early heroics, not yet twenty and by all accounts strikingly handsome, Fleetwood was of a quite different mettle from her dreamy, somewhat lacklustre husband. On the strength of their acquaintance as they rode around Penang, Eliza began a correspondence with this 'very fine young man' and referred to him frequently in terms which, while innocent enough in a young bride – 'he is a very great favourite of mine' – hinted at her capacity for a more dangerous infatuation. Unworldly and still painfully young, Eliza had married her first suitor while little more than a girl and had yet to reveal that she had the makings of a woman no less wilful than her mother. Pownoll, perhaps used to living in the shadow of a brother who was 'everything the fondest father can wish', gave no sign of resentment over her fondness for Fleetwood. He continued to write of his happiness with Eliza, 'the most amiable and virtuous of her sex'.[31]

These pleasantries were interrupted on the evening of 23 January by the arrival of a navy brig from Manila. Her alarmed captain reported that while passing through the Straits of Malacca he had been pursued by two heavy French frigates and escaped only by heaving all his cannon and shot overboard. That the *Manche* and *Caroline* had reached Ile de France was generally known (though not that they had been joined by *Venus* and *Bellone*). But here was the first evidence that they were out and hunting. More disturbing still was the fact that the China fleet was expected in the straits at any time. The two frigates plainly had intelligence of them and were lying in wait.

Not a moment was spared. That same night *Culloden* with Drury in the *Russel* and Fleetwood Pellew in the *Phaeton* sailed for Malacca, three days to the south. They did not find the French. But awaiting Pellew was news that caused him to alter his plans entirely. The China fleet had been delayed by two months. Rather than wait, Pellew handed over to Drury directly, returning to Penang and sailing two days later for Ceylon. Instead of the China ships, *Culloden* would escort home the Second Fleet. Admiral Drury would have the task of dealing with Hamelin's frigates.

Pellew was content. One son was seemingly bound for glory, the other for domestic contentment. As for himself, he had 'cheated Old Nick of his prey by leaving bile and liver in this vile hot country', and was going home 'abundantly rich . . . [to] cheerful society and a comfortable fireside'.[32]

One other item of intelligence reached Pellew just before *Culloden* sailed, a secret dispatch from Madras. It has been lost but a hastily scribbled note to Sir George Barlow from Pownoll hints at the contents.

> We have this moment heard of the unfortunate affair at Madras about the Army but we know you too well not to be certain who is in the right.[33]

In the intervening weeks, the long-festering quarrel between Barlow and General Macdowall had come finally to a head.

9

Sir George Barlow draws his sword

Madras, 5 January–9 March 1809

On Christmas Eve of 1808, at a remote garrison 200 miles north of Madras, a Scottish aristocrat in the scarlet uniform of the Army Commander-in-Chief stood on a dusty parade ground inciting a dishevelled corps to mutiny. That it did not immediately follow was no thanks to General Hay Macdowall.

The general's precise words have been lost but not the sense. He spoke not of the honour of army life, but the ills; and he told the soldiers that he understood their grievances, that they were justified, and that the Madras government was to blame. If this does not sound like an outright call to rebellion, it can be reasonably inferred that whatever he was so rash as to say to ordinary soldiers would have been expressed more freely with his officers in the mess when – wearing floral garlands as was customary for Christmas in India – they dined and drank late into the night.[1]

Macdowall's performance at Masulipatam, soon to be repeated at other garrisons, revealed in full the flaws behind that commanding appearance. After months of brooding, he had made final his decision to leave India and return to the clan seat at Castle Sempill, near Lochwinnoch in Renfrewshire. He was departing not as a leader, however, but as a vain and weak man, shaking his fist as he stalked from the scene of his humiliation. In falling back on the fellowship of the mess, even when it meant pandering to the prejudices of disgruntled junior officers, he fanned the flames of the unrest that was to follow.

Footsoldiers in India were not to be envied. An Indiaman hand could reasonably hope to be home in a year or so. A private soldier in the Company's Army endured the same voyage, even shared the seaman's duties, but he would spend years away and the odds on him getting home at all were less than even. While few died in battle, the mortality rate was ferocious. Wet conditions at Masulipatam's old Dutch fort – it was said that 'only a Dutchman or an alligator or a frog' would have chosen to live there – nurtured a virulent fever.

Unsurprisingly, the standard of recruits was not high. Madras complained: 'It is not uncommon to have them out of Newgate. Those however we can keep pretty much in order. But of late we have had some from Bedlam.'[2] The appearance of their officers was famously motley. 'Nothing could be more ludicrous than the dress of the Company's officers at that period,' wrote one of their number. 'Some wearing shoes and buckles on guard; others shoe strings; epaulettes not fastened to the shoulder, but hanging down upon their breast.'[3] They arrived in Madras as 'griffins', as the term for newcomers had it, with expectations of shaking the pagoda tree and returning home with the wealth of nabobs – and in truth some had done so. Far more frequently, the cost of setting themselves up entailed a debt from which there was no escape. 'You seem to think that I live like those satraps that you have read of in plays,' wrote one well-to-do officer to his family, 'that I never go abroad unless upon an elephant, arrayed in silken robes. I never experienced hunger or thirst, fatigue or poverty till I came to India. Since then I have frequently met the first three and the last has been my constant companion.'[4]

What distinguished Macdowall in this company, apart from rank, was his military status. He was one of that elite group of King's officers commanding in the Company's Army, and in drawing his sword on Sir George Barlow, so to speak, before ranks of ragamuffins in stained breeches and torn, unbuttoned redcoats, Macdowall betrayed the extent to which bitterness had reduced him as an officer and a gentleman. For some time now he had done 'nothing but abuse the Governor', as one local inhabitant put it.[5] Barlow was evidently inclined to pass off this latest statement as just more hot air. He would not, after all, have to put up with the general for much longer. It was known that Macdowall had sent his resignation to Lord Minto, who quite properly told him it would have to go to Barlow, and although he had been unable yet to bite this particular bullet, it was plain that the general would be leaving shortly – possibly with the Second Fleet.

Soon after returning to Madras, Macdowall issued invitations to a farewell ball. As such it proved an apt postscript to his tenure as Commander-in-Chief – a fizzing cocktail of resentment, envy and plain hatred for Sir George Barlow.

Many of Macdowall's guests had also attended Lady Barlow's debut. The general's fellow intriguer, William Petrie, sought out Charles Marsh, a barrister who had inherited Sir Henry Gwillim's mantle as resident firebrand. The trader William Hope was there as well and the ball may have served as something of a farewell for him too; the nabob of Madras, having made his fortune, was sailing home with the Second Fleet, to build a great pile on a hillside.

For all its sameness, the ball at Choultry Plain was an occasion, and accounts of what passed found their way around the country. Barlow himself may have attended, albeit briefly. Despite the hostile coalition arrayed against him, it would have been almost unthinkable that he should not have been invited. What is certain is that his wife was present. In the pleasant cool of a December evening, ladies wore their hair high and bodices low, and, as the band played quadrilles and minuets, a young English observer could take note of the 'great number of my lovely countrywomen, who display their charms to great advantage in the sprightly dances'.[6] Among those engaged most vigorously that evening was Lady Barlow. Her daughter, Eliza, wrote to Barlow in all innocence from Penang. 'I read an account of the late splendid Ball given by General Macdowall. I understand from the Admiral that my mother danced all the evening with her usual gaiety and was in high spirits.'[7]

One is bound to wonder what effect Lady Barlow's exertions had on the Governor and his authority, for whoever she had danced with all evening so gaily and spiritedly, it was not the embattled Sir George. His wife was now usually accompanied by his aide, Major Pratt Barlow – who had recently been promoted – and they were a familiar couple at social occasions. She was thirty-eight and he twenty-three, and though there was bound to have been some gossip – the fact that he was an army officer and a member of the forces confronting the Governor added a delicious piquancy to the spectacle that they provided – Madras may not yet have guessed how far Lady Barlow's affair had progressed. Still less did it imagine the truth about the child that she was now carrying.

Exactly when Lady Barlow and Major Pratt Barlow became lovers, only they ever knew for certain. Finally, when Sir George Barlow could no longer avoid the fact that his aide and his wife were, as he put it, 'together more than necessary or proper', and said so, he would retreat when she became 'very indignant'. For one of supposedly cold and aloof temper, Barlow is seen in these exchanges as a man of all too human parts. But it seems that the affair had begun in Lady Barlow's snug quarters of the *Mercury*, in which they sailed home together. The Major later confessed that he had engaged in

> a long course of criminal connection from the time of his coming home with the unhappy woman in the ship in 1806.[8]

While Lady Barlow herself would admit, with some fervour, to having been

> repeatedly criminal with Major Barlow on every opportunity which occurred.[9]

Since spending a summer together in London, and with it a handsome amount of Sir George's money – the lavish expenditure that had so troubled his brother William – the lovers had picked up where they left off on her return to Madras. Thomas Oakes, a member of the ruling Council, would later recall that Barlow and his wife led quite separate lives. 'Sir George's avocations from early morning to late in the evening at Government House rendered it impracticable for him to attend on Lady Barlow,' as he put it, discreetly but tellingly. In the meantime, the aide-de-camp had moved in at the mansion 'and always attended Lady Barlow when she rode out or went from home'. Despite the frequency with which they were together, Oakes insisted that he 'never entertained the slightest idea that there was any criminal connection between them'.[10]

Lady Barlow, whose blithe fecundity through all this can only be a source of wonderment, had fallen pregnant again directly upon being reunited simultaneously with her husband and her lover. Emma was born the following April. Who her father was seems to have been unclear to Lady Barlow herself, for she treated the child with the same distracted vagueness that she did the rest of her children. Only the fifteenth and last, a son named Frederick, was the subject of her unqualified affection. He alone was unquestionably a love child, having been conceived in the monsoon season of 1809. After this, Lady Barlow took gunpowder in order to bring about abortions at least twice when she fell pregnant.*

While Lady Barlow was obviously infatuated, her lover's conduct appears to have been calculated. Pratt Barlow had described his mentor as 'one of the noblest Characters England ever produced . . . an honour to his family and an ornament to his country'. The young officer was treated as part of Barlow's household, had spent liberally from his account in London, and been given promotion. Yet he was bitterly disappointed. A few weeks earlier he had written to William Barlow, whose recommendation had brought him to the Governor's service, with breathtaking audacity: 'I will say no more of my own situation here except that it is certainly neither what I wished nor expected. But as men in public situations have unquestionably the privilege of disposing of situations under them in any manner they think proper I have no right to complain. Nor do I.'[11]

The man whose neglect gave rise to his resentment could only have been Sir George Barlow, to whom he owed everything and whom he was now cuckolding. Major Barlow was a blackguard and although there is no evidence to link him to the seditious trend in the military, his attendance on Lady Barlow almost certainly contributed towards the open contempt of the Army, from the commander down, for her husband.

A week or so after Macdowall's ball, on the warm blue evening of 12 January, three Indiamen anchored off Fort St George. The three ships were the Madras contingent of the Second Fleet and, with only two weeks to interview and take on passengers before sailing to join the other ships off Ceylon, time was short. Captain John Eckford of the *Lady Jane Dundas* came ashore and was carried off by palanquin to the fort.

At 826 tons, the *Lady Jane Dundas* was to be the largest ship in the fleet and Eckford already had an agreement allocating quarters in her spacious stern to, among others, George Buchan, the chief secretary to the Governor and a most unusual man. Cast away on Madagascar as a

* Not the least remarkable aspect of sexuality in Company India was the unlikely conjunction of high temperatures and high libido. Lord Wellesley – who wrote somewhat insensately to his wife in England 'As for sex, one must have it in this climate' – was not alone in finding the sultry air an aphrodisiac.

lad of sixteen in the wreck of the *Winterton* in 1792, he had survived to be rescued, taken captive by French privateers, freed, and only then begun a career that had taken him to the top of the Madras Civil Service.[12] But it was for another reason that he stood out. Alone among the residents of Fort St George, Buchan was a man the Governor could turn to, his friend and confidant. And now, suffering ill-health from his time as a castaway, he was going home.*

Soon after Captain Eckford's arrival it became known that not only would Barlow's trusted aide be sailing in the *Lady Jane Dundas*, but his bitter foe too. General Macdowall had secured the other large section of the ship's great cabin. Having arranged the manner of his departure from India, Macdowall brought matters to a head. On 15 January he announced his resignation in a manifesto stating that his exclusion from Council by the Directors had placed him in a position 'so unexampled and so humiliating . . . as to excite the most painful emotions'.

> I have been offered an indignity, and my pride and sensibility would compel me to retire, even were the sacrifice greater, for I cannot submit to see the exalted station disgraced in my person.[13]

This blast was accompanied by a bout of sabre-rattling. A colonel of the 22nd Regiment of Light Dragoons presented Macdowall with a sword in the belief 'that in your hands it will never be drawn without cause or returned without honour'. A letter to this effect was sent to the *Madras Courier*. Macdowall's reply, vowing that the sword would 'never be wielded but in a just cause', was also printed by the paper.[14]

Colonel John Malcolm, one of the few senior officers dismayed by the breakdown of discipline and who had previously noted that Macdowall was 'very sparingly endowed with temper or judgment', compared the

---

* Buchan, a Scot, was a writer bound for Madras, at the time of the *Winterton* wreck. Along with a young third officer named John Dale, he came ashore in the land of the king of Baba. While Dale, as the senior surviving officer, took a yawl to the African mainland to raise the alarm, Buchan and others stayed with the friendly king. Months later Dale returned with help and provisions to the survivors, many of whom had died of malaria and privation. Buchan had survived but even then his adventure was not over. He was among a group captured on their onward voyage by a French privateer and taken to Ile de France. For all the enemy island's evil reputation, Buchan later expressed 'unqualified gratitude' for his treatment by the French.

commander's conduct at this stage with a man waving a torch over a powder magazine.[15]

He still had one more hand to play. For months the officer at the centre of the Tent Contract furore, Lieutenant-Colonel Munro, had awaited news of his fate. While regimental commanders demanded a court martial, and the Army's legal advocate ruled that he could not be charged, Macdowall had dithered. He did so almost to the last. On 30 January he summoned Munro and told him that the decision on a court martial would be left to his successor. A few hours later he changed his mind. Munro was placed under arrest, pending a court martial.[16]

That night Munro caused a terrific stir in the mess when he entered and 'had the impudent assurance to sit opposite to the Commander in Chief at dinner'. (Although under arrest he remained at liberty.) The next day he appealed to Barlow. This put the Governor in an impossible position – damned for interfering in army affairs if he took action, but duty bound to uphold the law. Barlow wrote respectfully to Macdowall on 24 January 'suggesting in the most earnest manner' that Munro be released.

The general replied that this request 'implied censure' of his actions and he could not comply 'without compromising the honour of the whole Army'. All chances of a compromise ceased at this point.

Barlow waited as long as he could before taking up the challenge. It was not until 27 January, the day before Macdowall was to embark on the *Lady Jane Dundas*, that a rider cantered up Mount Road to the Choultry Plain garrison, bearing an order for Munro's release. Macdowall complied – and then, in the haste of those last hours and a final act of bluster, drafted a General Order.

He said that only his imminent departure had prevented him from bringing Munro to trial for contempt. He then made a personal attack on Barlow for issuing 'a positive order . . . to liberate [Munro] from arrest'. This message he left to be copied and disseminated. His aide Colonel Capper, the mischief-making Adjutant-General, meanwhile drafted another General Order. He had precipitated the crisis by leaking Munro's report. Now he wrote a parting message to the Army on his friend's behalf that could only aggravate the tension.

Lt-Gen Macdowall cannot view his separation from a body of men he is sincerely attached to without suffering the most painful sensations . . . the whole tenor of their conduct has met with his entire approbation and he will boldly affirm, without danger of contradiction, that His Majesty has not in any of his dominions a more loyal, patriotic and valiant class of soldiers and subjects.[17]

Although the following day was a Sunday, Choultry Plain was abuzz with anticipation. Capper's deputy, Major Thomas Boles, arranged for Macdowall's General Order to be printed and that afternoon sent off copies under his own signature. This seemingly trivial action was to have severe consequences.

That same afternoon Macdowall was the guest at a farewell mess dinner. At about 4 p.m., after a final round of toasts, he left Choultry Plain with huzzahs in his ears and was borne down to the beach where a guard of honour awaited him. Saluting them, he became again the figure in the Raeburn portrait, all redcoat and breeches, his gold insignia and medals glittering in the sunlight – tall, upright, imperious. Then he stepped from the shingle into a boat sent from the *Lady Jane Dundas*, quitting the country where he had passed the greater part of his life. Later in his cabin he had a rare opportunity for reflection in solitude and, perhaps as the effects of the claret wore off, started for the first time to feel uneasy.[18]

The Indiamen were to sail in the morning. It was a clear night with a high moon and as the hands made their way around the decks, shaking out sails and making all ready, the ramparts of Fort St George were outlined as if in luminous white thread.

Watching all this with a sense of longing was the lone figure of George Buchan, who had 'walked out on the fortifications on a beautifully serene evening to see the fleet getting under weigh'. He would not, in the end, be sharing the great cabin with General Macdowall. A few days earlier Barlow had asked his friend to stay by his side during the crisis. 'The sacrifice was considerable,' Buchan wrote, but 'the feeling of gratitude and attachment to a revered friend could not allow me long to hesitate'. He went on: 'An old Indian said that he "loved to look at the sea, as the road to Europe" and this was a sensation at the time in my thoughts.'[19] And, just then, a fragment of verse came to his mind:

When the winds subside and the storms are laid,
The calm sea wonders at the wrecks it made.

Barlow was at his desk before dawn the next day. A copy of Macdowall's order had reached him during the night and he had summoned Buchan and the rest of the Council to an emergency meeting. At 6 a.m. they were in conclave at Fort St George with copies of both general orders before them. Something in Barlow now snapped. An order was issued as the meeting ended at about 8 a.m., summoning Macdowall before the Council.[20]

Macdowall, of course, was aboard a ship in the process of sailing, and the sequence of what followed is unclear. But when the fleet escort, HMS *Belliquiex*, signalled to weigh at 9 a.m., Barlow's letter had not been received. Later in the morning – the exact time is not known – cannons thundered out from Fort St George. This was a signal to stay the fleet. By now, however, the ships were moving towards the horizon. Perhaps, as a resident thought, they 'were too far gone to hear the guns'.[21] Perhaps the captains heard the cannons but mistook the signal for random firing. Either way, the attempt to recall Macdowall had failed.

What Barlow would have done with him had it been successful was a matter of feverish speculation. 'Some say the object was to detain the C in C, but that is hardly credible,' an observer wrote.[22] What the Army would have done was suggested in a letter to Barlow from a friend with an ear to the ground.

> Had the recall succeeded and the General been relanded under suspension, the Army were ripe for any measures ... You would have been lucky to have kept your seat.[23]

Whether or not he had considered the risk of a coup, Barlow now drew his own sword on the Army. Historians have puzzled why, given his reputation for iciness, he over-reacted at this point. Lady Barlow's amorous adventures may provide the key. The small, terrier-like figure in the Governor's robes had taken more than enough from the military.

The day after the fleet sailed he issued his own edict: Macdowall was denounced for 'acts of outrage' against the Government and dismissed. (This was no mere gesture; Macdowall had yet to actually resign and would only send a formal note some days later from a port down the coast.) Next Barlow turned on the two officers most readily identifiable with Macdowall's order – Colonel Capper and Major Boles. Both were suspended.[24]

As the news spread around regimental messes the effect was electrifying:

> Officers avowed themselves ready for any act of daring revolt. They encouraged one another in treason; they talked of fighting a tyrannical Government in defence of their rights to the last drop of their blood. Seditious toasts were given at the mess table and drunk with uproarious applause . . . The moral intoxication pervaded all ranks from the colonel to the ensign.[25]

Public sympathy, as was always likely in a garrison town like Madras, fell in behind the military. Barlow was isolated. 'Everybody condemns the Government and applauds General Macdowall,' one resident wrote.[26]

Events moved fast. Capper made a dramatic gesture – exchanging his army red coat for a civilian blue one and wearing it in public.[27] Secretly he called together a clique of senior officers at Choultry Plain. They sent a protest to Minto, demanding the removal of Barlow as Governor, and conveying a threat that they would otherwise take the law into their own hands. It was plainly seditious and, as one historian put it, 'a warning of mutiny'.

To Macdowall's cohorts it seemed that everything now depended on how the crisis was represented at home. As things stood, he would reach England knowing nothing of his dismissal and after Barlow's letters, sent by a fast-sailing packet, were in hand. The first blow might be decisive in establishing an advantage. It came down to a race for the India House.

Capper, as Macdowall's friend, was the obvious man for the mission – to pursue him with a warning of what had passed. On 7 February, a week after the general sailed, Capper was rowed out to an American ship, the *Atlantic*, 'in the hope of overtaking the fleet before they should leave Ceylon'.[28]

Amid the turmoil of these events it would sometimes be overlooked that Macdowall was not the only prominent figure to have left Madras in the three Indiamen. One individual in particular stood out among the sixty or so cabin passengers – roughly two-thirds of them army officers and their families – and that was William Hope.

Hope had come to India as a young private, had survived an era when the Madras Army had real enemies to fight – he may have been at the catastrophic 1781 defeat at Pollilur in which 2,000 British troops were slain – and although uneducated had an eye for opportunity. Somehow he acquired the capital to buy his way out of the Army and set up as a small-time merchant, selling essentials to newly arrived recruits. This enterprise turned in due course into the house of Hope & Co, and made its founder the richest man in Madras, with a fortune estimated at £100,000 (about £6 million at today's values). Hope might well have turned into what Lord Macaulay called 'a savage old Nabob, with an immense fortune, a tawny complexion, a bad liver and a worse heart'. His ethics were undoubtedly rugged. It may be recalled that in a duelling case brought before Sir Henry Gwillim, Hope had nobbled the jury to get two army officers acquitted of murder.

He had taken aboard the *Jane Duchess of Gordon* his wife, an Indian woman named Kezia, their four daughters – Kezia, Ellen, Anna and Caroline – and 'a very considerable portion of his fortune'.[29] Hope was returning home with all the swagger of a working-class lad who had ventured abroad and conquered. He would build a great house and, though he might be disdained by his social betters as a parvenu, he would still stand as an exemplar of a new egalitarian spirit. With his military connections, he would also be the dominant figure on the voyage home in a cuddy that resembled a regimental mess more than anything, with eleven officers around the dinner table – a major, four captains, three lieutenants and three ensigns.

They enjoyed a near-idyllic start to the voyage. The trio of Indiamen and their escort bent under the weight of a pleasant south-easterly breeze that ran them 114 miles along the Coromandel Coast on the first day, all under a pale warm sun – the *Jane Duchess of Gordon*, the *William Pitt* and the *Lady Jane Dundas*.

On 5 February the ships raced around Dondra Head, the southern tip of Ceylon, and on to Colombo. Here Macdowall went ashore and heard news that could only have cut him to the quick as a man, even as it must have overjoyed him as a soldier. Dispatches had just been received from Europe that Arthur Wellesley, his former comrade-in-arms, had struck a series of blows at the French in Portugal, culminating in a famous victory at Vimeiro.[30] Macdowall returned to his cabin to digest this information and the Madras ships sailed again – just down the coast to Point de Galle, the Second Fleet rendezvous.

If there was one thing that an Indiaman voyage offered it was opportunity for thought. Removed from the febrile atmosphere of the cantonment, the general started to reflect. Wellesley's triumphs rebuked him: as young blades they had drunk and served together, had matched one another step by step in promotion, but while Wellesley had gone from Indian victories to glory in Europe, Macdowall remained mired in mediocrity.

He might have suspected by now that he faced a rough reception at home. What he could not have imagined was that the most damning verdict on him would come not from the Directors but one of the officers he had left behind, who had observed his departure and thought of it as desertion. Macdowall, he wrote bitterly, 'soothed us with hopes of support and, when he had blown it into a flame, left us to fight our own battles'.[31]

Barlow saw what was in the wind when he heard about Capper's hasty departure. The Army was going to make representations at the India House. Very well, two could play at that game. Again he turned to his friend Buchan, who recalled: 'From the turn which things were taking, the Government of Madras was desirous that the Government should be fully apprised of the state of matters; and for this purpose it was thought proper that one confidentially informed on the subject should proceed to England.'[32]

Though Buchan was plainly the right man to represent Barlow in London, there remained the question of how – all that season's Indiamen having departed – he was to get there.

On 12 February the *Sir Stephen Lushington*, commanded by Captain Hay, came to off Fort St George after completing the outward voyage in just nineteen weeks, justifying her reputation as a flier. She was still due to proceed to Bengal when, three days later, Captain Hay was ordered to make ready for an immediate return to Europe. In less than two weeks, the *Lushington* was taking on passengers. No record exists of Captain Hay's negotiations with Barlow but, having been forced to cut short his voyage, he would have driven a hard bargain, especially when it was emphasised that time was vital. In the race to England, a single Indiaman – and a fast one at that – would have a big advantage over a fleet.

The settlement watched each new development agog. One resident offered a wryly ironic perspective:

> Madras is in a dreadful state. No two people hardly speak to each other. If you are asked what o'clock it is you must look grave, shake your head, pretend to be hard of hearing and answer 'Pretty well, I thank you. How is your family?'[33]

In fact there was talk of nothing else in the evening routs on Mount Road. One thing followed another. It became known that *Lushington*'s passengers were to include not only Buchan but Mungo Dick, a senior member of the Council and another Barlow aide. Almost immediately the Army detached Lieutenant-Colonel George Martin, a leader of the seditious movement, to join the ship and take further representations to the Directors. So intriguing a prospect did this ménage present that the *Lushington* was nicknamed Pandora's Box.[34]

She sailed on 2 March, a month behind the Madras Indiamen, but under orders to proceed home without stopping. After a few days of variable weather, she picked up a fresh trade blowing south-east by south and reeled off a succession of days when she ran around 200 miles from noon to noon. On 9 March she hit a short sharp squall, attended by thunder and lightning, but still managed 116 miles.

That same day a Madras resident sat down and wrote a letter full of foreboding about Barlow's confrontation with the Army. 'The business is by no means over. God knows how it will end.'[35]

And far to the south, the Second Fleet had reached Lat 20° 20'S, Long 72° 07'E, and run into severe weather.

10

'A perfect hurricane'

Point de Galle and at Sea, 7 February–15 March 1809

The Second Fleet mustered off Point de Galle early in February, like the clans of some great tribe, drawn from distant parts for an annual rite. Summoned by Admiral Pellew, ships came to the southern tip of Ceylon from around India with a precision that was one of the hallmarks of British seafaring. The nine Bengal Indiamen anchored in the bay on 7 February. The following day three Bombay ships came in from the opposite side of India. Not far behind were the three Madras ships. Finally, from distant Penang, came HMS *Culloden*.

In all these toings and froings, little attention was paid to the last passengers joining the fleet. But so far as the Honourable Alexander Johnston and his family were concerned, leaving Ceylon was proving anything but smooth. The Johnstons had been booked on the *Lady Jane Dundas*, only to be advised from Madras days earlier that their quarters had been occupied by General Macdowall. Johnston, who was needed at home on Crown business, was beside himself with anxiety.

Born into a long line of Scottish gentry, the lairds of Carnsalloch, Alexander Johnston was one of those endearing, and not uncommon, Celts who found their true home of the soul in the Orient. He was raised in India but his name will forever be associated with Ceylon where he cast the mould for a colonial regime well ahead of its time. As a child in South India, Johnston was educated by the missionary anthropologist, Christian Schwartz, grew up speaking Tamil, Telugu and Hindi and in the process 'imbibed a lifelong sympathy with the natives'. There was more to him than mere sympathy, however. Like Sir William Jones, the Calcutta orientalist, whom he resembled in many ways, he was an able jurist and a student of Asian people, cultures, religions and languages at a time when these subjects excited rather than repelled Europeans. He married Anne Campbell, another high-born Scot, and the young couple landed in Ceylon in 1799, where he had been appointed Advocate-General, four years after the ousting of the Dutch. Here his researches into the laws, customs and history of the inhabitants established him as an authority in these matters, while his promotion to Chief Justice gave him political influence.

Britain was now considering Ceylon's future as a colony and Johnston was about to proceed home to make recommendations to the King when he learnt that Macdowall had taken his place on the *Lady Jane Dundas*. Indiamen captains disposed of their cabin space as they wished to the highest bidder and Macdowall was a figure of influence. Every ship in the fleet was packed and it was only thanks to a Lieutenant-Colonel Walker leaving the *Earl St Vincent* and returning to Bombay – possibly under orders to make way for the judge – that accommodation became available. The Johnstons were rowed out to her on 10 February.[1]

It was a bright day in a dream-like land, one which few left without regret. Johnston and his wife had spent the past nine years on the island, where all five of the children accompanying them had been born, and they felt a pang of loss as the old town of Galle receded from view, the Dutch fort, its star-shaped bastions pink-blasted by tropical sun and black-streaked by monsoon rains, squatting among palm trees, the white line of surf against shimmering beaches and, beyond, valleys and mountains. Their relief at having obtained a passage was sobered by conditions on the *Earl St Vincent*. Every corner was occupied and the noise from a dozen children's voices was terrific.

Two days later, the unmistakable shape of a 74-gun ship of the line hove into sight. HMS *Culloden* had made a remarkable passage, having been swept across from Penang on a westerly current in just eight days.

She was followed the next morning by an American ship from Madras, the *Atlantic*. Colonel Capper had arrived a day ahead of the Indiamen with Macdowall.

Pellew had at this stage only an inkling of the trouble in Madras, but knew Macdowall was on an approaching ship. On hearing that the *Atlantic* had come in, and realising that she would have the latest news, he sent for her captain. After interrogating him, he dashed off a letter to Sir George Barlow marked 'Private'.

> Last night an American Ship from Madras anchored here. She brought Colonel Capper who, I find, landed instantly in great haste to seek General Macdowall. On my sending for the Master this morning, I learn from him that the Colonel landed and [has] not been seen since. The Master stated that he heard some displeasure of your Government had caused the Colonel's resignation or that you had suspended him – why he could not tell. But he believed signal guns had been fired from Madras to bring back the General . . . I am sorry to depart without knowing what this story is, but I shall get at it long before we reach Home and shall take care it is not related to the discredit of your Government.[2]

Capper stayed out of sight in Galle until the next morning when the Madras Indiamen were sighted, then had himself taken out to the *Lady Jane Dundas*. Macdowall, hearing what had passed since his departure, of his dismissal by Barlow, saw at last the gravity of his situation. Disgrace, possibly worse, awaited him at home. The best hope was for him and Capper to sail together and present a united front. Macdowall had taken over the entire great cabin and there was room for both of them. Capper's baggage was rowed out to the ship.[3]

Pellew, in the meantime, had traced another of the *Atlantic*'s officers and pumped him about events in Madras. By nightfall, Pellew was in the picture. In what followed he would act as a conciliator, but his loyalties were clear. Macdowall was an old acquaintance, a friend even, but Barlow was family.

The admiral sent a message across, inviting Macdowall on board and holding out the lure of a cabin on *Culloden*. The general replied, keeping him at arm's length, that he was obliged for the offer but was 'quite comfortable and snug' on the Indiaman. His words nevertheless betray a man deflated and increasingly uncertain.

> Your letter tells me you wished to see me, but I am not very well and have rather laid low since I heard of the extraordinary conduct of the Madras Government . . . the proceedings against me have abundantly vexed and distressed me . . . During the voyage [I] will

take an opportunity of stating the circumstances to you. I will not add more at present but trust you will allow the necessity on my part of not compromising the honor of the profession or the situation I held.[4]

Discernible now for the last time were the myriad small vessels – packets, galliots and cutters – that swarmed to *Culloden* like fish around a whale, linking the flagship with the Indiamen and the shore, carrying mail and orders, sustaining a communication network seemingly haphazard but somehow efficient. There was a final flurry of activity on the evening of 14 February when Pellew ordered captains to the flagship for their sailing instructions. At daylight the signal was given to weigh, bowers came up and sails were sheeted home. Even so, because of the manoeuvring required to bring so large and dispersed a fleet together, it was not until the following evening that all the ships fell in, leaving Galle bearing east-by-north-east about nine miles in a golden light.

The eighteen ships – eight more than the First Fleet – made an imposing sight, each a cloud of canvas lined with cannons and, with the appearance of men-of-war, a threat rather than a temptation for any French frigates. In the vanguard stood *Culloden*, a sight best conjured by the poet Samuel Coleridge in his description of another 74-gun ship of the line: 'a majestic and beautiful creation, sailing right before us, upright, motionless, as a church with its steeple – as though moved by its will, as though its speed were spiritual.'[5]

With the frigate *Terpsichore* bringing up the rear, they sailed in two lines abreast. As Commodore, Captain Maxwell in *Calcutta* stood ahead in the windward line, followed by *Bengal*, with Captain Sharpe. In addition to these two, there were five ships of 800 tons and more – the *Lady Jane Dundas*, *Hugh Inglis*, *William Pitt*, *Earl St Vincent* and *Jane Duchess of Gordon*. To leeward were the eight smaller Extra ships of between 530 and 630 tons – the *Indus*, *Huddart*, *Lord Eldon*, *Northumberland*, *Sir William Bensley*, *Sovereign*, *Euphrates* and *Harriet*. Also joining them was the *Atlantic*, whose captain had asked Pellew for protection.

Topmen in the crosstrees looked from horizon to horizon on the disc of a sea so enlarged by their heightened perspective that it came up to meet the sky – a boundless blue, pale above and deep below, with a breeze that cooled them as it filled the canvas beneath their feet with a low constant exhaling of breath. This was their element and for now it was in benign aspect. They had eaten their fill and tonight there would be grog and dancing on the forecastle. It was a moment of quick, exultant joy. They were homeward bound.

One who knew about it wrote mournfully: 'It is impracticable to give the inexperienced reader any accurate idea of the life in an East Indiaman, where a number of persons of all ages and classes are confined together in one place, with little to do, and few occasions of acquiring a single new idea.' It is this sense of confinement that is perhaps hardest for those of our times to grasp: for up to half a year, about 150 individuals of diverse social groups, from ship's boys to gentlemen, would never be further than 130 feet from one another. But they would still inhabit separate worlds – seamen up forward, gentry in the stern, others in steerage.

Most lubbers were struck by the sounds and smells, 'the cries of the sailors; the creaking of the ship's sides, the wind in the rigging; the lapping of water; it is universal, ceaseless. And then there are the appalling odours from which there is no escape, that detestable tar, the emanations from that odious gallery.'[6] Somehow, each person had to find a routine, a personal way of passing the time, but also a way that did not disturb the routine or sensibilities of another. A father advised his daughters:

> Nothing is so indelicate, indeed so indecent, as from the windows of ladies' cabins to see anything towing overboard or being hung out to dry; neither is anything more severely censured than loud talking, dancing over the heads of those in the great cabin, thus indelicately attracting the attention of persons in the next cabin or cuddy.[7]

Of how individuals spent the voyage of the Second Fleet little is known. Ships' logs, so detailed in noting wind, weather, speed, sea conditions, death and punishment, are silent on the doings of those whose names were entered in copperplate hands as passengers. It must be left to our imagination to envisage the cuddy of, for example, the *Indus*.

Passengers for England from Bengal

Lt-Col Murray	HM 67th Regt	Mrs P Tailhorde
Capt Butcher	HM 67th Regt	Mrs Benjafield, two children 4 & 1
Mr Francis Pierard	Hon Company's Civil Service	Mrs A Rolt, two children
Mr J With	Danish Officer prisoner	Three children, Tyler, Evans, Mclean
		Servants for Pierard, Rolt & Tailhorde

Joined the ship at Galle

Mrs Hannah Skipp*	Capt Wolfe
	Lt Perks

We are on firmer ground with the great cabin of the *Calcutta*. Here, indeed, was a cast drawn from a period drama. One would love to know what Jane Austen (who had some knowledge of seafaring with two brothers in the Navy) might have made of a floating drawing room containing five Bengal nabobs, including some of Hickey's old claret-drinking hearties, the two grieving widows, Harriett Arnott and Frances Parr, the only married couple, William and Emilia Scott – she the highly strung survivor of one Indiaman disaster – and the usual representatives of the Army and the Church, Major W. Fraser and the Rev. Paul Limerick.[8] Socially equivalent and familiar with one another, the passengers of the *Calcutta* were superficially the group most likely to make for a happy ship, and Captain Maxwell the commander best able to allay Emilia's fears.

The preponderance of military officers on the *Lady Jane Dundas* did not necessarily create a congenial company. That old literary seadog Captain Marryat thought there was 'no class of people who embark with more regret, or quit a ship with more pleasure, than military men'.[9] The reasons are not hard to fathom. Usually masterful types, they were reduced in all senses by *mal de mer*; no longer in command of men, or even of themselves, they were also obliged to submit to the discipline of another uniform. That said, the *Dundas*'s captain, John Eckford, was new to command and may have felt overawed by having not only General

* Young Mrs Skipp had gone out only the year before with her husband, George W. Skipp, a cadet but evidently no gentleman; he would later be cashiered. Mrs Skipp must have been powerfully moved to sail home alone.

Macdowall and Colonel Capper on board but Lieutenant-Colonel Alexander Orr. This was the officer who, seven years earlier, was involved in a secret inquiry instituted by Lord Wellesley into the liaison between the Company's Resident at Hyderabad, James Achilles Kirkpatrick, and a young noblewoman of the Nizam's court, Khair un-Nissa. Orr it was who, as an associate of Kirkpatrick, confirmed that the couple had fallen in love, beginning a romance of tragic and compelling consequences.* He was sailing home with his wife and two children.

A quite different tableau was presented by the nursery ship *Hugh Inglis*, where a trio of mothers ruled the roost amid the terrific row raised by twenty-nine children under the age of seven. The 'horrid screeches and crying of children,' noted by Hickey, 'or, what is full as bad, their vociferous mirth when playing their gambols in the steerage' must have been a trial for a childless couple, Mr and Mrs Mumford Campbell, of whom nothing is known beyond that they were in their early thirties and Campbell had just retired as magistrate at Rungpore.

Lack of privacy and confinement aside, the biggest problem was monotony. Handbooks like the East India *Vade-Mecum* offered hints on how to deal with it. Many voyagers, including James Wathen who sailed to Madras in 1811, found it best to make a virtue of routine.

> I rose generally at 5 and had many opportunities of enjoying the sublime spectacle of the Sun rising, to be seen to the greatest perfection at sea only. When the weather permitted I walked and conversed with the ladies and gentlemen on deck before breakfast; between breakfast and dinnertime I wrote the occurrences of the preceding day in my journal; and in the afternoon amused myself with drawing, writing and reading. Every period of the day being appropriated to a distinct employment, I felt the time pass away very agreeably.[10]

Meals were the fixed point in the day and, at the outset at least, captains' cooks would do their best to produce a handsome table: 'All kinds of fresh meats, exquisite curries, pies, tarts, puddings, etc.,' enthused one passenger; 'ill-concocted soups, queer-looking ragouts, and jelly the colour of salt water,' sniffed another. We have already noted the ceremonial

---

* This is the subject of William Dalrymple's *White Mughals*.

attached to dinner, served at two in the afternoon, when both sexes dressed as if for an event at Government House and the captain, in full uniform, presided at the centre of the table 'with an air of conscious dignity which is meant to be very imposing'.[11] Diners cast a wary eye over their new companions and single women were exposed to close scrutiny, as the diary of a young officer, George Elers, records.

> Of the two Miss Smiths, Jemima, the eldest, was a most incorrigible flirt, very clever, very satirical, and aiming at universal conquest. Her sister, Henrietta, was more retiring, and I think more admired; at least I know Colonel Aston was much struck with her pretty little figure and lovely neck . . . Mamma Payton, too, had her admirers. She was very quiet and matronly, and rolled about her fine black eyes at dinner in every direction. Without being absolutely vulgar, she had no polish or refinement, and had evidently not been used to fashionable company. As to poor Miss Chinnery, no one ever thought of her. Poor soul! She had neither beauty nor talent; but she was good-natured and inoffensive, and thankful *when* she received attention.[12]

Sex was less easily accomplished than flirting, particularly when cabins were partitioned by no more than a sheet of canvas. Still, motion and sea air were stimulants and some captains introduced codes of conduct to prevent single ladies making the kind of attachments that could cause tensions in the roundhouse. Some women were not inhibited. In one celebrated scandal, the niece of a member of Council confessed to having intercourse with three men on a voyage to Madras, including the captain.[13]

Meals offered more simple pleasures – a focus for the day's activities and a reminder of an orderly world beyond the horizon. Regimental bands played during dinner and again during the evening promenade, before a light supper at about nine and a few hands of whist followed by a general retirement. As a rule, captains required that candles should be extinguished by ten in order to minimise the risk of fire.

The routine of the Second Fleet was briefly broken on 20 February when they crossed the Equator and hands were given licence to mark the occasion with the curious mixture of ceremonial buffoonery and bullying known as Crossing the Line. Neptune's rites – involving bizarre dressing-up, conch-blowing and the ducking of lubbers – had been known to get out of hand, but there is no suggestion of excess on this occasion.

Instead it was the weather that turned nasty.

Like the First Fleet before, Pellew took the Outer Passage across the Indian Ocean. In every other respect, however, he followed a most unconventional course.

For a start they sailed due south from Ceylon. Most homeward sailings in the north-east monsoon season took a sweep eastwards before crossing the Tropic of Capricorn and bearing south-west for the Cape, which made optimum use of the prevailing winds and gave a wide berth to Ile de France during the hurricane season. Because Pellew sailed due south, he was always likely to pass closer to the island than was commonly thought wise.

Every fleet had a laggard. In this case she was the *Huddart*, hopelessly slow in company, the bane of other captains who would note grimly in their logs, 'Much detained by the *Huddart*'.[14] This was no reflection on her captain, William Nesbitt, who was a good seaman and had a gift, more rare among his kind, for making others at home in her. (On her outward voyage all thirteen passengers signed a letter thanking Nesbitt for his 'attention to the comfort of each passenger as well as for the very liberal and gentlemanly treatment we received'.[15] And an army couple in steerage, Private McLean and his wife, were well enough taken with the voyage to name their son, born on board, Huddart.[16]) Now he drove his crew hard to keep up so that when a stiff southerly filled topsails on 21 February, even the *Huddart* managed to reel off 140 miles.

They were still making fine progress for so large a fleet when, ten days after leaving Galle, a heavy bank of black clouds came up, bringing 'very hard squalls, very vivid lightning with thunder and hard rain'. They were at Lat 07° 10'S Long 83° 45'E and – though none knew it – close to the position where disaster overtook the First Fleet three months earlier, in 08° 27'S, 87° 75'E.

Although a few ships had sails split, and nervous passengers confined themselves to their cabins, the main effect was felt on the *Indus*. Captain Weltden had presumably not told his passengers that their ship was unseaworthy, but they would have been hard pressed to maintain their sang-froid over the hours that she was buffeted, when, he recorded, 'the ship lay dead in the water & the sea ran constantly over her & a great deal of water got between the decks.' Afterwards Weltden decided to lighten her by casting overboard stores meant for St Helena, then went on *Culloden* and reported to Pellew that 'he dreaded the consequences should they experience any very bad weather'.[17]

As the gale blew itself out, the air became heavy, sultry, and, from running along at seven knots, all eighteen ships lay with sails limp, becalmed. While captains stamped quarterdecks with impatience, a pause gave rise to contact between ships, which came alongside one another to exchange visits and be entertained.

> Gymnastic feats were exhibited, such as leaping, tumbling, balancing, etc. The sailors excelled in the hornpipe; some chaunted Dibdin's inimitable sea ditties, others amused their hearers with 'tales of wonder'. The lascars took part in these gambols, and exhibited tricks and dexterous deceptions peculiar to their country. The Chinese regarded everything with an observant eye.[18]

It was also at this time that Macdowall submitted to Pellew's invitation to join him on *Culloden*. The general came on board alone and was now a distinctly chastened man, admitting candidly in the admiral's cabin that he dreaded the prospect of having to appear in public at the Cape, which had a large British garrison. There was nothing mean-spirited about Pellew who, although in the opposite camp, was moved to see a fellow commander of men brought so low and later wrote to Barlow in an attempt at peacemaking. 'We had considerable conversation on the subject and I am quite satisfied he greatly regrets the circumstances and would give a great deal to retrace the ground he so imprudently and inconsiderately travelled out of his way to attain.'[19]

During the calm Pellew decided that something had to be done to keep the hands active, and a boat was set around the fleet, ordering each ship to hold gunnery practice. On 5 March sails were at last stirred by light airs and the ocean surface, overnight as flat as a plate, was broken by heavy swells, moving the ships on some thirty-one miles. Later a light north-westerly breeze came up, filling sails, and as it gained in strength the knotted log-line trailing in the wake of each ship marked their gathering speed: on 7 March they covered 76 miles; on 8 March, 128 miles; on 9 March, 178 miles. Pellew in the vanguard drew them on, making the most of the conditions. Some of the captains, however, were starting to feel uneasy about a course that was taking them steadily westwards and closer to the Ile de France.

Pellew was in many ways a contented man. It was his custom to 'walk in the stern gallery, bringing to mind all my dear friends at home, broiling as I am with heat'.[20] But one aspect of his command still rankled. He had failed to strike any sort of blow at the French. Above all, his plan for taking Ile de France had been rejected: that speck on his chart of the Indian Ocean had been a source of discomfort; it rebuked him; and its capacity for evil was evident again. That, at least, is one explanation for why he acted as he did now.

The fleet had reached a position of Lat 22° 20'S, Long 72° 07'E, roughly halfway across the Indian Ocean and some 04° or 05° to the west of where most of the captains would have expected to be. At this point, instead of setting a new course south-west towards the Cape, Pellew persisted in his westerly direction. They were holding roughly to 22°S latitude, just south of Ile de France, which stood at 20°S, and Bourbon, at 21°S.

Pellew never explained why he did this. It was nothing to do with the wind for, as Fairfax of the *Hugh Inglis* noted, that had been coming from the north-west, so it would have been natural to have shaped a more southerly course.[21] The simplest and most likely explanation is that the old battler, leaving the sea of his disappointment, was running close to the islands in the hope of a chance encounter with the French frigates.

If there was confusion among the captains over why he took them where he did, there was no doubt about the risk of sailing so close to Ile de France. From December to March was the season when hurricanes blew around the island, and all sensible mariners steered clear of it. The Indiamen captains would never criticise Pellew directly – that would have been unthinkable – but there was much muttering on quarterdecks. This is clear from the testimony of a majority of captains, who stated their course to have been too far to the west. Among them, Captain Campbell of the *Sovereign* pronounced loftily that had he been commander he would have given the island a much wider berth as he 'expected very bad weather

in March so near the islands and was never so near before by 02° or 03°'
(i.e. between 120 and 180 nautical miles).[22]

On 10 March the wind switched to the south-east and they ran almost
due west at a terrific pace. They were still some 600 miles east-by-south-
east of Ile de France, but converging rapidly, having covered more than
160 miles that day. During the night, the wind's shift brought in high seas;
and the weather began to deteriorate, as the *Huddart*'s log makes clear:

> 10 March: Strong trade throughout with squalls in the first and
> middle parts. Shipping a great deal of water.
> 11 March: A very strong trade throughout, the ship labouring much
> and shipping much water.
> 12 March: A strong trade throughout with very hard squalls at times,
> a very heavy sea running. Shipping much water. The weather too
> unsettled to perform Divine Service.

There had thus been four days of rough conditions – of wet, giddying
work aloft to reset and reef sails, and of lurching, heart-stopping fear
below, with ports closed and hatches battened – when on 14 March they
reached Lat 23° 30'S, Long 61°E. The fleet was now less than 200 miles
east-by-south-east of Ile de France. It had been blowing hard during the
night when, around daylight, all hell descended.

About two years earlier, in 1806, Admiral Sir Francis Beaufort had drawn
up the first known system of defining wind strength in the open seas,
ranging from a calm Force 0 to a hurricane Force 12. The Beaufort scale
would not be adopted by the Admiralty until 1838 and most British
seamen already had their own rough, broadly comparable, rules of thumb.
In home waters they might experience a gale, Force 8 on the Beaufort
notation of 39 to 45 mph, or a severe gale, Force 9 or above, which would
be judged by the senses – size of the sea, sound of the wind – rather than
any device. A modern account relates that 'a scream means the wind is
around Force 9 on the Beaufort scale. Force 10 is a shriek. Force 11 is a
moan'.[23] Few at this time would have known what sound Force 12 made in
the rigging, but there were other yardsticks. Beaufort's own description of
hurricane strength, as 'that which no canvas could withstand', was as good

as any for a wind of 75 mph and upwards.*

While conditions varied from ship to ship in the twin storms of 1808 and 1809, captains in both fleets used the term ' a perfect hurricane' to describe them. Some undoubtedly did encounter a genuine tropical cyclone – a ring of spinning thunderstorms, followed by an extraordinary calm at the centre, before a return to the demonic embrace of the eyewall. In order to understand what happened to the Second Fleet, however, it is necessary to envisage two roughly drawn groups of ships.

At dawn on 14 March, six Indiamen had fallen behind the leading group. They would experience a typical tropical storm that buffeted them and terrified their occupants, but did not threaten destruction.

Up front, *Culloden*'s log records that the *Terpsichore* and nine Indiamen were in sight. Although not named, they were the *Calcutta*, *Lady Jane Dundas*, *Bengal*, *Jane Duchess of Gordon*, *Hugh Inglis*, *Huddart*, *Indus*, *Lord Eldon*, and *Harriet*. It would later be suggested that Pellew ought to have signalled them to stow all canvas and heave to. This, indeed, was thought to be the wisest course to adopt in a hurricane – to ride it out under bare poles. But although the sea was swollen like a mountain range in motion, Pellew may not yet have believed that he was in the grips of a hurricane. He decided to run before it.

In such conditions it was for each captain to cope as best he could. 'Everybody shifted for themselves, looking only to their own preservation,' Pellew wrote later.[24] He might have sounded a more considerate tone. *Culloden* was in the best state of any ship, having recently been refurbished at Bombay and being well provided with hands: as a 74-gun ship of the line she had some 600 officers and men, more than ten times as many as the fleet's smallest ship, the *Lord Eldon*.

Under close-reefed mainsails, *Culloden* scudded along at an astonishing eleven knots. All through the morning winds strengthened, bringing heavy and frequent squalls of rain. Although the ships closest to her stayed in touch, by late afternoon the air had so thickened with spray and rain, and the sky so darkened, that another separation took place.

---

* Hurricane is a Caribbean Indian word for 'evil spirit and big wind', and it is with the West Indies that the term is generally associated, while storms of the same strength in the Indian Ocean are now called tropical cyclones and those in the Pacific typhoons. For the sake of consistency with the period, this narrative adheres to hurricane.

Culloden was last seen disappearing into the maelstrom followed by the four biggest Indiamen, *Calcutta*, *Bengal*, *Jane Duchess of Gordon* and *Lady Jane Dundas*.

The remaining five ships could no longer see one another either. They all fell behind for different reasons and found themselves in roughly the same vicinity. They were the *Huddart*, *Hugh Inglis*, *Indus*, *Lord Eldon* and *Harriet*.

On the *Huddart*, the storm had begun with a funeral. John Robinson, an invalid army officer, died early on in the blow and was dropped over the side in a hasty ceremony. Captain Nesbitt, who had always shown consideration for his passengers, made a personal entry in the log, 'His death regretted by all on board'.

Since then Nesbitt had wrought a wonder of seamanship by running with the lead group. He was as poorly served for crew as any ship, but his lascars had been forged into a capable unit, able to keep the sluggish *Huddart* up with the fleet. This may have been partly attributable to some expert help, for in addition to the usual mix in her passenger quarters (a Mr Stewart of the Civil Service, a Mrs Frazer, four army officers and nine children) she was carrying home two ship's captains. Having been in the country service, plying the merchant trade around India, Captains Young and Maugham were familiar with lascars, as they were too with the furies of the Indian Ocean, and it may well be that the *Huddart*'s struggle for survival was a tribute not just to one captain but three, working as a team.

As the furies gathered on the morning of 14 March, the foresail blew to shreds. An attempt was made to bend on another but the wind was too violent. At this point *Culloden* and the others disappeared. From noon, Nesbitt's log reads:

> Still the gale increas'd, the sea running exceptivily [sic] high and making frequent breaches over the ship. At half past three shipped a very high sea which upset most of the guns, stove the cutter to pieces on the larb'd quarter & tore with the weight of water the main stays'l to pieces.[25]

One cannon, overturned and sliding around the gundeck in a storm, was a lethal object. Half a dozen or so spelt certain doom. With the *Huddart* laid over and her deck canted to starboard, staying ropes were hacked away so that the guns on this side could be heaved overboard.

Men were then set to wearing the ship, bringing her head away from the wind. For some hours into the night the situation was stabilised. Although he had to keep all pumps going as waves continued to plough over the sides, Nesbitt noted with relief that his unloved ship was 'making very good weather of it, notwithstanding the violence of the gales & height of the sea'. She was scudding west-by-south-west when, just after midnight, she broached to, possibly by being pushed too hard, and was brought side-on to the wind.

> She was immediately laid over on her larboard beam ends, her side being entirely under water, her gunwale rail, gangboards etc were soon swept away and every thing on that side dashed to pieces and washed over board. Made every exertion to wear [turn the ship's head away from the wind] but without success, the fore stays'l & fore topmast stays'l blow'd to ribbands; attempted to set the jib but it was likewise instantly blown to pieces.

Desperate though the situation was, Nesbitt had the presence of mind to deal with another source of peril while she was canted over to larboard: 'Cut away and hove overb'd as many of our lee guns as we could possibly get at.' But while this balanced the starboard guns shed earlier, *Huddart* remained so far over that her larboard beam was usually under water, with sea surging around the hatches. Such was the slope of the deck that men could only step away from the pumps by handing themselves along by rope.

Nesbitt's log is nothing if not understated. For six interminable hours that night, 'from the time of our being brought by the lee at 1am till near daylight,' he wrote, 'the situation of the ship was very perilous'. His passengers had given up hope. They had been wet, sick and fearful long before death became an apparent certainty. Now, down in the darkness, awash and terrified, they waited for it. In a world drained of colour, they saw only shapes that shuddered dimly in the dark as another blow fell on the ship.

Quite when the first light of 15 March came no one was able to say. But the hour of deliverance was noted in the log as 8 a.m. when, quite suddenly, the wind dropped and the sea fell. With further pumping, she started to come up.

For the rest of the day Nesbitt took stock. All *Huddart*'s three masts had somehow been left standing and although her rigging was a fearful mess she had come through intact; a miserable sailer, she had yet proved a stout little battler. By evening the *Huddart* 'stood before the wind SW in the hopes of joining the fleet'.

In falling behind, Nesbitt had come within the orbit of other ships that had initially been with the leaders but, like *Huddart*, had lost sails or been brought to. Among them were the *Hugh Inglis* and the *Indus*. Both had been in difficulty beforehand, the *Hugh Inglis* because of her chronic leakiness, and *Indus* thanks to her ill-distributed load of deadweight cargo.

Captain Weltden of the *Indus* had said after the gale ten days earlier that he dreaded the consequences should his ship meet really bad weather. He was not exaggerating. The ordeal of those on the *Indus* may indeed have been compounded by the captain having some personal crisis. As he related, Weltden hove to on the morning of 14 March after *Culloden* disappeared into the storm.

> The sea was then running very high & the weather very thick with rain. The ship labour'd, the seas constantly beating over them, frequently going over the poop. A great quantity of water got down between decks altho' the hatchways were closely battened down.
>
> The sides began to work very much & the fore-rigging was giving way ... At 4pm it blew a perfect Hurricane ... In consequence of an application from the officers of the ship, determin'd to throw some of the saltpetre overboard. Expected every moment that we would go [down] as the ship rolled so very deep.[26]

How a small number of exhausted men, who had been at the pumps since daylight, managed to shift 300 bags of sodden saltpetre up on to the deck while the ship continued to plunge and roll was never spelt out. Weltden simply claimed that the bags were 'immediately thrown overboard & they soon experienced the benefit as the ship was much more lively'.

A different version of events was provided by Captain Campbell of the *Sovereign*, who claimed to have found the *Indus* in a dire state the next day, when Weltden – seemingly in petrified denial – said he was unable to make sail because water had covered the orlop deck, but at the same time refused all offers of help.* Two days later the ships were still together, bailing and carrying out repairs, when a heavy sea came up. Only then, according to Campbell, when he insisted that Weltden had to lighten the ship forward or founder, was the saltpetre thrown overboard and the *Indus* saved.[27]

Whose version was closer to the truth is an open question. Campbell's account, here and at other points, suggests pomposity; but Weltden continued to behave in a peculiar manner, at one stage defying orders at the Cape. The *Indus* should rightly not have been at sea at all, and the stress on her captain may have been translated into a form of breakdown.

The *Indus* was a ship that on any objective assessment should not have survived. So was the *Hugh Inglis*. Before the storm her leaks had required her to be pumped once daily. On 9 March this rose to twice, and on 10 March to four times. Nevertheless, when the storm began, Captain Fairfax decided that it would be dangerous to part from *Culloden* so near the Ile de France and he resolved to run with her. Fortunately, the *Hugh Inglis* was separated from the leading ships almost immediately.[28]

By some whimsical tide, she also escaped the worst of the gale that day. Fairfax wrote that she scudded easily before the wind and it was not until nightfall that she ran into real trouble. There was only one helmsman strong enough to grapple with these conditions and he may have become exhausted for, at about 9 p.m., the *Hugh Inglis* 'yawed to leeward and broached to on the starboard tack'.

For all his earlier misgivings about the crew, Fairfax now had cause to give thanks for they included a number of good lascars who proved 'very allert [sic] & equal to the situation'.[29] In half an hour or so they managed to wear and were soon running again south-west. The *Huddart*, put in the

---

* The orlop was the lowest deck in the ship, above the hold. Being below the waterline and sheltered from cannon fire, it was where the ship's surgeon operated and where civilians would be sheltered in enemy action.

same dire situation, had stayed down on her beam ends for six hours.

Even as the gale dropped Fairfax was given another fright. At daylight on 15 March he sighted a strange sail, apparently in pursuit of them, and which failed to answer the coded identification signal. The children were taken below as the ship was cleared for action. Whether the stranger was French or not, and what resistance the Indiaman could have put up, was never tested. The stranger edged away to the south and by noon was lost to sight.[30]

Like leaves they had been scattered and, as if cast to the same corner of a distant field, they started to come together again. Within a week, the *Huddart* fell in with the *Harriet*, which had also come close to foundering. The *Harriet*'s captain, William Lynch, related that, like the *Huddart*, she had survived because he had her guns heaved over the side. They were joined by the *Euphrates*, the American ship, *Atlantic*, and a few days later the *William Pitt*.

These ships had all been left behind when the *Culloden* and the four Indiamen closest to her ran. As a result, they had met just one violent storm in the twenty-four hours from daylight on 14 March. They had, in short, escaped the full fury of the hurricane.

Just how lucky they had been became apparent a few days later when another stranger was sighted four miles in the south-east. Through telescopes, it could be seen that she was a frigate – or the ruins of one. All her masts were gone, her rigging was cut away, her stern stoved in and her rudder useless. But what frigate was she? Not, it was plain, their escort *Terpsichore*.

Asked to identify herself, the signal came back. The shambles was HMS *Nereide* – the smartest ship on the Cape station and pride of her commander, Captain Robert Corbet. She, it happened, had been in the same latitude and encountered not one gale, but two. The *Nereide* was among those ships to have been at the eye of the hurricane.

11

'The most terrible of deaths'

At Sea, Lat 22° 20'S, Long 72° 07'E, 14–16 March 1809

Sir Edward Pellew was not a fanciful man. He was, though, warm-hearted and emotional – even sentimental when it came to his boys. He thought anger his worst vice. 'I would at times wish to believe myself possessed of a good heart but, alas, it is hidden among rubbish and vile passion of temper,' he once wrote.[1] He was, in fact, a man of imagination and some sensitivity, and in the long hours of the storm, when he thought it quite probable that he was about to die, he may well have reflected on the fate of his late enemy, Sir Thomas Troubridge. On the night of 14 March, *Culloden* was on her own with the fleet in her wake. She was also on the same latitude and now just a few degrees to the east of where Troubridge's flagship had gone down in another screaming gale two years earlier. The uncanny similarity of their circumstances was not lost on Pellew. Nor was the irony that he, widely thought to have destroyed Troubridge, was now seemingly going to meet an identical fate.

Rear-Admiral Troubridge, a great favourite of Nelson and St Vincent, had been sent to India in 1804 to share the Indies command with Pellew in an old settling of political scores. Pellew was the senior man, and the appointment was a clear affront. He went out on a limb, refused to acknowledge Troubridge and wrote to the Admiralty: 'I would rather command a frigate with her bowsprit over the rocks of Ushant all my life than command here on such terms. For heaven's sake, call one of us home.'[2]

Troubridge, whose high sense of honour was tarnished by a terrible temper, went almost mad with rage and brooded on plans for revenge, including challenging his foe to a duel. The feud resolved itself when – despite conduct that had left him open to a capital charge – the Admiralty

163

came down on Pellew's side. Troubridge was transferred to the Cape. He fled India in frantic haste, in HMS *Blenheim*, an old 74 that had been nearly wrecked a year earlier and was falling to pieces, ignoring Pellew's intention to give him another ship. *Blenheim* was last seen in a gale southeast of Madagascar, settling low in the water and flying signals of distress, on 1 February 1807.

A legend arose that Pellew had contrived Troubridge's death for, as his biographer noted, 'the picture of Pellew resolutely pushing his enemy into a sinking ship was more than imaginative minds could resist'. But Pellew bore Troubridge no malice, lamenting: 'Brothers could not agree as we were placed.'3

How they would marvel at home now, those idiots. As *Culloden* fought for her life, Pellew reflected thankfully that, unlike *Blenheim*, she was in good condition. But if she went down, here would be more fertile material for chatter – Pellew lost in the same manner as his old foe: two fighting admirals who were undone not by the enemy but hurricanes in the Indian Ocean. Had he, indeed, been a fanciful man, Pellew might have imagined Troubridge's ghost in the seas that flogged *Culloden*.

The first crisis occurred soon after the middle watch took over at midnight on 14 March, when a rogue wave, perhaps sixty feet high, smashed over *Culloden*'s stern. Its force was such that the ship, charging before the wind, was in immediate danger of broaching to – being turned broadside on to the wind and sea. As Pellew put it, she was

> poopt going 11 knots & had all her boats and quarter galleries washed away and lost her mizzen mast. *Culloden*'s after beams fell in on the Tiller & they could not steer the ship till 6 inches of the beams were cut away.4

Eliza Pellew was in her bed when the quarter gallery exploded in a spray of glass shards and sea that swept through the cabin. She remained composed, sitting up in her nightdress while having six men bailing water from under the bed, and the admiral remarked approvingly that 'she did not betray any feminine weakness, on the contrary was very heroic.' Her husband noted proudly, 'Eliza behaved amazingly well.' In contrast, her companion, the widow Mrs Cotton, was said to have been utterly terrified.

At daylight men were sent up to cut away the mizzen topmast, but before they could do so it blew off, carrying with it the gaff, the spanker and the whole of the mizzen rigging; and as the wreckage went over the side, it dragged away the boats on the starboard quarter. Soon afterwards it was reported that cannons on the lower deck were in danger of breaking free from their breechings; this threat, at least, was neutralised before it could create havoc.

Over the next twenty-four hours the weather followed a curious pattern. From the logs kept by Captain Pellew and the master, it would seem that there were periodic breaks in the storm, when the *Culloden*'s crew were able to start clearing some of the debris – and were rewarded with an extra allowance of beef and half a pint of arrack for their stout efforts – only for the blow to resume. At six in the evening Pownoll recorded 'More moderate with less sea', but then again at eight, 'Strong gales with rain at times'.5

Somewhat belatedly, Pellew's thoughts turned to the Indiamen. During one of the lulls, at daylight on 16 March, he ordered that the ship be brought to 'to await the convoy'. None of the Indiamen had been seen since the evening of 14 March and as *Culloden* had been flying along at around nine knots it was plain that they had been left behind. Pellew had no way of knowing that the hindmost group were in fact well over a hundred miles to the east. The storm had passed over them at dawn the previous day and they were now in the clear. But far from dissipating, the wind had acquired a new force, and was now bearing down on *Culloden*.

The second onslaught was signalled by a typical feature of hurricanes, a sudden and complete shift of the wind's direction – in this case from east-south-east to north-west. The *Culloden*'s crew was caught unawares and the ship was in immediate danger of broaching to. While they were still trying to bring her about, another giant wave came out of the lumpy grey sea and smashed over her stern, this time on the larboard side, and washed away the other quarter gallery.

There is no mention of how Eliza Pellew and her terrified friend, Mrs Cotton, responded to this second inundation of their quarters. But during the course of the night even Pellew started to entertain doubts as to whether the *Culloden* could take much more. Having so far believed this to be 'a most violent gale', he now revised his opinion. 'I may indeed call it, rather a hurricane,' he wrote.[6]

Rain came on harder than ever and as the wind strengthened it chased flying streaks of white foam across the sea until at some point the whole ocean seemed to turn white; the wind's force was tearing the crest off the waves. One who sailed through such a storm wrote: 'It became difficult to make out where the surface of the sea began or ended.'

It required a great deal to sink a wooden ship. As some of the First Fleet ships had demonstrated, a three-masted square-rigger could broach to and stay down on her beam ends for hours – could have water seven feet deep swirling around below, and still survive. Accounts from ships that did founder in mid-ocean are, obviously, rare. In one instance, however, HMS *Centaur*, a Third Rate caught in a gale in the West Indies in 1782, was kept afloat for days after being laid on her beam ends and smashed to pieces internally by loose cannons. Only when her pumps became choked was her fate sealed and on the seventh day she settled steadily in the sea, so that for a while she 'appeared little more than suspended', before finally foundering.*

On *Culloden*, the chain pump – a cyclical device that drew water up in buckets – was still in working order, as were the hand pumps. But she had taken a terrible pounding over the past three days. Late that night she 'strained and laboured in every part of the upper works and decks'. This created a new danger. Hull timbers were being worked apart and the caulking that sealed them breached. She was taking water in at various points, not only on to the orlop but in the lower gundeck.

The men were near the end of their collective tether. A number would certainly have suffered injuries of greater or lesser severity.[†] The ship was close to collapse as well. Pellew confided later: 'Had it continued six hours longer with the same violence, I believe she would have closed all our accounts in this life . . . Had not the old *Culloden* been in good condition, she must have gone down.'[7]

Instead, one final furious burst just before dawn on 17 March signalled

* Captain Inglefield of the *Centaur* was among eleven men to escape in a pinnace and sail to safety. The remainder of a crew of around five hundred died with the ship. See Duncan, *The Mariner's Chronicle*, pp.173–89.

† All the ships suffered casualties among their crews but only fatalities are mentioned in the logs.

the end. The wind started to moderate. Around noon, the hands again began setting the ship to rights. The sky cleared and the sea dropped and that night, for the first time in weeks, the *Culloden*'s crew could point to the brilliance above them, the Southern Cross dazzling on the larboard beam, and the sea, gone from black and malevolent to a luminous phosphorescence. Extra casks of beef were broken out, and an additional ration of grog was ordered for every man.

Celebrations in the stern were no less heartfelt. Mrs Cotton became intensely gay and promptly fell in love with another of Pellew's guests, an Army officer named Cochrane, who gave every indication of responding equally to her ardour.[8]

A course was set for the Cape. Thinking of the Indiamen, Pellew asked to be brought news of any sightings. Just after midnight on 24 March, under a bright moon, a lookout reported two strange sails, but they turned out to be American whalers. Ten days later, when they passed Cape Agulhas, the southern tip of Africa, he still had no intelligence of the fleet.

Four Indiamen had been close to *Culloden* at the onset of the storm and had tried to keep up with her. The *Calcutta* was sailing alongside to windward with the *Bengal* in her wake. Some way behind were the *Lady Jane Dundas* and the *Jane Duchess of Gordon*. All had up close-reefed main topsails and foresails and were going along fast.

That was on the evening of 14 March, and it was the last that was ever seen of them.

There was a curious if crude symmetry about each pair of ships: the two named after titled ladies, the largest in the fleet at 826 and 822 tons, disappearing together into the gloom; and the two named after Company possessions, near-identical products of the Wells yard – launched within a year of each other and with only two inches in length between them – and both deeply laden by the head. That symmetry would extend to the mystery of what happened to them. Most of the surviving Indiamen captains – who had hove to and therefore escaped the worst – concluded that they had simply been overwhelmed:

The four missing ships, when last seen, were following the Admiral under as much sail as the nature of the gale would admit, and there is every reason to suppose that they experienced, with the same violence as *Culloden*, the effects of the shift of wind. When the superior advantage of a line of battle ship in the strength of her crew is considered, it may be concluded that whereas the *Culloden* narrowly escaped, the gale proved fatal to the missing ships.[9]

Which is all well enough; but it assumes that all four ships made it through the night of 14 March. In fact, the other ship last seen running with them, HMS *Terpsichore*, almost went down herself that night – despite being strongly crewed – after being blown down on her broadside for several hours. All in all, the notion that four Indiamen stayed together in the rough vicinity of the *Culloden* until 16 March, while the rest of the fleet was dispersed over hundreds of square miles, is too pat.

One view offered at the time attracted little attention, perhaps because it came from one of the less-experienced captains. But Nesbitt of the *Huddart* had also been close to *Culloden* on the evening of 14 March, had been the last to see the missing ships, and had questioned Captain Gordon of the *Terpsichore*. At first he found it hard to imagine that the four finest Indiamen could have gone down when his own much-maligned ship had survived, but had his opinion 'entirely altered' by what he heard from Gordon.[10] Nesbitt's theory, expounded at the subsequent inquiry, forms the basis of the following account.

The *Lady Jane Dundas* and the *Jane Duchess of Gordon* followed *Culloden* into the black, mountainous crests of the night of 14 March. Like others they were ill-manned, but otherwise in good sailing trim and neither had the loading problems of *Bengal* and *Calcutta*.

In the stern of the *Lady Jane Dundas*, General Macdowall contemplated death. Since daylight the dreadful, vast shape outside the rear gallery had been rising and falling, growing steadily larger in the distance between the crests and the troughs, and although this evolution was almost imperceptible to the eye, it was felt in the increasingly violent blows that fell upon the ship. No dinner could be served and when darkness closed around them, Macdowall and Capper clung to chairs cleated to the floor as she shuddered, twisted and fell, their faces now illuminated only by a flickering candle. Capper would have been less than human had he not been cursing his last-minute decision to leave Madras and join his friend.

Similar scenes were to be found in each compartment of the great cabin, and, above it, in the roundhouse, where Colonel Orr huddled with his wife and two children and Captain Macpherson with his wife, and in steerage where the four Wintle children, William, Emily, Augusta and Harriet, were terribly alone.

That night, as the gale neared its ferocious peak, Captain Eckford decided to stop scudding. He had lost sight of the flagship late in the afternoon, so there was no longer any question of keeping up, and the longer the *Lady Jane Dundas* ran, the greater was the chance that she would broach to. As most captains had already done, he gave orders for the close-reefed main topsails and foresails to be taken in and everything made snug. Topmen went aloft, handed in the sails, and the *Dundas* slowed rapidly from around nine knots.

As she did so, the *Jane Duchess of Gordon*, which had been following under the same press of sail, came up out of the dark.

There was no visibility until the last moment, so there was no warning. In an instant, the impact of one wooden juggernaut, surfing down a wave into another, brought about their mutual destruction. In the shattering shock of the collision, masts snapped like sticks and the great oak timbers of the hulls splintered. Inside the ships, bulkheads collapsed with a series of thunderous cracks. Both went rapidly to pieces.

Though this ensured the death of everyone on board both ships, it was not necessarily sudden. Even after breaking up, sections of ship might stay afloat for some time, most typically the high stern quarter where the cabin passengers found themselves, suddenly and curiously, exposed to the tempest, drenched and wind-blown. For some time they were borne up in a part of the ship that was still vaguely identifiable by its shape but no longer familiar as their surroundings of these past weeks. Finally, piece by piece it disintegrated, until they found themselves floating and entangled among bits of wreckage.

On the *Jane Duchess of Gordon*, about a hundred and fifty souls were lost including twenty-seven cabin passengers. William Hope would not in the end build a great house in the country and lord it over his social betters. At the last, the nabob of Madras was reduced again to a humble station; although he was far the richest man on the ship, when the passenger list was published later, his name, totally unknown in England, was at the bottom, below eleven army officers and two gentlemen, John Hayes, Esq., and J.P. Moore, Esq. He was simply Mr W. Hope.

A similar number died on the *Lady Jane Dundas*, among them General Macdowall and the two colonels, Orr and Capper. In the minutes left to him after the ship broke up, Macdowall had enough time to reflect that he was being spared scandal and disgrace and, for a military man of his time and connections, death may have been preferable. He would not hear the damning verdict of the Directors: that he had 'encouraged a spirit of discontent and insubordination which it was his duty to repress', nor that his conduct had 'imperiously demanded our most prompt and decisive animadversion'.[11]

Arguably worse for Macdowall than any censure, however, would have been the consequences of his actions. A few months later, when Madras was on the brink of civil war, one of his old acquaintances in the settlement, unaware of his death, wrote savagely:

> He must be cursed by the Army as the chief cause of this disgrace
> and if he has a grain of feeling must reproach himself to the last hour
> of his life for the misery he has occasioned.[12]

To the last hour of his life, whatever agonies of conscience he did suffer, Macdowall was spared that.

Meanwhile the *Calcutta* and *Bengal* had continued to scud through the night. They had been closer to *Culloden* and were oblivious to the calamity that had occurred in their wake. Captains Maxwell and Sharpe had concerns enough of their own. Both feared their ships had been too deeply laden with saltpetre. On the other hand, they were the finest Indiamen of their type, beautiful products of the Wells yard. Somehow they had avoided the navy press, and in Maxwell and Sharpe they had the ablest commanders in the fleet.

Maxwell tried to keep his passengers' spirits up. All Indiamen captains strived for a confident demeanour – for, as one of them noted, 'landsmen are adrift at sea at the best of times, but in bad weather their ignorance magnifies the peril in their eyes; much depends on how the captain conducts himself' – but Maxwell was known for his way with anxious civilians.[13] That was just as well because there was no trace in *Calcutta* now of an Austen-like comedy of manners. The presence of Emilia Scott only made matters worse. Even if the term Jonah was never used, her previous brushes with death gave rise to what a captain sensitive to the mood in the cuddy called 'a general feeling of superstitious despondency'.[14]

Nothing could have prepared poor Emilia for the past twenty-four hours. Who could have imagined that she should find herself caught up in another Indiaman disaster? Certainly not her old acquaintance William Hickey.

Hickey was at his home, Little Hall Barn in Beaconsfield, some months later, writing his memoirs and recalling old India days, when he heard what had befallen many of his friends in the Second Fleet. It sent him back to his own experiences and the time when he was bound for Calcutta, a lawyer with a young wife, and a ferocious Indian Ocean storm blew up. His account is a compelling one, and we may picture him, an old man, adventures and travels over, rereading it and wondering at the final hours of his friends.

In great tribulation I returned to my cabin, telling Mrs Hickey to secure anything she was particularly anxious about and prepare herself to undergo severe trials. At seven each of us swallowed a dish of tea, the last and only refreshment we had for many subsequent hours.

At eight in the morning it began to blow hard, torrents of rain pouring down, rendering it almost as dark as night. Then was an order first given to take in top-gallant sails and reef topsails. The order was too late; the instant the sails were lowered they were blown to atoms. The sea suddenly increased to an inconceivable height, the wind roaring to such a degree that the officers on deck could not make themselves heard by the crew by the largest speaking trumpets. Between nine and ten it blew an absolute hurricane. The entire ocean was in a foam as white as soap suds. The ship began to roll with unparalleled velocity from side to side, each gunwale, with half the quarterdeck, being submerged in water each roll, so that we every moment expected she would be bottom uppermost or roll her sides out.

Thus buffeted about on the angry ocean, I told my poor Charlotte, whom I had secured in the best way I could and was endeavouring to support, that all must soon be over, it being quite impossible that wood and iron could long sustain such extraordinary and terrific motion. The dear woman, with a composure and serenity that struck me most forcibly, mildly replied, 'God's will be done, to that I bend with humble resignation, blessing a benevolent providence for permitting me, my dearest William, to expire with you, but oh! My dearest love, let us in the agonies of death not be separated,' and she clasped me in her arms.

The ship was apparently full of water, and seemed to be so completely overwhelmed that we all thought she was settling downward. Nevertheless the velocity and depth of her rolling abated nothing, tearing away every article that could be moved; not a bureau, chest or trunk but broke loose and was soon demolished, the contents, from the quickness and constant splashing from the one side to the other of the ship, becoming a perfect paste.

By two in the afternoon every bulkhead between decks except that of my cabin had fallen from the violent labouring. The folding door that opened into the great cabin was torn off its hinges and broken to pieces, exposing to our view the foaming surges through the great cabin's stern windows. If we look round the miserable group that surround us no eye beams comfort, no tongue speaks consolation, and when we throw our imagination beyond – to the death-like darkness, the howling blast, the raging and merciless element, expected at every moment to become our horrid habitation – surely, surely it is the most terrible of deaths![15]

In Hickey's case, the seemingly impossible occurred. The wind abated, the sea fell.

On *Bengal* and *Calcutta*, something similar happened. Two days of turmoil passed. By the evening of 15 March they were still in *Culloden*'s vicinity. Like her, they experienced a lull; like her too they had lost masts and were awash below. But as Maxwell and Sharpe surveyed the damage, optimism rose. The worst, it seemed, was past.

Those hopes were swiftly and savagely dispelled. The hurricane's sudden return from the north-west had caught *Culloden* unawares and caused severe damage. On the two Indiamen the effect was fatal. Manning was probably a factor: laid down on their leesides, they were unable to pump out water quickly enough and were gradually overwhelmed.

Their death throes were more prolonged than those of *Lady Jane Dundas* and *Jane Duchess of Gordon*. As water rose on the gundecks, passengers did what others had in similar circumstances – they joined the seamen and stood shoulder-to-shoulder at the pumps, hauling for all they were worth, drenched and exhausted.

In extremis, seamen often went below to break into the liquor stores, but that stage had been passed on *Bengal* and *Calcutta*. Everything below was already in pieces. There may have been an attempt to launch the ship's boats, although in all likelihood they were in pieces too. The upper deck was certainly awash and to retain their position men had to catch hold of ropes and stays, all in a last, dim hope that the wind would shift and allow the wreck to spring upright. Clinging for life to the slippery surface, they were mute as waves broke over them. From time to time a sea greater than the last would catch a man in an exposed position – and he would disappear over the side, a ghastly face in a flurry of limbs.

The ladies and gentlemen had retreated to the roundhouse, the highest internal point of the ship. At some point the water intruded. The sea was not cold, felt, rather, surprisingly warm. At first it churned around their feet, then washed away, only to return, and this time higher. Chairs had been cleated to the deck, but bureaus and tables were now being borne around the cabin. It made an odd sight. The stern windows were gone.

Contemporary accounts of ships in their death throes referred to 'the sufferers' praying, weeping and crying out for help. The truth may have been more prosaic. Robert Eastwick, a captain who spent a lifetime in Indian waters, left a record of his closest experience of drowning that is as convincing as it is understated. He was among a group of men, lying drenched and mute with fear, awaiting the inevitable on a sinking ship.

The gunner, a most respectable, good man, who had left behind him at Rangoon a wife and seven children, was next to me, and presently he moved and coiled his leg round mine. And although this seemed to weaken my hold, yet there was such a sense of companionship in his mere touch that I suffered it to remain. And so we all of us lay huddled like a cluster of limpets on a rock, the wreck rising and falling with a dull, lifeless motion, and great surfs breaking over her with sharp concussions, sending foam and spray flying high in the air.[16]

That expression of a human instinct for bodily contact at the last has a compelling ring of truth. In an image of the roundhouse on another doomed Indiaman – the *Halsewell*, lost in 1786 – the artist Thomas Stothard represented in a way neither facile nor sentimental, a company facing certain death. Individuals are displayed around a grim, dark little space. No one looks at anyone else; vacant, distracted gazes are fixed on another place. Some of the figures are defined by their isolation – a man, his face averted in horror, a young woman seated on the floor, her arms crossed in shivery dread. Others cling to one another for comfort – Captain Richard Pierce enfolds his two daughters. And, in a corner, a recumbent man, his face a mask of resigned despair, supports another lying across him. Stothard based the painting on survivors' testimony and though it is melodramatic for modern tastes, it chimed powerfully with an age that had knowledge of these things. Perhaps in this tableau we may glimpse something of the last hours of the *Calcutta*: Emilia Scott clutching on to the husband whose illness had brought them to this pass; and Harriett Arnott and Frances Parr, the widows united by the murder of their husbands and now sharing their final moments.

Hickey thought it the most terrible of deaths, but surely the most terrible thing about drowning was the fear of it. They had spent many hours imagining the unimaginable, so when the seas finally dragged them from timbers and ropes, and took them away into an immense place, it did not feel so strange after all. Their real sufferings were behind them. There was a final struggle and a brief agony gasping for breath, then just the salt water that had become everything and was the last thing of all.

12

Pellew's revenge

At Sea, Table Bay and the Downs, 15 March–12 July 1809

Why that tiny island was so productive of turmoil, nobody was sure. To sail past Ile de France in the south-west monsoon was to see a gem of the Indian Ocean, lustrous and green with a high interior of mountains shaped curiously like the stupas of oriental temples, or a row of jagged teeth. Some navigators said it was these peaks, protruding amid an empty ocean, which disrupted the monsoon wind when it switched to the north-east, thus setting in motion the forces that culminated in a Force 12 on Admiral Beaufort's scale. Others maintained that there was a wind unique to the island, a northerly monsoon, and it was this which – in passing over its adjacent warm and immensely deep waters – stirred its demons. Still others, plain superstitious, would have looked at that odd skyline again, shrugged, and concluded that it was simply a place that no seamen should go near.

It was a sight that had become familiar to Corbet and the *Nereide*, and in mid-March they were approaching it again. Three weeks had passed since their departure from Table Bay to resume the blockade and the prospect of spending the months ahead in zigzag cruising off Port Louis oppressed the ship. Corbet's promise of a new regime, the assurance to his court martial that 'the weeds of dissatisfaction having been rooted out, the soil will now bear more gentle tillage', was the subject of bleak humour at mess tables. Between 6 and 11 March, two men received twenty-six lashes each for drunkenness, six got twenty-four for neglect of duty, and two a mere twelve for insolence. One man was given six – although for what, only Corbet knew.[1]

There had been no beatings for four days when the *Nereide* encountered what the captain described at first as 'strong gales & dark gloomy weather with a heavy sea'. That was on 15 March. She was 370 miles south-west of Bourbon, and the hurricane was racing towards her from the east.

It arrived at about four the next afternoon, having destroyed four Indiamen in its wake a few hours earlier. Corbet's log records:

> At 5 strong gales carried away main staysail sheet & split the sail. At 8 strong gales with a heavy sea. Ship labouring very much. Fell overboard and was drownded a Black Boy. At 11.40 gale still increasing to a Hurricane. Put the helm up, found she would not fall off. Loos'd foresail which blew out of the Bolt rope. Righted the helm, tried her again with no better success. Gale violently increasing found it necessary to cut away the mizzen mast. Still she would not go off.[2]

Corbet later averred that any other frigate would have capsized and there is no reason to doubt him, for whatever his failings, seamanship was not among them. The wind was blowing 'harder than ever I had before seen it,' he wrote.[3] *Nereide* was so far down on her beam ends that the lee side of the quarterdeck was under water. The greatest danger now was of the remaining masts going over the side and, with the weight of wreckage, dragging her down. Corbet ordered the mainmast to be felled, and she righted.

Just after noon the wind dropped and for an extraordinary few minutes the air was calm. The sea, however, was not. A wave surged out of it, smashing in *Nereide*'s entire stern. Corbet, anticipating that the wind was about to return, had the fore-topmast cut down as well. Of the three masts and their network of rigging, only the lower section of the foremast now remained standing.

The captain, surveying the object of his pride, noted with horror: 'Thus in a quarter of an hour was the ship, from being in a most perfect state, become a wreck.'[4]

As in the case of all the ships to have been assailed by the hurricane, the wind came back suddenly from the north-west. The *Nereide* was driven along at eleven knots under a single bare pole, directly into a sea running vast from the south-east. Corbet could still barely believe it himself when he wrote to Bertie at the Cape: 'This, Sir, will give you some idea of the gale. I was in great alarm for the danger of scudding against the tremendous SE sea, but to my astonishment the NW wind so completely overpowered it that we did not feel any inconvenience from it.'5

In this fashion the frigate ran at between ten and eleven knots for almost twenty-four hours, until noon of 17 March when the hurricane blew itself out and the *Nereide*'s crew, exhausted and dazed, bent and set a new foresail. In the process, a topman named David Phillips was overcome, fell into the sea and was drowned. He had been a model hand, or at least an invisible one, being one of the few never to feel Corbet's lash. Apart from the 'Black Boy' mentioned in the log, seemingly some hapless lad taken on at the Cape, Phillips was the only death.

They spent days at anchor, clearing wreckage, and were still repairing the ship when a lookout sighted five strange sails. They were the battered remnants of the Second Fleet.

It would have been bad enough for any navy captain to be found in such a state by Indiamen. For one with Corbet's mania for smartness it was utterly galling, especially as they were from a group that had come through the storm in considerably better shape than *Nereide*. When Captain Graham of the *William Pitt* came on board and asked if he would convoy them, Corbet appears to have been somewhat ungracious. Graham recorded in his log that Corbet initially refused, 'in consequence of the disabled state of his ship', before agreeing 'as long as our sailing did not detain him'.6

Corbet later put it differently to Admiral Bertie. 'I conceived it my duty to see them in safety as far as my way was theirs and accordingly took charge of them,' he wrote. The benefit was, in fact, mutual as the Indiamen provided the wounded frigate with much-needed spars and hawsers. Once she had rigged a jury mast, they set a course for the Cape – the *Nereide*, followed by the *William Pitt*, *Huddart*, *Harriet*, *Euphrates* and the American *Atlantic*.

In all the thousands of square miles traversed by ships since the storm, it was almost uncanny how scattered ships continued to encounter one another in that vast space. On 25 March, four more of the Indiamen were sighted, *Indus*, *Sovereign*, *Lord Eldon* and *Northumberland*. They too fell in with the convoy, and at some point the captains were invited to join Corbet on the *Nereide*.

He became quite garrulous, telling them that in twenty years at sea he had never experienced such a storm and had believed *Nereide* to be doomed. As they talked it became plain that the further west a ship had been when the first gale came on, the more she had suffered, and as the *Nereide* had been in the most westerly position of all Corbet may have been feeling less touchy as they proceeded down south-east Africa. It pained him that he had been forced to turn back from Ile de France yet again, but Admiral Bertie had always been most amiable towards him – looked on him with great favour.

Another admiral had anchored in Table Bay, however, and he did not look on Corbet with favour. Sir Edward Pellew had just found out about the mutiny on *Nereide*, and he had a score to settle with her captain.

Lord Caledon, the young governor at the Cape, did not often receive distinguished visitors and when HMS *Culloden* came into Table Bay on 5 April with the daughter of a former Governor-General of India he made a tremendous fuss of her. The Pellew entourage were swept up to the Castle where Eliza and her husband were installed in a chamber with a splendid view of Table Mountain and treated with 'the most marked attention and hospitable kindness'.

Pellew in the meantime made it his business to find out what had happened on the *Nereide* since her departure from Bombay in November. He noted that instead of proceeding directly to the Cape, as he had ordered, Corbet had diverted to Ile de France. There was nothing to be done about that; his own orders had been superseded by those from Bertie. But the affair still left a foul taste in his mouth. The *Nereide* mutiny could and should have been averted.

Then Pellew read the court-martial proceedings, and what he found made his blood boil. All the suspicions roused by the petition to him were confirmed. Corbet, moreover, was not only a tyrant but deceitful. It turned out that at the court martial, he had misrepresented what passed at Bombay by producing a selective version of his correspondence with Pellew – one that omitted the admiral's marks of displeasure.[7] Pellew lost no time in pursuing the matter with Bertie.

It was bound to be an awkward business. The two admirals had been rivals in the same ocean. Bertie, moreover, had a reputation for being surly and brusque, and he had been irritated when Pellew tried to detain one of his most energetic captains at Bombay.[8] After what would seem to have been an icy meeting, Pellew wrote to Bertie on 8 April.

Sir, While the *Nereide* was in India I had great reason to be displeased with the disrespectful style of Capt Corbet's correspondence which I expressed to him in a letter of which a copy is enclosed for your perusal. Since my arrival here I find he produced a part of that correspondence on his late trial, accompanied with expressions of a similar tendency.

Had the *Nereide* been in port I should have called him to a publick account for his conduct, so derogatory to the duty he owed to his superior officer. Upon reading over the whole correspondence which is now before you it will appear that Capt Corbet's conduct has been well deserving of judicial animadversion which his absence only has exempted him.[9]

This letter was purely for form's sake. Pellew expected no support from Bertie and was keeping his powder dry for the Admiralty. At this stage, both believed that *Nereide* was still cruising off Ile de France.

The first survivors limped in two days later – the *Hugh Inglis* and *Earl St Vincent* with HMS *Terpsichore*. The frigate in particular bore marks of the storm and Captain Gordon related what would become a familiar litany, of a very narrow escape after being blown down on her broadside for several hours. Both the Indiamen had also broached to, the *Hugh Inglis* being especially fortunate to have survived in her leaky state.

The following day, eight Indiamen were sighted off Table Bay and paused for Captain Graham of the *William Pitt* to write to Pellew, giving their names and a brief résumé. They had just parted from HMS *Nereide*, he wrote, and were sufficiently patched up to proceed to St Helena. The exception was the *Indus* which needed further repairs.

Corbet, in the meantime, had broken off short of Table Bay and put in at the other side of the Cape peninsula. Simon's Bay, actually a cove within the larger False Bay, was also about twenty miles distant from Capetown, and Corbet stayed there. He was fully occupied with repairing his ship; it is also quite possible that, hearing of Pellew's presence in town, he was keen to stay out of the way.

But although they did not meet, Pellew had no sooner heard of Corbet's return than he wrote to him, excoriating what he called 'your contumacious conduct'.

> I regret that want of captains and the necessity of my immediate departure will not admit of my bringing you to a court martial for these marks of an insubordinate spirit . . . But altho' no legal animadversion can be passed, the Lords Commissioners of the Admiralty will not fail to be apprized of your very exceptionable conduct.[10]

This blistering epistle was signed, a touch ironically, Your Very Humble Servant.

Corbet, as ever, was far from contrite.

> So fully conscious am I of the rectitude of my intentions and the respect continually paid to my superiors, both in India, and ever, that I have to regret much the want of a sufficient number of members for legal animadversion, as I cannot suppose that any court martial could in justice pass a reprimand couched in as strong and severe terms as yours is.[11]

Significantly, however, he did not write this letter until four days after *Culloden* sailed and in that time he kept his head down. When he emerged, it was to send a bleating note to Bertie, accusing Pellew of 'an abuse of power, as well as most severe cruelty to a young officer'.[12]

Corbet always had a subjective notion of cruelty. Since the execution of Joseph Wilkinson, his bête noire had become a seaman named James Maxfield, who rarely got less than thirty-six lashes, whether for gambling, drunkenness or insolence. Another regular, Joshua Atherton, was given twenty for 'provoking gestures', so a spirit of defiance remained alive among the *Nereide*'s seamen.

But Bertie could not protect his protégé for ever. Pellew was about to forward a record of his dealings with Corbet to the Admiralty, including the

PELLEW'S REVENGE

men's original petition. While drawing attention to 'the improper tenor of Captain Corbet's language to a superior officer', his main intention was to expose him for the kind of brute who no longer found favour in the Navy. 'Their Lordships', he wrote with emphasis, 'should be acquainted with the facts in the petition.'[13] Their Lordships would indeed take note.

Pellew's vigour in pursuing Corbet was not matched by an equal concern for the Indiamen. Once the lame ducks of the fleet had appeared – the *Huddart*, the *Indus* and the leaky *Hugh Inglis* – Pellew's fears for the others were too easily assuaged. On the day *Culloden* left the Cape, he wrote to Sir George Barlow.

> You will be glad to hear that we have escaped with our convoy from the effects of a most violent gale (I may indeed call it, rather, a Hurricane) by which we were assailed on the 14th, 15th and 16th of March in Lat 23° 30'S, Long 61° 00'. A total separation took place and every body shifted for themselves, looking only to their own preservation, and more or less every ship suffered. The *Culloden* did not escape without great injury and loss; the particulars I have no doubt Eliza will convey to Lady Barlow. She had six men for a whole night bailing water from under her bed.[14]

Eliza, it transpired, had suffered some mishap, possibly a miscarriage, but was now 'well, cheerful and happy, and I believe in a way to repair her loss'. She and Pownoll rode out with a party of gentlefolk to the rolling vineyards around Constantia, source of the only Cape wine thought palatable by British visitors, and declared it all delightful – 'the weather, remarkably fine, adding to the beauty of the scene'. The widow Mrs Cotton was by now 'much adored by Capt Cochrane and adoring him'. Pellew remarked indulgently: 'Whether it will end in matrimony, I will not venture to say, and as both are past the days of imprudence, I have not thought it proper to interfere.'[15]

Having emphasised the severity of the storm, he then made light of the missing ships, telling Barlow blithely, 'they are, I consider, gone on to St Helena, which was the second rendezvous'. It was not long before he was disillusioned. The *Culloden* left Capetown on 14 April with the ships that had required most repairs and reached St Helena eleven days later. Seven Indiamen were at anchor, but of the *Calcutta, Bengal, Lady Jane Dundas* and *Jane Duchess of Gordon* there was still no sign. Now seriously worried, Pellew stayed another ten days in the hope that they might yet appear.

He was still there when 'Pandora's Box' came racing in. The *Sir Stephen Lushington*, bringing George Buchan with Barlow's dispatches from Madras, had departed more than two weeks after the Second Fleet but had caught up with them by sailing non-stop from Madras to St Helena in seventy-nine days. In crossing the Indian Ocean, she had regularly put 170 miles behind her from noon to noon, before slowing to around 60 miles a day as Captain Hay negotiated the treacherous passage around south-east Africa. On the final approach to the Cape, a fresh gale blew up in the south-east, sweeping them round it and into the Atlantic Ocean in a single exhilarating day when they logged 245 miles.[16]

Buchan went to see Pellew directly. Both were Barlow's allies and each was able to add something to the other's knowledge. Buchan learnt that the *Lady Jane Dundas*, on which he had been due to sail, had not been sighted for weeks. Pellew heard about the growing turmoil in Madras. He dashed off a note to Barlow, promising to join 'your confirmed friends' Buchan and Dick in opposing the 'incendiaries and malcontents' arrayed against him. 'We move off for England tomorrow . . . This will give us a good month the start of Macdowall and prepare every subject for the consideration of the Directors.'

The fleet sailed again on 9 May and now as the days passed pulses quickened. When a strange sail under English colours was sighted in the north, she brought recent news from Europe which Pellew sent around the ships: 'Austria at war with France. Spain going on well. King of Sweden dethroned.' Another stranger brought news of the Navy's victory at the Battle of Aix Roads and when they met a trio of whalers off Ascension, Pellew sent across to obtain a pair of large turtles for a celebratory dinner.*

In the Indiamen cuddies there was a growing sense of homecoming as the days grew longer and an English summer beckoned. They had

---

* In February 1809 a fleet led by the daring Captain Thomas Cochrane used fireships to attack a French squadron anchored near Rochefort in the Bay of Biscay, destroying four ships of the line and a frigate.

passed from one world to another and towards the end, on 5 July, when passengers came out for their quarterdeck promenade, it was to a stiff, salty breeze which flecked with white an ocean so dark, so different in its grey essence from the one they knew under the saffron-yellow evenings of the East, that it might have been a different element. With all sails filled, masts tilted and bows churning, the fleet covered 153 miles that day, rounding Ushant and leaving an unusually calm Bay of Biscay.

They scented England before sighting it – a heady, earthy, verdant smell. It brought joy, apprehension, anticipation, all the emotions of returning to the mother country after what, for many, had been decades away. At last on 12 July, with cheers from every deck, they came into the Downs, the anchorage off Deal in Kent, where most passengers disembarked.

In a typical ship's log, the moment of parting appears as a prosaic event:

> Sunny. Bright airs and calms. At half past 1pm the Purser went on shore with the Hon Co's despatches. The passengers left the ship at the same time.

But it was, nevertheless, a curious business – leaving these quarters where they had faced death and known deliverance, bidding farewell to people with whom they had experienced intimacy of a kind known to few. What they had seen as their dank smelly quarters had acquired the familiarity of homes. The wife of a junior officer cooped up in a horrible canvas partition in steerage for five months wrote:

> I had enjoyed much peace there in the absence of every comfort, even of such as are now enjoyed in jail. I used to say that there were four privations in my situation – fire, water, earth and air. No fire to warm oneself on the coldest day, no water to drink but what was tainted, no earth to set the foot on, and scarcely any air to breathe. Yet, with all these miserable circumstances, we spent many a happy hour by candlelight in that wretched cabin whilst I sewed and he read the Bible to me.[17]

Now, suddenly, in the way of human affairs, that all came to an end. Passengers left their ships and parted, never to meet again. The caravan had moved on.

Those leaving the *Hugh Inglis* included the twenty-nine child passengers, among them the three little girls evacuated from Bengal by Mrs Sherwood. Having completed one bewildering and frightening journey, they were just starting another in this strange new land.

Not everyone disembarked. On the *Lushington*, a man named George Halyburton, of whom nothing is known beyond the fact that he was a Madras merchant and had come home on his own, died in his cot at 10 p.m., having held on just long enough to see England again.

It took months for the full human cost to emerge. The seven ships lost in the two fleets had taken down with them about 1,200 lives. They included well over 800 seamen, perhaps 200 steerage passengers and some 140 cabin passengers. Among the latter, the largest category was children. At least forty-three of them had died, among them no fewer than six Moores on the *Bengal*, and the four Wintles on the *Lady Jane Dundas*.

Several individuals had, Hickey thought, been 'peculiarly marked by misfortune'. He had in mind Emilia Scott, seemingly destined to die at sea, and the widows, Harriett Arnott and Frances Parr. The same might be said of their ship. If any Indiaman ought to have been lost it was *Hugh Inglis*, but she had survived while *Calcutta*, the well-manned, shipshape *Calcutta*, had gone down. Small wonder seamen were a superstitious tribe. *Calcutta* might have been visited by the kind of witchy siren evoked by John Masefield in 'Mother Carey':

> She's a hungry old rip 'n' a cruel
> For sailormen like we,
> She's give many mariners the gruel
> 'N' a long sleep under the sea
> She's the blood o' many a crew upon her
> 'N' the bones of many a wreck;
> 'N' she's barnacles a-growing on her
> 'N' shark's teeth round her neck.

A fate no less whimsical had spared others, notably in the case of the *Lady Jane Dundas*. George Buchan would often reflect on how Barlow's plea for help had prevented him from sailing on the doomed ship. Also counting his blessings was Alexander Johnston whose place on her had been taken by General Macdowall.*

There was another group who had been preserved, and theirs was perhaps the most paradoxical fate of all. All seven of the doomed Indiamen had had hands pressed from them. At the time these men must have cursed what seemed a malign fate. Instead of going to certain death, however, they had been preserved. They would serve and fight, experience defeat and victory, in the battles for the Indian Ocean still to come.

Admiral Pellew's homecoming was spoilt by the Customs House whose officials swooped on his trove aboard *Culloden*. His live leopard escaped attention, and was subsequently much admired at Hampton House; but the affair made quite a flurry in the papers and the diarist Hickey, who had a deeply malicious streak, chortled that 'the gallant Admiral did not make a successful smuggler, having contraband to the amount of several thousand pounds'. What these items were was not specified. However, it made no great difference to Pellew. His fortune was intact.

He returned to find that the Admiralty, alive once more to the danger of Ile de France, was dusting off his old invasion plan. It must have frustrated him that he would have no part in carrying it through. He was honoured, taking the title Lord Exmouth, but he knew that the East Indies had not been his most distinguished command. And the Ile de France taunted

---

* George Buchan's second Indiaman escape – he had previously survived the *Winterton* disaster off Madagascar – struck him as proof of divine intervention on his behalf. He became most devout, following up his best-seller on the *Winterton* with a little volume entitled *Practical Illustrations of a Particular Providence (With Observations Applicable to Different Classes of Society)*.

Alexander Johnston's survival had a more material outcome. He went on to make the recommendations on which Ceylon's future administration was based. Universal popular education was set in train, slavery was abolished and trial by a jury of peers established for all religious groups. As Sir Alexander Johnston, he would return to Ceylon as a far-sighted and benign governor, and it is perhaps no exaggeration to say that the consequences of his voyage home with the Second Fleet proved crucial to the way Britain's relationship with that lovely island evolved in an atmosphere of relative harmony, tolerance and respect.

him. There is no certainty that he had put the fleet at risk in the hope of encountering Hamelin's frigates, but if that was not the reason, he was more culpable still for the loss of the four Indiamen.

There was much muttering at the India House. Captains who gave evidence at the subsequent inquiry made it clear they believed Pellew had sailed too close to the wind. For all that, other factors had contributed to the disaster as well. Pellew was a national hero and the Company's debt to him for the *Dutton* rescue was still remembered. The findings of the Shipping Committee were vague. There were no further repercussions.

Far more satisfying for Pellew was the outcome of the *Nereide* affair. Having considered the evidence, the Admiralty wrote a scorching rebuke to Corbet on 4 August, expressing 'high disapproval of the manifest want of management, good order and discipline' on his ship. The Sea Lords, having noted Corbet's belligerent defence at his court martial of 'starting', then went on to denounce the practice as 'unjustifiable and extremely disgusting to the feelings of British seamen'.[18] Beating men to their stations was prohibited once and for all. Costly though it had been, the *Nereide*'s crew had won a victory for all seamen.

An Admiralty broadside like this was usually enough to destroy a career. Had Corbet been in England at the time he would probably have lost his ship and that would have been an end of him. Instead, at the Cape, he was under the wing of an admiral who regarded him as indispensable. In the months ahead, Corbet and the *Nereide* would be constantly deployed as the momentum began to gather for an invasion of Ile de France.

PART II: CONQUEST

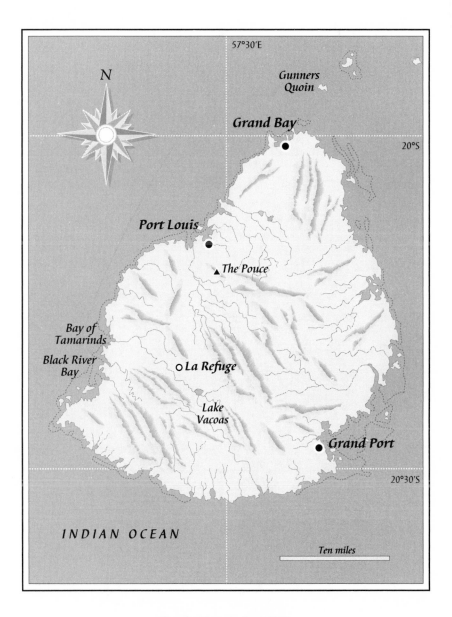

N

57°30'E

Gunners
Quoin

Grand Bay

20°S

Port Louis

▲ The Pouce

Bay of
Tamarinds

Black River
Bay

○ La Refuge

Lake
Vacoas

Grand Port

20°30'S

INDIAN OCEAN

Ten miles

Ile de France in 1809

13

Return to Ile de France

The Cape and Ile de France, 21 March–30 May 1809

From the day that the *Nereide* hove clumsily to at the Cape, a ruin of makeshift masts and shredded rigging, Corbet drove the men to get her back into fighting trim with the same furious energy that he exerted in a chase. There was no respite, let alone any question of shore leave. Corbet himself did not quit the ship. Having had his duty twice interrupted, first by a mutiny and now a hurricane, he was desperate to get back to Ile de France. His urgency is not hard to fathom. Corbet saw that Pellew's displeasure would have consequences in London and, though never doubting his own righteousness, knew he was sorely in need of distinction. Hamelin's frigates offered the prospect of action. All Corbet's misfortunes since taking command of *Nereide*, from the Plata fiasco to the mutiny, would be forgotten could he but seize his moment now.

It took just twenty-two days to make the *Nereide* ready for sea again, although all three masts had to be replaced, along with the entire rigging and sections of superstructure. While carpenters and sailmakers plied their crafts and hands swayed up new masts and yards, fresh beef and soft bread came aboard by the hundredweight, and a sort of harmony seems to have emerged from the joint endeavour of bringing the ship back into service. Only four men were beaten in three weeks, and those were for drunkenness. By 3 May she was prepared for sea.[1]

As the *Nereide* emerged from Simon's Bay amid squalls that blotted out the Cape Peninsula she was joined by HMS *Iphigenia*, the latest addition to the Cape squadron and an extremely important one. She was a new 38-gun frigate from the Chatham yard and her captain, Henry Lambert, was known as a gallant fellow, familiar with the Eastern Seas. He was also senior to Corbet by two years.

195

From the outset Corbet tried to outrun his companion. It was instinctive, an expression of primacy; Corbet could not behold a fellow captain without seeing a rival. He left Lambert behind briefly in a heavy swell on 5 May, and then, with a wind blowing strong in the north-west, ran off 222 miles and 232 miles on a course south-east-by-east, tinkering with sails constantly to lend speed to his wings. For a week there was not a sign of *Iphigenia*. Only on 13 May, after Corbet sighted a strange sail which he supposed to be an enemy, gave chase, cleared for action and boarded her (upon which she turned out to be an American bound for Canton) – only after this diversion did *Iphigenia* come up with him.[2]

The next day, *Nereide* slipped ahead again. Corbet in the meantime ordered a round of floggings: eight men were seized up to receive between twelve and thirty-eight lashes for neglect of duty. Whether or not this was for some perceived failing in the chase, all Corbet's demons were revived. Two days later, a main topsail sheet blew away in a north-westerly, for which three men were given twenty-four each. Beatings then followed on three successive days when eighteen men received up to three dozen, mainly for neglect but also for Corbet's other obsession, dirtiness.

Twenty-seven days after leaving the Cape, he recorded in his log: '30 May: Steady breezes and fine. At 11.50 land bearing NW, extremes of Ile de France.'

That day they fell in with the sloop *Otter*. The tidings she had to impart dashed Corbet's hopes. Hamelin's *Venus* had recently slipped out with the *Manche*. The four French frigates were now cruising in the Bay of Bengal and could not be expected back for months. All that lay ahead of *Nereide* was a resumption of that interminable trawling off Port Louis.

A pall descended on the ship. Three days later, in a mass flogging, Corbet ordered 10 men to receive a total of 220 lashes.

The great mystery about the Ile de France, as everyone agreed later, was why Britain neglected it for so long. Even at the time the question perplexed a great many people, not least Bonaparte himself. In January 1808, the Emperor received an emissary from the island, René Decaen, brother of the Governor, and asked why the English had not yet invaded it.

'I think because each time they have been about to do so, something has happened to distract their attention in India or Europe,' Decaen replied.

'Oh, that's it,' a baffled Bonaparte said. 'I have never been able to understand why they didn't take it. It's sheer idiocy on their part.'[3]

He had a point. William Pitt had spelled out the strategic imperative twenty years earlier when he declared: 'As long as the French hold the Ile de France, the British will never be masters of India.'[4]

Why then had nothing been done? At least three invasion plans had been drawn up since 1796, most recently Pellew's. René Decaen's analysis, about Britain's distractions, was not far wide of the mark, but there were other factors as well, notably the dual nature of power in the Indian Ocean. The East India Company had most to lose from the French threat and had the forces in India to deal with it, but persisted in hoping that the Government would grasp the nettle first. The Government had more pressing concerns. Ultimately, it was always going to require joint action. The strategists' view was that the Company's Army could not conquer Ile de France and its twin bastion of Bourbon without His Majesty's forces. And nothing at all could be done without the Admiralty.

But there were other factors in this apparent neglect that arose from British ignorance. Firstly, no survey of the island's coastline had ever been carried out with an eye to invasion: Port Louis, lying in the north-west, faced to the leeward of the prevailing winds and having strong defensive batteries, could not be attacked from the sea. In the absence of other intelligence, Pellew's plan had been to approach Ile de France from the south and land troops at the old Dutch harbour of Grand Port, setting them off on a march across the island.[5]

Secondly, and more crucially, the British had an exaggerated idea of what would be required to succeed. Charles Decaen, the Governor, had pulled off a brilliant bluff, creating an illusion that Ile de France and Bourbon were formidably defended.

Mauritius, as it is now known, is a volcanic fragment thirty-nine miles from north to south and twenty-nine miles from east to west. The circumference is 130 miles. It is inseparable historically and geographically from Réunion – Bourbon as it then was – which is a little bigger and lies some 130 miles to the south-west. Filaments of France, they lay 10,000 miles and a four-month voyage from the motherland, lush dots in an empty ocean, without resources or riches whatsoever beyond a lustrous, slightly weird, beauty. They nevertheless always loomed large in strategic terms, lying directly between the Cape and India, and in the path of the prevailing monsoons.

As with so much of the Indian Ocean, the Portuguese were the first Europeans there, finding both islands uninhabited and calling them the Mascarenes. Then came the Dutch, who settled the smaller of the two in 1638 and named it Mauritius after Count Maurice of Nassau. They discovered a vivid wildlife – including a large, flightless fowl, *Raphus cucullatus*. Even seamen found this creature disgusting to eat – the Dutch called them *walgvogels*, or nauseous birds – but it was live meat. Being gawky and earthbound it was also easily hunted. Its decline hastened by the introduction of dogs and rats, the poor dodo became extinct long before the Dutch withdrew in 1710 to concentrate their resources at the Cape of Good Hope.

For years Mauritius had something of a Caribbean flavour, an outpost abandoned to slaves, renegades and pirates expelled from the West Indies. Then, in 1722, the French came, renamed it Ile de France, and – because they needed a refuelling station en route to their Indian colony of Pondicherry, south of Madras – stayed. They were much blessed in an early Governor: Bertrand-François Mahé de La Bourdonnais, a son of Brittany and a man of many parts – sailor, engineer, and visionary.

La Bourdonnais was the colony's true founder. He shifted the harbour from the old Dutch settlement of Grand Port to a bay in the north-west where he built a fort, barracks, warehouses and, in time, a charming and surprisingly sophisticated capital, Port Louis. More slaves were imported from Madagascar and Mozambique to grow sugarcane, cotton and indigo. Bourbon provided yet more fertile soil for cultivation. And because the islands lay on the trade route to the East, they prospered as entrepôts where ships of other Western trading nations, America and Denmark, would call to obtain goods. Ile de France was always the more important, however. By the beginning of the nineteenth century its population was roughly 82,000, the vast majority slaves. The French, about 5,000 of them, were rich and cultured, living a somewhat gamy belle époque in which gambling, duelling and corruption were rife.

As well as providing a regional headquarters, Port Louis was France's base for seafaring operations, its 'Gibraltar of the East'. From here the great admiral Pierre André de Suffren set out to fight four bloody battles against Sir Edward Hughes in 1782 that ended without either gaining control of the Indian Ocean.

Bonaparte's rise revived French ambitions in the East. The islands were the fortified bases from which he intended to make thrusts against British interests in India. His grand plan, for a full-scale invasion of the subcontinent through Egypt, had been thwarted by Nelson's victory at the Nile. But he was far from having given up his designs in the Indian Ocean when he sent out General Charles Decaen in 1803.

Decaen had been one of Bonaparte's favourite young generals during the Revolutionary wars. The Emperor believed that the surest way to destroy Britain was to have her expelled from India and it was with this mission that Decaen was entrusted as Captain-General of French territories in the East, with headquarters in Pondicherry. His timing was unfortunate. The Peace of Amiens broke down before he landed, Pondicherry was captured and Decaen had to repair to Port Louis, still vowing to 'act against the English whom I detest because of the injury they have done to our country'.

Ile de France was hardly suited for the purpose. The populace, long left to their own devices, had been suspicious of the motherland ever since envoys of the Revolution landed declaring all men equal, including the 70,000 or so plantation slaves, and were sent packing back to France. The island, moreover, was intrinsically vulnerable. It could not feed itself, being dependent on produce from Bourbon. And while Bonaparte had promised that Decaen would receive troops and ships, his priorities were, as always, elsewhere. Because the islands had to secure their own lines of shipping, the shortage of vessels for defence and transport became critical.

The French Navy was another of Decaen's problems. Its commander in the Indian Ocean was Admiral Charles Linois, an aristocrat who, in the so-called Battle of Pulo Aor in 1804, fled with his squadron from a richly laden fleet of Indiamen in the belief that they were men-of-war. Fine French commanders did exist but without enough ships they would always be unequal to challenging the English squadrons in India or at the Cape. Far more damage to British interests had been done by Robert

Surcouf, 'le Roi de Corsaires', by drawing on the islands' privateering tradition and setting aside foolish notions of *gloire*. When an English captive once challenged him with the words 'You French fight for money while we fight for honour', Surcouf shot back: 'A man fights for what he lacks most.'

Decaen, it must be added, did little to help his own cause. A military man and an instinctive authoritarian – even Bonaparte thought him 'utterly devoid of tact' – he was soon at odds with the extravagant, self-indulgent local elite. He then fell out with his sea commanders. Although Admiral Linois, whom he arranged to have sent home, was no great loss, his dispute with Surcouf was disastrous. It may be recalled that Surcouf had sailed home at the end of 1808, never to return.

By then Decaen had seen the withering of his hopes. Bonaparte had let him down. When René Decaen went to Paris in 1808, he took news of the sepoy mutiny at Vellore. With the Madras presidency in turmoil, it seemed to Decaen that the situation was ripe for fomentation among France's old allies, the rulers of Mysore, a state some 250 miles west of Madras that had lost its independence in a battle with Company forces at Seringapatam in 1799. It happened that Bonaparte's ambitions in India had just revived and, as a result of Decaen's intelligence, he told the Navy to investigate whether a squadron of three ships of the line and six frigates could be ready by September to carry 4,500 men to Ile de France. They were to be followed by another 15,000 men, the whole force then proceeding to India.[6] He got so far as proposing to Tsar Alexander that Russia might cooperate in a second attack, from Persia.[7] Almost immediately, however, he became distracted by events in the Iberian Peninsula, where Britain had joined Portugal and Spain in an alliance against France.

Decaen was left lamenting a lost opportunity, writing to Bonaparte 'with all the sadness of a wounded soul'. More and more he came to see that his duty would lie in defensive, rather than offensive, operations. And so he set about disguising the real vulnerability of his tiny colony.[8]

Although the blockade, instituted in 1808 with the vague hope of starving Decaen into submission, brought English ships into a curious proximity – they were clearly visible from Port Louis as they traversed the horizon – their captains knew little about the island beyond that it was encircled by battlements of coral reefs. At the same time their involvement in prisoner exchanges enabled Decaen to create his illusion. English ships would bring prisoners, usually captured at sea, to Ile de France and receive in exchange British captives, also taken in merchant ships. In a shrewd campaign of disinformation, Decaen saw to it that prisoners were fed with false intelligence before being freed. He had thus duped the enemy into believing his garrison to be far stronger than it was. British intelligence estimates were that Ile de France had between 1,500 and 2,000 National Guard and a militia of up to 10,000. The true number was probably no more than 800 troops and about 3,000 militia.9

One man, Decaen knew, could destroy this carefully nurtured deception. Although an outsider, he had spent years on the island, had won the confidence and affection of the inhabitants, and knew almost as much about its morale and military strength as did Decaen himself.

On an opal-clear day in March, 1809, a week after the hurricane that almost destroyed the *Nereide* had hurtled southwards and spent itself in mid-ocean, an English sea captain sat down on a hillside on Ile de France with two young French boys and, as he often did, instructed them in the arts of navigation. It was an arcadian scene, a plantation set within a tapestry of forests that wreathed themselves around extinct volcanoes and down into valleys – and here, at a simple timber homestead, a handsome, curly-haired young man schooling two lads in astronomy, algebra and geometry. It was somewhat curious too – an Englishman, after all, teaching his enemies' children while a merciless war between their countries raged across the world. Not just any Englishman either. Captain Matthew Flinders of the Royal Navy was one of the age's great navigators, the explorer and cartographer of the coast of Terra Australis. He was also a prisoner, now in the sixth year of his captivity on the island.

Whether 'my scholars', as Flinders fondly called the sons of his foemen, recognised his eminence is not recorded. But that day he would have struggled to retain the attention of two spirited lads. They had returned in the morning from Port Louis which was buzzing with excitement. An especially large and fine 44-gun frigate had arrived from France. After months of isolation, and shortages that had brought the island to the edge of despair, here was evidence that Bonaparte had not forgotten them.

The following day brought further intelligence of the ship and her captain. Flinders was astonished by the coincidence. He wrote in his journal:

> We learn at noon that the frigate arrived is the *Venus*, which sailed from Cherbourg Nov 9. She is commanded by Captain Hamelin, whom I knew at Port Jackson when he had the *Naturaliste*.[10]

Hamelin's arrival buoyed him. While charting Terra Australis, Flinders had encountered Hamelin and Nicolas Baudin on a French expedition engaged in the same task. Rivals, they yet shared the bond of a common endeavour and Flinders had done what he could to help the French when they were plagued by scurvy. Now coincidence had brought Hamelin to Ile de France as Commodore of French Navy operations in the Indian Ocean.

That night Flinders sent a message to him. Had Hamelin brought news from France, perhaps even an order for his release, and might he expect a visit from his fellow seafarer?

The answer, as so often before, was crushing. 'Captain Hamelin does not appear to have brought anything that concerns me: he desires to see me, but fears to displease the Captain-General in coming for that purpose.'[11]

The Captain-General – always that implacable obstacle. 'It is inconceivable, the animosity of this barbarian to me,' Flinders wrote in anguish. This 'barbarian' was General Decaen.

A series of misfortunes had brought Flinders into Decaen's clutches. A protégé of Sir Joseph Banks, the naturalist and explorer, Flinders was sailing home in 1803 after completing the first circumnavigation of Australia when he was forced to put in at Ile de France. He foresaw no difficulty. So far as he knew, England and France were at peace under the Treaty of Amiens.

His first meeting with Decaen was disastrous. Not only had war resumed, but the anglophobic Decaen suspected that he was a spy exploring the island's coast. Offended by Decaen's manner, Flinders refused to accept an invitation to dinner. Decaen replied icily that the invitation would be renewed when Captain Flinders was at liberty. By 1809 Flinders had had more than five years to ponder on the imprudence of the snub.

His captivity had caused ripples. Pellew campaigned from India for his release, as did some eminent Frenchmen such as the explorer Louis de Bougainville. In 1806 Bonaparte signed an order for Flinders to be freed and restored to his ship. This did not reach Ile de France for well over a year and when it did, Decaen metaphorically tore it up. Circumstances, he told the Emperor, had changed. Flinders, 'appearing to me to be always dangerous, I await a more propitious time for putting into execution the intentions of His Majesty'.[12]

It is hardly surprising that Flinders fulminated at 'this barbarian'. The Governor seemingly was acting out of simple spite. In the years that Flinders spent on Ile de France, he never saw that Decaen was doing his best for his country. Since their initial misunderstanding, Flinders had acquired knowledge that did indeed render him 'always dangerous'.

Despite a jaw like a frigate's bow, Matthew Flinders stood out among his swaggering contemporaries for an almost feminine sensitivity. To the journal that he kept throughout his captivity he confided his longing for Anne, the wife to whom he had been married just three months before sailing for the Antipodes. He worried about the wasted years of his navy career. What troubled him most as a dutiful man of his time, however, was his inability to fulfil his commission; his work in Terra Australis – journals, notes and charts – remained in his trunk, its importance known only to himself.

It could never be said that his confinement was rigorous, however. From 1805 he lived with the D'Arifat family at their aptly named homestead La Refuge, an exquisite spot in the high interior of the island, with permission to roam up to two leagues (about six miles) among plantations of coffee, maize and plantains. The air was pearly cool, fragrant with flowers and cloves. Flinders would climb the Pouce, one of the stupa-like mountains above Port Louis, and wander rivers, waterfalls and the volcanic basin around Lake Vacoas, which contained fish, including eels which he proclaimed 'large enough to take down a deer'. He resumed work on his charts, and was much consoled by the possession of a flute; when his hosts proffered scores by Pleyel, Haydn and Mozart, he fell on them.

Music formed the basis of his first friendship on the island. Thomas

Pitot, a Port Louis trader, invited him to musical evenings where they joined others in quartets. Initially language was a barrier because Flinders spoke no French, but at La Refuge the four D'Arifat children became his 'scholars' and while he instructed the boys in navigation and the girls in English, they taught him French. He was candid in his liking for female company and with Madame D'Arifat, a kindly matriarch, he formed a friendship that was as touching as it was durable.

> Madame and her amiable daughters said much to console me, and seemed to take it upon themselves to dissipate my chagrin, by engaging me in innocent amusements and agreeable conversation. I cannot enough be grateful to them for such kindness, to a stranger, to a foreigner, to an enemy of their country, for such they have a right to consider me.[13]

While Flinders's circle of friends widened, he was often reminded of the ambiguity of his position. Occasionally they forgot their manners and abused the English in his presence. And when a risibly distorted account of Trafalgar brought rejoicing – 'our great Lord Nelson and other admirals lost their lives and seventeen sail of English men of war are said to have perished' – he had to swallow his misery.

Flinders had a keen eye for the peccadilloes of this little society, noting how an *affaire* would be regarded with knowing indulgence. He liked flirting himself and wrote amusingly of resplendent Frenchwomen displaying their charms – 'the shoulders and bosoms and nearly half the breasts were uncovered' – at Port Louis's gay and stylish theatre.

> Such an array in an English theatre would create uproar. The modest would be offended, the prudes would break their fans, the aged would cry Shame! the libertines would exult and clap, and the old lechers would apply to their opera glasses.[14]

Always he was thankful for the genuine warmth shown to him by the island's inhabitants. And his one real friendship touched him deeply. After an idyllic day with Pitot, sitting by a waterfall and discussing natural history, he wrote movingly of finding himself 'a prisoner in a mountainous island in the Indian Ocean, lying under a cascade in a situation very romantic and interior, meditating upon the progress which nature is

1 Admiral Sir Edward Pellew, simply 'the greatest Sea Officer of his time' according to a contemporary authority. This portrait, by Samuel Drummond, was painted in 1816, after Pellew's return from his most celebrated later command, the freeing of Christian slaves in Algeria, for which he was created Viscount Exmouth.

2 Captain Fleetwood Pellew leading a boarding party against the Dutch at Batavia in 1806. 'A prettier exploit I never saw,' wrote a doting Sir Edward. 'What father could have kept his eyes dry?'

3 Lieutenant-General Hay Macdowall, Commander of the Madras Army. The conquering hero of Sir Henry Raeburn's portrait was in fact a deeply flawed leader, 'very sparingly endowed with temper or judgment'.

4 Arriving at Madras. Riding to the beach in a *masoolah* was a fraught, often risky, experience shared by all Indiamen passengers.

5 Capture of the French frigate *Nereide* by *Phoebe* in 1797. Commissioned into the Royal Navy and placed under Captain Robert Corbet in 1806, the *Nereide* became a byword among seamen for brutality, a hell afloat.

6 Sir Nesbit Willoughby. Indestructible and volatile, he was known by his men as 'the Immortal'.
7 Commodore Jacques Hamelin, the French commander in the Indian Ocean.
8 *The Loss of an East Indiaman* by J. M. W. Turner, *c.* 1818. The subject of this terrifying canvas was long thought to be a man-of-war but recent research indicates that Turner's inspiration was the wreck of the *Halsewell* Indiaman.

9 The *Essex*, a classic East Indiaman of 800 tons, at anchor in Bombay. Beyond the stern gallery lay the comparative luxury of the roundhouse and great cabin, occupied by privileged passengers.
10 The Battle of Grand Port, a French engraving of the sinking of the *Sirius*.

11 Captain Matthew Flinders, a portrait executed during his six-year captivity on Ile de France.
12 Sir Josias Rowley in later life as an Admiral.
13 *The Bombardment of Algiers* by George Chambers. This episode, in 1816, was the climax of Admiral Pellew's later career.

14 *A Sailor Returns in Peace*, by Thomas Stothard.

continually making; and in company with a foreigner, a Frenchman, whom I call, and believe to be, my friend.'[15]

It was his outdoor pursuits that started to provide him with a strategic oversight of the colony. He cut a path through the forest around La Refuge to high ground overlooking the Bay of Tamarinds and the west coast, and from his eyrie monitored the British blockade after it was instituted in 1806. Over the next two years, Flinders made increasingly frequent references in his diary to the appearance off Port Louis of 'English cruizers'. He noted the consequences as well – severe food shortages as the blockade cut off supplies from Bourbon, followed by a souring of the popular mood. Friends kept him abreast of events in Port Louis, of Decaen's increasingly frequent rages. In their isolation, many still believed in the French victory of Trafalgar; but a realisation was dawning that much of what passed for news from Europe was tainted. It was whispered that Bonaparte was no longer received with adulation in public.

Flinders also had acquaintances among the military. He knew about troop numbers and the quality of the officer corps, which in his judgement was not very high. When Decaen decided to raise a new regiment raised from the slave population – much to the settlers' disquiet – Flinders heard about that as well. He saw the island's vulnerability. 'If attacked with judgment it appeared to me that a moderate force would carry it,' he wrote.[16]

Early in 1809 a general sense of abandonment prevailed. On 8 March, Flinders wrote: 'Every person seems now convinced that the blame of the war does not rest with England but attaches to the ambitions of Bonaparte.'

Thus were matters poised when his old acquaintance, Jacques Hamelin, came in to Port Louis on 21 March.

Being confined to La Refuge, the English sea captain was unable to join the cheering crowds and it would appear that he was never given the opportunity to see Hamelin, who remained apprehensive about antagonising Decaen. But Flinders received the usual reports. He heard that Hamelin's orders had come from Bonaparte himself, and that he was to 'chase, capture or destroy all the enemy ships you may meet'. A new French challenge had been issued for supremacy in the Indian Ocean.

The Division Hamelin consisted of the Commodore's ship, *Venus*, a new 44-gun frigate, the *Bellone*, another new 44, and *Manche* and *Caroline*, both of 40 guns. That stark description does little to convey the threat they represented. The much-vaunted superiority of French ship design and building is thought by some historians to have been exaggerated. Hamelin's frigates, however, were the best of their kind, which is to say as good as any afloat and in a quite different class from anything in Bertie's ageing Cape squadron. They were the biggest and fastest frigates yet seen in these seas, copper-bottomed for speed and wear. They were also the most heavily armed. Corbet's *Nereide*, for example, had 36 guns firing 12-pound balls. All four of the new French frigates had 18-pounders. They also fulfilled what the naval historian N.A.M. Rodger has called the only useful measure of quality in warships – fitness for purpose. Hamelin's ships were as equipped to strike at England's commercial lifeline as they were to resume the battle for the Eastern Seas.*

It was not merely for its ships that the new division stood out. France's Navy had been short of fine commanders since the revolutionary purges and, in these waters, none had matched the great De Suffren. The Division Hamelin, however, represented a new generation and included outstanding officers. Hamelin himself, a chivalrous man highly regarded by Flinders, was perhaps not the ablest of them. However, in captains like Jean Feretier of the *Caroline*, Dornal de Guy of the *Manche* and Victor Duperré of the *Bellone*, England faced formidable foes, while Pierre Bouvet, a privateer with a colourful past that included escaping from a Thames hulk, would prove the most combative of all.

---

* The two largest French ships, *Venus* and *Bellone*, bore comparison with the super-frigates with which the United States had launched its Navy more than a decade earlier, which were also of 44 guns (at least nominally). However, three of the Americans, the *Constitution*, the *United States* and the *President*, were even larger and more heavily armed than the French ships. *Constitution*, for example, was 204 feet long with thirty-four 24-pounders and twenty 32-pounder carronades, and with a crew of 450. She and the similar *United States* inflicted shocking blows on the Royal Navy in single-ship actions when the two countries went to war in 1812. British frigates, designed for blockade duty, and therefore to stay at sea for long periods, were lighter and had fewer men. Typically, a large Royal Navy frigate of the day, like the *Sirius* to be met later in this narrative, was 148 feet in length with twenty-six 18-pounders and a crew of 240. Historians have pointed out that British captains had severe difficulties handling such frigates and fighting their guns at the same time against larger and better-manned enemy ships supposedly of the same class.

By the time of Hamelin's arrival the hurricane season was nearing an end and British ships could be expected to return any time. *Bellone* and *Caroline* had already gone out when, late in April, Flinders heard that they were to be followed by *Venus* and *Manche*. Decaen had gone down to the port to send Hamelin on his way. 'My young friend Aristide writes to me from town that *Venus* and *Manche* had been visited by the General and were to go out in search of English ships.'[17]

What kind of ships the French were to search for was not stated, but their intention must be to strike at Britain where she was vulnerable, her trade. They would pick up where Surcouf had left off. All four frigates were bound for the Bay of Bengal and the Straits of Malacca.

14

'A mongrel kind of gentleman'

Bengal and Ile de France, 25 April–9 August 1809

Just as Hamelin's squadron left Port Louis in search of prey, a Third Fleet of Indiamen was gathering where the Hooghly oozed a thick brown slick out into the north-western corner of the Bay of Bengal. Temperatures had started their rise towards the catharsis of monsoon when a pinnace from Calcutta, bearing Captain John Dale and his passengers, came twisting down that curry-coloured smear to where the *Streatham* lay in Saugor roads.

Dale was one of the undisputed heroes of the Eastern Seas. Sixteen years earlier, as a callow third officer on the *Winterton* Indiaman, he had rescued a situation most others would have regarded as impossible, after the wreck of his ship off the west coast of Madagascar. Now aged thirty-nine, Dale looked every inch the commanding officer – strikingly tall and broad-shouldered, with a strong head of prematurely grey hair and level gaze. It was just as well that his adventures had put steel into him, for he had learnt from Pellew's successor, Admiral Drury, that he would be sailing without a navy escort. The man who had almost single-handedly brought to safety a hundred survivors of an Indiaman wreck was to commodore one of the richest fleets of recent times through seas patrolled by Hamelin's ships.

Dale stooped to enter his cabin, a neat little compartment with a cot, a bureau covered by charts, pistols and a sword. Like the man, it was somewhat austere, with no visible indulgence, no sign, for example, of the silver jug presented in gratitude by the *Winterton* passengers to the officer 'to whose indefatigable exertions we owe our lives'.

Later that afternoon, 25 April, he went forward to join his passengers for dinner. His exploit was well known and it would have been strange had those assembled at the table – Alexander Wright Esq. and his wife, Elizabeth, and

211

Captain Bean of HM 17th Regiment with his wife, Martha – not asked him for
an account. It was a fine tale – good enough for his friend and fellow survivor
George Buchan to have turned into a best-selling book – and Dale could have
held his company spellbound, relating how he had found himself the senior
officer among 230 castaways on a tropical island; of leaving his charges in the
care of the king of Baba, a benign monarch who wore a scarlet cowl and sat
beneath a tamarind tree; of setting off in a yawl for Africa, 600 miles across the
Mozambique Channel; and of how, four months later, after marching another
200 miles up the African coast, he raised the alarm at the Portuguese outpost
of Quelimane before returning with help to the emaciated survivors, almost
half of whom had died of malaria.[1]

Whatever Dale related in the cuddy about his adventures past, it is safe
to say that he confided little about his concerns for the present. And
concerns he undoubtedly had. The five Indiamen had finished loading –
not just saltpetre but a fabulously rich cargo of silk, an investment on
which London fortunes were riding. But their navy escort, the sloop
Victor, would see the Indiamen only out of the bay. At that point Dale
would assume command.

Given the value of the cargo, and the recent arrival of Hamelin's frigates
in the bay, this might seem curious. Since Pellew's departure, however, the
state of the Indies squadron had gone from bad to worse. Admiral Drury's
ships were as sickly as the men who sailed them and had yet to manage an
encounter with the enemy. Just days ago Drury had written to the
Governor-General, Lord Minto:

> At the moment there are five ships in dock and except the *Russel* and
> the *Modeste*, scarcely an effective man of war is to be found in India.
> The only two frigates I have recently been able to collect were
> despatched in pursuit of two of the enemy's cruizers in the eastern
> seas without reserving to myself a single ship for the execution of any
> emergent service.[2]

At the same time tensions between the Navy and the Company over
impressment had reached a new high point, culminating a week earlier in
the most disturbing incident yet.

* * *

The Indiaman *Asia* was at anchor off Madras on 18 April when a midshipman 'ragged and dirty' came on board and demanded: 'Call your hands out. I have come to press your men.' James Walker, the *Asia*'s chief officer, replied mildly enough that impressment was normally the job of a lieutenant rather than a midshipman, and refused to assemble the hands until the young man produced his warrant.[3]

That afternoon he returned, still unkempt – in a lieutenant's uniform but with dirty trousers and no stockings – and still without a warrant. What he did have were three boats of armed men from the *Dasher* and *Procris* sloops, and when Walker still refused to turn out his hands a seaman with a pistol roared: 'You bugger of a chief mate, I know you well and I only wait for orders to blow your brains out.'[4]

At this turn of events, Walker sent a boat to summon the *Asia*'s captain, Henry Tremenhere, but it had barely put out before coming under musket and pistol fire from the navy boats. Shots were also fired at the *Asia*'s officers, standing on the poop. Walker, understandably alarmed, beat to quarters and ordered the other officers to arm themselves.

Ashore, Tremenhere had heard the commotion coming from his ship and ran down to the beach where he 'distinctly saw a coxswain take a deliberate fire at the *Asia*'s boat'. Barely able to believe his eyes, he set out in a *masoolah* and came on board at the same time as Captain Mansell of the *Procris*, with whom he had shared the Captain's House at Fort St George until that very morning. An icy exchange followed. As Tremenhere related it:

> Captain Mansell told me he intended to press five men but after what had passed he should certainly take fifteen. He said the ship's company were at quarters and the officers had armed against a King's ship. I told him I was sorry for it but could not have supposed that he would have [taken men] as we were living in the same house together without giving me a hint of it.[5]

Tremenhere had already lost seventeen men in a press and was damned if he would give up more. He produced a letter of protection. Mansell ignored it, had the hands turned out and said he'd prefer volunteers but, one way or another, would have fifteen of them. No one volunteered. In the end Mansell took just ten. But a few hours later an officer from *Dasher* came and took five more.

213

It might be thought that Tremenhere was thus entirely justified in complaining to a board of inquiry about overweening navy officers grown intoxicated with 'notions of honour and consequence attached to them from being in HM service'.[6] However, these same officers took their lead from their commander – and in Drury they had a new admiral whose lip curled at the mention of 'India captains, merchants and Parsees'.

If the *Asia* incident showed how dangerously frayed tempers had become, it also succeeded in reviving debate about the number of hands that could legitimately be pressed from arriving Indiamen. As things stood, ships of 800 tons were required to furnish fifteen men and those of 500 tons ten men. In practice, as the *Asia* and others that season showed, an 800-ton ship could lose more than thirty men and still have no legal redress. But when the Governor-General, Lord Minto, responded to the *Asia* incident by proposing a law that would 'draw a line over which the Navy must not step', Drury hit the roof. He wrote to the Admiralty:

> The captain of an Indiaman is but a mongrel kind of gentleman or officer – turbulent, insolent and overbearing. Their conduct should be severely reprehended by the Court of Directors and the most rigid means adopted to punish them for their repeated outrages against His Majesty's flag.[7]

Three weeks later, on 1 June, Tremenhere was guiding the *Asia* into the Bengal roads when a squall blew up and drove her on to a sandbar. She went to pieces in a few hours. Here at last was unequivocal evidence of an Indiaman wrecked for lack of men to handle her. The *Asia* affair would prove a watershed and lead to a new navy regime on pressing.

Dale's fleet of five weighed on 29 April and worked down the Hooghly, emerging into the sea under clear skies with a southerly breeze. They were three large Indiamen of 800 tons, *Streatham*, *Europe* and *Monarch*, and two of the smaller Extra ships, *Lord Keith* and *Earl Spencer*. The good weather held for just a week before the logs started to signal an ominous pattern. On the *Streatham*, Dale noted:

> 7 May: Great swell from S. Ship pitching violently. Impossible to have prayers.

8 May: Strong gales. Ship labouring & pitching excessively.

15 May: Great sea. Ship plunging very deeply.

16 May: Strong monsoon with repeated squalls & great sea. The ship very uneasy.[8]

The *Streatham*, like virtually every Indiaman that season, had suffered severely from the press. Before sailing, Dale, joining in a chorus of captains' indignation, had written in protest to Lord Minto that he could not be sure of his ship's safety. Now there were echoes of the Second Fleet. Beating into the wind – working a ship against the prevailing direction by a series of tacks – required strong hands, and the conditions were proving too much for *Streatham*'s Chinese and lascar crew. Although the logs show that on 16 May the fleet covered sixty-eight miles, it had been driven north rather than progressing south and was at Lat 15° 05'N, Long 87° 10'E, roughly where it had been a week earlier, and not yet south of Madras.

Three days later, they had moved south by a single degree (sixty nautical miles) when another alarm was raised. Captain Hawes in the *Monarch* signalled that his ship had sprung a leak and, making eighteen inches of water an hour, was too far gone to be repaired at sea. As commodore, Dale had to decide how best to proceed. He wrote: 'Captain Hawes telegraphed me to say that *Monarch*'s leak was getting worse hourly, that he was desirous of making immediately for Penang but could not venture alone for the state of the ship.'[9]

There was nothing else for it but to detach another ship to escort her to safety. Dale sent a note across to the *Earl Spencer* and the following day these two ships set a new course for the sanctuary of Penang. In twenty-two days there had been drama quite sufficient for an entire voyage but this was merely the beginning.

The three remaining ships, *Streatham*, *Europe* and *Lord Keith*, continued to struggle against countervailing winds, tacking but still being pushed northwards, so that while the log-line recorded them covering 320 nautical miles in the next four days, they progressed only from 10° 42'N to 10° 27'N while moving fewer than 3° west to 89° 02'E, and therefore advancing by about 150 miles. On 30 May, Dale had to reduce the daily water allowance from five to four pints per man to preserve supplies.

At that point, still some 500 miles east of Ceylon, the *Streatham*'s log

comes to an abrupt end. For events the following day it is necessary to turn
to the record kept by Captain Peter Campbell on the *Lord Keith*:

> 31 May: At daylight saw a strange sail bearing SW, distance 6 or 7
> miles. At 6am the Commodore [Dale] made the private signal which
> she did not answer. Got everyone to quarters at quarter past 7.[10]

Dale, earlier trials forgotten, watched grimly as the stranger came on. His
worst fears had been realised – an undermanned Indiamen fleet, without a
navy escort, had been ambushed by one of the new French frigates.

On the Indiamen, all became bustle. Cabin partitions were dismantled,
cots and furniture stowed. Ports banged open, barefoot men ran out the
guns. Anxious women hushed their children and were taken below to the
orlop where they might suffer in heat of 120°F but could not be harmed by
cannonballs or flying timber. On *Streatham*'s quarterdeck, gentlemen
passengers hefted the unfamiliar weight of cutlasses and handled pistols
while being given impromptu and somewhat belated instruction in their
use by Captain Bean of the 17th.

In the weeks after departing from Port Louis, the French frigates had
separated. Hamelin's *Venus* and the *Manche* were also in the Bay of
Bengal, but some degrees to the east. The frigate that had intercepted the
Indiamen was the *Caroline*.

From her quarterdeck, Lieutenant Jean Feretier could see how he was
gaining on the Indiamen and savoured the moment. He knew his strength,
knew his enemy's weakness and knew that a sumptuous prize was in the
offing. A junior officer, he had inherited the *Caroline* when her previous
commander died at sea, and now he had his opportunity.

The 40-gun *Caroline* was one of the two lighter French frigates. She
handled beautifully, with a crew of 330 plus 50 soldiers, and in addition to her
twenty-eight standard 18-pounders, mounted eight 36-pounder carronades
and ten long 8-pounders. The Indiamen were poorly manned and totally
outgunned: the *Streatham* had thirty 12-pounders, the *Europe* twenty-six,
and the smaller *Lord Keith* only twelve long 6-pounders. Manning and
firepower were not the full story, however. Such was the English ascendancy
at sea that three Indiamen might have been capable of prevailing against a

single enemy frigate. But Feretier was one of a new breed of French officers who had learnt a vital lesson from an uninterrupted sequence of English victories – that battles were won by gunnery as well as seamanship.

Feretier had another advantage. The Indiamen had sailed with an American ship, the *Silenus*, which requested protection before breaking off for the Carnicobar islands where she fell in with the *Caroline*. America was neutral and, notwithstanding that he had sought an English escort, her captain gave Feretier details of the Indiamen, their rich cargo, miserable manning and probable route.[11] His calculation was accurate enough to have brought the Frenchman directly to them.

Feretier bore down first on the *Europe*, passing her with a well-directed broadside that destroyed her rigging, carried away her foremast topsail yardarm and left her crippled. It was skilled gunnery by a humane commander, aimed at inducing surrender rather than taking life. Feretier then passed on to *Streatham* and hit her equally hard.

Dale had formed his ships in line of battle as best he could and his British hands were ready to fight. But they accounted for no more than 44 of the *Streatham*'s 133-man crew (about 120 men were needed to fight each side of a 36-gun ship) and the others, mainly Chinese, showed an understandable reluctance to stand to the guns. Dale soon noticed that no fire was coming from the lower deck.

> I sent the chief officer below to encourage the people at the guns. He returned shortly after to inform me that the Chinese & Portuguese who were stationed on the gun deck could not by any exertion of the officers be kept to their stations, deserting as soon as brought back.[12]

The *Streatham*'s fire was still effective enough for a ball to take the head off *Caroline*'s master – 'a most excellent officer,' lamented Feretier. 'The same shot', he added coolly, 'carried off half my hat and wounded me slightly in the cheek.'[13]

In retaliation Feretier directed his fire right at *Streatham*. Holes were blown in her port side, sending splinters the size of table legs scything across the deck. The fight was wholly unequal and after half an hour Dale struck his colours. Feretier turned to the third ship, the *Lord Keith*.

Captain Campbell's crew were assisted by the male passengers, Messrs Case and Adams, in bringing several guns to bear on the *Caroline* while she was engaged with the *Streatham* and they had managed to get off several shots before the frigate came up on them. Once again the French gunnery was immediately on the mark. The *Lord Keith* was raked at sail height and had the foremast and maintops shot away, her sails shredded.

Now Feretier returned to the crippled *Europe*. Captain William Gelston was not able to get off any fire at all. 'The petty officers & Europeans did behave with great courage, but as for the Lascars, they were only in the way,' he wrote.[14] Faced with being blown to pieces, he quickly surrendered. In less than two hours it was all over.

The whiff of powder and eddy of smoke still hung heavy on the sea as two boats carrying officers and men rowed across to take possession of the *Streatham* and *Europe*. At this point Campbell perceived that he might make his escape as, although the *Lord Keith* was in a bad way, Feretier had his hands full. 'It was thought most prudent to make such sail as the state of our rigging would admit,' Campbell wrote.[15] By knotting and splicing, the *Lord Keith* managed to slip away and by nightfall was out of sight. After a hasty consultation, at which it was decided that her present course might bring them again into contact with the enemy, she started east for Penang. There she arrived on 9 June.

Feretier proceeded to show that he was a gallant foe as well as a dangerous one. All courtesy was shown to Dale and Gelston, while the passengers received 'particularly kind and attentive treatment' from the prize crews. Although notionally prisoners, life for the civilians on the Indiamen stayed much the same while the ships bore south-west – smoothly now under following winds. Seven weeks later they approached the French islands, but instead of proceeding to Port Louis, where he might have run into the blockade, Feretier set a course for Bourbon. *Caroline* brought her prizes into St Paul on 22 July.

The prisoners were taken ashore where captains Dale and Gelston made a point of writing a letter, thanking Feretier for his gracious conduct. The gentry were put up with local families. In the meantime the Indiamen were unloaded, and gave up their silken treasure.

Matthew Flinders could not credit the first reports – 'two prizes, said to be Company's ships valued at 3 millions of dollars'. French intelligence of this kind, as he noted, was 'always exaggerated'. A week later, however, a friend wrote confirming the value.

The news set off wild celebrations in Port Louis, as Flinders recorded:

> The guns were fired and placards fixed up announcing the rich prizes at Bourbon and the payments of the bills of exchange by the government, both which have diffused the greatest joy throughout the island, for the administration here was almost at its last shifts for money.[16]

From a French point of view, it was not just a financial lifeline but a terrific tonic for morale. In the eight years to 1801, just seven Indiamen had been taken – less than one a year. Now a lowly lieutenant had captured two in a day. Decaen promptly promoted Feretier to captain.

The news took weeks to reach Calcutta but when it did there was an outcry, and merchants dusted off a self-evident truth. As they put it in a petition to the Government: 'As long as the islands of Mauritius and Bourbon remain in possession of the Enemy, effectual protection of our ships cannot be afforded.'[17]

15

'The enterprizing Captain Corbet'

Ile de France and Bourbon, 8 June–23 August 1809

While the *Caroline* had been engaged in her bountiful cruise, a quickening in the movement of English ships off Ile de France became perceptible to the lonely figure who haunted the hills overlooking the sea. During the mild, rainy month of June, scarcely an evening went by that Matthew Flinders did not jot down in his diary 'Cruizers as yesterday', or 'Cruizers the same', as they criss-crossed the horizon between Port Louis and Black River Bay, about twenty miles down the west coast. As a navy captain himself, Flinders took a keen interest in the commanders and it was not long before he was struck by the activity of one ship in particular.

Blockade sailing was a devil of a business. There could scarcely ever be enough ships and, even if there were, they were unlikely to be in the right place at the right time. The way the *Caroline* had slipped unhindered back to Bourbon with her prizes was proof of that. Pellew had stipulated that to adequately patrol the two islands – with hundreds of miles of coastline, half a dozen anchorages and 130 miles in between them – would require two ships of the line, six frigates and four sloops.[1] In practice, no such force had ever been available. At present, in the absence of Commodore Josias Rowley, whose dilapidated flagship, the 64-gun *Raisonnable*, was being refitted at the Cape, it consisted of the horrible old *Leopard*, which was good for nothing besides acting as a supply ship, three frigates, the *Sirius*, *Iphigenia*, and *Nereide*, and the sloops *Otter* and *Sapphire*.

Among them, it was the *Nereide* that caught Flinders's eye.

By now Ile de France was short of food as well as most other resources and awaited with almost desperate anticipation the occasional ship from France able to slip through the blockade. At a time of year when the weather held few terrors, neutral vessels, American, Danish and Swedish,

223

were also plying these waters. Corbet, in short, had ships on which to exercise his flair in the chase and the *Nereide* had been turned into a potent instrument of sailing excellence. Corbet's brilliance at intercepting and boarding had proved itself when he acquired the first intelligence of Hamelin's appearance in the Indian Ocean. Now, within days of returning to Ile de France, the *Nereide* was engaged in a succession of chases that occupied the men and gave an outlet to Corbet's energies.

To what extent this accounted for the change that became discernible in Corbet himself is open to conjecture; there were, as we shall see, other factors at work as well. But for the first time in our story, he began to demonstrate his other side as a navy officer – the commander whose ability and energy had once impressed his superiors as much as his cruelty estranged his men.

The early life and background of Robert Corbet are as much an enigma as everything else about the man. Even the year of his birth is unknown. Although it was long believed that he came from an old Shropshire family, recent research points to an obscure line of Irish clergy from Wexford. Either way, he lacked glittering connections.

There is no known portrait of him. By all accounts he was short and dark, and it is tempting to imagine him as a sizzling tinderbox, a furious black-browed figure beneath a cocked hat. But the legends that attached to him are as suggestive of an icy and obsessive rigour as they are of rage. One of his officers, who admired him, wrote that Corbet developed a system of order 'such as enabled a subordinate promptly to trace to its source whatever evil sprung up amongst us'.[2] Certainly there was more to him than mere anger. Corbet lusted for honour as some men lusted for women, blindly and destructively. If he was hated by a great many, he was esteemed by a few, for he seemed to incarnate the virtue prized above all others by the Navy – zeal. A zealous officer, it goes without saying, was brave; he was also able, energetic and devoted to the Service body and soul. All these qualities Corbet possessed.

The key event in his career thus far had occurred in the Mediterranean under the eye of Nelson, who praised him in dispatches for capturing a large French privateer while he was a lieutenant commanding the sloop

Bittern, and in 1805 promoted him to post captain. The great man wrote: 'Your conduct and perseverance merit my entire approbation.'[3] It was heady stuff for a young officer and Corbet would spend the rest of his unhappy life trying to recapture that glory.

He had always overstepped the norms of punishment, an indiscriminate resort to 'starting' having been noticed while he commanded the *Bittern.* But for all his unquestionable cruelty, he was no simple brute. He was alive to his men's health requirements and saw to it that they were well fed; the provisioning of *Nereide* was unusually good. On occasion, he showed that he could address men effectively, rousing them to action through pride rather than fear. He insisted that he was no tyrant, and evidently believed it.

Essentially, however, Corbet was remote from the real values of Nelson's Navy. To the elements that won great battles, gunnery and teamwork, he was seemingly blind. And here perhaps lies one of the keys to an understanding of him. He had never participated in a major action and, in the absence of a reactive foe, had never had his obsessive assumptions tested. This may account for his neglect of gunnery. One can scan, week by week, the pages of *Nereide*'s log without a hint of the great guns being exercised, let alone fired at targets. As for teamwork, the kind of fond male companionship on which the Navy thrived, Corbet had no truck with it. An aloof, solitary figure, he almost invariably ate alone in his cabin while his officers messed together. He was equally reluctant to mix with his fellows, rarely leaving the ship to dine or receiving other captains on board.[4]

To a lonely disposition and a love of order verging on the fanatical must be added another affliction of tortured souls down the ages. He was a martyr to rheumatism. It had first surfaced while he was a junior officer and was so bad by 1804 that he sent a plea to Nelson in an atrocious scrawl that, suffering 'excruciating pain', he might take six weeks leave to 're-establish a constitution much broken'.[5] Nothing else of his sufferings is recorded; but they had evidently not made him more sensitive to the pain that he could inflict on others.

Early on the afternoon of 8 June *Nereide* passed up the western coast of Ile de France in company with the sloop *Otter.* They had just rounded

Gunner's Quoin, a great wedge of rock that resembles a shark's head rising from the sea a mile or so off the island's northern tip, when a lookout shouted down that a strange sail was approaching from the east. She turned out to be a brig and, although under English colours, changed course on sighting *Nereide*. Corbet made all sail and gave chase. The brig weaved east-north-east in what was plainly a desperate attempt to flee. After two hours, as *Nereide* closed in, the occupants put a boat over the side in a last, vain effort. Corbet later recorded the outcome in his log.

> Made sail after the boat, fired a gun & brought her to. Found 12 French prisoners on board her which had made their escape from Bombay prison in an open boat along the coast of Malabar as far as Cannanore, then ran away with the above Brig & was bound to the Isle of France. Took every person out of [the boat] and set her on fire.[6]

They came up the side like condemned men, despairing and dishevelled, and were taken below where accounts of their escapade were heard with much marvelling and shaking of heads, for it would have been a tough Nereide who was not moved by the story of men who, enemies or not, were ordinary hands like themselves who had escaped prison, ventured more than 500 miles in an open boat, then seized an enemy vessel and voyaged another 3,000 miles to within sight of sanctuary, only to be captured at the last thanks to this savage twist of fate. It was, indeed, an epic, melancholy tale and even Corbet was impressed enough to make this detailed note of it. The *Nereide* resumed her cruise, and only ten days later a second chase began.

> 19 June: Fresh breezes & squally with showers of rain. At 4, a strange sail in the NW. Made all sail in the chase. At 6 still in chase. Chase suspicious. Trimm'd sails occs'lly. At 9 carried away the Stbd Fr T Gallant Backstay. Made & shortened sail as necc. Midnight still in chase.
> 20 June: Fresh breezes and cloudy. Still in chase. Fired several guns at her. At 2 shortened sail & boarded the chase. Proved to be *L'Agile* from St Malo bound to the Isle de France.[7]

L'Agile was a handsome prize, a brig laden with supplies for the beleaguered island. Corbet now had two groups of prisoners on *Nereide*, and allowed them to write letters that were sent in to Port Louis under a flag of truce.

Flinders's captivity had become something of a cause célèbre. Like all navy officers, Corbet knew of his eminent colleague's unwarranted captivity and seized the opportunity to intercede personally. His prisoners were instructed to write that he was willing to free them, provided that Decaen released Flinders and any other British captives.

The Governor was deaf to these pleas but it would appear that some of the captives had families on the island and they approached Flinders. Would he, they asked, take up their relatives' case with Corbet? The navigator was in an awkward position. He sympathised with anyone forcibly separated from family. At the same time, he saw that the responsibility for any prisoner exchange lay with Decaen. Instead, he wrote to one of Corbet's prisoners, a midshipman named Berten.

> Sir, Without having the honour of being known to you, I take the liberty of addressing you this letter. Prisoner since near six years in this island, I have received much attention, civility, and friendship from many of your countrymen ... Your respectable aunt Madame Herbeck is one of those worthy persons whose conduct has excited my esteem, and it is at her instance that this letter is written. If, therefore, it can be of any use in procuring your speedy exchange, or in softening the hardships of your situation, I request you will make it known that your relations are known to and respected by me. To that purpose you are at liberty to shew this letter to any of my brother officers of His Majesty's Navy, who will much oblige me by rendering you service.[8]

Corbet's overture came to nothing. Decaen remained obdurate and the Frenchmen taken in the brig and *L'Agile* were transferred to a sloop bound for the Cape.

Apart, that is, from one who managed to slip unnoticed over the side.

A few days later, on 29 June, Flinders recorded the outcome. A French prisoner, he noted in his journal, had come ashore 'after four hours' swimming from *Nereide*'.[9] The man's identity is unknown; still, it may be permissible to imagine that one of those involved in the great escape from Bombay attained his freedom after all.

* * *

227

L'Agile was sent to the Cape as a prize. When she disappeared over the western horizon, she had a small crew from the *Nereide* headed by a master's mate named Daley, as well as the French captain and two of his officers. The men from the *Nereide* were hands whom Corbet saw as no great loss but whose loyalty could be trusted, such as the elderly sailmaker Hector McNeil. Not for the first time, Corbet had misjudged his men.

Three were Irish – Thomas O'Hara was a twenty-two-year-old from Tyrone, Alexander Baird, twenty-three, from Londonderry, and David Masey aged twenty-one. A fourth, James Buckle, was American. Little else is known about them, other than that none had figured in the *Nereide*'s previous convulsions; nor had they been particular victims of punishment, although O'Hara had just been given twenty-four lashes for the unusual offence of 'buying cloathes'. Their nationalities, rather than any suffering at Corbet's hands, may have accounted for what followed.

Ile de France had long provided a haven for British renegades. One fugitive from the infamous *Hermione* mutiny had ended up there, serving in a French frigate, and the privateer Surcouf often had British hands on his ships. More recently, Decaen had been recruiting prisoners to his short-handed militia. Irishmen, in particular, were encouraged to defect by being told that Bonaparte supported an independent Ireland. A number of prisoners from HM brig *Seaflower*, taken off India by the *Manche*, had gone over, as had Catholic troops in the Company's Army, captured in the two Indiamen.[10] Although quite what followed *L'Agile*'s separation from *Nereide* cannot be known for certain, some speculation is thus warranted.

L'Agile's captain quickly identified the Irish accents among the prize crew. It would not have been hard to seduce O'Hara, Baird and Masey. From the tops they had seen the French island in all its lush verdancy, had talked among themselves of a life in such a place, where the hard work was done by slaves and service on a privateer brought rich rewards. If they resisted the captain's coaxing, the promise of a society free and egalitarian, it would not have been long before they reminded themselves of the brutal regime to which they had to return.

A few days into the voyage, the three Irish hands and Buckle surprised their shipmates at the change of the watch. Daley, the master's mate, was killed. McNeil and the rest were overcome and clapped in irons. *L'Agile*'s captain was restored to his ship and a new course set – for Bourbon.[11]

In naval terms it was a mutiny, the second involving *Nereide* in five months.

The dread of the *Nereide*'s crew for their captain had in the meantime acquired a certain resonance among the island's inhabitants. As Flinders put it:

> Captain Corbet is more feared here than any of the other cruizers; it is in effect him who has taken most of the vessels here; and in general he appears suddenly and immediately finds something to do. He appears to be a very active and enterprizing officer.[12]

A few weeks later, Flinders noted the arrival of another English ship off the island, the 64-gun HMS *Raisonnable*. Commodore Josias Rowley had resumed his command of the blockade.

If ships' captains can be said to speak through their logbooks – and there is a case to be made that they were mirrors of the true character – it is hard to imagine two more different types than Rowley and Corbet. Everything that Corbet did was meticulous, but a struggle – with his ship, his men, the conditions, himself. Apart from the grisly frequency of beatings, his logs stand out mainly for painstaking detail in sailing procedure. Rowley was born to the sea, and it showed in his casual ease with command and his way with men. His logs are notable for the frequency of gunnery practice and the rarity of floggings.

This is not to say he was careless of discipline. He had the ability, though, to inspire by example rather than to compel through fear. Rowley, in the words of a fellow captain, was 'so just in distinguishing merit, and so temperate and judicious in correcting guilt, that he won affection as well as respect'. He also possessed the gift of all great commanders. One of his contemporaries, Captain Basil Hall, wrote of him in words which define that capacity to excite the devotion of fighting men, and to lead them into hell: 'The officers and men under his command would have engaged at his bidding in actions of the most desperate character. They loved him.'[13]

The 'Nelson touch' was a phrase coined for the great commander's method in battle; but it also has connotations of love and brotherhood, as well as a spark capable of salvaging victory from defeat. In that respect, it could be fairly said that Rowley had the Nelson touch.

His grandfather was an Admiral of the Fleet and his uncle, Sir Joshua Rowley, a Vice-Admiral in whose ship he first served as a boy of twelve. There was no whiff of nepotism about the Rowleys, however, and Josias's rise was steady rather than spectacular. A few months before Trafalgar, he took over one of Nelson's old ships, the *Raisonnable*, but was consistently unfortunate: instead of being with Nelson, he had been involved in an action off Cape Finisterre; later he was caught up in the messy failure of Popham's mission to South America. Rowley was now aged forty-four, and on the verge of the defining operation of his life. For although the British Government was still far from having resolved on actual invasion, there was a new interest in testing how readily the French islands might fall. In the words of a magisterially fence-sitting dispatch from the Admiralty, the Commander at the Cape, Admiral Bertie, had been authorised to proceed with occupying Ile de France and Bourbon 'if it shall appear that the said islands, or either of them, is likely to surrender to HM Arms'.[14]

A first step had recently been taken with the occupation of Rodrigues, a tiny island 350 miles east of Ile de France which had wood, water and a small French population able to supply visiting ships with vegetables and livestock. Rowley's orders from Bertie were twofold: to intensify the blockade; and to establish with Lieutenant-Colonel Henry Keating, who was in charge of the force on Rodrigues, whether the islands were indeed 'likely to surrender to HM Arms'.

Raisonnable sailed from Simon's Bay on 16 June under a squally south-easter that was boisterous enough three days out to precipitate six young bullocks overboard.[15] This loss of the last fresh meat this side of Rodrigues occasioned much grumbling about carelessness and the buggers in charge of the beasts. But as the squalls died and the skies cleared, so spirits lifted, and although the old 64 had to be coaxed along like an elderly relative, Rowley got the most out of her, to the extent that the days followed one another in sweet-sailing emptiness, more than 150 miles reeling off from noon to noon as the Cape sank further behind and the sea brightened to a luminous light sapphire.

We have seen so much of the dangerous and brutal side of seafaring that there is a risk of forgetting that it had a counterpoint. Life was hard for all common folk in the early nineteenth century and the man who went to sea for King George, though he might have been pressed, had an assurance of food and liquor, shelter and companionship, and even medical care. He had a chance for advancement, to gain the esteem of his fellows, and to win prize money. It is, therefore, not so surprising that he was, at his best, a proud fellow whose highest ideal was a loyalty that bound together his mates, his ship, his country and his king. Just as the soldier of Bonaparte's army bestrode European battlegrounds with a sense of invincibility, England's sailor roamed the seas with a conviction that no foe could stand against him. This was his domain and when he set out with a following wind under such a man as Rowley, when he stood in the yards surveying the vast blue below, feeling his strength and the breeze on his skin, he had purpose. He may even have been happy.

Routine was his lodestar. The rotational watchkeeping system varied the time that he was on duty in any twenty-four hours – four-hour spells spread among three watches – but in every other respect his life had a constant, reassuring rhythm dictated by the ship's bell, tolling on the half-hour as a signal and a summons: eight bells at 4 a.m., marking the end of the Middle Watch, rousing him to the muster, a stowing of hammocks and the scrubbing of decks; another eight bells at midday, end of the Forenoon Watch, a call to dinner and grog; then four bells at 6 p.m., end of the first two-hour Dog Watch, for supper with another pint of grog.

Only one incident was sufficiently out of the ordinary to be included in Rowley's log on the three-week passage, and that was the surgeon's feat of catching a shark nine feet long which, on being eviscerated, was found to contain fifty-nine little ones. When Rodrigues was sighted on 7 July, not one man in a crew of almost 500 had been flogged.

Rowley's purpose on Rodrigues was to take on supplies for the ships already engaged in the blockade, and to meet Colonel Keating, who had been kicking his heels for months with his 600-strong force of HM 56th Regiment and the 2nd Regiment of Bombay Native Infantry. The meeting proved a great success. Rowley and Keating were men of similar temperament and, unusually for their rival services, struck up an immediate rapport. When Rowley raised the possibility of a strike against the islands Keating enthused.

A week later *Raisonnable* anchored off the northern tip of Ile de France to join the rest of the squadron. Over the next few days, captains cast off their nankeen jackets and white duck trousers, and donned breeches, silk stockings and blue coats before being rowed across to the flagship and an audience with the Commodore. No record survives of these briefings but two elements emerge. Firstly, Rowley laid out his plans. Secondly, he took Corbet aside for a frank talk about his way with the men.

Rowley's strategy was based on a limited resumption of cruises between Bourbon and Ile de France while still concentrating the squadron's limited resources off the latter. His intention was to keep the *Bellone* bottled up in Port Louis, where she had been for weeks, but to be prepared for the return of Hamelin's three other frigates; had he but known it, the *Caroline* had just captured the Indiamen, some 1,500 miles to the north-east, while the *Venus* and *Manche* were cruising off the Nicobar Islands. Rowley also had one or two ideas for provoking the French and testing their reflexes.

His captains were a mixed bag. Samuel Pym had the best ship, the *Sirius*, a 38-gun frigate armed with 18-pounders. Pym was among the senior commanders, although far from being the most capable. Henry Lambert of the *Iphigenia*, another 38, came highly praised, having served under Pellew in India where, captaining the *San Fiorenzo* in 1805, he captured the frigate *Psyche* after a bloody running battle. Of Corbet's zeal there would never be any doubt; he would have happily tackled two French frigates on his own. Another captain also stood out as a regular fire-eater.

Nesbit Willoughby, of the 16-gun sloop *Otter*, scarcely looked the part, being 'tall, lean, pale, gloomy and irascible'.[16] He came from the aristocracy – an old Nottinghamshire family with vast estates and the great Elizabethan house of Wollaton Hall – and was arrogant, touchy and highly strung. For all that, he was a true creature of the elements.[17]

Willoughby joined the Navy aged twelve and spent his entire career on a course running so close to the wind that it could only have ended in death or glory. Twice as a young lieutenant he was found guilty of insolence towards his captains, first being confined for a year, then being dismissed the Service. Always he was redeemed by his warrior qualities and a gift for the spectacular, which he exhibited first in boarding a Dutch ship at the Battle of Copenhagen and in action against the French in the West Indies. Restored to the Navy and given the *Otter* in 1808, he was sent out to the Cape where Bertie, who had been his first captain, regarded him indulgently. In this he was fortunate for, like Corbet, he was a ferocious flogger, declaring that 'it was as much pleasure to him to punish a man when he comes to the gangway as it was to go to his breakfast'.[18] Like Corbet, too, he had a petition circulated against him by his crew, and had been tried by court martial at the Cape for cruelty directly after him. Whether because Willoughby's regime paled by comparison, or because Corbet was one of the adjudicators, he was acquitted.

Despite their similarities, Corbet and Willoughby were physical and temperamental opposites. Corbet – short, dark, intense, living only for the Service – was genuinely hated by those who served under him. The languid Willoughby, on the other hand, had a theatrical streak which made him popular with his men and a rakish flair with women; he had enjoyed success among the beauties of Rodrigues. But he, too, was desperate for honour. Both now in their early thirties, Corbet and Willoughby eyed one another with a dark jealousy.

Corbet, clearly, had made the bigger mark so far. Willoughby could not match his rival for seacraft but, with new orders to provoke the French wherever possible, on land as well as sea, he was to make a specialisation of daring, irregular operations. On 14 August, finding two French merchantmen and a gunboat sheltering under the batteries at Black River Bay, midway down the west coast of Ile de France, he put off from *Otter* shortly before midnight in the gig, followed by a lieutenant in the yawl and a midshipman in the jolly-boat. Guided only by a glimmering from the shore, they slipped silently into the harbour.

Willoughby's intention was to carry the gunboat, then seize the two merchant vessels, a brig and a lugger, and take all three out under the nose of the battery. Such was the darkness, however, that they boarded the wrong ship. The alarm was raised and an unholy tumult followed in which the French opened fire and 'threw up fire-balls of a superior description which illuminated the whole river'. Under sustained fire the raiders had to withdraw with just one prize; they were lucky that only one of the *Otter*'s crew was killed.[19]

Not much had been achieved, but it was the first English raid on Ile de France and it shook the inhabitants. Flinders, who heard the explosions in the night, reported a growing sense that invasion was inevitable. Even the news that Bonaparte had occupied Vienna after two great victories over the Austrians excited 'much more sadness than joy', he wrote.

Corbet, perhaps galvanised by Willoughby's escapade, hove to off the east coast of Bourbon a few days later, exchanged fire with a shore battery and sent in a boatful of Marines who drove off the defenders, blew up three magazines and withdrew.

Although Corbet's energy never flagged, one aspect of his usual regime on *Nereide* had in the meantime undergone a transformation. It could scarcely have been coincidental that, since their talk after Rowley's arrival, floggings had stopped. Not dropped off, but stopped. From handing out dozens a day, Corbet had ceased to lash. When, on 2 August, William White was found among the animals on the orlop and got twenty-four for 'beastliness' – an offence that merited a thrashing on any ship – he was the first since the *Raisonnable* joined the blockade.

Rowley knew Corbet well, had served with him in the Plata fiasco. There are few documents that cast light on their relationship, but the indications are that it was one based on mutual respect. Rowley got the best out of Corbet, just as he did from the rest of his men. The image of *Nereide*'s captain as a brute drawn from nightmare has always to be balanced by his doppelgänger, the earnest, insecure man, anxious to recapture the heady heights of youth when he had been singled out for praise by the great Nelson. At Rowley's prompting, Corbet had tempered discipline and was starting to justify his earlier promise.

Just when the news was received that turned everything upside down is not clear. Around the second week of August, however, Rowley learnt that the *Caroline* was back, that she had two prizes, and that she had brought them triumphantly into Bourbon without opposition. What followed illustrated the difficulty of maintaining an effective blockade. Rowley diverted some of the squadron to Bourbon, in case Hamelin too should choose this time to return. Captain Duperré of the *Bellone*, seeing his opportunity after being long confined at Port Louis, seized the moment. It happened that Flinders was at his lookout post as *Bellone* came out.

Thursday 17 August. Cloudy. In the evening saw a ship under full sail steering for Bourbon, and another which crowded all sail after her, about 3 leagues astern. We suppose the first to be the *Bellone*, and the latter to be an English frigate in Chase.[20]

For once Flinders was mistaken. The English ship in pursuit was *Raisonnable*. They continued to run through the night but by dawn *Bellone* was five miles ahead and, although Rowley had every scrap of canvas up, his dilapidated flagship was never going to catch one of the fastest ships afloat. At noon he wrote mournfully: 'Chase drawing away from us.'[21]

It was a painful but valuable lesson. The entire squadron had been unable to contain a single frigate. The *Bellone* was out, and about to join Hamelin in creating mayhem.

The only good news in this dismal chapter of events was the arrival of another of His Majesty's frigates. The *Boadicea* was a hugely valuable addition to Rowley's force, 38 guns and 18-pounders at that, the closest that any English frigate came to matching Hamelin's firepower. With the *Raisonnable* nearing the end of her useful life and soon to follow the *Leopard* home, Rowley identified the *Boadicea* as his next flagship.

He also resolved on action that would genuinely test French resistance and go some way to avenge the twin embarrassments caused by *Caroline* and *Bellone*. A message was sent to Rodrigues, inviting Keating to join the Navy in a raid on Bourbon – to storm the port of St Paul and recover the Indiamen. The army man could not have been more pleased, 'offering to embark with his troops in the most handsome manner'.[22]

Rowley set out his plan in a dispatch to Bertie: 'I considered it practicable that the place might be carried with the assistance of troops from Rodrigues . . . I have therefore detached the *Nereide*, *Otter* and *Sapphire* to bring them down & as soon as they arrive shall proceed to the attack.'[23]

Another reason to attack Bourbon had just been discovered. Willoughby, as he wrote to Rowley, had been cruising off the island on 23 August when a brig was seen to windward making for St Paul. With barely a breeze in the air and no prospect of catching her under sail, Willoughby's senior lieutenant, John Burn, ventured that she might be cut off by boat. Burn with 'great perseverance and laborious pulling, boarded her'. The brig, it turned out, was *L'Agile*, the French vessel taken by Corbet, last seen heading for the Cape with a prize crew. Willoughby was spitting with rage as he spelled out how four treacherous seamen from *Nereide* had 'murdered Mr Daley prize master & ironed the rest of the party sent by Captain Corbet'.[24]

'I am sorry to inform you', Willoughby went on, 'that the mutineers escaped by taking to their boats, tho' Lt Burn chased them close upon the beach.'

The mutineers may have escaped, but they were trapped on Bourbon and Rowley's taskforce was poised to attack.

16

Battle on Bourbon

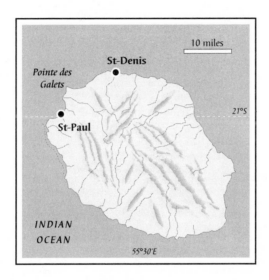

Bourbon in 1809

Bourbon and the Cape, 19 September–12 December 1809

Rowley's plan was for an extended foray, rather than an invasion. Seizing Bourbon's main port, St Paul, would nevertheless be a real test – of both French mettle and British capacity to land a sizeable military force on the islands. Whatever the upshot, it would provide lessons for what must follow on Ile de France.

The *Raisonnable*'s great cabin on 19 September offered an image of camaraderie rare between blue- and red-coated officers. The fellowship that had been observed between their respective commanders, Rowley and Keating, fused with the prospect of action, produced an air vibrant with energy. Five other vessels lay near by, about ten miles off Bourbon, and, since midway through the forenoon watch of a hazy, sultry day, barges, gigs and jolly-boats had put off from *Nereide*, *Boadicea*, *Sirius*, *Otter* and *Wasp*, coming alongside for their occupants to clamber up the flagship's side and be brought aft. Now they stooped over charts of Bourbon laid out on Rowley's desk – the Captains Corbet, Willoughby and Pym, and Keating with the officers of HM 56th Regiment and the 2nd Regiment of Bombay Native Infantry.

The slight, intense figure of Corbet was prominent in the discussion and planning. He argued animatedly that a force of Keating's size might go round Bourbon 'debarking in the different quarters and destroying the batteries and artillery, rendering the island useless to [the French] and of great consequence to us for refreshment in the blockade'.[1] He was in high spirits, still elated by the success of his recent foray against Bourbon's eastern battery.

Despite these urgings, Rowley opted for caution. They did not know the full armed strength on Bourbon, or how it was distributed between

St Denis, the principal town, and St Paul, the heavily defended harbour on the north-west shore. What he did know was that the *Caroline* and her prizes were still at the latter. He would direct the attack here. Once the batteries had been stormed, the town seized and the ships secured, there would be time enough to consider his next step.

Keating's 370 troops would be landed on a beach seven miles from St Paul and steal up on the crescent of seven batteries guarding the bay. The critical task of going in under the cover of dark and landing them was entrusted to Corbet – singled out by Rowley for 'his perfect acquaintance with the coast as well as his known skill and activity'.[2] Willoughby, somewhat piqued but always keen for a scrap, volunteered to command a navy landing party. He would support Keating with 230 Marines and seamen.

At sunset the following day, 20 September, the squadron came to, still some miles from St Paul. The whole 600-strong force was mustered on *Nereide*, she having been equipped with barges and cutters from the other vessels, hoisted on temporary davits around the ship. After sunset she went ahead alone.

They were almost betrayed by the weather. Overnight the wind dropped and *Nereide* failed to reach the landing stage of Pointe des Galets on schedule, so that as dawn washed the beach in an orange glow, hundreds of troops had yet to disembark. But it was now that Corbet's ability in handling his ship was seen. Darting about the quarterdeck, barking orders, he succeeded in bringing her in quicker and closer than any other member of the squadron could have done. In the landing, he showed an eye for potential mishaps, and a sense of timing crucial in avoiding them. And there can be little doubt that the crew of the *Nereide* responded keenly. Their captain's newly lightened hand had transformed the ship. A lieutenant on *Raisonnable* noted how the landing was completed 'with a celerity peculiar to the gallant Captn Corbet'.[3]

At 6.30 a.m., as daylight came up on the dark figures beetling along the coast, Corbet was able to signal Rowley: 'Troops on shore and near the first battery.'

The first and second batteries fell by 7 a.m., just as the inhabitants of St Paul woke up to the landing and as the raiders were advancing after a lightning march around Pointe des Galets. Defenders took up positions behind a stone wall at the town's edge with eight 6-pounders, blocking the way to the third battery. Down in the port, guns from the *Caroline*, *Streatham* and *Europe* were brought to bear on the attackers in a fire that Keating reported was 'chiefly grape and well directed'.[4]

The fight was short and sharp. The Bombay troops made a breach in a series of charges carried 'in the most gallant manner', driving the defenders back, and now the third battery fell. As the crackling of small arms subsided, the cannons' boom swelled. Willoughby's Marines had taken possession of the big guns and turned them on the French ships in port. Within an hour the remaining batteries fell and Rowley was able to take in the squadron, bringing more fire to bear on the *Caroline*.

Raisonnable's log recorded the end of resistance within three hours of the landing: 'At 8.55 the *Caroline* hauled down her colours & also the two Indiamen. All firing ceased.'[5]

Army and Navy vied in praising one another for their joint victory. Rowley thought it impossible to do justice to 'the skill and gallantry of Lt-Col Keating' or the 'bravery shewn by the troops in successively carrying the batteries'.[6] For his part, the colonel acknowledged Rowley's 'judicious arrangements' but reserved his highest praise – 'the happy termination and ultimate success of this enterprise' – for Corbet's slick seamanship in the landing.[7]

Casualties for so dashing an operation were light – fifteen dead and fifty-seven wounded. In the *Raisonnable*, young Lieutenant Walters cheered: 'Thus was executed, by the superior skill and judgment of a few clever men, plans that treble the force would have failed in under inferior commanders.'[8]

Their coup went beyond seizing the only safe harbour on Bourbon. The *Caroline*, thus far the most successful of the French frigates, had been captured intact, and the two Indiamen, *Streatham* and *Europe*, had been retaken.

But Corbet still had one or two other trophies in mind.

The defenders had fled to the hills behind St Paul as Marines from *Nereide* moved through the town, examining the bodies of the dead and wounded. They had their orders and though the bloodied figure tried to conceal himself, he was recognised immediately. A cry went up, 'Seize the traitor.'

Thomas O'Hara, the twenty-two-year-old Tyrone mutineer, had fought in the defence with the desperation of one who knew his life was at stake. His idyll, a free man on this sweet island, had lasted just a few weeks before the familiar shape of his old ship hove into view like the goddess of retribution, Nemesis herself. Wounded in the fighting, he was abandoned by the other *L'Agile* mutineers in the retreat. He was clapped in irons and brought into Corbet's brooding presence.

But though navy justice was sometimes capricious, it still had entrenched notions of fairness. There was no question of O'Hara being tried on the spot and strung up from the nearest yardarm. Corbet reported the capture to Rowley with grim satisfaction but applied merely for O'Hara's court martial for his 'abandoned crimes'.[9]

Also discovered at St Paul were John Dale and William Gelston, captains of the *Streatham* and *Europe*, in a house near the port where they had spent the past four months. Dale's experiences had echoes of those of Flinders on Ile de France. He had been confined to town but otherwise left to his own devices, mixing freely with the inhabitants and receiving friendly treatment 'such as will ever claim my esteem and gratitude'. Dale was disappointed that his incarceration on Bourbon had prevented him meeting Flinders, but left some books to be sent to him, including a *Naval Chronicle* relating the saga of his detention.

To his liberators, Dale confirmed that O'Hara was far from being the only defector on Bourbon. As well as the other *Nereide* men in the *L'Agile* mutiny – the Irishmen Baird and Masey, the American Buckle – they included Irish sailors from *Seaflower*, the brig captured off India by the *Manche*. 'I never conversed with any of these men,' Dale reported, 'but understood they gave as a reason for entering into the French service that they had been starved into it.'[10]

That evening, after destroying the batteries, Keating's troops returned to *Nereide*. In the morning an emboldened French force collected on the heights, threatening to advance and recover 'an extensive government store of considerable value'. They withdrew when the British landed again, but in a hasty conclave Rowley and Keating agreed that the store should be destroyed. Willoughby and his Marines carried out this task with relish.[11]

Sadly, the store turned out to be of more than mere 'considerable value', containing the entire treasure trove of silk from *Streatham* and *Europe*, worth the equivalent of £17 million. The resulting bellows of anguish that would come later would be not only from Leadenhall Street, but Rowley and his officers, who watched blithely oblivious as their prize money – about a quarter of the value – went up in smoke before their eyes.

General Desbrulys, the Governor, had fled, leaving the town in confusion and fear. Retribution was in the air and local slaves seized the moment to turn on their masters – an incident which, as Flinders related, caused alarm on Ile de France where Decaen had raised a new regiment from among the slave population.

> It appears that a part of the slaves at St Paul revolted, and did some mischief. They demanded arms of the English, and offered to burn the town, but Commodore Rowley kept them on board the ships, and after the attack ceased, sent them back to their masters, with information of what they had offered to do. The instigators of this insurrection were shot to the number of eight. This news appears to cause a great sensation here, and to convince the inhabitants of the impolicy of arming the slaves for the defence of the island which has been adopted by General Decaen.[12]

Next day Desbrulys cut his throat, leaving a note that he could expect no mercy from Decaen. 'I do not want to be a traitor to my Country, but I have no wish to sacrifice the inhabitants by a useless defence of this open island … Death on the scaffold awaits me. I prefer to execute myself. I commend to Providence and to kindly souls my wife and children.'[13]

Local people, led to expect the worst from the British, had in the meantime been surprised by their 'mild and lenient treatment' and were imploring the intruders to stay as they too feared 'the rage and violence of General Decaen'.[14] Formerly, Bourbon had been left to its own affairs, a bread basket for its more metropolitan, less fertile, neighbour. Now, according to Dale, the islanders felt neglected and oppressed, and spoke with open hostility towards Imperial France in general and Decaen in particular.

Although St Paul had surrendered, Bourbon itself was not won. Keating believed that between 1,500 and 1,800 men would be needed to occupy and hold it against any counter-attack from Ile de France. Another great cabin conference gave rise to a spat between Corbet and Willoughby. The latter, having redefined himself as a land commander, was all for pressing home the advantage by offering surrender terms to St Denis. Corbet declared loftily that it would be 'cruel to seek such a step knowing we were unprepared to give them protection . . . from the enraged military government of Ile de France'.[15]

Ultimately, the decision rested with Rowley – who had seen in the Plata disaster how a distant force could over-reach itself. His orders from Bertie had been to test French defences and this he had done. Another factor had also to be considered: a new hurricane season was at hand. Rowley wrote to Bertie that if a sufficient force could be assembled to land by December, Bourbon probably would fall without a struggle. 'Certainly the inhabitants are much dissatisfied with the present government. At any rate we have easy access opened whenever it shall be considered expedient to attack and we have done everything possible to conciliate the inhabitants.'[16]

This dispatch was entrusted to Corbet, a generous gesture in a naval tradition that brought distinction upon the bearer of glad tidings. Rowley had singled out Corbet for special praise and when he sailed for the Cape, taking the mutineer O'Hara to his just deserts, he would have drawn satisfaction deeply into his nostrils with the warm air.*

The *Nereide* left Bourbon on the last day of September and so smooth was her run to Africa that the Natal coast was sighted on 12 October. Once Cape Agulhas was rounded the wind dropped completely, however, and Corbet – bursting to deliver his news – had the gig lowered off the

---

* Thomas O'Hara continued to evade navy justice. Brought to trial at the Cape a few weeks later, he complained that all the witnesses necessary to his defence had been sent back to England. He was landed at Woolwich nine months later and given into the custody of the Marines. Once more his witnesses proved difficult to trace. There matters rested. And continued to rest, while Thomas O'Hara somehow disappeared from the Navy's view. What became of him is beyond establishing with certainty, but a trail running through Admiralty records suggests that the authorities started to confuse him with another Irishman, one Bernard McCue, a mess servant at Woolwich who, having left a trail of incompetence behind him, got the local postmaster to write a letter on his behalf, 'making application for his discharge in order that he might entirely get out of the way . . . leave this country and proceed to Ireland'. Woolwich was only too pleased to be rid of him. There is no certainty that Thomas O'Hara and Bernard McCue were one and the same. What can be said is that O'Hara was never court-martialled. One of the more legitimate objects of Corbet's vengeful spirit, he was one of the few to escape it. (See Admiralty Indexes ADM 12/141, 12/150 & 12/152 for the links that connect O'Hara and McCue.)

mountainous ridge known as the Twelve Apostles on 17 October to be rowed the last six miles in to Table Bay.

The arrival of *Nereide*'s hot-footed captain at his door that evening brought a rare smile to Admiral Albemarle Bertie's sour countenance. He was not a good-humoured man at the best of times and a series of personal setbacks had turned him into a downright bear. Corbet's report provided a rare opportunity to bask in reflected glory and he dictated a dispatch to their Lordships that judiciously blended triumph with urgency. He was, he wrote, 'in hourly expectation', of the arrival of the *Caroline*, scourge of the Company ships, and the recaptured Indiamen.

> All the batteries at St Paul were successfully stormed and completely destroyed in a most gallant and masterly manner by the joint operations of Capt Rowley with HM squadron under my command and a detachment of the Force stationed at Rodrigues under Lt-Col-Keating. This has been an enterprise planned with judgment and executed with promptitude and gallantry. The object has been completely effected and the troops are returned to Rodrigues.[17]

The cause of Bertie's sulkiness at this time is not hard to find. The admiral had set his heart on a sea-led operation against the French islands – a project which, it was now evident, had every opportunity of success under Rowley and held out the prospect of honours and ennoblement, perhaps a baronetcy, for himself. Rowley had set a December deadline. It was already mid-October and the opportunity was slipping away. And all the while Bertie was plagued by this confounded business in Madras.

This business in Madras had, of course, been rumbling away for months. Just that week, however, fresh dispatches had arrived from India. Bertie was summoned to the Castle by Lord Caledon, Governor at the Cape, and told that a number of garrisons – precisely how many was not yet known – had mutinied against the presidency and were threatening to march on Madras. Sir George Barlow's government was in danger, perhaps even his life. To meet the threat he, Caledon, was authorising a mobilisation of the Cape regiments to go to the rescue, and Bertie's ships would be needed to escort them.

The admiral did his best to resist. He was not at liberty, he said, to divert any ships from the French islands where it was plain, from the latest intelligence, 'that steps may be (should they not already have been) taken for offensive operations'. With a hint of menace, he added that ships might encounter hurricanes at this time of year and 'on their fatal effects I need make no comment to Your Excellency'.[18]

Caledon was not to be fobbed off. He had no doubt, he replied, that 'the perilous state of India' required their support, adding acidly: 'Allow me to make the observation, of what consequence can the Isles of France be to Great Britain if she loses her Empire in the East?'[19]

There was no good answer to that and so plans went ahead for sending 1,900 infantry, 300 dragoons and 90 artillerymen to Madras in transport ships, with navy escorts in the form of *Nereide* and the *Otter*.[20] Ile de France would have to wait.

One setback was followed by another. Bertie, who made enemies with careless ease, had just acquired a very bad one indeed in William Shield who, as the Navy's resident Commissioner, controlled all ships' supplies. A seemingly mild-mannered family man, Shield took exception to what he termed Bertie's 'violent and indecorous conduct' in their dealings.[21] A sulphurous feud was to have severe consequence, not least for Bertie himself. An early broadside was fired now, over the Cape squadron's newest acquisition.

In appreciation of Corbet's efforts, Bertie had awarded him the captured *Caroline*, renamed *Bourbonnaise* after the action at St Paul. She was a real plum, the finest frigate on the station, yet now in need of some re-equipping. But when Corbet applied to Shield for supplies that included a best-bower – one of two main bow anchors – the latter demurred. Corbet, astonished, stormed into Shield's office and, according to Shield, used abusive language and threatened to horsewhip him.[22] Shield lodged a complaint with Bertie, then dug in his heels and started to raise objections to other aspects of refitting the *Bourbonnaise* from supplies held at the Cape.

The upshot, incredible though it seems, was that in order to re-equip his ship for service, Corbet had to take her back to England. Beside himself with rage, Bertie wrote to the Admiralty:

> I have been compelled to send to England this powerful Frigate, notwithstanding her perfect state & the loss of her services, [as] well as those of an Officer whose local knowledge would have been eminently useful in the event of hostile operations against the Isle of France & Bourbon.[23]

Shield, far from contrite, continued to wield his authority with every sign of malice and against the interests of the Service. He refused to provide Corbet with roundhouse furniture for *Bourbonnaise*, or the crew with hammock cloths, needed for a winter passage to England. More culpably still, he declined to act on a report that *Nereide*'s foretopmast was sprung and should be replaced before she was used to escort troops.[24]

Almost the most astonishing aspect of this bizarre affair is that Shield escaped from it unscathed. Either he had powerful allies in London, or Bertie had even more enemies than he knew. Their feud continued to fester for months as accusations and protestations passed slowly between the Cape and the Admiralty. But when it came to resolution, the disapprobation of their Lordships would fall not on Shield, but Admiral Bertie.

Corbet was piped off *Nereide* on 9 November. After all that had passed between captain and crew – mustered on deck as the slight, saturnine figure passed over the side for the last time – the moment came in almost banal fashion, a log entry concluding 'Midnight, light breezes and cloudy', and below it a scratchy signature, 'Robt Corbet'. He took with him into *Bourbonnaise* many of her best hands and his enforcer, the bosun's mate, Moses Veale.[25]

He left a baffled remnant. For weeks the Cat had remained in its sheath. But any idea that Corbet's basic approach to discipline may have altered had been dispelled only days after the *Nereide* anchored in Table Bay. A few hands, celebrating their return after a victory in which they had played no small part, were found drunk. Nine men got two dozen. But Corbet saved his final brutal flourish for James Maxfield – always a regular, whether for gambling, drunkenness or insolence – who received sixty.

Relief among the *Nereide*'s crew at his departure was tempered by the fact that he was being replaced by another tartar. When next they sailed it would be under Nesbit Willoughby, who was rewarded for a warlike performance at St Paul with his first frigate command.

The *Bourbonnaise* sailed for England on 12 December. Corbet had seemingly been cheated of his destiny on Ile de France. But he would be back, to write a final chapter to the war in the Eastern Seas and create a navy legend.

Commodore Hamelin's cruise

Ile de France and Capetown, 10 November 1809–24 August 1810

The loss of Corbet's zeal, as well as his knowledge of the islands, was soon brought home to Rowley. Commodore Jacques Hamelin had not had an especially fruitful cruise in the *Venus* so far, but he was about to make life more difficult for the squadron than ever.

On 10 November a trio of Indiamen, 185 days out of Portsmouth bound for Calcutta, were midway across the Indian Ocean and, at a position of Lat 00° 56'S, probably preparing for the high jinks of Crossing the Line. It was a pleasantly mild day for these latitudes and, having left the Ile de France in their wake weeks ago, those on board may have been looking forward to their arrival in Bengal after what had been a long but entirely trouble-free voyage. That evening a sail was sighted – as it transpired, the *Rattlesnake*, an 18-gun sloop from Madras.

Commodore John Stewart of the *Windham* received a lieutenant on board and, after initial relief that the Navy had not come to press his crew, listened gravely to a report that two French frigates were in the vicinity. Stewart sent messages across to the other Indiamen, *Charlton* and *United Kingdom*. 'I have reason to apprehend our meeting an Enemy of superior force,' he wrote.[1] Over the next week each ship exercised her great guns as they passed north until, on 17 November, they reached 06° 03'N – east of Ceylon and just a few degrees south of where the *Caroline* had intercepted Dale's fleet in June.

At dawn of a thin calm morning, 18 November, three strange sail were sighted about twelve miles distant. They were Hamelin's *Venus*, the 40-gun *Manche*, and the corvette *Creole*. Despite these absurdly one-sided odds, Stewart decided to attack. He addressed the crew from the quarterdeck, pointing to the *Manche* and telling them that she was to be their prize. She was too heavily armed for a straight fight, of course, but she was some distance ahead of *Venus* and *Creole* and Stewart said he intended to get in close and board her before the others came up.[2]

The plan was breathtaking in its effrontery. The *Manche*'s 38-pounder carronades were not known as 'smashers' for nothing and at close quarters *Windham* would be quickly reduced by good gunnery to a splintered ruin. In the matter of numbers, the frigate had twice as many hands as the Indiaman. Stewart was putting his faith in a detachment of about 200 troops spread among his three ships.

His speech was reportedly cheered by the men before they went to their stations.[3] A passenger similarly circumstanced wrote: 'I could not help admiring the alacrity of the seamen – one would have thought by their looks and cheerful bustle that they were preparing for some jovial entertainment or grand festival.'[4] The response of the *Windham*'s passengers is not recorded. Those who were hustled below included a gentleman named Hunter, his sister, Mrs Scott – described as 'a worthy Scotch lady of the old school' – two sisters, the Miss McCargs, and two other young ladies, the Misses Barton and Button.[5]

Stewart's fellow captains watched all this aghast. Although he had ordered them to follow him into action, they did so with obvious reluctance and as *Windham* closed with the Frenchman, it was seen that *Charlton* and *United Kingdom* were not coming on at the same pace. Not to put too fine a point on it, they had shortened sail and fallen some miles behind.[6]

Over the next two hours *Windham* exchanged heavy fire with *Manche* whose aim, fortuitously, was found wanting, so many balls hummed harmlessly overhead. But Stewart could not get close enough to board. Each time the *Windham* neared her, the frigate bore up and made sail. Eventually, Captain Dornal de Guy, perceiving his foe's determination, wore round on the starboard tack to evade him one last time before breaking off at noon to rejoin the *Venus*.[7] Four of the *Windham*'s crew were dead and the Indiaman had sustained a battering but it had been a gallant little action. Captain William D'Esterre of the *United Kingdom* wrote in his log that Stewart had 'behaved most nobly'.[8]

Windham remained in the background of the cannons blazing redly in the night as the French frigates set off in pursuit of less troublesome quarry, the other Indiamen. Stewart, in no position to come to their defence and perhaps feeling let down, tried to make his escape. At 11 p.m. on a still, clear and bright night, the *Windham* bore away to the north-west.

Now it was the *United Kingdom* and *Charlton* that had their hands full. 'The French frigates and corvette were standing after us with all sail, bearing very fast,' D'Esterre wrote. 'At half past 12am Sunday morning commenced action, both frigates firing on us.'[9] In less than an hour both Indiamen had struck, *United Kingdom* with three men dead. The two captains were taken on board the *Manche*. In the meantime, *Venus* set off in pursuit of the *Windham*.

Stewart managed, despite the damage to his ship, to elude Hamelin for the rest of that day. Brought up from the orlop, Mrs Scott and the other ladies observed the desperate efforts made to escape: guns were cast overboard to lighten the load and running repairs made to rigging as the *Windham* raced on and on, into the night. And through the next day and night. Then yet another. Somehow, a damaged Indiaman was staying ahead of one of the fastest frigates afloat, thanks to the skill of her captain and the energy of her crew.

These exertions were followed admiringly from the *Venus*'s quarter-deck, where her officers were drawn to the spectacle in a spirit of fraternity. Hamelin remarked that 'every credit was due to *Windham*'s captain' while his juniors marvelled: 'They did not conceive it possible that any ship could have escaped for so long.'[10]

Only on the morning of 22 November – four days after the French were first sighted – did Hamelin bring *Windham* to bay. Stewart had retained a few guns, so that even then he was capable of a last gesture of defiance. A volley thundered out. The balls passed over the *Venus*. An answering fire brought the Company's colours fluttering down.

Stewart still had one more lesson for his foes. A prize crew went across to *Windham* while her captain, passengers and crew were welcomed on *Venus* by Hamelin. Two weeks later they caught up with *Manche* and the other captured Indiamen and were within ten days of Port Louis when the sky turned red, the weather thickened and a furious wind came on to blow. One year after the storm that destroyed the First Fleet, a new hurricane season was about to announce itself.

At daylight on 20 December, Hamelin found his ship alone and in peril. All three of *Venus*'s topmasts had been torn away and, thanks to a delay in closing the ports, water in the hold was seven feet deep. Her crew, in fatalistic acceptance that she would founder, had retired to their cabins. At this point Hamelin, recalling the skills of his prisoners, swallowed his pride and sent for Stewart. The nineteenth-century naval historian William James related that Hamelin

> requested that [Stewart] would endeavour with his crew to save the French frigate; but he, at the same time, wished him to give a pledge that he and his men should not take possession of the frigate. Captain Stewart refused to give the pledge, but replied that M Hamelin must take his chance. The French captain gave up the charge of his frigate to the British captain and crew, his prisoners. By great exertions on the part of the latter, the wreck of the frigate's topmasts was cleared and the water in the hold reduced.[11]

James is the most partisan of British naval historians. Making due allowance, it is apparent that Captain John Stewart, a man of prosaic name, was an exceptional seafarer. Like John Dale, John Ramsden and some of the other Indiamen captains encountered in these pages, he was an outstanding representative of that forgotten species of Britain's seafaring past, a rebuke to the superior spirit of their navy counterparts with their haughty notions of 'mongrel gentlemen' and distinctions between 'the art of war and the art of gain'.

What had become of his own ship was not clear, for the *Windham* had parted from them during the gale. But now, in the final week of 1809, the *Venus* was nearing home.

The storm spent itself before reaching Ile de France. Even so, Rowley knew a new hurricane season was upon him, and that he was taking a calculated risk. Since the Bourbon operation he had resumed the blockade, but by the end of December *Raisonnable* had been at sea for six months and Rowley was pushing his luck. If there was still no sign of Hamelin in a week or so he would, in all prudence, have to order the squadron back to the Cape.

The last day of 1809 was cloudy and hazy, with airs that stirred lightly overhead as *Raisonnable* stood about twelve miles to the north-west off Port Louis. In the mid-morning, provisions were being taken across to the *Leopard*, which may account for an apparently sluggish response to the sighting of a sail in the north-east; possibly Rowley was lulled by the presence in the vicinity of the frigates *Sirius* and *Boadicea*. The sail was spotted at 10.40 and it was past noon when, the log records, *Raisonnable*

> made all sail in chase. At 6 chase anchored in Black River. Shortened sail and Hove to.[12]

It was utterly galling. By the time *Raisonnable* was under way, the French frigate – though her identity was not known, her nationality soon become plain – had passed them to the north and was beating down the west coast. Six hours into a hopeless chase, Rowley had to watch as the *Venus* entered Black River Bay and anchored under the battery's shelter. Months of cruising had failed to prevent Hamelin's return.

Bad though this was, worse followed. Two days later, Rowley made his log entry between gritted teeth.

> At daylight saw six strange sail. Made all sail in chase. At 11 the chase got into Port Louis. At 11.10 saw them at anchor.[13]

This time the frigates were the *Manche* and *Bellone* and the four sail with them were prizes – such prizes, indeed, as altered the strategic balance at sea. The *Manche*, under Captain Dornal de Guy, had in tow the Indiamen *United Kingdom* and *Charlton*. They had passed without ill-effects through the storm that assailed Hamelin. The *Bellone*'s booty was even more impressive. Since escaping from Port Louis four months earlier, Captain Duperré had captured and burnt five merchant brigs in the Bay of Bengal, as well as taking the 18-gun sloop *Victor* and a large if ageing Portuguese frigate of 52 guns, the *Minerva*, soon to be renamed *Minerve*.

Rowley was furious with himself. Even Nelson had been known to make mistakes in blockading but Rowley suspected that he had been duped by an old trick – lured from Port Louis by Hamelin so that the prizes could slip in behind him. At the same time he viewed one member of his squadron even more severely. Captain John Hatley commanded the finest ship in the blockade, the frigate *Boadicea*, yet she had been ineffective in both chases. Nothing was to be done for now but to return to the Cape, leaving the French captains to their celebrations. But Rowley had resolved that when he came back, it would be with *Boadicea* as his flagship.

The arrival on the island of British civilians caused a stir at La Refuge. 'There are six ladies on the *Venus*,' Flinders wrote excitedly.[14] He was soon disappointed. Though the Indiamen passengers were taken to a nearby plantation on their way to Port Louis, he was not allowed to meet them. Since the incursion on Bourbon, he had been under virtual house arrest, and Ile de France in a state of near-paralysis.

Apart from dismay at finding the enemy at the gate, the inhabitants had been shocked by how easily resistance on Bourbon had been swept aside. Then there was the loss of the cargoes on which hopes for the economy had been resting, and the way that Bourbon's slaves had made common cause with the English. The implication was not lost on Decaen, who hastily demobilised his regiment of slaves.

The strain had taken a toll within Flinders's little circle. A six-year acquaintance with a neighbour named Chazal – who painted one of the few existing portraits of the explorer – never recovered from a furious row after the Frenchman 'reproached the English government with injustice and inhumanity in a most prejudiced manner'. Even in the invasion-charged air, however, his friendship with the worthy Pitot, among others, endured. Flinders liked women – fondly, innocently – none more so than his hostess Madame D'Arifat and her daughters. Superficially, time still seemed to pass amiably enough, between music, chess and instructing his young scholars – and an occasional windfall of the *Gentleman's Magazine*.

Still Flinders could not be reconciled to his exile – to these surroundings, no matter how alluring, or these friends, no matter how warm – while cut off from what gave his life meaning, the notion of duty. He still agonised over his inability to complete his mission, to present the Admiralty with details of his discoveries, especially as Nicolas Baudin, who had been with Hamelin in Australia, had recently published his work.

His other pain was private. He had been married to Anne for almost nine years now, of which they had spent just three months together. Yet still he addressed her with all the tenderness of fresh love. Replying in August to one of her letters – which had been three years in reaching him – he wrote:

> I continue to remain in the same friendly and estimable family of Madame D'Arifat, where I am treated as a son, except that they shew me more attention. How often have I ardently wished that thou my dearest friend and best love wast here with me in the midst of these worthy persons; like me thou wouldst find in them a mother, brothers, and sisters . . .
>
> Preserve then for me, my only love, thy heart, thy kind affection, thy health, for the happy, happy day when Providence shall place to suffer our reunion; and be fully assured that nothing can change the constant love and tender friendship, with which I am thine own. Mattw. Flinders.[15]

Perhaps the most remarkable aspect of Flinders's captivity is that he persisted in enduring it. The proximity of the English ships whose movements he noted from his eyrie, and the help offered by friends, would have made escape easy. During one particularly black spell of depression, in 1808, he had come so close to it that he wrote farewell letters. Why, then, did he not seize the chance? It always came back to honour. He had given his word as an officer to observe his parole.

Decaen was blind to his dilemma. Their dealings would always be marked by mutual incomprehension. The beleaguered Governor had become convinced that his captive had gathered intelligence of a kind crucial for an English invasion. Though Flinders never knew it, Decaen believed that in recent months he had 'several times managed to go out at night, had made soundings along the coast, and had transmitted information to Bengal'.[16]

In the months that followed, Decaen appears to have recognised that the game was up. The fire went out of him. Unpopular, his administration bankrupt and his despotic ways increasingly questioned, he saw that an invasion was almost certain and resigned himself to it. When Hamelin claimed the Indiamen cargoes as prizes for himself and his men – a presumption that in years past would have cost him dear – the old autocrat objected briefly, then backed down.

Hamelin had not actually distinguished himself much in the action. It had been De Guy's *Manche* rather than the *Venus* that stood out in capturing the Indiamen. Two other captains had proved their merits as well. In taking an English Navy sloop and a Portuguese frigate, Duperré of the *Bellone* had largely made up for the loss of the *Caroline*. He was promoted to Commodore of a new division that included *Victor* and *Minerve*. Pierre Bouvet, a former spy and corsair, had also shone on the brig *Entreprenant*. He was given *Minerve*.

At the same time Decaen demonstrated a rare generosity of spirit to Captain Stewart of the *Windham*. In recognition of their assistance in saving the *Venus*, Stewart and his crew were allowed to go to the Cape directly. There they were astonished and delighted to be restored to their ship. The *Windham* had not been lost in the storm, as feared, but recaptured by one of the blockading squadron.

Flinders had also perceived that an invasion was now only a matter of time. Of the mood at the India House, he remarked shrewdly: 'The taking of five Company's ships in so short a time may fix their wavering determination.'[17] In the meantime, he noted that Decaen had adopted desperate means to raise funds from the population:

> Mr Martin-Monchamp read an address to the inhabitants and an exposition of the extreme distress to which the government was reduced by the retaking of the Company's ships at Bourbon . . . Mr M said that he found much goodwill amongst the inhabitants but not much money . . . I recommended jokingly sending away all the English prisoners and me amongst them, as the first step to reform.[18]

In fact, Decaen had promised that if relief was not forthcoming from France within six months, he would resign. Detaining Flinders had lost its rationale.

The 28th of March 1810 was a rainy day at La Refuge. Flinders rose to begin his usual routine, lessons for the boys in astronomy and making notes on the magnetism of the Earth, when a rider cantered up to the homestead with a letter. Flinders read it, and then did so again. There was no mistake. Decaen had authorised 'my return to my country upon condition of not serving hostilely against France during the present war'.[19]

There followed a hectic few days. Letters of congratulation poured in from friends. Freed from restriction, Flinders went to Port Louis where he was embraced by supporters. A dinner was given in his honour to which the Indiamen passengers were invited and at which they made a tremendous fuss of him, in particular the worthy Mrs Scott from the *Windham*. Flinders was delighted at being able to converse with his countrymen again, even though the man who had come to the island unable to speak a word of French now had some difficulty in making himself understood in English. This somewhat dreamlike social whirl continued for a week or so, with the expectation that Flinders and the rest of the captives were about to be released into the *Harriet*, a cartel from Bengal. Flinders's journal poignantly captures the flavour of a heady moment in which notional enemies came together as friends.

Friday, April 6. Cloudy threatening weather. Went out in a great cavalcade of chaises, palanquins and horses to Chimere. Our party was numerous and some appropriate songs were sung, in one of which was a verse complimentary to the English whom friendship had brought there, and a wish that before a year the two nations might be united as we were at that time. It is my friend Thomy [Pitot] who is always the poet of the occasion. Dancing went on till two in the morning when we supped, and the dancing afterwards continued to daylight. Of my countrymen there were Messrs Hope and Hunter, Mrs Scott, and the two Miss McCargs: Their polite and complaisant conduct, as well as their talents, have done honour to our country among the French people. Much thunder and lightning during the day and night.[20]

Weeks passed. The blockade resumed, with Rowley now in *Boadicea*. On 7 May, Flinders was allowed to board the *Harriet*, but more weeks went by. Not until 13 June, the day that his sword was restored to him, did the *Harriet* sail and Flinders enter his freedom.

At the moment of departure he felt the paradox of his liberty: 'My heart is oppressed at the idea of quitting my friends here, perhaps forever.' And his farewell to Madame D'Arifat had a special tenderness: 'Adieu then, my dear lady and friend. May God of his infinite goodness bless and preserve you and yours. This is the fervent desire of your most affectionate, obliged and devoted friend and humble servant, Mattw Flinders.'[21] Six years, five months and twenty-six days since his first, all-too-blithe, sight of that shoreline, Flinders watched Port Louis fall away in the dying of the evening light.

The moment that he started to put all that behind him came the following day when, in full uniform again, Captain Matthew Flinders of His Majesty's Navy was piped on board HMS *Boadicea* and given three rousing huzzas. Rowley was there to welcome him and that evening they did him proud at dinner in the great cabin, joined by Colonel Keating and three captains of the blockading squadron. Over bumpers of claret Flinders learnt that the invasion of Bourbon was in hand. A force of 3,650 troops was approaching from Bengal.

The original intention had been that Flinders would go to Bengal himself. Instead, as the bearer of intelligence from behind enemy lines, he set off for the Cape that very night in the *Otter*. Decaen had not underestimated his potential for doing harm.

Capetown was in the midst of winter and it was foggy and wet on the afternoon of 14 July when Flinders pulled up at the admiral's residence in a chaise. Bertie greeted him gruffly and wasted little time in small talk about his captivity before getting down to business.

Flinders set to work, making notes about the islands, their military depositions and financial situation. He drew sketches of Port Louis, the town and the port, and of the north-west coast, including Black River Bay.[22] Perhaps the prime value of his intelligence, however, was on the question of morale. Ile de France, he reported, was ready to fall like ripe fruit. Decaen was utterly discredited. The military was unpaid and, in some cases, of suspect loyalty. Resistance was likely to be minimal and in all likelihood the civilian population would welcome the English as liberators. Only Hamelin's frigates stood in their way.

All this chimed favourably with preparations already in hand. For Flinders had arrived at the Cape to find his earlier judgement vindicated:

the taking of five Indiamen in so short a time had indeed 'fixed the wavering determination' of the Company. Not only was a force descending on Bourbon, but another was being mustered to invade Ile de France itself.

18

Christmas at the India House

London and Plymouth, 19 December 1809–24 June 1810

The winter that clutched the heart of England in 1809 was the harshest that anyone could remember, a hoary blanket that froze land and water, man and beast, and dispelled memories of the relatively mild seasons of the previous twenty years. It heralded the coldest decade in Britain since the 1690s. Jane Austen, living at Chawton Cottage in Hampshire, wrote that December of the dreadful cold: 'Everything seems to turn to snow this winter.'* In London, the Thames froze over, and a blazing fire set to keep the Hanoverian family warm at St James's Palace succeeded to the extent of burning down the King's private apartments.

But there was a particular iciness to the Arctic blast that blew down Leadenhall Street and chilled the self-proclaimed Grandest Society of Merchants in the Universe. The India House, the severely classical structure opened in 1800 and decorated with figures representing Commerce, Industry and Integrity, was, as a historian of the Company has written, often 'wholly self-deceived in the matter of its own prosperity';[1] and, that winter of 1809, the weakness of its financial underpinning became chillingly apparent. It had taken many months for the sequence of calamities at sea to be borne here by the winds. Now they came, like sorrows, not singly but in battalions, and the India House shook to its foundations.

In December, the Directors finally accepted that no further hope could be

* By a curious coincidence, Austen received a visit that month from Admiral Bertie's wife, who was hoping to see Frank Austen, a rising star in the Navy. It was not a success. Mrs Bertie, the novelist remarked sweetly, 'put up with us very kindly', adding: 'She lives in the Polygon, and was out when we returned her visit, which are *her* two virtues.' (Letter to Cassandra Austen, 9 December 1809.)

entertained for the survival of the missing seven ships of the First and Second fleets, and the Shipping Committee was directed to investigate the twin disasters. In the week before Christmas, a succession of carriages came clattering to a halt outside the India House and debouched bewigged gentlemen in blue jackets, buff waistcoats and breeches, cocked hats, swords, all topped off with black velvet capes. These grand figures then disappeared within, among the echoing corridors and statues of such Company heroes as Clive and Coote. The results were less impressive than the formalities. All seventeen surviving captains told their stories, and compelling stories they were; but their evidence amounted to no more than a description of the twin hurricanes. As to how similar disasters might be avoided in future, they had little to suggest other than steering well clear of Ile de France between November and March, which was not exactly a novel idea.[2]

Still believing that there was more to be learnt, the Directors opened another avenue of inquiry, this time into Indiaman design. Although the full range of their study is beyond the scope of this book, it focused on recommendations made in 1796 by the Company's master shipwright, Gabriel Snodgrass, for the introduction of a continuous upper deck. Snodgrass argued that a ship whose forecastle and quarterdeck were joined, and which therefore did not have a deep waist, became more proof against heavy seas because water that came on board would more readily drain off. On a deep-waisted ship, on the other hand, the water was taken in and became trapped below decks, inclining her more to founder or capsize. Snodgrass's simple logic had been incorporated into the latest Indiamen. Now his theories were examined again.*

What the inquiry did do was give the Company hard evidence about the dangers of pressing Indiamen crews, and this time the Admiralty had to face the issue squarely. The number of men who could be taken from a

---

* It was claimed by George Millett, a former Director who had once been a captain himself, that some of the flush-decked ships in the Second Fleet, such as *Northumberland*, *Euphrates* and *Sovereign*, had a very much easier time of it than waisted ships like the *Huddart*, which almost foundered. However, while it is true that some of the lost ships were deep-waisted and design may have been a factor in their foundering, the *Huddart*'s crisis was caused by other factors, and the *Sovereign* and *Northumberland* both shipped a great deal of water despite being flush-decked. Certain ships simply encountered worse weather than others, as their logs show. Summing up the debate, the maritime historian Northcote Parkinson concluded that the 1809 catastrophes probably hastened the transition to flush-decked ships but noted that these had faults of their own.

ship of 800 tons was reduced from fifteen to ten, and from one of less than 600 tons from ten to six. These numbers were to be strictly observed and certain ranks of men, such as carpenters and caulkers, were to be given absolute protection.[3] Admiral Drury, who had recently inveighed against the insolence of Indiamen captains, was implicitly rebuked.

Having just about come to terms with the hurricane losses, the Company learnt at Christmas of the captures of the *Streatham* and *Europe*, the two most richly laden Indiamen yet to sail for home. At that stage the Directors were spared the knowledge that three more ships had just been taken – the *Windham, United Kingdom* and *Charlton* – but even so the toll was unprecedented: eight ships destroyed (including the *Asia*) and two taken, all within six months. Four more had been lost in other incidents in the same period.*

The Directors returned from tables groaning with turkey, venison and steamed puddings to Leadenhall Street, and a diet of more wretched tidings. A meeting on 16 January was presented with the grimmest commercial report in living memory, an outpouring of fear, bafflement and outrage:

> We fear we must conclude that 12 of our ships have been lost by the visitations of Providence and 2 have been captured by the enemy, a series of losses which the most cautious foresight could not have considered within the bounds of probability, an unexampled accumulation of sorrow to Families and a destruction of property to the value of £2 million in ships and goods.[4]

This amount, some £120 million at present-day values, may even have been on the low side.† For the Company, at a precarious stage, it was crippling. The report went on: 'The losses will cause derangement of our finances at home as we had estimated that the sale proceeds of these

---

* They were the *Travers*, wrecked in the Andaman Islands on 7 November 1808; the *Britannia* and *Admiral Gardner*, which went aground on the Goodwin Sands, 14 January 1809; and the *True Briton*, 'parted Company in the China Sea and not heard of again' on 13 October 1809.

† According to the commercial report, the purchase cost of the silk was £282,000, that of the lost and ruined saltpetre £393,000, or more than £40 million at current worth. The discrepancy between the £675,000 cost of the goods and the £2m lost to the Company is down to the value that their sale would have realised, and the cost of replacing the lost ships.

cargoes would assist us in the discharge of the Bills of Exchange which have been drawn upon us to such an unexampled amount in the last year.'5

Even that was not the end of it. News of the Madras Army's troubles had been causing concern for months and enough was known of General Macdowall's mischief-making for the Directors to have wholeheartedly endorsed Sir George Barlow's dismissal of him for 'conduct highly reprehensible and having a distinct tendency to encourage a spirit of discontent & insubordination'.6 Though Macdowall was dead, just before Christmas reports reached London that showed the poisonous effect of his legacy. Several garrisons had started to march on Fort St George, threatening to overthrow Barlow.

As the New Year dawned, bleak and bitter, a terrible new story started to circulate. Sufficiently credible to be believed by Charles Grant, the chairman of Directors, this was to the effect that the Army had taken Barlow out and shot him.7

As a Company history records, 'India stock rapidly fell, and the Directors took fright.'8

The White Mutiny has lingered long in the background of this story. It created a great stir at the time and cost many innocent lives. If it is not dealt with in any great detail here that is because it fell short of the worst expectations. What had put the fear of God into administrators and shareholders was the shock of finding that white officers would be so oblivious to their responsibilities that they would hold the country to ransom. Minto thought that 'greater perils have, perhaps, never threatened the possessions of the Honourable Company or the British Empire in India'.9 In the end, there was no enemy at hand, French or otherwise, to exploit an incendiary situation. And the Army pulled back from the brink just in time, leaving everyone, including the officers themselves, shocked and mystified as to quite what had happened.

Macdowall, it will be recalled, had sailed for home in January. Matters rumbled on until May, when Barlow suspended a clique of senior officers who were demanding his dismissal. On 21 July, six regimental commanders wrote to him, demanding a pardon for all suspended officers and an amnesty for acts of insubordination. Around the same time, reports reached Madras that three northern garrisons had mustered 30,000 men near Secunderabad to march on Fort St George. It was these reports that created the shock waves felt at the Cape in October and London in December.

This crisis in the north was resolved by a solitary officer, Colonel Barry Close, a figure of great renown in the Indian Army, who confronted the mutinous white officers by riding among sepoys on the parade ground, declaring that he represented the Company *Bahadur*, or ruler, and expected them to be faithful to their salt. The officers considered firing on him, but could not nerve themselves to it and in the face of this masterful sangfroid they quailed.

A second crisis, involving garrisons in the west, came to a head on 10 August when, in a lethally confused situation, sepoy regiments advancing towards Seringapatam on the orders of their mutinous European officers were intercepted by King's dragoons. The officers fled while their men were cut to pieces. Up to 400 sepoys died. The stain of this episode – at the site of the Madras Army's most famous victory, against Tipu Sultan of Mysore in 1799 – was compounded by the officers' cowardice. For all their blood-curdling threats and avowals of honour, when the smoke cleared there was just one white fatality – a lieutenant who died of fatigue. The massacre did, however, shock the officer corps out of their madness. On 23 August the last of them surrendered.

There followed a ritual purification, a series of courts martial of the twenty-one most culpable officers, who might well have been taken out and shot but instead were cashiered. In all but five cases, they were later restored with no discernible injury to their careers. (One became a Director of the Company.) The ghastly prospect of a civil war within the Company's territories in India had passed.[10]

Barlow, whose almost childlike naivety in matters concerning his wife was combined with a flinty resolve in political affairs, had handled the crisis with aplomb. A loyal officer wrote: 'He neither assumed any boastful air, nor showed any despondency; but with that firm, modest tone which true courage always inspires, he determined on making no concessions nor taking any particular precautions for his personal safety.'[11] One relieved Madras resident said that had the mutineers known Barlow was 'so great a man, they would never have put him to the trial', before adding prophetically: 'Gentlemen in Europe will not be able to appreciate his

conduct properly because none but we who were here know the difficulties
he had to contend with.'[12]

So it proved. Lord Minto arrived from Calcutta on 11 September to take
charge, having decided that the Army and Barlow were irreconcilable.
Seeing which way the wind was blowing, Barlow sent for Captain Robert
Eastwick, a respected seafarer in the country trade. As Eastwick put it,
Barlow was 'very anxious to send his despatches home so that he might
receive the credit of the affair. He offered us 5,000 pagodas* to take them.'[13]
The problem was that Minto wanted to make his own impression on the
Directors and put pressure on the owner of Eastwick's ship to take his
report rather than Barlow's. It was received at Leadenhall Street early in the
New Year, and the subsequent celebrations dispelled some of the winter
chill. One official remarked that 'during the many years he had been at the
India House, no despatches had ever been so anxiously awaited, nor, when
read, given such unqualified satisfaction'.[14] By the time Barlow's report
arrived it was old news. Minto had established himself, rather than Barlow,
as the Company's saviour in Madras. It may not be stretching a point to
suggest that from this point, Barlow's career was doomed.

There was no single defining point, no moment of decision at which the
might of Britain – the Navy, the Army and the Company with all its resources
– was mobilised against the Ile de France. The catalogue of disasters had
stirred a new warlike spirit at the India House and Whitehall was in
agreement that something must be done; but the momentum lay elsewhere,
in India and at the Cape, and the pace of correspondence between there and
London made coordinated decision-making impossible.

The key decision, taken in London during the summer, had been to
explore whether the French islands were 'likely to surrender to HM
Arms'. From that point it became a matter of commanders on the spot
taking the initiative. The ease with which British forces landed on
Rodrigues and Bourbon had demonstrated the weakness of French
military defences. What was required now was someone with the
authority of a proconsul and the bottom of an aristocrat to take the
decisive step. For all his virtues, Barlow would never have dared had he

* The pagoda was the coinage of the Madras presidency, worth about eight shillings.

still been Governor-General. This was where Lord Minto justified his appointment. While London shivered and at last resolved on invasion, Minto had set the process in train.

Early in 1810 he wrote to the Cape, stating that the islands 'shall be taken possession of in HM name & on behalf of the British Crown', and applying to Sir Henry Grey, the military commander, for troops, and Bertie for naval support.[15] To his wife he confided that he was taking action because the blockade had failed and because of the Company's severe losses. The raid on Bourbon, 'an enterprise which was conducted and executed in a very masterly manner', showed the way forward. On the recommendation of Rowley and Keating, 2,000 men had been mustered at Madras and would soon set sail to occupy Bourbon.

> A second expedition must be sent against the Isle of France, and a much larger force: including those going now, about 10,000 men . . . It will probably depart from India in August.[16]

The force would consist of HM and Company forces, drawn from garrisons around India and the Cape, and be transported in a huge fleet of Indiamen and smaller ships.

That same month, the Company, having reached its own point of resolution, mustered a ten-strong fleet of Indiamen at Plymouth. They included six survivors of the previous season's hurricanes – *Ceylon*, *William Pitt*, *Northumberland*, *Huddart*, *Euphrates* and *Tigris* – and were to sail for India with orders for Minto. This time they would carry neither silk nor saltpetre, but soldiers to mount an invasion.

The fleet sailed on 15 March, escorted by HMS *Africaine*, a 40-gun frigate, under Captain Richard Raggett; but they had got only as far as Palma when she was directed to return. The Admiralty had decided she was to have a new commander.

Captain Robert Corbet spent much of that cruel winter in his room at Blake's Hotel in Jermyn Street, wrapped in a cloak and grieving for his former life and the *Bourbonnaise*.

She had come home like a bird on the wing, covering the more than 8,000 nautical miles from Capetown to Plymouth within sixty days. No sooner would a stranger be sighted than *Bourbonnaise* went off in pursuit. These strange sail invariably turned out to be friendly, as Corbet was no doubt aware all along; it is as if he was simply pleasuring himself in exercising this flyer of a ship, testing how much he could get out of her. He had gone back to some of his old ways since quitting Rowley's command, having had seventeen men flogged over the two months at sea. This was not notably harsh by most standards, however, let alone his own.[17]

Of his presence in England that year there is no record apart from a few terse notes in his spidery hand to the Admiralty, one complaining of the 'considerable expense' he had incurred in being forced to bring the *Bourbonnaise* home and requesting reimbursement. Corbet's family history is as much a mystery as everything else about the man; he was married body and soul to the Navy and, even were his parents alive, it is hard to imagine him making a pilgrimage to the family home in Wexford. He kicked his heels, hanging around the Admiralty. His 'plum' had been sent away for overhaul.

Corbet was still under a cloud. In the autumn the Admiralty had fired its broadside deploring 'the manifest want of management, good order and discipline' on *Nereide* and he knew he might not be given another command. Who or how an intercession was made on his behalf is not known. But the Indiamen had been at sea for a week when it was pointed out that the only navy officer to have landed troops on a French island in the Indian Ocean, who had won praise from Bertie and Rowley, and who was the acknowledged specialist in those waters, was in London. And so a packet was sent after them to Palma, recalling HMS *Africaine*. Captain Raggett was to be superseded.[18]

Corbet's orders were to follow the Indiamen to Madras. Once they had taken on forces for the invasion, he was to escort them to the Ile de France, and 'from his intimate acquaintance with the locality, superintend the debarkation of Troops'.[19]

His reputation was enough to trigger unrest even before he came on board. The *Africaine* was at anchor in Plymouth when her crew made grim discovery of their new commander's identity. None had served under him before but during a visit between ships in port, an old *Nereide* seaman reportedly told them that Corbet 'had conducted himself in [his] former ships in a very oppressive and tyrannical manner'.[20] The purser wrote with foreboding on 21 June: 'A most violent prejudice has arisen in the minds of the ship's company against the appointment of Capt Corbet.'[21]

Mutiny on the *Africaine*, as on the *Nereide*, was preceded by a round robin, petitioning for Captain Raggett to be restored and stating that the men would 'go cheerfully anywhere in the world with him and even accept a cut in pay' if only they could be spared service under Corbet. While there was no question of this being granted, the Admiralty saw that the matter required tactful handling. Corbet was kept in the background while three senior officers went on board to parley with the crew on 22 June. Rear-Admiral Sir Edward Buller and Captains Thomas Wolley and George Cockburn were standing on the quarterdeck when the hands were ordered aft. What charge, they were asked, did they have to prefer against their new captain? No one answered, but there were cries of 'No Corbet!'

> They were then mustered by the open list and individually the same question was put, all answering in the negative but still raising the cry of 'No Corbet!' It was explained how certain they were of being seriously punished . . . that everything would be overlooked if they received their captain without disaffection; and that any well-founded complaint would be attended to.[22]

The frigate *Menelaus* was ready to send Marines across to seize the lot of them when the crew at last declared their 'readiness to receive Captain Corbet and to do their duty'.[23] In the afternoon Corbet came on board and they were turned up to hear him read his commission. As he stepped forward, the cries of 'No Corbet!' went up again. The purser, John Tapson, watched with alarm. 'This capricious and now downright mutinous conduct was no longer to be borne,' he wrote.[24]

The situation was saved by Captain Cockburn who collared one of the dissenters, a fellow named Elliot, put him in a barge, then

> walked forward and by a firm but conciliatory address to some of the best seamen, pointing out the irrevocable fate of their shipmate being conveyed by the barge should they persist in their conduct. He induced them to promise, if Elliot was restored to the ship, that they would return to their duty. The barge was recalled, the prisoner liberated and the captain's commission read.[25]

Corbet was not exactly emollient but nor was he overweening, and in the circumstances his words were not ill chosen. Addressing his new crew for the first time, he said:

> You perhaps expect I should promise not to use the cats. If you do not do your duty I will flog you well. I suspect you are a set of cowards, afraid of a brave man commanding you. Depend upon it, I will avail myself of the first opportunity of enabling you to vindicate yourselves from this suspicion by shoving you under the enemy's fire.[26]

Corbet recognised the resonance with the *Nereide* mutiny. When they sailed on 24 June, the Marines stayed aft, defending the captain's quarters, and at the ready.

There is no definitive source for events on HMS *Africaine* over the next three months – which may help to explain how what might be called the Corbet mythology later flourished as it did. Crucially, the log was lost, so there is no means to test the two eyewitness accounts. One, by Jenkin Jones, a master's mate, was written years later as part of a campaign to salvage Corbet's reputation and, being partisan, has to be treated with caution. The other, Purser Tapson's private journal, is dispassionate and fair-minded, but silent on some points.*

Both agree that the first month at sea passed in a state of tension. The hands ignored the usual rituals while crossing the Equator on 21 July, which Tapson put down to 'a pretty strong symptom of the continued sullenness and sulkiness of the Crew, who made no application whatever for permission to enjoy the fun so generally indulged in'.

Matters came to a head over a Marine given thirty-six lashes for drunkenness. On being cut down he used 'highly insubordinate language', for which Corbet had him clapped in irons, intending to submit him to a court martial once in port. A few days later a letter was thrown in at the quarter gallery window, threatening that if Corbet did not 'relax in

---

* In addition, there is Captain Basil Hall's anecdotal account in his *Fragments of Voyages & Travels* series, based on navy gossip and therefore interesting as to how the Corbet myths evolved but, as Hall conceded on being confronted in print by Jones, factually flawed.

the severity of his discipline, his life would be forfeited'.[27] He opted immediately for a test of strength.

After ordering the officers to buckle on side arms and the Marines to load their muskets, Corbet

> read the letter to the ship's company, telling them that not-withstanding this threat it was his fixed determination to be a great deal more severe than he had ever been, and in order that they might not think this an idle threat, he intended to give the mutinous Marine 8 dozen Lashes, which was more than double the number he had yet inflicted on any man since he had assumed command – that if it was their intention to prevent it by opposing their force to his authority, now was the moment to try, by rescuing the Prisoner. He assured them he did not doubt the issue of it. With the Officers and Marines he would 'pitch them overboard like a flock of sheep'.[28]

Several petty officers now approached Corbet, declaring that the men knew nothing of the threat. A suspect was dragged forward and when the letter was found to resemble examples of his handwriting, 'the poor wretch appeared as much frightened as if the nooze [sic] was already round his neck.' But Corbet – perhaps sensing the moment ripe for an act of mercy – pronounced the evidence insufficient to identify the fellow as the writer, and dismissed him with a ringing admonition: 'I shall take the trouble of reading to you, Sir, the last speech of the chief mutineer in the *Temeraire*. I would advise you to think upon it, lest you find yourself one day in his position!'[29]

Turning to the crew again, Corbet warned that 'call him Tyrant or what they pleased', he would not be intimidated. The Marine was then seized up, the relevant Article of War read, and the bosun handed out 8 dozen lashes. Each of the 96 blows sent its own signal to the watching men. As Tapson remarked:

> If the People had before this entertained any doubts of the Nerve and determined character of their Captain, they must no doubt have been undeceived.[30]

For some days his guard stayed up. Marines remained under arms and the gunroom officer kept a brace of pistols by his cot, exercising especial vigilance at the change of the watch at midnight and 4 a.m. Gradually, 'caution relaxed and confidence in the orderly conduct of the crew was restored'. Routine, the seaman's friend, asserted itself and the hands 'cheerfully and smartly performed their duty'.

Corbet was clear in his own mind that he was sailing towards the defining moment of his life. With his career rescued from ignominy, he walked with sure-footed certainty. The young master's mate, Jenkin Jones, observed him closely over the weeks that he drove *Africaine* south towards the Cape. Jones, who would go on to become a captain himself, was an uncritical admirer of Corbet. 'Habitual alacrity was certainly indispensable in all who served under his command,' he wrote; but rather than brute cruelty, it seemed to him that Corbet's method involved 'constant attention to minute arrangements, a proper devotion to duty' and rigorous order. By the time *Africaine* rounded the Cape, on 19 August, the ship was in a state of efficiency and her crew were seemingly reconciled with their commander.

Another three weeks brought them to Rodrigues. Here Corbet met his destiny.

Reports had just reached the island of a cataclysmic battle between English and French frigates. Although details were sketchy and confused, what he heard was sufficient for Corbet to tear up his commission. He would not, after all, follow the Indiamen to Madras. He would, instead, in Jones's words, 'do what no ordinary-minded man would have dared to do – namely, deviate from the orders given to him by the Admiralty by bearing up for Ile de France'.[31]

19

The Battle of Grand Port

The Cape and Ile de France, 21 May–29 August 1810

Thousands of miles ahead of the *Africaine*, the ten-strong Indiaman fleet was approaching the Cape on 21 May. Nothing much had changed since the last time these ships sailed together and there were the usual grumbles about the old *Huddart* which was found 'a considerable detention to the fleet'.[1] The *Hugh Inglis* had suffered an outbreak of smallpox and was under quarantine. Otherwise their run down the Atlantic had been free of incident and the *Ceylon*'s roundhouse passengers, Mr and Mrs Welland, congratulated themselves on their progress. Having left their Wimpole Street house in February, they had reached the halfway mark of their journey back to Patna, where Abraham Welland was a judge.[2]

Off Simon's Bay the fleet divided. Six ships that were collecting troops in India carried on.* Those taking on soldiers at the Cape – the *Ceylon*, the *William Pitt*, the *Euphrates* and the *Astell* – came in to anchor. Passengers set off in coaches for Capetown, and found it in a state of high excitement.

Reports had been received that the invasion of Bourbon was under way. In the meantime, the 24th and 33rd Regiments were to board the Indiamen and would proceed to Madras where a huge fleet – some sixty sail – was being gathered to bring 10,000 troops halfway back across the ocean to Ile de France. All this had to be done before the new hurricane season in December. Even today, as a strategy of military projection, it is impressive. At the time it was breathtaking, and Capetown was thrilled to be involved. A feast of patriotic fervour came to a climax with a ball enlivened by pretty Dutch girls to mark the King's birthday, and a service

---

* They were the *Hugh Inglis*, *Huddart*, *Northumberland*, and *Tigris* (bound for Madras and Bengal) and the *Sir Stephen Lushington* and *Alexander* (Bombay).

279

at St George's Cathedral that sent the soldiers on their way with an hour-long sermon on the evils of drink.3

Just before they sailed disturbing intelligence reached Bertie: yet another heavy frigate, the *Astree*, had joined Hamelin's squadron, and Robert Surcouf was feared to be returning in a new ship.4 Bertie briefed the Indiamen captains, adding that Duperré's *Bellone* had been last sighted eight days' sail north of Ile de France. His admonition that they should 'keep a high southern latitude', in other words well to the south of both islands, came with added emphasis: he could not spare them a navy escort.

As the Wellands reboarded *Ceylon* their attention would have been drawn to another Indiaman at anchor near by. She epitomised all the dangers that lay ahead. In recent months the *Windham* had been captured by the French *and* caught in a hurricane in the very waters into which they were about to venture. Having been retaken by one of the blockading squadron, brought to the Cape and restored to Captain Stewart, the *Windham* was also bound for Madras. She was among five Indiamen carrying troops that sailed from Simon's Bay on 13 June.

The bad weather started that afternoon, a heavy sea from the south with squalls and low visibility. Water swirled across decks, pouring through hatches on men wallowing in misery and vomit. Conditions below were atrocious, even by the wretched norms of Indiamen. *Ceylon* and *William Pitt*, which would normally have carried up to 150 troops, had almost double that number, plus camp followers (20 women and children) and seamen. On each ship, 450 souls were spread over two areas of deck roughly seventy feet by thirty-five feet. Between them, the five Indiamen had 1,300 military passengers, each with a living area of a little over ten square feet.

Later that day they were still battling towards the eastern end of Simon's Bay (or False Bay as it is now known) when darkness fell and the *Euphrates* struck a rock at Cape Hangklip. Soon she was 'taking upwards of 2ft in the hour, all pumps at work'. Had not the *William Pitt* sighted her distress signal and stood by through the night, she might have foundered. As it was, the *Pitt* escorted her to safety in calmer conditions.5 But the voyage had started ominously; and the five Indiamen were already reduced to three.

The *Ceylon*, *Windham* and *Astell* ran up the coast into more bad weather off Natal where a wind shift to the south-west brought a gale. *Ceylon*'s captain, Henry Meriton, a renowned mariner, knew this coast and how many ships it had destroyed.* 'A very heavy sea made us labour greatly,' he wrote. 'Some seas were really dangerous and I judged it prudent to bear away for the Mozambique Channel.'6 It was a difficult decision because it ran counter to Bertie's advice and would take them into the French cruising latitudes, but as they bore north the skies cleared. For two weeks, the Wellands and other passengers forgot their anxieties about storms and enemy frigates as they hissed between Africa and Madagascar, in pleasure, under an awning on the quarterdeck,

> with all the sails set that the masts can carry, the sea as blue as blue can be, pretty little clouds, the motion smooth, the flying fish following the ship, leaping and darting in and out of the water, the never-to-be-forgotten sunsets – all the calm beauty, the elegance of form and colour which nature is full of.7

This idyll ended as the ships emerged from the channel and neared the island of Mayotte on 3 July. Three strange sail were sighted, 'astern on the starboard tack coming up very fast'. Two frigates and a corvette, they hoisted English colours. Meriton was not fooled. 'I made signal to my consorts to haul our wind on the starboard tack, to prepare for action & that the strangers were enemies.'8 They were indeed – *Bellone*, *Minerve*, and *Victor* – and under such a press of sail that they swelled almost perceptibly in the glasses of the officers watching them come on. Meriton did a rapid calculation, then telegraphed his colleagues. Escape was impossible and he thought it best to 'bring on the action before the day was spent'.

If anyone was up to the challenge it was Henry Meriton. Born on the Thames at Rotherhithe, he was a tough, taciturn man who had spent all but ten of his forty-eight years at sea and had featured in two notable episodes in the Company's maritime history. In 1786, he was among the few to have escaped from the wreck of the *Halsewell* off the Devon coast and wrote a best-selling account of it. More to the point, he was the only

---

* The coast of south-east Africa has been a shipping graveyard since the time of the Portuguese navigators. The wrecks of the *Dodington* (1755) and the *Grosvenor* (1782) had made it notorious among Indiamen captains.

Indiaman captain who could boast of capturing a French man-of-war. In the 1,200-ton *Exeter*, he chased down the *Médée*, a 36-gun frigate, in 1800 – to the chagrin of her captain, who could not believe that his conqueror was a merchantman. Like Dale of the *Streatham*, Meriton was held in high enough regard to be entrusted with command of a fleet in the absence of a navy escort.

At least he now had the services of another real fighter. On the *Windham*, Captain Stewart shook his head in disbelief at having encountered French frigates for a second time, then began to consider how best to resist. To Meriton's signal, he replied: 'If we make all sail and get into smooth water under the land, we can engage to more advantage.'9

The Indiamen presented a warlike face, their guns rolled out and decks bristling with musket-bearing soldiers. But the days when the mere appearance of an English ship could frighten the French into submission were past and the Indiamen's 12- and 18-pounders were hopelessly outmatched by *Minerve*'s 32-pounders and *Bellone*'s 42-pound carronades. Meriton's report of the action survives:

At 2pm the first frigate [*Minerve*] came up on our weather quarter & hove to just out of gunshot. We formed a close line ahead – *Windham* in the van, *Astell* rear. The frigate came up abreast, fired one shot which struck the *Windham* & directly fired her broadsides which struck the *Ceylon*, when the contest commenced & a heavy and well directed fire was kept up by all our three ships. The frigate fired at us alternately and the corvette [*Victor*] fired principally at the *Ceylon*, and in the first hour very much disabled us in our masts, sails, rigging. Action was continued with great spirit on both sides for the first two hours, frequently within musket range.

At 4pm the frigate shot forward & to windward, as if to board the *Windham*, observing which the *Ceylon* and *Astell* closed to support her. The discharge of musquetry from our three ships was so severe that the enemy could not load their guns and she fell astern.

At half past four her main and mizzen topmasts went overboard close by the Cap, but before we could reap the advantage the other frigate [*Bellone*] came up on our lee quarter and opened up a tremendous fire of grape. The wind by this time having abated & the swell much fallen, almost every shot did execution. *Ceylon* had become quite unmanageable, every brace, bowline, halyard being shot away. Our sails were entirely useless, being cut to pieces.[10]

The Indiamen crews had been encouraging one another, exchanging three cheers each time they passed.[11] But the firestorm from *Bellone* settled matters. Meriton was severely wounded in the throat by grape and the chief officer had scarcely taken command before he too was hit. At 7.20 p.m., *Ceylon*'s colours were struck by the senior officer standing.

With Meriton out of action, Stewart tried to get Captain Hay of the *Astell* to join him in boarding *Bellone*, but Hay had also been wounded and his chief mate saw an opportunity to escape. As the *Astell* extinguished her lights, Stewart realised what was afoot and renewed his fire, keeping it up long enough for her to slip away, before trying to follow in the dark. It was not to be. *Windham*'s rigging was too far gone for another epic chase.

The French were far from unscathed, having lost sixty dead and wounded, mainly on *Minerve*, an unprecedented toll from an action with merchantmen. Among the ninety-six Indiamen casualties, Meriton survived and went on to praise 'the zealous and honourable support given by my consorts'. The Directors were impressed enough to pay each captain £500 and generously reward the men.[12] The unpalatable fact was, though, that two more Indiamen had been taken, *Windham* for the second time, and 600 troops lost to the invasion.

That same day, 3 July 1810, almost 1,500 miles to the south-east, Commodore Rowley sailed from Rodrigues with a fleet for Bourbon. This time they were coming to stay.

Rowley, in his flagship, *Boadicea*, had a squadron of four other frigates: the *Sirius* under Samuel Pym; *Iphigenia*, Henry Lambert; *Nereide* under Willoughby; and a recent addition, the *Magicienne* commanded by Lucius Curtis. They were escorting fourteen transports carrying 3,650 troops under Colonel Keating. On 7 July the force landed at six points around Bourbon, meeting even less resistance than anticipated, so that within forty-eight hours the island had surrendered and Robert Farquhar was installed as Governor.

It may well be that, had Keating and his forces sailed directly for Ile de France, he would have taken that as well, thereby saving the Navy much discomfort and humiliation. However, events were dictated by the pace of communication, each development requiring transmission to Minto in Calcutta. Keating's orders were to secure Bourbon and await the 10,000-strong force mustering in India. Whatever Flinders had said about the island's readiness to surrender, the planners were taking no chances.

Rowley stayed at Bourbon. His decision later drew criticism in some quarters, but his reasons were sound: Bourbon had replaced Rodrigues as the platform for invasion and he needed to be near Farquhar and Keating. There was no reason to suppose that the French frigates were any readier for battle now than they had ever been. But perhaps he ought to have considered the combustible mix of personalities going to Ile de France.

The senior captain was Pym of the *Sirius* who, to judge from his record in the Indian Ocean, was an unimpressive, possibly incompetent, commander. Pym certainly had his hands full with one of his subordinates – for though Willoughby's courage was the stuff of legend, it was never far from bravado; while Rowley had managed to keep him in check, he could be a commander's nightmare. Willoughby had previously clashed with Corbet and now tried to overawe Pym. It is only fair to add that he had become a thoroughly intimidating figure, as much for his appearance as his reputation, having recently suffered a disfiguring wound when a musket blew up in his face, exposing his windpipe. His life lay in the balance for days, and when he rose again, his men – who now regarded the lean, pale, dyspeptic figure with something like wonderment – began calling him 'the Immortal'.

Rowley's orders were for *Iphigenia* and *Magicienne* to return to Port Louis while *Sirius* and *Nereide* sailed to Grand Port, at the southern end of Ile de France. English strategists had long seen this as the best site for an invasion and Pym was to establish a foothold here.

Seen today, Grand Port is one of the loveliest spots on the island – the ruins of the old Dutch town set against a backdrop of mossy mountains, hunched along the skyline like crouching green lions, the waters lapping placidly around a bay of sparkling turquoise. For mariners its pleasing appearance is deceptive, however. Beneath the glittering surface lie random shoals of coral at depths of between ten and twenty feet; and the reason that the bay is so clear, so calm, becomes apparent when one looks out to the white-creaming reefs that guard the entrance. About four miles offshore lies the Ile de la Passe, a shard of land a few hundred yards long which, in 1810, was topped by a little fort and a battery of 24-pounders.

This was the objective that Pym and Willoughby approached on 13 August. *Nereide* had been left some miles behind and, when *Sirius* reached the Ile de la Passe soon after nightfall, Pym sent in five boats with seventy men who took the battery and seized the French signal codes before they could be destroyed. Willoughby, who had come to regard land operations as his province, was furious – 'an unfair proceeding', one of his officers called it.[13]

After an icy exchange Pym sailed to join the Port Louis blockade, leaving the firebrand in charge of Ile de la Passe and of fomenting agitation on the mainland. In commando-style fashion, Willoughby launched an incursion at the head of 170 troops, and ranged unresisted up the east coast, distributing propaganda leaflets signed by Governor Farquhar that related the fall of Bourbon and gave warning of the impending invasion.

> Inhabitants, we are ready to land on your coasts with a formidable force by sea and land. To what purpose would you make a sacrifice by opposing the troops of His Britannic Majesty who only desires to take you under His gracious and royal protection! . . . Our Government is generous, it rewards the cultivator and the workman, as well as the sailor and the soldier. The French pay in paper and bills of exchange, and we pay in Spanish coin.[14]

Willoughby was still ashore when, on 20 August, a French squadron was sighted on the horizon, making for Grand Port. He had to make a hard five-hour pull in the gig to get back to *Nereide* in time to organise a warm reception for them.

On the approach to Grand Port, Mr and Mrs Welland took an evening turn on *Ceylon*'s quarterdeck. Though captives, the personages of the roundhouse had been impeccably treated by the officer in charge, a Lieutenant Moulac, and retained their cabin and privileges. It was 15 August, the anniversary of Bonaparte's coronation: the Emperor's health had been drunk, guns fired, and *Minerve* sailed round the fleet with a band blaring out tunes on the poop. National prejudices had been set aside, for the music was provided by the band of the 24th Regiment and Mrs Welland was quite taken with the spectacle laid on by the enemy: 'All the ships had their colours hoisted and altogether displayed a most Triumphant scene.'[15]

Mrs Welland was one of those formidable ladies of early Empire, imperious, obstinate and utterly certain of her opinions. Mr Welland was not short of opinions himself – he had not hesitated to give Captain Meriton, no less, the benefit of his insights into navigation, as well as some 'rules and instructions' for fighting an Indiaman. But it was his spouse who loomed the larger of the two. In a later age Mrs Welland would have been called a battleaxe. In her own she may be likened to Mrs Bennet, with bile.

Though flattered by Moulac's chivalry – '*so* attentive,' she thought – Mrs Welland became most indignant at dinner when he spoke confidently of reaching Ile de France without being molested by English ships. Was this not proof, she demanded to know, 'that our Frigates, which are supposed to be completely Blockading the Place, must be extremely neglectful?'

In fact, it was precisely to avoid them that Duperré was taking his prizes to Grand Port, where the English rarely cruised. On 20 August it came into view – the bay and mountains lying at the end of a channel, the white line of reefs at its entrance and the fort on Ile de la Passe.

The first thing to arouse suspicions was the sight of a strange ship at anchor. Mrs Welland recalled:

> We remained in a state of anxiety for some time, not knowing whether it was English or French. We were ordered down to the Bread room, and most of the Gentlemen with us, where we remained an hour, when we were sent word we might come up, for the ship had shewd French colours and had answered all the signals. So we ascended out of this vile hole.

The coded signal from Ile de la Passe was: 'L'ennemi cruise au Coin de Mire' ('The enemy is cruising off the Coin de Mire' – or Gunner's Quoin as it was known by the British).[16] Satisfied, Duperré lined up his squadron in triumphant show to enter port – *Victor* and *Minerve*, followed by the prizes *Ceylon* and *Windham*, then *Bellone*.

Mrs Welland and her husband had returned to their cabin and were at a gallery window, 'amusing ourselves looking at the land and ships', when there came a roar of guns and, as Mrs Welland noted crossly, '*Balls* fell into the sea a short distance from us'. Turning to the judge, she remarked: 'There is surely some mistake, for they never would fire Balls in a salute for the Commodore.'

At that moment a fellow passenger, Robert Saunders, entered looking apprehensive. 'I hope I am not alarming you unnecessarily,' he said, 'but I think you'd better go back to the bread room.'

Willoughby had them at his mercy. Deceived by the coded signals and oblivious to their peril, the French were passing under the guns of the Ile de la Passe at about 1 p.m. when the Tricolour came down, the Union flag was hoisted, and he gave orders to open fire.

As balls dropped around the leading ship *Victor*, her captain panicked and struck his colours. Just then disaster struck at the Ile de la Passe. In the switching of colours a flag caught fire, fell on a cartridge box and set off an explosion that disabled five guns. Cannon fire continued to come from *Nereide* but it was ill-directed. In the confusion, Captain Bouvet in *Minerve* ordered *Victor* to rehoist her colours and they sailed into Grand Port, followed by *Ceylon* and *Bellone*. One ship bore away – *Windham*. Duperré's squadron had escaped unscathed.

Under a flag of truce, Willoughby demanded that *Victor* be surrendered to him under the laws of war, to which Duperré replied: 'If he wants my corvette, he can come and take her.' Privately, he was less self-assured, telling Bouvet that as more English frigates were bound to descend on Grand Port, they ought perhaps to destroy their ships to prevent them falling into enemy hands. Bouvet was made of sterner stuff replying:

> You have your frigate from the Emperor. I have received mine from the Captain-General [Decaen] and will set it on fire only if he orders it. I doubt that you have the right to dispose of your frigate without permission. Write to the General.[17]

A report was sent across the island to Port Louis where Decaen ordered

Hamelin to sail south immediately with the *Venus*, *Manche* and the new frigate *Astree*, then set off himself on horseback for Grand Port to put fire into Duperré's belly. He arrived just before dawn on 22 August and went on board the *Bellone* to relate that Hamelin was on his way.

In the meantime, Mrs Welland had emerged from her third sojourn in the *Ceylon*'s bread room to learn that an English invasion was thought to be imminent. Fearful civilian captives were pleading to be sent ashore and even Mrs Welland was subdued when she summoned the gallant Moulac. 'He came looking jaded and uncomfortable. I said I would depend upon his telling me whether we ran any risk of our other Frigates coming round and having an action in the night, for *that*, I thought, was more than I could just now bear. On his honour he assured me it was impossible.'[18]

Early in the morning of 23 August, the Wellands were set down on a pebble beach milling with French soldiers, and had some possessions pilfered before two cavalry officers took them in hand 'with the elegant manners and all the ceremony of the most polished courtiers'. Brought to a chateau, Mrs Welland was horrified to find that they would have to share a room with two other couples and a lieutenant-colonel of the 24th. The gentlemen slept on the floor but the beds, infested with fleas, were just as uncomfortable.

That afternoon cannon fire was heard from the bay. It continued with unremitting violence into the night. Battle had been joined at Grand Port.

Willoughby had sent a boat telling Pym that the French were bottled up in Grand Port, and boasting, quite unwarrantedly, of having 'touched the frigates up in style'.[19] Pym hastened down the coast, having ordered the *Iphigenia* and *Magicienne* to follow.

An incident en route, trivial in itself, is revealing of Pym's insecurity. At Black River Bay, they sighted the *Windham* which was recaptured by one of *Sirius*'s lieutenants without a shot being fired. Pym – who had an unedifying tendency to claim the credit for his officers' actions – reported this little affair in epic terms. 'I have this moment recaptured the *Windham* from under the batteries at Black River and altho they kept up a very heavy fire I am happy to say our damage is very trifling.'[20]

Even had it not been for their earlier quarrel, Pym's lack of self-assurance and Willoughby's arrogance made them ill-suited partners in an attack. The tone was set as *Sirius* joined *Nereide* off Ile de la Passe on 22 August. Willoughby sent the signals: 'Ready for action' and 'Enemy of inferior force'.[21] With a foe twice their strength, lying in wait among coral reefs, this was little short of lunacy. In an atmosphere heavy with braggadocio, Pym was being goaded.

Not to be outdone for boldness, Pym stated later: 'I saw the enemy's position and judged I could make an easy conquest by an immediate attack.'[22]

He went briefly on board *Nereide* and again there was a locking of horns. Willoughby, having volunteered to lead the way in, was now determined on it as a matter of honour. Pym was equally insistent on precedence, and he was in charge. But only one individual on either ship knew the treacherous waters of Grand Port – a black 'pilot' on *Nereide*, a local man recruited by Willoughby and dubbed John Johnson. Willoughby refused to give him up, instead sending across *Nereide*'s master William Lesby to pilot the *Sirius* – although, as Lesby and Willoughby both later admitted, he 'had very little knowledge' of the reefs.[23]

Late in the afternoon, as the two frigates advanced down the channel and just ten minutes before they would have gone into action, the *Sirius* hit a shoal – or, as Pym put it plaintively, '[Lesby] run me on the inner point of the narrow passage'. To this misfortune Pym attributed everything that followed. He averred that had he been able to get *Sirius* alongside *Bellone* 'all the Enemy's ships would have been in our possession in less than half an hour', and he blamed Willoughby for what he called 'the loss of Glory'.[24] He may have been right.

Even so, things could have been a good deal worse. *Sirius* was hauled off overnight and at 10 a.m. of a calm, dazzlingly bright day, *Iphigenia* and *Magicienne* were seen beating up the channel. With two more 36-gun frigates, Pym now had better than parity with the foe. His strategy was to take all four ships into Grand Port, bringing them to within pistol-shot – 'as close as possible without laying on board' – and wither the enemy with their fire. Pym himself would deal with the main threat, the *Bellone*. Willoughby was to divide his fire between *Bellone* and the sloop *Victor*. Lambert in *Iphigenia* would drop alongside the other French frigate,

Minerve. Curtis in *Magicienne* would join in raking her and deal with the Indiaman *Ceylon*.

Before sailing, there was a conference on the *Nereide* at which Lambert and Curtis consulted the black pilot, Johnson. They claimed later that he gave them to understand that they could steer directly to their appointed stations 'without fear of grounding'. Nevertheless, the *Sirius*'s brush with the reefs the previous day ought to have indicated caution.

They were all to follow in *Nereide*'s wake. Pym had, 'with some difficulty', agreed to go in after Willoughby.[25]

At 4 p.m. on 23 August they weighed. The men had been fed and given their ration of grog and now, with a slick orderliness amid the bawling from loudhailers, they eased themselves along the yards, unfurled the sails and then, with that unnerving mix of jaunty optimism and flinty bloodlust that defined Nelson's Navy, went to their battle stations. Hammocks were stowed in netting along the upper decks to absorb shot. Below, galley fires had been extinguished. In the cockpit, surgeons laid out their saws and tourniquets. Under full sail, the four frigates pushed down the channel towards Grand Port in single file.

One Frenchman watched admiringly how the English ships came on 'so graceful, so well handled and so audacious'.[26] For all their menace, there was something lyrical about the scene, four sail arched against a tropical evening sky in a place of luminous beauty.

The French ships were anchored in a crescent, broadside on, behind a reef from which warning buoys had been removed and which lurked below like an invisible but deadly barricade. The *Bellone*, according to Bouvet, 'occupied an excellent position, protected by the highest peak of a patch of reefs over which there were only twelve to sixteen feet of water'.[27] The *Minerve*, *Ceylon* and *Victor* lay on either side of her.

Directed by the pilot, *Nereide* passed up the channel. But at the crucial moment Pym could not bring himself to run in after Willoughby and steered out of his wake, as if to pass. This time his error was fatal. Going at four knots, *Sirius* struck on a reef known to the French as Grand Banc Sud. 'She thumped a little and then lay still,' the carpenter recalled.[28] She was still ten cables, about 2,000 yards, from the French anchorage, and out of range.

The evening sun was directly in the eyes of the advancing English and, glittering off the sea, obscured any discoloration from the reefs lurking just below the surface. This was *Magicienne*'s downfall. She was scything along when she too went aground. Curtis managed to warp her stern a little, but she then became stuck fast, still 500 yards distant from the enemy.

Lambert in *Iphigenia* negotiated the shallows and came alongside the *Minerve*. He had just got off their third broadside, however, when the cable holding her at anchor was blasted away and she drifted off behind *Nereide*, her line of fire obscured.

That left only the *Nereide* – the tragic, doomed *Nereide*.

Whatever blame was due to him for bringing about this fiasco, Willoughby never flinched from his responsibility. He directed the helmsman to the place forfeited by Pym, alongside *Bellone*, and bestrode the quarterdeck – a gaunt figure, tall and distinctive in blue gold-buttoned coat and cockaded hat, chatting imperturbably to young John Burn, his first lieutenant. Burn had distinguished himself in every action in which they had been involved. 'My gallant Burn,' Willoughby called him, and that was high praise. Another bond had been forged between captain and crew. He was not the paternalistic sort of commander who encouraged and cajoled his men. He flogged, barked and glowered. But, as he later made clear, he thought the *Nereide*'s crew were to be trusted; and they trusted him, if only because he seemed indestructible – 'the Immortal'.

Nereide dropped a cable's length away from *Bellone*, about 200 yards, and soon after 5 p.m. the guns began to roar in a series of thunderous cannonades – twenty-six 12-pounders against forty-four 18-pounders. Each ship was enfolded in billowing clouds of smoke that rose and blotted out the land and sky, so that soon there was only the bucking of cannons and blood-running decks.

It would be suggested later that *Nereide* was betrayed by poor gunnery, a legacy of Corbet's command. This was untrue. The gunners' aim was good and both the *Victor* and *Bellone* were cruelly hit. Their cables were cut, as were those holding *Minerve*, and all three drifted on to shoals. Duperré was wounded and Bouvet left his ship to command the *Bellone*, taking some of his men and additional armaments.[29]

But the crucial moment occurred when a rope holding *Nereide* at anchor was shot away and she swung round, bow on to *Bellone*'s broadside. From 6 p.m., in the dying light, *Nereide* was repeatedly raked by balls that passed up her length, smashing through bulkheads, scattering bodies and guns.

There is no shortage of description of the effects on the human body of an 18-pound cannonball. Men were likely to be torn in two or dismembered by a direct hit. The scything motion of chain-shot or bar-shot – usually directed at masts and rigging – had an even more pulverising effect. Langrage and grape made not so gross a dispersal of human tissue but, like shotgun pellets, spread out over a wider area and hit more targets. By far the majority of wounds, however, were inflicted by wooden splinters. A ball striking, say, the quarterdeck rail, reproduced the effect of a grenade, releasing a hailstorm of lethal wooden shards like shrapnel.

None of this quite explains what occurred on the *Nereide* – the type and level of casualties, or the rate at which they occurred. The most probable factor was the repair of her superstructure after the hurricane when, because no oak was available, large sections were replaced with fir.[30] Whereas seasoned oak could, to a limited extent, absorb shot, the fir of *Nereide*'s bulwarks simply exploded, multiplying the shrapnel effect.

From holding her own, broadside-to-broadside, *Nereide* had come head on to the enemy. She had lost the use of her main guns and was turned in a minute from a man-of-war into a charnel house. The balls that raked her below left some discernibly human bodies screaming among remains that smeared the ship's sides or lay distorted in slicks of their own blood. Smoke and nightfall quickly closed in to blot out the scenes; the screams went on.

More deadly still was the quarterdeck, where Willoughby and his officers stood defiantly exposed, upright as statues, directing the men through loadhailers while fragments of metal and wood swept over, around and through them. Willoughby was the first to fall, caught in the head by a splinter that gouged his left eye from its socket. He was carried from the quarterdeck just after 6 p.m. No sooner had Lieutenant Burn taken command than he fell, mortally wounded. Lieutenant Henry Deacon stepped forward – and promptly fell too with twenty-two separate wounds. Others lying dead or wounded on the quarterdeck included the master, Lesby, and the bosun, John Strong.

All this happened so fast that William Weiss, an acting lieutenant standing on the forecastle, did not realise that he was the last officer left standing until being told that Willoughby wanted to see him. Weiss, who had not been in action before and watched in shock as the perfect order around him was turned into a shambles of upturned guns and collapsed rigging, found Willoughby in the master's cabin, head swathed in a bloody cloth.

> He desired me to tell him the state of the ship. I told him the quarterdeck and forecastle guns were rendered useless by being dismounted and most of the men belonging to them killed or wounded. The ship being between the enemy and *Iphigenia*, we were receiving the fire of both.[31]

The surgeon, a gory figure who had just disposed of Willoughby's eye, entered and said that men were being brought below very fast and that if the ship was not moved there would soon be no one left standing. *Nereide* had been in action for about an hour.

Willoughby told Weiss to cut the springs – cables holding her at anchor – so she might drift out of her deadly exposure. This was done by about 8 p.m. and had the effect of moving her on slightly. Still *Bellone*'s guns blazed at her out of the night.

Next Willoughby sent Weiss in a boat across to *Sirius*, requesting support.

Pym had watched mortified as his attack disintegrated. *Sirius* could not be budged, nor could *Magicienne*. That left the *Iphigenia*, but when Pym sent a message for her to go to *Nereide*'s help, Lambert had to reply, 'It is not possible to warp towards her in consequence of a shoal between us.' Pym, his hands tied, sent Weiss back to Willoughby with orders that he should 'abandon *Nereide* and come on board *Sirius*'. This invitation to escape the inferno was treated with disdain. Willoughby replied to Pym that

> he could not leave his ship while any of the officers and men were left on board but would thank him to send boats to take out the wounded as soon as he could.[32]

No more help came. The *Nereide* drifted until her stern became caught on a reef and there she wallowed, her hull holed like a skin with pox, masts shot away, superstructure shattered. A handful of men stood by the guns, insufficient in number to fire them but – conditioned to having every action ordained – unwilling to quit their posts. On being told of this, Willoughby was moved by 'the effect on a ship's company, the whole of the principal officers being killed or wounded', and he sent to say that anyone still able to walk or drag themselves should go below and shelter in the ship's bowels.[33] On the upper decks only bodies were left. *Nereide*'s guns had long been silent. At 10.30, Willoughby ordered the colours to be struck.

In the dark, however, the French had no way of knowing this. Once more Weiss set off in the boat, to inform *Bellone* that 'we had struck, being entirely silenced and a dreadful carnage on board'. The boat was soon hit and, in danger of sinking, he turned back. When the French did cease firing, shortly before midnight, it was more a response to collective exhaustion than an act of mercy.

The *Nereide* was left in total darkness. Squalls blew up in the night, and from the upper decks came a rhythmic creaking and a flapping of shredded canvas as well as the cries and laments of the wounded.

The scene at daylight of 24 August was recorded by a French officer:

The calm of the morning allowed the rise and fall of tide to carry to and fro, around our ships, the bodies of hundreds of victims broken by death.[34]

The French were not unscathed. 'Our ships lay riddled, their bloodstained decks covered with debris,' he went on. 'Our crews, wild-eyed and half-naked, seemed utterly exhausted and were well-nigh unrecognisable with wounds and powder. On the other hand the English frigates, so audacious the day before, were lying there in far worse condition than ours.'

Even now Bouvet on the *Bellone* remained unaware of *Nereide*'s surrender and when, soon after daylight, a Union flag was seen fluttering from her mizzen – it had been nailed there – the bombardment resumed. At length someone on *Nereide* noticed the flag and the mast was felled. Only then did *Bellone* cease firing.

The French lieutenant sent on board said he found *Nereide* 'in a state impossible to describe'.[35] But a midshipman named Wantsloeben did his best:

We had to take great care not to stumble over the dead, dying and wounded, who were often covered by the scattered limbs of their poor shipmates. On reaching the afterpart of this floating tomb, we perceived an object covered with the Union Jack. M Roussin lifted it carefully and, to our great surprise and admiration, found Captain Willoughby, seriously wounded in the cheek and more or less unconscious. M Roussin spoke to him but he did not reply. The expression of this brave English captain, meeting mine, seemed to be pensively appraising the purity of his patriotism in having selected the national flag as a suitable death shroud.*

We went down to the battery where the same scene met our eyes. More men dead or dying; guns dismantled and their carriages broken; planking stove in; gun ports destroyed. On reaching the middle of the ship, or cockpit, we saw numbers of wounded men, prostrated by their cruel sufferings and being cared for by the doctors. Further off, near the mizzen step, some forty men, the most senior of whom was a midshipman, were sitting huddled together, their heads buried in their arms. They said that since the previous day, they had called out that their ship had surrendered, that all their officers including their commander were killed or wounded, but that each time the men making the attempt had been killed by our gunfire and that, as they had no longer the least hope of defence, they had sought refuge where we found them.[36]

Willoughby would take a terrible pride in asserting that *Nereide* 'lost as great a number of officers and men as ever were lost in a British frigate'.[37] Of the 281 men on board when she went into action, no fewer than 230 were casualties. Among the 92 dead were a number of Corbet's old scapegoats, including William Williams, a Thames man, and John Watkins, from Greenock, both of whom had joined her in 1806 and been lashed from Rio to the Cape and Bombay and then back. Another, William Wiggins, the fifty-three-year-old American who had testified against Corbet at his court martial, clung to life for four weeks before dying. A number of good Irish Catholics had also fallen for England, including Thomas Hussey, Joseph Dodd and Patrick Hodgkins.[38]

Nereide was named after a mythological figure, a nymph or mermaid – a

---

* Wantsloeben's observation was somewhat premature. Willoughby was to live for another forty years.

creature of ambiguous elements: seductress, fatal lover, a siren who lured men to their deaths. The allusion was hauntingly apt. A ship – like the men who commanded her, and to just as enduring effect – acquired a reputation for her disposition; not just her sailing abilities, but that indefinable accretion of myth and folklore among an intensely superstitious fraternity that imbued her, as a living creature, with human characteristics.

About thirty men had endured all that had befallen *Nereide* these past years, among them James Burns, captain of the maintop, and able-bodieds like Thomas Kirk and William Morris, who would in due course return home to be paid off with sums typically of around £21 11s 7d.[39]

How they recalled their old ship if they ever met again in a tavern, we can only imagine. That her shadow followed them to their graves there can be little doubt. But she and they had suffered together for the last time. A total wreck, the *Nereide* never sailed again.

The *Nereide* had acquired a certain grisly glory in defeat. For the other three English frigates the Battle of Grand Port brought little besides embarrassment or shame.

During *Nereide*'s death throes Pym sweated blood to free *Sirius*. He was not wanting in energy, but rather in coolness and sense, and his next error was perhaps the most serious. Around dawn, a lieutenant came across from *Iphigenia* and told him that Captain Lambert proposed to board and carry the *Bellone*. This, he argued, was a last opportunity to turn defeat into victory, if only Pym would send all available men to assist him. *Bellone*, *Minerve* and *Victor* had all gone aground and were, briefly, vulnerable.

Pym refused and forbade Lambert to attack. Instead, he was ordered to warp out *Iphigenia* from the battle zone and help to get *Sirius* off.[40] From this point the squadron was doomed. Because of the squalls blowing against him, it took Lambert all day and into the evening to warp *Iphigenia* into position, no doubt cursing his superior every yard of the way. The chance for a counter-attack had passed.

From *Bellone*, Bouvet sent a message to Decaen: '*Nereide* is ours. If I receive an anchor of 1,000lb and cordage, the three others will suffer the same fate. Vive L'Empereur!'[41] His rejoicing was premature. Whether or not his request was honoured, *Bellone* also remained aground for the time being, enabling Pym to deny Bouvet his prizes.

The *Sirius*, it became clear, was not to be moved. As an officer observed dolefully: 'She never budged an inch again.' *Magicienne* could not be shifted either. About 500 yards from the French ships, she had been able to deploy only five guns and, since *Nereide* fell silent, she had become their sole target. Captain Curtis reported to Pym that 'his men were falling very fast and that she was filling abaft'. Although casualties were, in fact, quite light compared with *Nereide*, the position was hopeless. Pym recalled: 'I gave him an order to abandon *Magicienne* during the night and burn her in the morning, but from Captain Curtis again representing that his ship was filling and the useless loss of his men, I allowed him to put the order in force that night.'[42]

An odd sense of propriety persisted to the last. Pym's order read: 'You will set His Majesty's Ship *Magicienne* on fire with her colours flying.' The crew put off in boats for *Iphigenia*. At 7 p.m., *Magicienne* was set ablaze and that night blew up with spectacular effect.

Sirius was next. Pym waited until the *Iphigenia* had warped into place, then 'sent my crew on board & Lt Watling and myself set fire to the ship'. The *Sirius* disappeared in a blazing flash and clouds of smoke at 11 a.m. on 25 August.

Not until the next day could Pym bring himself to start his report to Rowley, a strangled cry of misery – 'sorry I am to say that the captain every officer & man on board *Nereide* are killed or wounded . . . two more ships destroyed to prevent them falling into enemy hands . . . I have given up the command to Captain Lambert' – that concluded: 'P.S. I feel too much distress on this occasion to go into particulars.'[43]

Squalls were still blowing the following morning when *Boadicea*, approaching from Bourbon, sighted a boat on the weather beam and hove to for an officer to come aboard and pour out his story. Rowley's dispassionate note records the disaster in almost prosaic terms:

> The officer of the boat informed us of the loss of the *Sirius*, *Magicienne* & *Nereide* in Action with the Enemy, the two former having struck upon rocks not known.
> Fresh breezes & dark cloudy weather.[44]

Sixty miles to the east, at Ile de la Passe, the final blow was descending.

Iphigenia had finally warped down the channel to the island and, while the little battery remained in English hands, it was fair to assume that the French still in Grand Port would not hazard an immediate attack. At daylight on 27 August, however, three ships appeared in the south – the *Venus*, the *Manche* and *Astree*. It had taken Hamelin six days to tack down from Port Louis against contrary winds. Lambert tried to negotiate a strategic withdrawal, offering to give up the Ile de la Passe 'to stop the effusion of blood' if *Iphigenia* was allowed to depart, but Hamelin was having none of it.

Rowley came within sight of Ile de la Passe on 29 August and had signalled *Iphigenia* – unaware that she was in French hands – to ascertain how matters stood when Hamelin's frigates appeared to windward, making the answer all too obvious. Realising that he was in possession of the last English frigate in these seas, Rowley – displaying a common sense that had deserted his captains – 'thought it prudent to tack off', as he put it in reporting these calamities to Bertie. *Boadicea* was chased all the way back to Bourbon.

Set against the great actions of the age, the Battle of Grand Port might have been passed off as an ugly but small-scale setback in a distant theatre. It did not involve great fleets, like Copenhagen, the Nile or Trafalgar. Nor did it change the course of history. Even so, it created no end of a rumpus at the time.

No more comprehensive defeat can be imagined. It was, in truth, more of a debacle. Rowley's five frigates had at a stroke been reduced to one. Four captains were captured and the Commodore had been forced to flee. More than 2,000 seamen were dead, wounded or taken. Symbolically, it was hugely significant – the only French naval victory of the Napoleonic wars, which made it not so much a defeat as an apparent violation of the natural order. Moreover, with one exception, English ships had failed to put up their usual fight. There was an uncomfortable disparity between the toll on *Nereide* and the losses on the other frigates: *Magicienne* had eight dead and thirty-two wounded; *Iphigenia* five dead and twelve wounded; the *Sirius* had no casualties at all. Writing decades later, the Francophobe historian William James was still grumbling: 'No case of which we are aware more deeply affects the character of the British Navy than the defeat it sustained at Grand Port.'[45]

On the French side, Grand Port entered legend. It was inscribed on the Arc de Triomphe. It inspired canvases of shattered enemy ships and a rash of verse, including some doggerel declaimed to an attentive audience in Port Louis a few weeks later.

There was indeed cause for rejoicing. Total French losses were 36 dead

Brave Duperré, va poursuivi	Duperré, Victor, thee we hail,
Ta carriere intrepide	And mark thy brave career!
Contre toi que peut Willoughby	E'en Willoughby could not avail
Que peut sa Nereide.	Nor Nereide's might strike fear!
Deja Decaen entendu ton cri	There Decaen goes! He shall not
Et sous l'arrain qui tonne	fail
Il rira, volera	To reach the battle zone,
Combattra	And help to win the day,
Pour l'honneur et Bellone.	Whilst we will pray
	For Honour and Bellone.[46]

and 112 wounded, most of them on the *Bellone*, including Duperré, hit in the face by grapeshot. Capture of the *Iphigenia* brought the number of French frigates to six, against Rowley's one. Decaen had been offered a glimmer of hope.

Severely wounded, Willoughby was carried to Maison Robillard, a chateau lying at the end of a palm-tree-lined drive which had been turned into a holding centre for prisoners and a makeshift hospital. He was laid in a bed beside Duperré and the two recovering foes exchanged handshakes and talked over their battle.

Mrs Welland was less sympathetic. On being told that Willoughby had nailed his colours to the mast, she remarked witheringly: 'I wish this nonsense had saved his ship.' She and the others had heard news of the English defeat with undisguised incredulity. 'Our Gentlemen could not believe that we were not successful.' What made it worse was that they had to hear this dreadful intelligence related by Frenchmen.

Civilian prisoners were soon sent off on palanquins twenty miles across the island to Port Louis. Having recovered from the shock of being left 'at the mercy of Caffrey Bearers' who fed her wild raspberries, Mrs Welland remained there some weeks, sorely testing local hospitality with her waspish verdicts on everything from the food: 'the most uncongenial kind of mixture, olives, a raw Artichoak or Prawns'; to the customs: 'the Revolutionary style of Matrimony has been adopted here, and the Women [are] by no means correct'.

The Wellands were still at Port Louis when news came of the sighting of a strange English ship. She was a frigate, *Africaine*, but it was her captain's name that struck a chord here and moved one French captain to declare that he would willingly give up all the captured ships if only this threat could be removed. Even Decaen was dismayed, dashing off a despatch to the War Ministry in Paris about the unexpected return of

Captain Corbet, the soul of all the destructive attacks made upon our two islands. [47]

Corbet had heard at Rodrigues of the disaster at Grand Port and turned back to Ile de France.

20

'For shame, hoist the Colours again!'

Bourbon, 12–13 September 1810

Dawn came up on 12 September with a prospect that might have come to Robert Corbet in his dreams. After three months at sea, the scent of land, of earth, trees and vegetation, hung on the warm morning as he looked out from *Africaine*'s quarterdeck on Bourbon and the neat port of St Denis, bustling with military activity. This was his country's newest possession, a conquest in which he had played no small part. What made Corbet's pulse race, however, his eye gleam, were two ships in the distant offing. They were frigates and they could only be French.

Nineteen days had passed since the Battle of Grand Port, and a week since Corbet got wind of it at Rodrigues. What he needed first was a briefing on how matters stood. Before hastening ashore he ordered Lieutenant Joseph Tullidge to make *Africaine* ready for battle.

Governor Farquhar almost collapsed with relief at seeing him. The plans conceived for invasion had been founded on British naval power. Now the French were masters of these waters and the hurricane season was just weeks away. Far from British ships besieging Ile de France, the French were blockading Bourbon. Rowley in *Boadicea* was bottled up at St Paul, fifteen miles to the west, by the two frigates espied by Corbet – *Astree* and *Iphigénie* (the captured *Iphigenia*). As for Hamelin's other frigates, Farquhar said, heaven only knew where they were or what mischief they might be up to, but they could appear on the scene at any time. Thank God, he might have added, that Corbet had turned back at Rodrigues.

A message was transmitted to Rowley. Help was at hand and *Boadicea* should rendezvous with Corbet at Pointe des Galets, a headland roughly midway between their respective anchorages, so they might 'make sail simultaneously in pursuit of the Enemy'.[1]

From his return to *Africaine* that day, Corbet's actions suggest a man transfigured. Everything had, at last, fallen into place, presenting an opportunity of a kind that came to few officers. That he would seize it, he had no doubt; for if one thing stands out about Corbet at this time it is the assurance with which he acted. Lesser men were bound by lesser horizons. He was, so far as he was concerned, one of Nelson's true disciples – a visionary commander, ruthless and bold – and fate and his own judgement had coincided to produce the moment in which he would prove it.

Almost as much as glory, he sought vindication. Much had changed at the Admiralty, where the methods that made him something of a throwback to an earlier, more brutal age, had all but destroyed his career. What others thought of as cruelty, he saw as efficiency. Now that his moment had come, he was convinced that he would be vindicated. Another navy captain, Basil Hall, who became fascinated by Corbet and wrote a study of him, commented:

> It was well known that the most earnest desire of his heart was to fall in with an enemy of equal or even superior force in order that he might prove how efficient his [disciplinary] plan really was. He hoped to furnish a triumphant practical answer to his brother officers who often advised him to adopt a less rigid system.[2]

Was there another figure in the background of Corbet's visions? Was he haunted by his bitter rival, Willoughby, whose zeal on Corbet's old ship was already being spoken of in hushed tones? Zeal. That was the essence of it all for Corbet. Great navy officers were a blend of qualities. In *Men of Honour*, his fine study of Trafalgar and the making of the English hero, Adam Nicolson defined these as Zeal, Honour, Boldness and Love. The word that recurs through Corbet's career is zeal. There was something of the Old Testament in him. Nicolson cites an extract from William Blake's prophetic text, *The Marriage of Heaven and Hell*, as a summary of Nelson's method in battle, but the words also resonate with Corbet's whole career. They might have served as his epitaph:

Energy is eternal delight.
Prudence is a rich, ugly old maid courted by Incapacity.
The tygers of wrath are wiser than the horses of instruction.
Without contraries is no progression.
The road of excess leads to the palace of wisdom.
He who desires but acts not, breeds pestilence.
The wrath of the lion is the wisdom of God.[3]

Nicolson has noted in passing Corbet's similarity to the Nelsonian ideal – his daring, his extremeness, his ruthlessness, his courage – and yet his distance from it. Here his surviving letters to Nelson are illustrative. Two years before Trafalgar, when Corbet was captaining the sloop *Bittern* in the Mediterranean, he questioned one of the great man's orders (it was admittedly ambiguous) and provoked his wrath. Corbet was mortified, the monster of the quarterdeck reduced to a bleating boy: he had sought clarification only 'in order to guide my weak judgment', he wrote. 'No impertinent or inquisitive request to Your Lordship's letter was ever thought of by me.' Nelson's disapproval, he concluded, 'cannot fail to remain a source of the utmost uneasiness to Your Lordship's Most Faithful & Most Devoted, Humble Servant'.[4]

Nelson forgave the transgressor. He noted his zeal, praised his action against the privateer *Hirondelle* with those words that imprinted themselves on Corbet's soul – 'Your conduct and perseverance merit my entire approbation' – and granted him leave for treatment of the rheumatism that was his cross. When Corbet left the Mediterranean in mid-1805, missing Trafalgar by five months, he wrote thanking Nelson for his constant consideration, signing himself 'With the Truest Gratitude and Respect'. He could see greatness of spirit, but not emulate it. What Corbet had always lacked, and always would, was his hero's gift of humanity. The glaring paradox of this man who worshipped Nelson was that he remained quite oblivious to what made him so great a commander, his ability to give and inspire love.

Early in the afternoon of 12 September, Corbet returned to *Africaine*. The French frigates had drawn off, allowing further breathing space. He made all sail towards them, at the same time raising the Commodore's pendant in *Africaine* – a ruse intended to convince them that she was the *Boadicea* and disguise the fact that there were now two British frigates in the offing. By all accounts *Africaine* had been cleared for action 'with alacrity and spirit' and there is every reason to believe that, contrary to much subsequent naval legend, her crew went forth with eagerness to battle.[5]

At around 4 p.m. *Africaine* was approaching from the east as *Boadicea*, converging from the west, rounded Pointe des Galets. The French, lying to the north, had seen them before they sighted each other and were running to the north-east. For the first time since Grand Port, Rowley could see he had parity or better with the foe: as well as *Africaine*, he was followed by the sloop, *Otter*, and the brig, *Staunch*. Bouvet, who had emerged as the best fighting captain on the French side, had taken over the *Iphigénie* and besides two frigates had just the brig *Entreprenant*. He also had one other card up his sleeve, however. *Iphigénie* mounted heavy 18-pound French cannons, moved into her from *Bellone*.[6]

Corbet estimated that the French were seven or eight miles ahead. Under topgallants and with a wind fresh from the east, the sweet-sailing *Africaine* was gaining on them. The *Boadicea*, on the other hand, having set out from a westerly direction, was struggling head on to the wind and falling behind. From early evening, Corbet had the testing task of staying up with the enemy and at the same time retaining contact with *Boadicea*.

Hours more in the chase lay ahead when he announced that there would be no evening grog. 'It shall not be said that we wanted Dutch courage to thrash these Frenchmen,' he said. 'Strike the spirits into the hold.' There was apparently no demur and Corbet then 'hailed the decks to let the men sit down between the guns, tell long yarns and appoint agents for their prize money'. The master's mate Jones paints an image of the scene which, while idealised, may be allowable.

> A merrier night I have seldom passed than that – between the guns, surrounded by a brave, humorous, contented and confiding crew. The pencils of such men as Marryat would have found ample materials from what was narrated in Jack's best style on the *Africaine*'s main deck on that occasion. They all knew and showed they knew that a better seaman or more skilful and brave officer than Corbet was not to be found.[7]

306

The *Africaine* closed rapidly. She was a beautiful sailer, scything along at nine knots close-hauled, and although *Astree* and *Iphigénie* had topgallants and staysails set, she had them within range well before midnight. According to Tapson, 'as it was not Capt Corbet's intention or wish to strike the first blow until *Boadicea* should be in a position to support us, he shortened sail, and continued to increase or diminish the canvas as occasion required'.[8] A gun was fired and a blue light burned every half hour to indicate their position to Rowley.

But Rowley – six miles in the rear and still hindered by the easterly wind – was having difficulty staying in touch. A squall had blown up and through a dark, rainswept night, he could make out little, as an entry in *Boadicea*'s log indicates: '6.20 lost sight of the chase. 6.30 lost sight of *Otter* and *Staunch*. At 7 saw a flash NE. Burnt a blue light. 8.15 saw a flash. At 9 saw 2 flashes. At midnight squally with rain at times.'[9]

The crucial moment came after midnight.

At 2am very light winds. At 3 observed *Africaine* commence action. 3.30 observed a very heavy firing from 3 ships in close action.[10]

Those very light airs had settled matters. Rowley was becalmed. Corbet, throwing caution to the wind, had seized his moment.

Accounts of that night added a final layer to the dark mythology attaching to Corbet's name. For decades afterwards stories would circulate with the decanter at navy dinners and captains' tables, acquiring resonance and momentum until they started to make their way into print. All this came to a head some thirty years later when Jenkin Jones, by then a captain himself, published a pamphlet intended to silence some of the uglier tales and vindicate his hero. Still the myths endured. To some extent they still do.* Jones's missionary fervour – 'I feel proud to have served under Captain Corbet; his memory will ever be sacred to me' – means that his evidence is not always reliable. The best and coolest source for these events is the little-known journal of John Tapson.

* Patrick O'Brian's treatment of the Corbet legend in *Mauritius Command* may even have given a new lease of life to it.

By midnight it became clear that the *Africaine* was on her own. 'A heavy squall came on,' Tapson wrote,

> and so black and thick was it that we lost sight of the Enemy. After it had cleared away it was found that they had availed themselves of it to bear up and run before the wind. Our helm was of course put up to close with them. At 2.30am they again suddenly hauled to the wind, which brought us within half Musquets shot of the nearest ship's weather quarter (*Astree*).[11]

Corbet's heart beat with a savage joy. 'It is said that he deemed himself at this critical moment of his fate the most fortunate of men to possess such an opportunity for distinction,' a fellow captain wrote. 'He exclaimed in the greatest rapture: "We shall take them both! Steer right for them! And now my brave lads, stand to your guns and show them what you are made of!" '[12] Jones presents him as a more measured figure, shouting through a loudhailer: 'Fire your guns as you bring them to bear. Take cool aim and do not throw a shot away.'[13]

The opening broadside was fired at about 2.20 a.m., as *Africaine* came up on *Astree*'s weather quarter at musket range. Flames in the dark illuminated briefly the apple-cheeked hulls of the two ships and the ghostly shadows of canvas.

Less than ten minutes into the action – the *Astree* had just fired her second broadside – the *Africaine*'s quarterdeck was hit. A flash, a thud, and Corbet lay in the flickering light of a lantern, a widening pool of blood pumping from his right leg. Men ran to his side bearing more lanterns.

First reports had it that he had been shot from behind by one of the crew. This story gained sufficient credibility for it to be repeated in the standard histories of the day, albeit with caveats. It will not bear much scrutiny. Corbet's principal wound was caused by a ball from *Astree* which took off his right foot, 'a little above the ancle [sic]'.[14] At the same moment, a chunk of the gunwale through which the ball had just passed came spinning through the air, smashing his right femur in a number of places.

Corbet was borne away, passing his command to Lieutenant Tullidge, a courageous officer but one in awe of his hypercritical captain. It was generally agreed that the prudent course now would have been to drop astern and await Rowley in *Boadicea*. According to Tapson:

Such would have been done by [Tullidge] had he felt himself at liberty to act to the dictates of his own judgment – but Capt Corbet had, on being carried off the quarterdeck, given him positive orders to 'stick to them and give it to them'. Tullidge considered that if he did not obey in the most strict manner Capt Corbet would be very apt to impute it to a wilful disobedience, or (which was infinitely worse to a gallant heart like his) a too-great regard for his personal safety.[15]

Meanwhile the *Astree* had set her mainsail 'to shoot ahead out of our fire', at which the *Africaine*'s crew set up a cheer. (This spawned another myth – that the crew had cheered to see their captain carried away wounded.) As soon became apparent, it was a forlorn triumph.

Tullidge made sail to go alongside *Iphigénie*. Had he pursued *Astree*, she might have struck while *Iphigénie* was still off to leeward and unable to manoeuvre into a firing position. Instead, *Africaine* came broadside on to *Iphigénie* while *Astree* was placed in a raking point across her bows. The French directed grape and langrage at her masts and rigging where they wrought havoc, so that by the time Tullidge tried to slide away from the fire 'it was found impossible to move a single yard, every brace and bowline having been shot away'. At the same time the wind had dropped. Tapson recorded:

No hope therefore now remained of being succoured by *Boadicea*, and no alternative but to hammer away at an Enemy double our own numerical force and, from the relative superiority of their position at least 4 times that force – for only the two bow chasers on the forecastle could be brought to bear on *Astree* and the 6 aftermast guns on the *Iphigénie*.[16]

After an hour of this, Tullidge had been wounded four times – somehow he remained on deck – and Robert Forder, the other lieutenant, was below with a musket ball in the chest. At 4 a.m. the master, a man named Parker, had his head removed by a round shot, while the senior army officer, Captain Elliott, also lost his head, to grapeshot.

In the absence of any other officer, command of the forecastle guns had fallen to the young master's mate, Jones, who was also wounded. He recalled cannon smoke drifting across a deck puddled and smeared with blood. Most of the bodies had been tossed over the side or taken below.

I manned, remanned and manned again the only two guns which would bear on the *Astree* until my heart sickened at ordering men to the slaughter – everyone having been killed or wounded. The cheerful alacrity with which at my order they quitted the comparatively safe guns to serve where death seemed almost inevitable, excited at the moment (and the impression made under such circumstances on a young mind is indelible) my warmest admiration. Had I felt it to be my duty to order for a fourth time the guns to be manned I have no doubt the order would have been promptly obeyed; but to have given such an order in that stage of the conflict would have been an unjustifiable expenditure of the lives of brave men.[17]

The slaughter in the dark . . . the obdurate spirit . . . a helpless frigate being withered at close range – the *Africaine* had acquired a terrible resemblance to the death throes of *Nereide*.

At around 5 a.m. Corbet lay in the cockpit, sweating in agony. His right leg had been amputated at the knee. The thigh, fractured in a number of places, was a bloody bandaged mess tied off with a tourniquet. The whole leg would almost certainly have to come off; but the wound was not necessarily mortal; Corbet had been saved by the exertions of his surgeon, a sickly and disabled man named James Campbell who had been with him on *Nereide* and who, over the past three hours, had performed miracles of hasty butchery in his gloomy cell. The recovery of many severely wounded men was testimony to this.

At that hour, Tullidge concluded that the ship could no longer be defended and struck the colours. Out of 295 men, 50 had been killed and 126 wounded. This was fewer than *Nereide* – 92 dead, 138 wounded – but still unconscionably high for an English man-of-war.* There could be no question that the *Africaine* had acquitted herself in the highest tradition of naval gallantry.

When Corbet was told, he flew into a state of 'raged vexation' and burst out:

For shame, hoist the Colours again! Fight and go down! Fight and go down![18]

---

* These may be compared with those on, say, Nelson's flagship at Trafalgar. A First Rate with a crew of some 800 men, the *Victory* suffered 54 killed and 79 wounded, a casualty rate of roughly one in six. On *Africaine* the rate was almost two in three, on the *Nereide* no less than four out of every five.

Tapson put it charitably. Corbet, he wrote, was either unaware of the extent of the carnage, or was overwrought. In the 'excitement occasioned by his wound on his naturally irritable Temper, added to the mortification and chagrin at the idea of surrendering to an Enemy, he was become reckless of life'. It may be closer the mark to conclude that, cheated of his chosen destiny, he sought immolation of everything, ship and men. All that was left to him was matching the bloody example set by Willoughby on *Nereide*.

Tullidge – with four wounds a gory, haggard figure himself – spent some time pointing out the futility of further resistance. Eventually, if not convinced, Corbet was persuaded that the 'Colours had received no Tarnish'. And yet, 'his proud and lofty spirit could ill brook the idea of falling into the hands of the Enemy'. He sent Tapson, the only man able to speak French, up on deck with Tullidge to receive the French officer. It was the last they saw of Corbet.

The ceremony was brief and grim, with none of the usual courteous ritual. When Tullidge proffered the sword to the French officer, 'the Brute rudely snatched it' and virtually pushed him and Tapson towards the *Iphigénie*, barking '*Embarquez toute suite.*' They were better received on the quarterdeck by Bouvet – 'a perfect contrast to the Ruffian we had just left' – who expressed the hope that his opposite number, Rowley, was well. It transpired that Corbet's ruse of hoisting the Commodore's pendant had indeed deceived the French into thinking that they were in action with *Boadicea* and that the second English ship – still becalmed some miles off in the dawn light – was the Indiaman, *Windham*.

On hearing the true identity of his antagonist, Bouvet became concerned. It turned out that by an extraordinary coincidence he knew Corbet

> having been taken a Prisoner by him some years before in a corvette in the Mediterranean when Capt C commanded the *Bittern* sloop, and having been detained some weeks on board, had had an opportunity of observing and appreciating his professional Merits.[19]

The immediate question was what to do with the *Africaine*. Within minutes of her surrender, all three masts had come crashing down and, to all intents and purposes, she was a wreck. Bouvet still sent on board a prize crew to attempt to bring her in to St Paul. And so Corbet was left on his ship with about twenty Frenchmen and eighty Africaines.

* * *

From this point there is no first-hand account. All the officers had left the ship. Jones's narrative ends and Tapson, captive on *Iphigénie*, based his on what he was able to glean later. The absence of sources no doubt contributed to the rumours that started to fly almost as soon as Corbet was found later that day, dead in Tapson's cot. 'The blood in it [had] completely saturated all the Bedding.'[20] The tourniquet, untied, lay beside him. The body, slight and white, was cold.

Tapson established that after the surrender, Corbet had been moved from the orlop, where the surgeon and his assistants remained feverishly busy, to the purser's cabin and put in a cot. There he lay in agony. Pain was nothing new to one who had been a martyr to rheumatism for years, but he did not endure it well. 'He appears to have borne the acute bodily pain with but little patience or fortitude [Tapson wrote] notwithstanding his brave and daring Spirit.'[21]

Corbet's physical suffering was all the worse for his grief of mind. To him came the overwhelming injustice of it all – the ball that had cut him down before he could carry through his strategy, and so early in the action that it added a hint of malign mockery to his fate. Others would pose the same agonising question on his behalf. 'Who will say what steps he would have taken had he kept the deck?' Jones wrote. Might he have pursued *Astree* and secured a famous victory? There is every reason to suppose that the question tormented Corbet's final hours.

The theme of revenge as a factor in his death is a persistent one. It was taken up by Captain Basil Hall, a popular author of seafaring yarns who was as appalled as he was intrigued by the stories he had heard about Corbet. Hall never accepted that he had been shot by his own men but repeated a variation of the betrayal story that he heard from other officers. This was that during the battle, his men 'read to [Corbet] the bitterest lesson of retributive justice that perhaps was ever pronounced to any officer'.

> To prove how completely they had it in their power to show their sense of the unjust treatment they had received . . . they folded their arms, and neither loaded nor fired a single shot in answer to the pealing broadsides which the astonished enemy were pouring in upon them . . . They were cut to pieces rather than fire one gun to save the credit of their commander.[22]

This ridiculous tale provoked Jones finally to write his pamphlet, and lay that particular myth to rest. Hall insisted, however, that the manner of Corbet's death had had a profound impact on navy discipline, forcing captains 'to think upon the danger as well as the folly of urging matters too far'. He also spoke of 'several versions of this terrible story current in the Navy'.

The most terrible revenge story of all was perhaps too strong meat to be openly repeated at the time: of a ship in which normal order has been lost, officers removed, men confined below, a hated captain lying in agony, alone until a figure slips into the cabin, exchanges looks in which fear and hatred mingle, then a quick movement and the tourniquet is cast aside. It is just about feasible; there were one or two men on board who would have been happy to see Corbet dead, notably the Marine who got ninety-six lashes. But such a script smacks more of our age than theirs.

Central to it is the notion that Corbet was as brutal on the *Africaine* as on *Nereide*, for which there is no evidence. *Africaine*'s log was lost, and with it the punishment record; but Corbet had curbed his worst ways. Tapson never described him as cruel. Arguably, Corbet's most terrible act on *Africaine* was wanting to embrace a holocaust – to 'Fight and go down!' – without any regard to his men.

On how he met death, it is again Tapson whose version rings most true. A devout and high-minded man, he wanted to believe that when the tourniquet came off it was 'by some accidental circumstances, Capt Corbet rendered insensible of it from the feverish state of his mind, too exhausted to call the attention of his Attendants to the fact'. But he could not in all conscience do so.

It must be confessed that a consideration of all the circumstances leads to the opinion that Capt Corbet was his own destroyer ... We need not wonder that during [a] phrenzy he did loosen the Tourniquet, both to put an end to his bodily pain, and to avoid the mortification of being carried into a French port ... It is to be hoped that it was effected during a moment of Delirium, and that the great Creator of all things will not in consequence call him to account for an act so apparently replete with rashness and temerity, and so directly opposed to His sacred Command.[23]

Corbet had never showed any outward recognition of a Creator. His faith was in the Service and it is probable that, just as his hero Nelson died serenely, thanking God for having done his duty, he who had no belief or hope of Redemption took his own life in despair because, presented with a single opportunity, he had failed in his.

21

A close run thing

Madras and Ile de France, 28 August 1810 and after

Thousands of miles across the ocean, on the day that Corbet killed himself, apprehension hung as heavy in the air of Fort St George as humidity before the monsoon. Sir George Barlow sat at a desk, faced with piles of dispatches and surrounded by sweating aides, his apparent unflappability tested once more. Minto had swept imperiously back to Calcutta, leaving Barlow to handle the detail of the invasion, and he was grappling with figures, of ships and men, that, no matter how he calculated them, refused to add up. If Barlow was not a very worried man, he ought to have been. In logistical terms, he had a want of tonnage. Put another way, there were not enough ships to carry the troops.[1]

The invasion of Ile de France had become a disaster in the making. Sending a 10,000-strong force against a tiny fortified island in mid-ocean would have posed a test of logistics and resources at the best of times. Never mind that the Army included officers who had recently mutinied against their own government; nor even that, thanks to the capture of the Indiamen, there were not enough transports to take them all. Departure had been so delayed that it was clear the fleet would be entering the hurricane season. Where the troops were to land was anyone's guess, now that Grand Port had proved a death trap. And all the time, the planners were suffering under the delusion that Britannia still ruled these waves, rather than Bonaparte.

Barlow's transport crisis resolved itself by a happy vagary – the appearance off Madras of another fleet of Indiamen. Unaware of anything untoward, they came to on 29 August intending to pick up supplies and continue to Calcutta: eight ships that included the First Fleet veterans, Henry Sturrock of the *Preston* and John Ramsden of the *Phoenix*.* They

* They had sailed from Portsmouth on 14 April, a month after the first Indiamen designated as transports.

were immediately summoned by Barlow. By chance (or misfortune) some of those who had been there at the outset of this stormy era were about to be drawn into the final act.

Two years had passed since Sturrock returned Lady Barlow to her husband. A less agreeable interview followed this time, as Barlow told Sturrock and the others that he was commandeering their ships. Passengers, cargoes, private trade – all would have to be deposited in Madras, and the Indiamen given just enough time to take on men and provisions before turning about and sailing with the 'Expedition'.

Sturrock fumed. His passengers – *Preston*'s usual assembly of the Company's finest and their wives – blustered at the cost and inconvenience of it all.[2] Ramsden was more philosophical, but he could not fail to point out the ominous precedent. The expedition could not reach Ile de France before the end of November. Had Barlow forgotten what had happened to the First Fleet in the third week of November two years earlier?

In reply, all Barlow could do was refer him to Minto's decision: the invasion must go ahead this year. As Minto admitted, he had been *'damnatus obstinatus mulier* on this point'. Even he, however, had to acknowledge the risks. 'If the troops do not rendezvous in time to attack by the middle of November, it is not entirely prudent to attempt it later, for the violent hurricanes which seem to live in those islands and to come out, like swallows, at certain seasons, sometimes are experienced in November.'[3]

As the troops would certainly not now rendezvous before mid-November, the expedition had already passed the point of prudence. The chaos of embarkation emphasised the point. Sturrock watched in dismay on 18 September as wave after wave of sepoys were borne out to *Preston* by *masoolahs* and came up the side like a horde of pirates. At the end of the day there were 630 of them on board and, he noted despairingly, 'the ship was so crowded it was impossible to move or to do anything'.[4] This deadly crush was relieved when Major-General Henry Warde, in charge of embarkation, came on board, blanched, and ordered 225 men to be taken off at once.[5] That still left more than 400 crammed into every corner. After landing craft were hoisted up and laid on deck there was barely room for men to pass in single file. When Sturrock considered how they would handle the ship in a storm, his blood ran cold.

Conditions were marginally better on *Phoenix* where the 300 soldiers – regulars of HM 69th Regiment rather than sepoys – had the equivalent of a quarter more space. But looking out from the quarterdeck over the turmoil, 'the people so numerous and so noisy', Ramsden reckoned grimly that he would do well to avoid an outbreak of disease.[6]

Among the flotilla of smaller transports was one named in honour of the Governor's wife, which gave rise to some ribald humour about army officers entering the *Lady Barlow*. Though the lady herself cut a less visible public figure in Madras these days – she had recently given birth to a son, Frederick, her fifteenth child and the only one she could be quite certain was by her lover – she remained a subject of unbridled gossip. Even now Barlow failed, or chose not, to confront her. He had preoccupations enough.

Barlow had opposed the expedition from the outset. It was all very well for Minto to opine with the airy cool of the aristocracy, 'We ought not to fail, although War is a fine lady and too capricious to be entirely depended upon.'[7] Barlow enjoyed none of Minto's immunity. He had noted how rapidly the Directors' support for his handling of the mutiny had evaporated and knew that, should the invasion run into trouble, his part in it would be found wanting. Standing on the battlements, the guns roaring as the fleet departed on 23 September, he thought himself well shot of the whole affair. Since Corbet had failed to appear to escort the fleet, Admiral Drury was delivering the transports to Rodrigues.

Barlow would have been less sanguine had he known of the latest setback. Five days earlier, the Commander-in-Chief of the Army had been captured by the French off Bourbon.

Whatever passed through Rowley's mind as dawn came up on the aftermath of Corbet's folly, showing yet another frigate lost to him, yet another of his captains undone by impetuosity – and in the cabin's privacy he had every reason to shake his fist at the heavens – there is no hint of it in the stark entry in *Boadicea*'s log for 13 September: 'Obs'd French Colours flying on board the *Africaine*, the 2 Enemy Frigates to be *Iphigénie* and *Astree*.'

It was a terrible blow, as bad in a way as Grand Port. Again Rowley was left commanding the sole British frigate in these waters and again he was obliged to resist an impulse to attack – at least until he had support. Later that morning he rejoined the sloop *Otter* and brig *Staunch*. Then he made sail back towards the foe.[8]

It is revealing of French *esprit* that, even at this point, having been twice victorious and with a chance to deliver the *coup de grâce*, to take *Boadicea* and stop the invasion in its tracks, they flinched. As Bouvet, commanding the *Iphigénie*, explained it: 'I thought it best not to wait for the enemy in the unrigged and dismantled state in which I found myself. I was therefore compelled, much to my regret, to abandon to him my prize, although but a hulk, filled with the dead and dying.'[9]

In fact, Bouvet left in such haste that his prize crew were abandoned, along with eighty or so unwounded Africaines, and Rowley was gifted the frigate lost only hours earlier. As he drew near another extraordinary thing happened. Men were seen leaping from *Africaine* into the sea and swimming towards *Boadicea*. They came swarming up her sides and were brought aft. The Africaines were making a demonstration. Just as they had once roared 'No Corbet! No Corbet!', now they wanted to show their eagerness to serve a commander whose reputation lay on the opposite tack. Lay them alongside those French frigates again, they shouted, and they'd serve them out, all right. If nothing else, the mettle of these men, and evidence of the enemy's lack of resolve, gave Rowley heart.[10]

The body in the purser's cabin was dealt with discreetly. Rowley made no mention of its disposal – a hasty burial at sea wrapped in Tapson's blood-caked cot – and, in his letter to Bertie, he passed quickly if regretfully over the loss of 'my gallant friend Captain Corbet'.

> He was wounded early in the action & died a few hours after it ceased. In him the service has lost one of its best officers.[11]

But Rowley could not conceal the ultimate flaw now exposed in Corbet's 'system'. For all his brilliance in the chase, he had never fought a determined, equal enemy and his neglect of gunnery had cost *Africaine* dear. Her roundshot was found to be used up but because of the gunners' misuse of their quoins – the wooden wedges used to adjust a gun's elevation – balls had gone too high or too low. *Iphigénie*'s losses were only nine men killed and thirty-three wounded, *Astrée*'s one dead and two hurt. Even the partisan Jones admitted that the firing had been inept, noting:

'Our shot would probably have done more execution if the practice of gunnery had been in 1810 what it is today [i.e. 1839].'[12] This overlooked the fact that some officers were already cultivating the practice, Rowley among them.

Starting back to Bourbon, Rowley struggled to preserve an appearance of calm while in a state of 'extreme anxiety and mortification'.[13] At every step he had been let down by subordinates and it is a mark of his character that no hint of recrimination or self-pity ever found its way into his dispatches; the closest he came to acknowledging disaster was a passing reference to 'the present critical position of our affairs'.[14]

Despite the appalling turn of events, Rowley's superiors had confidence in him. Governor Farquhar said: 'From my knowledge of the judgment and character of Commodore Rowley I feel sanguine of his being able to defeat the Enemy's plans.'[15] Bertie spoke of Rowley's 'active, intelligent mind', his 'zeal, judgment, perseverance, skill and intrepidity'.[16] A fellow captain paid tribute to his 'magician's touch' with men and ships.[17] All these qualities were required in the situation in which Rowley now found himself.

First, he sent the only ship he could spare, the transport *Emma*, to cruise from Ile de France to Rodrigues. The expedition, Rowley knew, had just left India, or was about to, and the *Emma*'s orders were to intercept the invasion fleet if possible 'to warn of the French peril & the comparative state of our naval force'.[18]

His next priority was to make the most of his resources. Hamelin had six frigates and although three of them, *Bellone*, *Minerva* and *Iphigénie*, needed repair, that still left the *Venus*, *Manche* and *Astree*. Rowley had two, one a mastless wreck that somehow had to be made fit for service, despite an almost total absence of timber or cordage. Having towed *Africaine* to St Paul, he set about having *Windham*'s masts shifted to her, with the willing help of Keating's soldiers. This rare inter-service comradeship between two commanders was another of the gifts that Rowley brought to the campaign.

He was at anchor a few days later when the event occurred that changed everything. Three ships were sighted off St Paul on an easterly course for Ile de France. From what could be made out, two were frigates which 'appeared to have suffered in their masts and rigging'. Here, in fact, was the aftermath of an action; and while it might seem impossible, after all that had gone before, for another English captain to have over-reached himself, that is precisely what had happened – the captain, indeed, of the ship carrying Major-General Sir John Abercromby.

Abercromby, Commander-in-Chief of the expedition, had sailed in an advance party with his staff from Madras to survey the coast of Ile de France and establish a suitable landing place. Insensible of the disasters that had befallen Rowley's squadron, they approached Port Louis on 17 September in HMS *Ceylon*, expecting to find British ships.* When Captain Charles Gordon espied instead the harbour bristling with enemy frigates, he bore up for Bourbon but two ships raced out in pursuit. They were Hamelin's *Venus* and the *Victor*.

'I was in a dilemma,' Gordon wrote, 'whether I was to make sail and gain the island, which I could have done readily, or if I was to shorten and receive them.' The presence on board of the Commander-in-Chief might have been thought to compel caution, but Gordon's response was typical of the hubris afflicting British officers:

The painful impression of Flying from the Enemy resolved me to adopt the latter.[19]

There is no need to dwell on details. He put up a stout resistance, engaging *Venus* for an hour when, having suffered in the rigging, he made sail belatedly 'in the hopes of reaching [Bourbon]'. They had almost attained the sanctuary of St Paul, when *Ceylon*'s topmasts fell. Abercromby and his staff were made prisoners and another British frigate taken in tow.

Hamelin started back for Ile de France. Had he reached Port Louis, the course of the campaign might have been altered. As it was, he had encountered Rowley.

To all intents and purposes the war for the Indian Ocean was lost and won that day, 18 September 1810, by a tilting in the scales of fortune. First,

* HMS *Ceylon* was a 32-gun India-built frigate, not to be confused with the Indiaman of the same name.

Hamelin was within Rowley's striking distance. Furthermore, the wind now shifted in Rowley's favour after he'd spent hours pinned in St Paul bay, helplessly watching the French and their prize recede into the distance. The third stroke of luck was the parting of a towrope securing *Ceylon* to *Victor*. It took an hour to reattach her, and the delay was critical. *Venus* had also suffered in the action, losing her fore and main topmasts, and their chance of regaining Port Louis was gone. Rowley wrote: 'Having the advantage of a fresh breeze, we soon increased the enemy.'[20]

The hands, the old Africaines among them, cheered as they gained. There was a debt to be repaid, for Grand Port as well as the *Africaine*, and they could see that moment approaching at around noon when they were piped to their mess tables. *Boadicea* had taken on fresh beef and vegetables that morning and they ate heartily with their grog.[21]

Just before 3 p.m. *Venus* stopped running. Through his glass Rowley saw *Victor* cast off the towrope and make sail eastwards, evidently to summon help from Port Louis. At the same time Hamelin raised his commodore's pennant and *Venus* bore up to meet *Boadicea*.[22] Hamelin's action was notable for chivalry rather than strategy. He had opted for a duel of honour, Commodore versus Commodore, flagship against flagship, when he may have done better to consolidate his forces – *Venus* lining up with *Victor* and *Ceylon* against *Boadicea* and the approaching *Otter* and *Staunch*. Hamelin's was the more powerful ship, with 18 pounders against 12 pounders and a crew of 480 against the *Boadicea*'s 300. But she had lost her topmasts and, if she did not strike hard and fast, would be outmanoeuvred.

They came at one another, *Boadicea* and *Venus*, the silence of distilled concentration among men crouched at their guns broken by trumpeted orders and a flapping from the yards as canvas was hauled in, then a turn of the wheel and the two ships were alongside one another in thunder and lightning. It had taken all day to reach this point; but now, late in the afternoon, the climax came with sudden savagery. A broadside flamed out from *Boadicea*, the guns were hauled in on their trucks, freshly shotted, flintlocks set, the carriages trundled out again, and within four minutes a second volley burst from the English frigate.

It was enough. Rowley's record of his triumph was as starkly matter-of-fact as his accounts of disaster:

At 4.30, hoisted our broad penant. At 4.42, run alongside [the *Venus*]
& opened our fire upon her. At 4.50 she hauled down her colours.[23]

In the eight minutes between the commencement of fire and Hamelin's
surrender, *Venus* had suffered nine dead and fifteen wounded. She had
managed a single broadside to *Boadicea*'s two, and wounded just two
men. Rowley's insistence on gunnery practice had proved itself.

The moment Hamelin's pennant fluttered down marked a turning
point, and both men knew it. Had *Boadicea* been taken, it is hard to see
how the expedition could have gone ahead. With both the commodore
and the Commander-in-Chief as prisoners, and not a single British ship
left capable of countering the French, the advancing fleets would have
been perilously exposed. Hamelin had recently captured a vessel loaded
with supplies that would have patched up his wounded ships. Bolstered
by *Boadicea* and *Ceylon*, a French squadron of eight frigates could have
wrought havoc. Instead, those few, intense minutes tipped the scales.
Rowley won two ships, notably the *Venus*, Abercromby was freed, and the
French lost their capacity to thwart the invasion.

Another tide turned at the same time. Seamen, troubled by the
mysterious and unfamiliar experience of defeat, cheered and slapped each
other on the back. *Nereide* and *Africaine* were avenged. A winning captain
had taken a grip and restored navy pride. Rowley was their talisman, a
harbinger of victory and prize money. Morale rose like a tropical swell.

There is no record of the moment that Hamelin offered Rowley his
sword. The French Commodore had nothing to be ashamed of – had
proved himself a decent, generous foe. But though no doubt courteous, it
was an encounter of contrasting cultures. Hamelin had been affected by a
long-prevailing French ethos in the Indian Ocean. Not since the 1780s and
the days of De Suffren, had a French commander sought battle. Like his
compatriots, Hamelin had become used to the easy pickings of merchantmen. He was a fine seafarer, as his voyage with Baudin to Terra Australis
attests. Like Surcouf, the model corsair, he had a keen nose for prizes. But
what France had needed at this point was a fighting commander rather than
a privateer, and that he was not.

A comparison with his foes is instructive. In reflecting on the
recklessness of men such as Willoughby and Corbet, the contemporary
historian William James declared: 'Ten frigates, lost like the *Africaine*,

weigh less, as a national misfortune, than one frigate given up without any, or even with an inadequate, resistance.'24

It seems an absurd statement, a bombastic expression of nationalism typical of its author. As a sentiment, it also reflected a dangerous notion of invincibility that had infiltrated the Navy since Trafalgar, which had been at the root of the madness at Grand Port and would continue to affect its officers. And yet it captures something of the bloody determination that made great victories possible. The sacrifices of *Nereide* and *Africaine* had not been entirely pointless, for they had taken three of Hamelin's frigates out of action. More importantly, they had unnerved the French.

In *Venus* were found supplies from the captured storeship, a vital infusion of ropes, spars and materials that transformed Rowley's capacity to refit. This seemed to clinch the shift in fortunes, as he wrote to Bertie on returning to Bourbon with *Venus* and *Ceylon* in tow. 'They have both arrived in these roads [St Paul] where, I trust, we shall in a few days have them and the *Africaine* in a state for service which will again restore us to our accustomed ascendancy in these seas.'25

Only one thing now stood in their way. The weather.

The task of bringing together simultaneously forces from four points around the Indian Ocean was always going to be tricky. Minto's somewhat breezy timetable had been for ships from Calcutta, Madras and Bombay to gather at Fort St George and sail in a single fleet for Rodrigues, where they would, it was hoped, meet up with a further force of brigade strength coming from the Cape. In the event, the thirty or so ships that had departed under Barlow's fretful eye were the Madras and Bombay divisions. They were late, but still well ahead of those from Calcutta and the Cape.

The Madras fleet soon fell further behind schedule. Fears of bad weather gave way to a new concern when the pleasant wind that carried them south for the first week dropped, to be replaced by light airs and calms. Day followed day and that vast assembly drifted listlessly, canvas hanging limp. Sometimes ships barely moved: on 2 October, they covered just nineteen miles; on 5 October, only twenty-nine miles and they were not yet within 10° of the Equator.

Meanwhile bodies were being heaved overboard almost daily with what logbooks noted dutifully as 'the usual ceremony'. Most Indiamen lost between eight and a dozen of their European troops, roughly one in every thirty. As for the sepoys, their deaths were not recorded, but the ratio was almost certainly far higher. Some idea of the tumult prevailing on the decks of even well-ordered ships like the *Phoenix* can be gathered from a note entered by Captain Ramsden in his log every Sunday: 'People so numerous & so noisy as to make it utterly impracticable to perform Divine Service.'[26]

Ramsden may have been careless of their spiritual health, but he could not have been more attentive to their physical wellbeing. Almost daily he recorded 'washed and fumigated orlop with [gun] powder'. As a result a private who died on 19 October was the last of only four men lost on *Phoenix*. That day, too, the wind picked up.

For a week the conditions veered between sunshine and squalls. Two captains in particular scanned the horizon for black clouds. Ramsden and Sturrock monitored their position constantly and would have noted keenly the conditions on 27 October, when they reached 08° 15'S, 84°E, close to where the First Fleet struck disaster two years earlier. Where the hurricane had raged, a sweet breeze cooled a golden evening.

Even better followed, a steady trade that came up abaft – and now cream appeared at their bows, and sails furled with a crack. After five weeks, the miles were being reeled off, faster each day: 103 miles on the 27th . . . 130 the next day . . . then 135 . . . and on the 30th a startling 163 miles. This exhilarating final dash almost made up for their delayed departure, so that the notional deadline for arrival had just passed when Ramsden was able to record:

Nov 6: At sunset, island of Rodrigues bearing SWbW abt 8 miles. Fine.

Thousands of sickly, dizzy troops disembarked to recover. Their officers were summoned to meet General Abercromby who, since his release, had been awaiting them with rising impatience. Of the Calcutta and Cape fleets there was still no word.

* * *

The Calcutta fleet, of seventeen sail, had been due to sail on 5 September, allowing an optimistic two months for the voyage. Troops were still embarking two weeks later in an operation of such haste that often there was no time to list their names. Conditions were utterly atrocious. The same *Hugh Inglis* that, in the Second Fleet, had defied all the odds by bringing safely home 29 children, was now taking on 440 soldiers of HM 22nd Regiment (368 privates, 35 NCOs, 17 drummers, 13 lieutenants, 3 captains, and 2 majors). The smaller *Huddart* had 300 men of HM 14th Regiment. Not surprisingly, men died at regular intervals from the time that they sailed from Saugor roads on 10 September. The *Huddart*'s execrable sailing offered little prospect that time could be made up.

The situation of the Cape fleet was even worse. It had not yet departed.

Admiral Bertie went ahead early in September in the frigate *Nisus*, having no inkling of events at Grand Port. It was not until 23 September that dispatches reached the Cape 'containing the disastrous intelligence of the destruction of our squadron'. Lord Caledon, knowing that 600 men had already been captured in the Indiamen, immediately ordered that the 2,000 about to sail in four transports should disembark, while he considered 'the train of possible calamity to ensue from this unhappy event'.[27] He could not even be sure that Bertie himself had not been taken.

Bertie, in fact, might well have been taken. He remained unaware of the Grand Port defeat when the *Nisus* reached Ile de France and, 'to our astonishment, [we] saw nothing of our own vessels'. Fortunately, the remaining French were too subdued to tackle another intruder so *Nisus* was able to peel off for Bourbon, arriving on 5 October to hear from Farquhar how Rowley, 'tho' reduced to one frigate against five of the enemy [had] restored the Naval Balance in the course of ten days'.[28]

Bertie handled his last command with some flair. His career had just collapsed, the long-running feud with Commissioner Shield having come to a bruising climax which proved his downfall.* But he had a chance to go out with guns blazing, and he took it well. His first order was for *Venus* to be renamed *Nereide*, in honour of 'a glorious resistance almost

---

* Relations between the two men had reached an impossible state. Bertie, claiming that he had put up with 'insults unparalleled in the Naval service', demanded the Admiralty's backing. When it was not forthcoming, he requested his own recall. He returned to a cold shoulder and although his services in Mauritius were eventually rewarded with the baronetcy he had long coveted, he was given no further command.

unparalleled even in the brilliant annals of the British Navy!' He honoured 'the gallant Corbet whose eagerness to check the triumph of an exulting enemy impelled him to an unequal contest'.[29] Rowley, too, was lauded to the skies. Behind this public morale-building, Bertie disposed ruthlessly of his only rival for the juiciest prize. He had no intention of sharing honours with another admiral, and, as the senior man, ordered Drury back to Madras. Drury declared himself 'insulted and injured' and sailed off in a choleric rage, dying soon after he reached India.

Almost everything was now in place. Rowley had been off conducting the first survey of the island's coastline in a series of depth-taking operations at night. Having abandoned the idea of a landing in the south, Rowley had identified one of the few spots undefended by coral reefs, rocks or batteries and in reasonable proximity to Port Louis. This was the beach of Mapou Bay, at the northern tip of the island and about fifteen miles from the capital, opposite the vast rock of Gunners' Quoin. Here the force would be landed.

Only the remaining troops were now wanting. Transports were still arriving in dribs and drabs: six small transports from Bombay; the Indiaman *Euphrates*, almost wrecked at Cape Hangklip. But of the Calcutta and Cape fleets there was yet no sign. (The Cape ships were actually still hundreds of miles away because Lord Caledon had taken a month to decide that it was safe for them to proceed.)

On 16 November, the wind stirred briskly in the east, bringing with it a thunderstorm that lasted through the night and tore the sky with lightning.[30] Whether or not this ominous reminder of the season helped to make up Bertie's mind, he decided that they could wait no longer. Abercromby was reluctant to launch an invasion with only half his Army. Bertie insisted. The troops could be reinforced by sailors, he said, but to delay further would imperil the entire expedition.[31]

The skies turned from black to blue and the sun was radiant when Bertie signalled all commanders to *Africaine* for orders. It was still shining on 22 November when about forty ships, one of the largest fleets ever mustered in the Indian Ocean, raised sail. By 8 a.m., with a light breeze stirring, they stood on for the Ile de France.

The next day the first gleam of reflected canvas appeared on the north-east horizon . . . three sail . . . then six . . . a dozen. Not before time, the Calcutta fleet had arrived.

* * *

Had it not, would the outcome have been any different? Almost certainly not. Once Rowley regained the initiative, success was always going to come down to the weather and the landing. After the fleet covered the run from Rodrigues to Ile de France in four days with 'light trades & pleasant weather throughout', the final phase unfolded with unexpected ease.

As a spectacle it was imposing, for all that. From 26 November, when the first sails off the northern shore were reported to Decaen, to 29 November, when the armada filled the sea, they grew – men-of-war, Indiamen, transports, country ships and auxiliaries – until they resembled a floating forest around Gunners' Quoin. Figures vary. The Calcutta fleet had swollen the number of ships to above fifty, but more were still arriving. By most estimates, from sixty to seventy sail were poised to launch their troops.

The island facing them rose in layers of lushness topped off by volcanic peaks – menacing and lovely at the same time. All that could be seen was verdant vegetation. Of defence there was no sign, let alone of an enemy still mistakenly believed to number 10,000. Nor was there any change in the weather. The 29th of November was 'one of the finest days that could be chosen, the breeze being particularly favourable' and from 10 a.m. landing craft were hoisted out – flat-bottomed boats, cutters, barges, launches, pinnaces and yawls. An officer on board wrote:

> The division moved towards the shore, presenting a magnificent and interesting spectacle. While pulling to the beach, we could not but feel the most lively anxiety for the event, and continued gazing intently till we saw the troops land, form and advance without a musket being fired.[32]

The first wave of fifty craft brought ashore 1,555 troops and two howitzers. In the distance a rolling blast was heard – as it turned out, a magazine being destroyed at Grand Bay, two miles to the west. Thereafter the landing continued uninterrupted.

The precise number of British troops disembarked over those two days is not known. Figures vary, from about 6,300 European soldiers and 3,000 sepoys, to about 7,000 of the two combined.[33] They were joined by 2,000 navy sailors. Whether from a notion of service or a desire to witness history, some Indiamen officers and men volunteered to go as well.

329

Captain Nesbitt and eighteen of the *Huddart*'s hands went ashore 'to assist at the guns'. So, unfortunately, did Captain Yates of another Indiaman, the *City of London*, who 'burst a blood vessel shortly after he landed with his seamen to work the guns & died'.[34] The only other known casualty during the landing was Thomas Palmer, a soldier who had been ill for days and died on the *Huddart* as his mates disembarked.

Decaen, it is said, was surprised by the choice of landing place – it was one of the few parts of the island without a ready source of fresh water for troops – and believed initially that it was a diversion.[35] This might account for his own somewhat tardy response. On 30 November, the day after the landing, an advance guard under Colonel Keating had marched south about ten miles through open country without encountering any resistance. They were within five miles of Port Louis when they came to the Tombeau river.

Some 1,800 Frenchmen and five artillery pieces had been mustered astride the road to Port Louis when Decaen rode out at the head of his cavalry. In attempting to get close to the enemy to inspect their strength, he was wounded in the leg and withdrew, leaving the defence to General Martin Vandermaesen. No more than a few shots were exchanged that evening, leaving the invaders in anticipation of the battle for Port Louis that would surely begin in the morning.

At dawn they ate the last of their rations and formed up. Abercromby launched a routine flanking movement on either side of the road while the main body moved forward in a frontal assault on the French guns. An officer who witnessed it wrote:

> A cannonade commenced from the enemy's lines which though pretty brisk for a time, totally ceased by half-past nine. I found that the advance guard had had a sharp brush with the enemy, who were strongly posted but were forced to retire, leaving two guns, some tumbrils, and a few wounded men behind them. The weather was uncommonly fine, but the troops complained of a grievous want of water.[36]

The next day, as Abercromby was enjoying a shave and a clean shirt on board *Africaine*, a flag of truce came out from Port Louis. That was it. The invasion was over.

As the culmination of months of bloodshed and bravery, effort and suffering, planning and sleepless nights, it was a bewildering anticlimax. A military culture that revered grand, hard-fought and bloody victories did not know quite what to make of it and though there was undoubtedly relief, there was also a perverse sense of deflation. The number of British soldiers killed in two days of hostilities was put at twenty-eight and even that number may have been embellished for form's sake. Two or three times as many had died on the voyage.[37] What glory, it was argued, accrued from such feeble resistance? Captain Philip Beaver, the officer in charge of the landing, grumbled: 'The only stand they made scarcely merited the name of a skirmish. Will anyone be found to rise in the Commons and move a vote of thanks on this occasion?'[38]

It was always the case that once the French lost their grip at sea, the game was up. Flinders had said there would be little or no resistance, and he was right. Having been so long neglected by his Emperor, Decaen saw no reason to make a useless sacrifice. He had a duty to avoid disgrace, but no more. The frigates had not stirred from Port Louis.

All that remained was for the terms of surrender to be negotiated. Decaen stipulated that he, his officers and troops should not be treated as prisoners of war, but be allowed to return to France, and do so in Duperré's ships. This last article was dismissed as 'altogether inadmissible', but in other respects the terms agreed by Rowley and General Warde were generous, providing for the transport home of all French combatants.[39] 'They are actually allowed to march with their arms, their eagles and fixed bayonets,' fumed the glory-denied Beaver. 'What can justify such concessions?'

Bertie reported the conquest to the Admiralty with palpable satisfaction:

> I have the honour to announce the capture of the Isle of France and its dependencies, comprehending the extirpation of the Naval Force of the Enemy in these seas and the subjugation of the last remaining colonial territory of France.[40]

The Ile de France was no more. The new rulers immediately restored to it the name formerly used by the Dutch, and by which it has been known since, Mauritius.

Four navy captains were among those freed, one of whom had enjoyed great fortune in surviving yet another close shave. Decaen had wanted to have

Willoughby shot for distributing seditious material – Farquhar's pamphlet – among the population, but Duperré interceded and saved his former adversary's life.[41] 'The Immortal' had also made a remarkable recovery from his wound, though he would wear a patch over the left eye for the rest of his life; his friend Colonel Keating sent him a note jesting that 'your female friends seem to think that your Beauty must be injured'.[42]

The courts martial were held over four days from 10 December as Pym, Lambert, Curtis and Willoughby were called to account for losing their ships. Whatever recriminations there had been during their captivity, the four closed ranks now. Pym was fortunate in being absolved by his fellows, and Willoughby in particular may have had to grit his teeth when he was called as a witness by the accused.

> Pym: Were my actions marked with ability?
> Willoughby: They were marked with ability.[43]

It helped that *Nereide*'s black pilot, Johnson, could not testify. Pym was able to blame him for the *Sirius*'s grounding: the pilot, he averred, had given 'too positive assurance that there was no danger in our way'. As the poor fellow had been shot by the French after *Nereide*'s capture, he was unable to demur. And it may not be unduly cynical to suggest that the presiding captains were content to go through the motions. Pride had been restored, after all, and there could be no suggestion of the accused being guilty of the most heinous sin, cowardice. The court finding 'no blame attributable to Captain Pym for the loss of *Sirius*', he was acquitted.

Lambert and Curtis were more readily exonerated. That left Willoughby, who had set the disaster in train with his signal to Pym, 'Enemy of Inferior Force'.

His explanation, wholly unconvincing, was rejected by the court which pointed out that 'the Enemy evidently *was* superior'. But thereafter proceedings moved smoothly on to an account of heroism on *Nereide*, with which there could be no quibbling whatsoever. Willoughby's signal was described as 'Injudicious', but the court concluded: '*Nereide* was carried into battle in a most judicious, officerlike and gallant manner, and the court cannot do otherwise than express its high admiration of the noble conduct of the Captain, Officers and ship's Company during the whole of the unequal contest.' Willoughby's acquittal came with the unprecedented imprimatur: 'Most Honourably'.

No other findings were likely. Nevertheless, there was evidence aplenty of the flawed heroics that had become typical of the Navy since Trafalgar. A new generation of French officers had shown that overweening English confidence was misplaced; and the importance of gunnery had been underlined. Both lessons were overlooked, and the cost would be even higher two years later in war with America. While Grand Port could be swept under the carpet of a redemptive victory, the defeats suffered by the Navy in single-ship actions against America in 1812 caused a sensation on both sides of the Atlantic. The historian N.A.M. Rodger wrote that in Britain 'the Navy and the public were shocked to discover that they were not invincible. People who thought the Navy was being ruined by aristocrats, or brutal discipline, or slack discipline, hastened to attribute blame accordingly. The Admiralty issued an implicitly critical circular reminding captains of the importance of gun drill.'[44]

Rodger concludes that there was no single factor to explain the pattern of setbacks and puts down one famous American victory, the capture of the frigate *Java* by the formidable USS *Constitution*, to superior firepower. No blame, at least, could be laid at the feet of the English captain – none other than Henry Lambert, erstwhile commander of *Iphigenia*, who might have turned the tide at Grand Port if Pym had listened to him. Some captains were born unlucky. Lambert was killed by a musket ball in the breast.

For the Indiamen captains there was no glory, nor was there an early return to England. Ramsden and Sturrock, on their last voyages, had anticipated being home by spring. Instead they were caught up in another Company adventure that detained them for an entire year.

The *Phoenix* and *Preston* weighed with *Huddart* on 10 December for Bengal, where they were drafted into the expedition being prepared to seize Java and deny Bonaparte a last refuge in the Orient. Batavia fell in July and the ships were back in Bengal by October, finally able to collect the cargoes that would bring Ramsden and Sturrock comfort, perhaps even a certain luxury, in retirement. But it was still a long haul from the time they bore away from the Hooghly for the last time in September and came to in the Downs in mid-summer, 1812, with three other survivors of the First and Second fleets – *Huddart, William Pitt* and *Hugh Inglis*.*

Ramsden, now forty-four, was duly reunited with Mary, the wife he had met in the fateful voyage of the First Fleet. They remained childless but had a good number of years together. Ramsden became a stalwart of the Indiaman captains' club. Sturrock continued to exploit his aristocratic connections to good effect and is last sighted four years later, in partnership with the Lady of the Manor at Woolwich, Dame Jane Wilson, in the local ferry company. Neither Ramsden nor Sturrock ever wrote a memoir. Nor, so far as is known, did any other Indiaman captain, which is much to be regretted. As a breed, they are forgotten.

Although the inhabitants of Mauritius did not exactly welcome the British as liberators, they did entertain high hopes of the benefits that would flow from occupation. Farquhar, whose propaganda leaflets had helped to raise their expectations, was installed as Governor with the task of fulfilling them. The new regime was not demanding. The islanders were given the option of returning to France with their possessions, or taking a vow of allegiance to the Crown. The vast majority stayed, with rights of religion, law and customs intact. British squeamishness about slavery was not translated into action for another twenty-five years, and even then abolition was accompanied by compensation of £2 million to the plantation owners.

But the French inhabitants did not embrace their English rulers. Farquhar was popular enough, a genial administrator who persuaded them that the disappointment of their hopes – free trade turned out to have its limitations – was no fault of his. Some took up their grievances with the one person in England who had their best interests at heart and who they dared to hope might be sent out to govern them. Though this hope was not fulfilled, Matthew Flinders never betrayed their cause. He campaigned long, and in the end successfully, for the release of Mauritian prisoners on

---

* Those on board that day included two slaves from Mauritius who had stowed away on the *Hugh Inglis* in hopes of reaching the land of abolition. Natives of Madagascar, they were treated with cautious hospitality on being discovered, then accepted as crew and dubbed John and Florrie. They left the ship at Blackwall with a few pounds in their pockets, and disappeared off into the melting pot of London's docklands.

Thames hulks, and corresponded until his death with old friends like Madame D'Arifat and Pitot.

One of his letters put a finger on what might be termed the paradox of the islands.

> In the case of peace, I hardly think it possible that your islands should be given back. Both the Government and the Company are well aware of their importance. Nevertheless, they certainly are of no *positive* advantage to England; and this I consider to be their greatest misfortune.[45]

The 1815 Congress of Vienna did, in fact, return Bourbon to France, of which it remains an improbable part to this day. Mauritius was retained, emerging as a society reshaped. Having abolished slavery, and found insufficient workers left to sustain the sugar industry, the British introduced indentured labour by Indian peasants, a system little different from the one it had replaced. Still, the island did eventually grow prosperous, as well as evolving into one of the most tranquil, mature and stable democracies of the Commonwealth.

Pitt was soon proved to have been right. Control of the Indian Ocean did indeed bring dominance, ushering in an era of unfettered imperial expansion. British trade, power and, finally, governance, spread across all India and thence through the Far East. Meanwhile, confirmation of the Cape's strategic value was to lead in time to colonial advance in Africa.

The Company's shipping resumed a more tranquil passage of the Eastern Seas, and not only because the French had been purged. The hurricane season of 1808–9 had been a freak and nothing like the sinking of seven ships in two storms ever occurred again. Indiamen losses became infrequent. This was in part because the time for the Navy's greatest need of their crews had passed. It was also thanks to improvements in Indiaman design and building that arose directly from the disasters. From 1810, new regulations stipulated that key structural components must be made of iron, including the 'knees' securing beams to hull timbers. In future, no ship should be simply torn apart by the sea.

Larger Indiamen of 1,450 tons increased the freights of textiles and spices being brought from India, and tea and silk from China. Another commodity also found its way to London wharfs in larger quantities – one less conspicuous and desirable to consumers, but more precious to the strategists seeking Bonaparte's downfall.

In 1808, the year in which this story began, the Company had contracted to supply 6,000 tons of Bengal saltpetre to the Government. By the time that Mauritius was taken in 1810, that quantity had doubled to more than 12,000 tons. As Wellington's battles started to turn the tide in the west – Ciudad Rodrigo, Badajoz, Salamanca, Vitoria – while Bonaparte was throwing the Grande Armée to the wolves of the Russian winter in the east, an uninterrupted supply of the purest form of saltpetre represented a real strategic advantage. One historian has suggested that the superiority of Britain's Navy was partly due to the potency of its gunpowder, estimated to be greater than that of the French by a factor of six to five.[46] It may not be stretching a point unduly to suggest that a contribution, not only to the war at sea but the battle for Europe, was made by the Indiamen that fought their way through the hurricanes of 1808–9 and brought their cargoes of saltpetre safely home.

Epilogue

With the passing of that era of storm and battle, the winds that had borne out seamen and soldiers, adventurers and administrators, carried them again home.

Captain Nesbit Willoughby dragged his scarred and battered body back to London where it was deemed too frail for further navy service. He then devoted the rest of the war to proving the doctors wrong. To pursue Bonaparte, he went to St Petersburg where, on presenting his credentials as a land commander, he was accepted into the Russian Army in 1812. Within a few months he'd seen his cavalry unit routed by the French, been captured and found himself caught up in Napoleon's retreat from Moscow. Once more he survived – privation, fever and nine months in a French prison, before escaping.

By now the Admiralty, recognising what sort of character they were dealing with, restored Willoughby to the Captains List and for four years he commanded a frigate in the West Indies. The fire within continued to burn, but more moderately. He was knighted, promoted to Rear-Admiral, and made naval aide-de-camp to a young Queen Victoria. Something of a roué in his youth, he never married and spent his later years at his home in Portman Square, writing religious tracts as well as trying to advance young officers' careers, in memory of 'my gallant Burn', the youthful Lieutenant John Burn killed on the *Nereide*. Although Willoughby died aged seventy-two in 1849, his nickname, 'the Immortal', remained apt.

Josias Rowley, quite properly, did better out of the campaign than anyone else. Admiral Bertie, assured of his own baronetcy, sent him home with the dispatches that secured one for the real hero of Mauritius as well. Rowley's subsequent course saw him raised to Vice-Admiral and Commander-in-Chief in the Mediterranean, where he served with all the modesty and disdain for showmanship that he had always evinced. Avoidance of the limelight might have cost him more honours. One contemporary noted that if his glory had not been won in so distant a theatre, 'the renown of Sir Josias Rowley would assuredly have proved not less general in the country at large than it is in the Navy'.[1] Like Willoughby he never married, but lived to a pretty ripe seventy-seven at a grand old pile, Mount Campbell, in Co. Leitrim, Ireland.

Rowley tried without success to help one of those whose destiny was linked less happily with Mauritius. On reaching England in 1810, Matthew Flinders was reunited with the wife to whom he had stayed devoted during two years at sea and seven as a captive. Flinders found personal happiness with Anne and their union quickly produced a daughter. He was also briefly a London lion, paraded and introduced to the future William IV. But his treatment by the Admiralty was thoroughly shabby. His years in Decaen's hands were not recognised as service, despite his achievement in mapping the continent he had started to call Australia, and the representations made by Rowley on his behalf. Flinders was passed over for promotion and put on half pay. That did not stop him assisting French prisoners financially, as well as campaigning for their release.

Over the next four years, Flinders threw himself into publishing an account of his explorations. He had always been highly strung, however, and this, along with anxiety over money, started to destroy his health. Aged forty, he was dying even as the work went into production. The first copy of the two-volume classic *A Voyage to Terra Australis*, published on 18 July 1814, was rushed to his bedside and placed in his hands by Anne, but he was already unconscious. The next day he started up, called out 'My papers!' and died.

The Admiralty neglected his widow as badly as it had him. Anne Flinders was left to raise their daughter on the meagre pension of a post captain. Suggestions by the King and Sir Joseph Banks that something ought to be done came to nothing and she lived in something approaching poverty until her death in 1849. Belated recognition came from the colony of New South Wales, which Flinders had literally put on the map, in the form of a £100 annual pension for their daughter.

338

The year after Flinders's death, London society was gripped by a scandal the like of which few could recall. When Lady Barlow's long-concealed liaison finally burst into the open it did so spectacularly.

The trigger was the recall of Sir George Barlow as Governor of Madras. As he had feared, the Directors went from 'complete and decided approbation' of his handling of the White Mutiny to deciding his 'continuance inexpedient'. At the end of 1813 Barlow, his wife and Major Pratt Barlow sailed home in the Indiaman *Rose*. By now it is hard to think that Barlow was unaware of his wife's infidelity, especially as during a three-month stopover at St Helena he noted how the lovers 'often walked or rode out together and never evinced any desire that he should join them'. In an age when divorce was tainted with disgrace, it may be that Barlow had decided to ignore the affair that had by now been going on for seven years.

What might be overlooked in Madras would not, however, pass in London. Two months after the Battle of Waterloo, while Sir George was in church with the children, Lady Barlow was discovered by the governess in the sitting room of Wood Lodge in Streatham, kneeling beside the major with her hand inside his military pantaloons. The governess had the temerity to ask how often she had 'been criminal', to which her ladyship replied candidly: 'Lord, Miss Page, I don't know!' The major tried to bluster his way out of trouble, proclaiming: 'My character is too well known for anyone to injure me.'

The indications are that even now Barlow might have turned a blind eye, but for the intervention of his brother, William, who had long had his suspicions about Lady Barlow and declared: 'Her wickedness exceeds all belief. Of all the cases of domestic perversion ever heard of, this is the most shocking.' Two days later, Lady Barlow was sent to a friend in Bath, her arrival heralded by a note of terrible bleakness:

> Madam, Will you have the goodness to break to my wretched mother that her disgraced and guilty daughter is come to her for protection and advice, sent by Sir George Barlow. If she can receive me for the night and my unfortunate child [Frederick, the youngest, now aged six] or let me know what her wishes are I will receive them under any name she may please to address me. I dare sign no name.

339

Pray meet me at mother's door where I may expect to be by seven tomorrow evening and there you will have the goodness to inform me what my mother's determination is respecting me.[2]

The scandal leaked out in *The Times*, and when the divorce came before the King's Bench in the spring of 1816, London was avid for details. Despite the judge's avowed intention that 'no more of the circumstances should be stated than are necessary', all the above facts were laid before the court, along with Lady Barlow's confession to a lengthy 'adulterous and criminal intercourse'. While the major's counsel pleaded that he was 'by no means in affluent circumstances and is mostly in debt and in want of money', Barlow was granted damages of £2,000. The criminal pair were forbidden to marry.

Barlow settled an annual income of £100 on his former wife – which was not ungenerous, if hardly what she was used to. The major went on to reveal unexpected depths of character. He did not abandon the fallen woman – now plain Elizabeth Barlow, and fifteen years his senior – but set up home with her in Kensington where they lived for twenty years. He attained the rank of colonel, but they were short of money up to her death in 1836, when she was aged sixty-six and he fifty-one. What became of Pratt Barlow and their son Frederick thereafter is not known.

Barlow himself retreated to the Surrey countryside with a mean-spirited Company annuity and no public recognition whatsoever. The prime minister, Spencer Perceval, promised to make him a peer but was assassinated before he could do so. Meanwhile some of Barlow's old foes from the Madras Army had returned and circulated hostile pamphlets which, possibly in conjunction with his cuckolding, attached a stigma of failure to him that his total withdrawal from public life did nothing to dispel. The verdict of history was harsh: the *Dictionary of National Biography* concluded that Barlow was 'an able man and a good servant, but failed utterly when placed in a government at a crisis' – a view completely at odds with the record. It took another Madras Army officer, Colonel John Malcolm, who had been no friend to him, to pass a more apt judgment. 'No man has ever served [the Directors] with purer principles of honour, nor more active industry.'

For one known for icy aloofness in office, Barlow's personal papers offer a poignant alternative view of the private man. A bundle of letters from his former wife are among them, written over the period when their union had produced fourteen children in nineteen years, and her fond expressions are, in places, underlined and marked in his hand. The marks were probably made for the divorce case to cite evidence of alienated affection. Still, it is consistent with a pattern of lifetime attachment that he kept them until his death.

There is another, much larger, file, marked 'Letters from My Children', and here it is possible to discern the outlines of solace. Barlow remained at the centre of a vast family circle – his other children, from George, a hero of Badajoz and Waterloo, to the last, Emma. Most had families of their own and while this very considerable Barlow tribe continued to be engaged in the Army, Navy, Church and Company, the house in Farnham was a nucleus to which its members would return. At least two of his sons went out to Bengal and when their children were sent home, they came to grandfather Barlow's care. He was no mighty nabob, flaunting his wealth and tales of grand old days, but a shy, retiring patriarch who treasured family gatherings, visits, and tidings of his scattered clan. He passed thirty quiet years in Surrey, with his memories of Fort St George and dawn over the Indian Ocean, before dying in 1846 aged eighty-three, quite forgotten.

Robert Corbet was less easily forgotten and he and his methods remained a source of heated debate. In 1830, almost twenty years after his death, a new storm over Navy discipline gave rise to an angry exchange in the letters columns of *The Times*. The respective positions were spelled out first by a correspondent, styling himself Medenae, who raised the old spectre of 'starting' and posed a rhetorical question, 'What must have been the suffering of men when under an ill-tempered fool or knave', before citing 'Corbet of the *Bittern* and who was killed in the *Africaine*', as both, but 'more knave than fool'.

This brought a furious response from one, 'H.J.B', who averred that it would have been a bold man who made such a statement while Corbet was alive. H.J.B., who claimed to have been on the *Nereide* during her voyage from Bombay, went on: 'A man of more chivalrous honour or kinder heart never existed, but it was his conviction that the superiority of the British Navy over every other arose from discipline.' The writer made no mention of the fact that the voyage had ended in mutiny, implying instead that Corbet co-existed with his men in egalitarian fraternity, and citing an anecdote in supposed support of his claim that 'in discipline Captain Corbet made no distinction':

> In my hearing he told a gentleman passenger, whom he saw sitting on one of the quarterdeck carriages of a carronade, 'Sir, if His Majesty had intended the quarterdeck of his ship to be made a lounging place he would have directed it to have been furnished with chairs and sofas instead of carronades'. 3

As for discipline, the comparison was absurd. But the exchange indicated the way that Corbet continued to polarise opinion in death, just as he had in life. The debate, not to say gossip, in naval circles went on, culminating in the publication almost thirty years after he was killed in Jenkin Jones's exculpatory pamphlet, *Character and Conduct of the Late Captain Corbet Vindicated*. It made no discernible difference. Corbet was remembered mainly as a tyrant, with which there can be little quibble.

His old Nemesis, Sir Edward Pellew – or Lord Exmouth as he now was – was not forgotten either. The old warrior joined the landed gentry, buying the vast estate of Canonteign outside Exeter, but soon tired of fireside comforts and was back at sea within a year. He commanded in the Mediterranean before going on to what proved to be the highlight of his later career – a mission in 1816 to liberate thousands of Christian slaves in Algiers.

A junior officer provided an engaging portrait of Pellew, once renowned for agility in racing his men to the tops, still active on the flagship:

> My astonishment was increased to see his Lordship, who is about sixty-five years old, and of a stout body, during the battle, with a round hat on his head, a telescope in his hand, and a white handkerchief round his body; running from one place to another, directing all the people as actively as any young man on board.4

During this campaign Pellew evidently had a premonition of death and wrote to his eldest son Pownoll, who had long lived in the shadow of the favourite, Fleetwood, a healing and touching letter to be delivered in the event of his death. It reads in part: 'When this reaches you the Father who loves you will be no more . . . Be a protector to your family. United you will all be invulnerable, Divided ruined . . . I assure you my Dear Pownoll, you are all alike dear to me . . . God bless you, be virtuous and you will be happy, so prays, Your affectionate Father.'5 In the event, Pellew carried out his mission with panache and returned to more honours and plaudits from Europe – the freed slaves were mainly Italians and Spaniards – and a viscountcy at home.

Pellew continued to provide handsomely for his eldest son, giving him the Canonteign estate. Pownoll built a fine house and became MP for Launceston. He and Eliza had had three children – prompting him to observe fondly, 'she enters most fully into all the amiable and endearing maternal character'. Then, five years after her mother's disgrace, Eliza stunned everyone by emulating her.

For some time she had been idly dismissive of her husband's domesticity, complaining that 'we live in a very stupid part of the country'. Once drawn to the more dashing brother – 'my very great favourite Fleetwood' – Eliza was still looking for excitement. She found it at last in the form of a young lieutenant of the 36th. They started a passionate affair in Brighton and when his regiment was sent to Cork, in June 1820, she threw up everything and followed him. An impossible situation was resolved when they eloped. Eliza, it was reported

> very suddenly discharged her English servant, paid off her lodging, parked her trunk and disappeared in a post chaise. At the same time a certain officer had been noticed absent from his Regiment. They spent a couple of days at an Inn & then [went to] Bantry.6

This information came from one grieving father to another. Both were mourning not death but loss – the failure of hopes and happiness, so bright on a day in Madras twelve years earlier when their respective offspring were wed. Few things in his private life more became Pellew than the letter he wrote to Barlow at this time, betraying no anger, no hint of recrimination at Eliza's behaviour, only sympathy. 'We did all that parents could do to secure the happiness of our children,' he wrote. 'I can only assure you, my dear Sir George, that I feel as much distress as you can possibly do.'7

Pellew's sorrow for his oldest son was compounded by the failure of his favourite's career. Fleetwood Pellew had been assiduously – and prematurely – advanced by his father. Always too quick with the lash, Fleetwood's harshness caused an ugly mutiny in 1813 and a decline from which not even the old admiral's influence could save him. Pellew's indulgence of his boys had, in the end, served neither well. His nepotism may have turned the Sea Lords against Fleetwood, who then spent thirty years on half pay. Given a command again at sixty-one, he promptly provoked another mutiny and was recalled.

As Viscount Exmouth of Canonteign, Pellew lived on, not at the estate of his title but at West Cliffe House, a quite ordinary home for one of his wealth and station but which had the virtue of looking out to sea from a small hill above the port town of Teignmouth. Here he endured, in the words of his biographer, 'indignantly into an age of sedition and reform and all manner of evil, outliving his generation and despising the ways of younger men'. He died aged seventy-seven in 1833. His flaws were plain, but they were aspects of a generous, warm disposition.

As a commander, he suffered from the comparisons that were inevitably made with Nelson. But comparisons were inappropriate. Pellew did not care for delegating, which was essential in a fleet commander; nor, although he had a great gift for friendship, was he seemingly able to inspire other captains as Nelson did. He should be remembered rather for his own genius, which was for solo command. In action against a single foe of superior strength, and for seamanship, he had no peers. 'The greatest Sea Officer of his time' was how John Croker, First Secretary at the Admiralty for more than twenty years, described him, and, in that time and at that place, that was as fine an epitaph as any.

Notes

Chapter 1: Admiral Pellew's strategy

1. L/MAR/B 307E, log of the *Preston*. As well as a daily record of weather, sailing conditions and incident, each East Indiaman logbook contained a list of passengers taken on the voyage
2. ADM 51/1866, log of the *Culloden*, 4 August 1808
3. Ibid.
4. Parkinson, *Pellew*, p.376
5. Ibid., p.370
6. Ibid., p.329
7. Roger, pp.556–7
8. L/MAR/1/23, folio 170, random shipping notes
9. Ibid., folio 28, Ramsay to the Admiralty, 8 May 1806
10. Hickey, Vol iv, p.415. The petition, in its entirety, covers pp.415–19
11. ADM 1/180, Pellew to Pole, 26 September 1808
12. Parkinson, *Pellew*, p.370
13. Ibid., p.376
14. Ibid., p.369
15. Ibid., pp.370–9
16. *Madras Courier*, 31 August 1808
17. Dodwell, p.182
18. *Madras Courier*, 31 August 1808
19. MSS Eur, Barlow papers, F176/52

Chapter 2: A petition from Bombay

1. ADM 1/60. The original intelligence was reported by Corbet to Bertie on 16 July 1808
2. ADM 1/180, Pellew to Pole, 22 February 1808
3. ADM 1/181. Petition dated 28 August 1808, attached with letter Pellew to Pole, 25 June 1809

4. ADM 1/5392, Corbet's court martial papers, letter from Corbet to Pellew, 31 August 1808
5. ADM 1/181, Pellew to Corbet, 22 September, 1808
6. ADM 1/5392, Corbet's court-martial papers, Corbet to Pellew, 31 August 1808
7. ADM 51/2590, log of the *Nereide*
8. ADM 1/181, Pellew to Corbet, 19 September 1808
9. L/MAR/B 143D, log of the *Lord Eldon*, 30 October 1808
10. ADM 1/5392, Corbet's court martial, Corbet to Pellew, 5 November 1808
11. MSS Eur F151/20, Munro papers, Gahagan to Munro, 9 October 1808
12. MSS Eur F176/36, Barlow papers, evidence of Thomas Oakes
13. Lawson, p.266
14. See MSS Eur F176/36, Barlow papers, the divorce of Sir George and Lady Barlow
15. Penny, p.63
16. Old Madras is affectionately and vividly recalled by a number of chroniclers. See the volumes by Henry Davison Love (1913); Henry Dodwell (1926); George Elers (1903); Major Charles Kirby (1867); F.E. Penny (1900); James Wathen (1814)
17. Hickey, Vol iv, pp.322, 342-4
18. For an overall view of the slide towards rebellion by the Madras Army, see Cardew, *The White Mutiny*.
19. The Barlow papers at the British Library provide an extraordinarily broad, and uncommonly candid, profile of a dynasty of Company servants
20. For Barlow's career and Wellesley's tribute, see O/6/7 at the British Library (APAC)
21. Cardew, p.30
22. MSS Eur F176/7, Barlow papers, Letters from William Barlow
23. *The Times*, 7 December, 1815
24. MSS Eur F176/15, Letters from Lady Barlow to Sir George
25. MSS Eur F176/7, William Barlow to Sir George, 12 August 1807
26. Ibid.

Chapter 3: General Macdowall's grievance

1. Hickey, Vol iii, pp.240-1, 288, 321; Vol iv, pp.150, 190-1
2. Longford, pp.86, 89
3. Cardew, pp.40-1
4. Ibid., pp.46-7
5. Kirby, Vol ii, p.13
6. Cardew, pp.46-7
7. Kaye, Vol i, p.460. The officer concerned was Colonel (later Sir John) Malcolm
8. Ibid.
9. Kirby, Vol ii, p.14
10. MSS Eur F151/20, Munro papers, Thackeray to Munro, 2 September 1809
11. MSS Eur C240 contains dozens of letters home from Mary Symonds and her sister, Elizabeth, Lady Gwillim, as well as one or two from Sir Henry Gwillim, and is a rich source for Madras social life in the early nineteenth century
12. MSS Eur C240, from Betsy Gwillim, c.February 1802

13. Ibid., from Mary Symonds, 4 March 1807
14. Ibid., from Betsy Gwillim, c.May 1805
15. Ibid., from Mary Symonds, 2 February 1805
16. Minto, p.23
17. Keay, p.169
18. Elers, p.172
19. See Dalrymple, p.433
20. MSS Eur C240, from Betsy Gwillim, 10 September 1806
21. H431, folio 127, British Library (APAC). The papers in H430 and H431 give a detailed picture in correspondence of this fascinating affair
22. MSS Eur C240, from Mary Symonds, c.November 1806
23. H431, folio 305, British Library (APAC)
24. Wathen, p.36
25. H431, folio 383, British Library (APAC)
26. ADM 51/1866, log of the *Culloden*
27. This is evident from the tone of Pellew's letters to Barlow. See Appendix D in Cardew's *White Mutiny*
28. MSS Eur F176/43 & F176/44 of the Barlow papers contain letters from Eliza Pellew and Pownoll Pellew respectively to Barlow, dated 22 October 1808

Chapter 4: 'Sir Henry Gwillim embarks . . . and the Devil go with him'

1. A fundamental resource for a study of the East Indiamen is Anthony Farrington's *Catalogue of the East India Ships' Journals and Logs, 1600–1834*, held at the British Library and a few other specialist libraries. It contains details of each individual ship, her maker and specifications, with the dates and destinations of each voyage
2. *Madras Courier*, 14 September 1808
3. L/MAR/1/23. Evidence of captains. This is part of the inquiry held by the Shipping Committee in December 1809 into the disasters that befell the First and Second Fleets. Many of the East India Company's shipping files were destroyed for want of storage space and this is one of the very few to have escaped intact
4. Each complete Indiaman log, in addition to details of the voyage and a list of passengers, contains details of the crew
5. L/MAR/ 1/23
6. Parkinson, *Trade in the Eastern Seas*, p.296
7. Ibid., p.196
8. The Indiamen and their commanders are a neglected area of Britain's maritime past. Anthony Farrington's *A Biographical Index of East India Company Maritime Service Officers 1600–1834* (The British Library, 1999) is a starting point for tracing the careers of captains and officers. For the service, see the books by Cotton (1949); Keble Chatterton (1933); Miller (1980); Sutton (2000); and Parkinson's *Trade in the Eastern Seas*.
9. MSS Eur F151/20, Munro papers, Gahagan to Munro, 9 October 1808
10. MSS Eur C240, from Mary Symonds, c.November 1806

11. L/MAR/B 175I, log of the *Phoenix*
12. MSS Eur C240, from Betsy Gwillim, 6 March 1805
13. Quoted in Parkinson, *Trade in the Eastern Seas*, pp.283–4
14. Cardew, pp.175–82, *The Case of Mr R. Sherson*
15. L/MAR/B 175I, log of the *Phoenix*, 14 November 1808
16. MSS Eur C240, a letter from Sir Henry Gwillim, 15 January 1809, makes this clear
17. Hickey, Vol iii, pp.18, 22
18. L/MAR/B 175I, log of the *Preston*, 21 November 1808
19. L/MAR/1/23. Evidence of Capt Ramsden
20. Mary's marriage to Ramsden is mentioned in passing among her papers in MSS Eur C240

Chapter 5: 'Not heard of again'

1. L/MAR/B 239B, log of the *Diana*, 22 November 1808
2. Ibid., 23 November
3. L/MAR/B 239B, log of the *Diana*, 23 November
4. Ibid., 11 March 1809
5. L/MAR/B 291C, log of the *Ceylon*. Also the evidence of William Harris in L/MAR/1/23
6. Eastwick, pp.258–9
7. L/MAR/B 291C, log of the *Ceylon*, 22 November 1808
8. Ibid. The information about their marriage is included under the List of Passengers
9. L/MAR/1/23. Evidence of Capt Ramsden
10. Ibid. Evidence of Capt Macdougall
11. L/MAR/B 307E, log of the *Preston*
12. L/MAR/B 211E, log of the *Ann*
13. ADM 1/61. Bertie to Pole, 22 January 1809
14. L/MAR/1/23. Evidence of Capt Ramsden
15. Ibid.
16. These partial passenger lists were published in the *Madras Courier* of 19 October 1808

Chapter 6: 'A cabal in the maintop'

1. ADM 51/2590, log of the *Nereide*, 6 January 1809
2. ADM 1/5392, court martial of Capt Corbet, extracts of letter Corbet to Pellew, 5 November 1808
3. ADM 1/60, Bertie to Corbet, 2 November 1808
4. ADM 1/61, Corbet to Bertie, 18 December 1808 & ADM 51/2590, log of the *Nereide*
5. ADM 1/5392, court martial of Capt Corbet, evidence of the Accused
6. Ibid.
7. Ibid.
8. Roger, p.489
9. ADM 1/5392, court martial of Capt Corbet, evidence of George Scargil
10. Ibid. Evidence of the Accused

11. Ibid.

12. Ibid.

13. Ibid. Evidence of Moses Veale

14. Ibid. Evidence of the Accused

15. ADM 51/2590, log of the *Nereide*, 29 July–12 August 1808

16. ADM 1/181, protest dated 26 August 1808, enclosed with letter Pellew to Pole, 25 June 1809

17. Ibid.

18. ADM 1/5391, court martial of Joseph Wilkinson and others, evidence of Lt Noble. It is an oft-repeated error in naval studies that the cause of the *Nereide* mutiny was the desire of the men to go to the Cape in the belief that they would receive a more sympathetic hearing from Admiral Bertie than they had had from Pellew. In fact, the reverse was the case

19. Ibid.

20. Ibid. Evidence of Lt Blight

21. Ibid. Evidence of John Smith

22. Woodman, p.134

23. Roger, p.452

24. ADM 1/5391, court martial of Wilkinson and others. Corbet betrayed his animus for these five at the hearing

25. Ibid., Corbet to Bertie, 26 January 1809

Chapter 7: Justice at the Cape

1. MSS Eur C240, Letter from Sir Henry Gwillim, 15 January 1809

2. Quoted in Worden, p.97

3. All references from ADM 1/5391, court martial of Wilkinson and nine others

4. ADM 1/61, Bertie to Pole, 18 February 1809

5. All references from ADM 1/5392, court martial of Capt Corbet

6. This is from Laughton's précis of Corbet's life in the *Dictionary of National Biography*

7. ADM 1/5392

8. ADM 1/61, Bertie to Pole, 18 February 1809

9. Ibid., Bertie to Johnston, 25 January 1809

10. Ibid., Johnston to Bertie, 26 January 1809

11. Ibid., Pringle to Bertie, 28 January 1809

12. Ibid., Bertie to Pringle, 5 February 1809

13. H430, folio 453 & H431, folio 415, British Library (APAC)

Chapter 8: 'One of the most wicked places in the Universe'

1. MSS Eur F176/15, Barlow papers, contains letters from Eliza to her father dealing with her childhood in England

2. Quoted in Dalrymple, p.33

3. Ibid., p.407

4. MSS Eur F176/43, Barlow papers, Eliza to Barlow, 20 November 1808

5. Ibid., F176/44, Pownoll Pellew to Barlow, 31 January 1809

6. Hayter, pp.51–2

7. There were many contemporary accounts of the *Abergavenny* disasters, mainly because there were survivors and because it occurred so close to home. The most recent retelling is by Alethea Hayter

8. Hickey, Vol iv, p.477

9. L/MAR/1/23, the surviving captains testified to this effect

10. Kincaid, p.73

11. Parkinson, *Trade in the Eastern Seas*, p.198

12. L/MAR/1/23. Evidence of Capt Franklin

13. *Bengal Past & Present*, Vols ii, vii, x & xvi

14. Hickey, Vol iv, p.447

15. *Madras Courier*, 20 April 1808

16. Hickey, Vol iv, pp.353–4

17. L/MAR/B 231D, log of the *Hugh Inglis*, 19 August 1808

18. Graham, p.87

19. Kincaid, p.79

20. L/MAR/1/23, folio 223, Pellew order dated 29 August 1808

21. Ibid., Summary on Pressing and Manning

22. Cited in Bowen, p.173

23. E/4/905, folio 299, British Library (APAC)

24. L/MAR/1/23. Evidence of Capt Hooper

25. Ibid., narrative of Capt Weltden

26. Ibid., Sundry Notes, folio 150

27. Hickey, Vol iv, pp.382 & 367

28. L/MAR/1/23, Opinion of Missing Ships

29. Ibid., narrative of Capt Weltden

30. Ibid.

31. MSS Eur F176/43 & 44

32. Quoted in Parkinson, *Pellew*, p.379

33. MSS Eur F176/44, Pownoll Pellew to Barlow, undated

Chapter 9: Sir George Barlow draws his sword

1. Cardew, p.51

2. Quoted in Dalrymple, p.25

3. Elers, p.54

4. Quoted in Dodwell, p.186

5. MSS Eur F151/20, Munro papers, Thackeray to Munro, 2 September 1809

6. Wathen, p.36

7. MSS Eur F176/43, Barlow papers, Eliza to Barlow, 29 January 1809

8. MSS Eur F176/36 contains the searing papers of the affair and subsequent divorce proceedings

9. Ibid.

10. Ibid.

11. MSS Eur F176/21, Barlow papers, Capt Barlow to William Barlow, 20 October 1808

12. For an account of the *Winterton* castaways see Hood

13. Cardew, p.54

14. *Madras Courier*, 8 February 1809

15. See Minto, p.207

16. Cardew, p.56

17. MSS Eur F151/20, Munro papers, folio 41, copy of Col Capper's order

18. Macdowall's letters in Appendix D of Cardew's *The White Mutiny* are indicative of a change of heart

19. Buchan, p.144

20. MSS Eur F151/20, Munro papers, Gahagan to Sir John Craddock, 4 February 1809

21. Ibid.

22. Ibid.

23. Cardew, Appendix D, Pellew to Barlow, 15 February 1809

24. Cardew, p.62

25. Kaye, Vol ii, p.243

26. MSS Eur F151/20, Munro papers, Gahagan to Craddock, 4 February 1809

27. Ibid., Gahagan to Craddock, 19 February 1809

28. Ibid.

29. Wathen, p.81

30. A report to this effect was published in the *Madras Courier* of 12 February 1809, and had already been received in Ceylon

31. MSS Eur F151/20, Munro papers, unsigned letter to Munro, 12 March 1810

32. Buchan, p.144

33. MSS Eur F151/20, Munro papers, unsigned letter, 9 March 1810

34. Ibid.

35. Ibid.

Chapter 10: 'A perfect hurricane'

1. L/MAR/B 209F, log of the *Earl St Vincent*. Johnston told the Royal Asiatic Society in 1827 that he had initially booked a passage on the *Lady Jane Dundas* and that although he had been spared his valuable collection of manuscripts had gone on board her and been lost. Transactions of the RAS, Vol I, Appendix A

2. Cardew, Appendix D, Pellew to Barlow, 14 February 1809

3. Ibid., Pellew to Barlow, 8 May 1809

4. Ibid., Macdowall to Pellew, 15 February 1809

5. Quoted in Nicolson, p.52

6. Quoted in Parkinson, *Trade in the Eastern Seas*, p.224

7. Quoted in Cotton, p.72

8. Although in most cases passengers' names are known from logbooks, those who were travelling on the ships that were lost are named in the final pages of Hickey's memoirs

9. Quoted in Parkinson, *Trade in the Eastern Seas*, p.224

10. Wathen, pp.8–10

11. Quoted in Parkinson, *Trade in the Eastern Seas*, p.289
12. Elers, p.47
13. Kincaid, pp.62–3
14. L/MAR/B 209F, log of the *Earl St Vincent*, 8 June 1808
15. *Madras Courier*, 12 October 1808
16. L/MAR/B 217D, log of the *Huddart*
17. L/MAR/1/23, narrative of Capt Weltden
18. Wathen, pp.10–11
19. Cardew, Appendix D, Pellew to Barlow, 14 April 1809
20. Parkinson, *Pellew*, p.371
21. L/MAR/1/23, Opinion of Course Steered
22. Ibid.
23. Junger, p.133
24. Cardew, Appendix D, Pellew to Barlow, 14 April 1809
25. L/MAR/B 217D, log of the *Huddart*
26. L/MAR/1/23, narrative of Capt Weltden
27. Ibid. Evidence of Capt Campbell
28. Ibid. Evidence of Capt Fairfax
29. Ibid.
30. L/MAR/B 231D, log of the *Hugh Inglis*, 16 March 1809

Chapter 11: 'The most terrible of deaths'

1. Parkinson, *Pellew*, p.367
2. Ibid., p.359
3. Ibid., pp.373 & 364
4. Cardew, Appendix D, Pellew to Barlow, 14 April 1809
5. ADM 51/1866, log of the *Culloden*
6. Cardew, Appendix D, Pellew to Barlow, 14 April 1809
7. Ibid.
8. Ibid.
9. L/MAR/1/23, narrative of Missing Ships
10. Ibid., narrative of Capt Nesbitt
11. E/4/904, despatch to Fort St George dated 15 September 1809, British Library (APAC)
12. MSS Eur F151/20, Munro papers, Thackeray to Munro, 2 September 1809
13. Eastwick, pp.260–1
14. Ibid.
15. Hickey, Vol iii, pp.19–22. This is an edited version
16. Eastwick, p.72

Chapter 12: Pellew's revenge

1. ADM 51/2590, log of the *Nereide*
2. Ibid., 16 March 1809
3. ADM 1/161, Corbet to Bertie, 11 April 1809

4. Ibid.

5. Ibid.

6. L/MAR/B 184J, log of the *William Pitt*, 21 March 1809

7. This is apparent from the letters in ADM 1/5392, Corbet's court martial, and the complete correspondence sent subsequently by Pellew to the Admiralty

8. Bertie wrote to the Admiralty complaining that as a result of Pellew's measures 'it must be a matter of great uncertainty when I am joined by the *Nereide*, if she comes at all'. ADM 1/60, Bertie to Pole, 12 December 1808

9. ADM 1/61, Pellew to Bertie, 8 April 1809

10. ADM 1/61, Pellew to Corbet, 12 April 1809

11. Ibid., Corbet to Pellew, 18 April 1809

12. Ibid., Corbet to Bertie, 16 April 1809

13. ADM 1/181, Pellew to Pole, 25 June 1809

14. Cardew, Appendix D, Pellew to Barlow, 14 April 1809

15. Ibid.

16. L/MAR/B 274F, log of the *Sir Stephen Lushington*, 19 April 1809

17. Sherwood, p.245

18. From J.K. Laughton's entry in the *Dictionary of National Biography*

Chapter 13: Return to Ile de France

1. All details from ADM 51/2590, log of the *Nereide*, 11 April–6 June 1809

2. Ibid.

3. Quoted in Parkinson, *War in the Eastern Seas*, p.310

4. Addison and Hazareesingh, p.43

5. Parkinson, *Pellew*, pp.351–3

6. Scott, p.311

7. Zamoyski, pp.33–4

8. See Scott, chapter 26

9. Parkinson, *War in the Eastern Seas*, p.449

10. Flinders Electronic Archive, Private Journal, 21 March 1809

11. Ibid., 24 March 1809

12. See Scott, chapter 25

13. Flinders Electronic Archive, Private Journal, 6 October 1805

14. Ibid., 25 July 1805

15. Ibid., 21 October 1805

16. Quoted by Scott from *Voyage to Terra Australis*, Vol ii, p.419

17. Flinders Electronic Archive, Private Journal, 25 April 1809

Chapter 14: 'A mongrel kind of gentleman'

1. For an account of this episode, see Hood

2. ADM 1/180, Drury to Minto, 25 April 1809

3. ADM 1/180. Evidence of James Walker, sworn 18 April 1809

4. Ibid.

5. ADM 1/180, Tremenhere to Alexander Falconer, undated, April 1809
6. Ibid.
7. ADM 1/180, Drury to Pole, 8 May 1809
8. L/MAR/B 185B, log of the *Streatham*
9. Ibid., 26 May 1809
10. L/MAR/B 187, log of the *Lord Keith*
11. James, p.282
12. L/MAR/1/23, folio 191, Dale's report dated 4 September 1809
13. Hood, p.233
14. L/MAR/1/23, folio 192, Gelston's report dated 5 September 1809
15. L/MAR/B 187, log of the *Lord Keith*
16. Flinders Electronic Archive, Private Journal, 9 August 1809
17. O/6/4, Merchants and Agents petition, 19 October 1809, British Library (APAC)

Chapter 15: 'The enterprizing Captain Corbet'

1. Parkinson, *War in the Eastern Seas*, p.447
2. See Jenkin Jones, *Character and Conduct of the Late Captain Corbet Vindicated*
3. *Dispatches & Letters of Vice-Admiral Lord Nelson*, Vol vi, p.51
4. As well as the ever-revealing log of the *Nereide*, two men who sailed with Corbet wrote about him. John Tapson's unpublished journal, at the William L. Clements Library at the University of Michigan, is the most valuable source, but Jenkin Jones provided the necessary corrective to simplistic conclusions
5. ADD MSS 34925, folio 129, Letters to Nelson, British Library
6. ADM 51/2590, log of the *Nereide*, 8 June 1809
7. Ibid.
8. Flinders Electronic Archive, Letter to M Bertin, 1 July 1809
9. Ibid., Private Journal, 29 June 1809
10. Flinders and Dale both attest to the fact that some captives defected, though neither was censorious
11. ADM 35/2970, the *Nereide*'s paybook, identifies the mutineers. See also ADM 1/62, Willoughby to Rowley, 30 August 1809
12. Flinders Electronic Archive, Private Journal, 10 January 1810
13. Hall, p.326
14. ADM 1/61, Bertie to Lord Caledon, 19 October 1809
15. All details from ADM 51/2751, log of the *Raisonnable*
16. Quoted in Austen, p.128
17. This remarkable figure of English naval history still awaits an adequate biographer
18. ADM 1/60, enclosure of petition with Bertie to Pole, 30 September, 1808
19. Austen, pp.134–5
20. Flinders Electronic Archive, Private Journal, 17 August 1809
21. ADM 51/2751, log of the *Raisonnable*
22. ADM 1/62, Rowley to Bertie, 28 August 1809
23. Ibid.
24. ADM 1/62, Willoughby to Rowley, 30 August 1809

Chapter 16: Battle on Bourbon

1. ADM 1/62, undated report by Corbet
2. ADM 1/62, Rowley to Bertie, 29 September 1809
3. Quoted in Parkinson, *War in the Eastern Seas*, p.367
4. ADM 1/62, Keating report on the attack on St Paul, dated 29 September 1809
5. ADM 51/2751, log of the *Raisonnable*, 21 September 1809
6. ADM 1/62, Rowley to Bertie, 29 September 1809
7. ADM 1/62, Keating report
8. Quoted in Parkinson, *War in the Eastern Seas*, p.367
9. ADM 1/63, Corbet to Rowley, 22 September 1809
10. ADM 1/62, Dale to Bertie, 15 November 1809
11. ADM 1/62, Keating report
12. Flinders Electronic Archive, Private Journal, 4 October 1809
13. Quoted in Austen, p.134
14. ADM 1/62, Dale to Bertie, 15 November 1809
15. ADM 1/62, undated report by Corbet
16. ADM 1/62, Rowley to Bertie, 30 September 1809
17. ADM 1/62, Bertie to Pole, 20 October 1809
18. ADM 1/62, Bertie to Lord Caledon, 16 October 1809
19. ADM 1/62, Caledon to Bertie, 17 October 1809
20. ADM 1/62, Caledon to Bertie, 22 October 1809
21. ADM 1/63, Shield to Pole, *c*.February 1810
22. ADM 1/63, Corbet to Bertie, 29 November 1809
23. ADM 1/63, Bertie to Pole, 8 December 1809
24. ADM 1/63, Bertie to Pole, 11 January 1810
25. ADM 35/2590, paybook of the *Nereide*

Chapter 17: Commodore Hamelin's cruise

1. L/MAR/B 277E, log of the *United Kingdom*, 10 November 1809
2. IOR/G/9/2, ff 428–32, minutes of an inquiry into the defence of the *Windham*, British Library (APAC)
3. James, pp.293–4
4. Quoted in Parkinson, *Trade in the Eastern Seas*, p.222
5. The *Windham*'s log with its record of passengers was lost. The names were noted by Flinders in his private journal, 31 March 1810
6. IOR/G/9/2, minutes of an inquiry etc., British Library (APAC)
7. James, pp.293–4
8. L/MAR/B 277E, log of the *United Kingdom*
9. Ibid.
10. IOR/G/9/2, minutes of an inquiry etc., British Library (APAC)
11. James, p.295
12. ADM 51/2751, log of the *Raisonnable*, 31 December 1809
13. Ibid., 2 January 1810

14. Flinders Electronic Archive, Private Journal, 3 January 1810
15. Ibid., Letter to Anne Flinders, 27 February 1809
16. See Scott, Chapter 25
17. Flinders Electronic Archive, Letter to Charles Desbassaynes, 14 March 1810
18. Ibid., Private Journal, 11 November 1809
19. Ibid., Private Journal, 28 March 1810
20. Ibid., Private Journal, 6 April 1810
21. Ibid., Letters, 14 May 1810
22. Ibid., Private Journal, 14 July 1810 and Letters, to Rowley, 19 February 1811

Chapter 18: Christmas at the India House

1. Parkinson, *Trade in the Eastern Seas*, p.2
2. The complete papers relating to these hearings are contained in L/MAR/1/23
3. Cotton, pp.54–5
4. E/4/904, folio 449, Commercial Report, 16 January 1810
5. Ibid.
6. Ibid., folio 64, response to letters on military affairs, 15 September 1809
7. Philips, pp.70–1
8. Ibid.
9. Minto, p.222
10. Cardew's *White Mutiny* is the sole full-length treatment of this episode
11. Quoted in Morris, p.309
12. MSS Eur F151/20, Munro papers, letter from Thackeray, 2 September 1809
13. Eastwick, pp.248–9
14. Ibid., p.250
15. IOR/G/9/2, folio 156, undated memo from Minto
16. Minto, p.243
17. ADM 51/2177, log of the *Bourbonnaise*
18. See James
19. Tapson Journal, 24 June 1810
20. Ibid., 21 June 1810. Both Tapson and Jenkin Jones, the other first-hand source, agree that none of *Africaine*'s crew had previously served under Corbet
21. Ibid.
22. Jones, *Character and Conduct of Captain Corbet Vindicated*
23. ADM 1/828, Buller to William Young, 22 June 1810
24. Tapson Journal, 21 June 1810
25. Jones, *Character and Conduct of Captain Corbet Vindicated*
26. Ibid.
27. Tapson Journal, 21 July 1810
28. Ibid.
29. Jones, *Character and Conduct of Captain Corbet Vindicated*
30. Tapson Journal, 21 July 1810
31. Jones, *Character and Conduct of Captain Corbet Vindicated*

Chapter 19: The Battle of Grand Port

1. L/MAR/B 231E, log of the *Hugh Inglis*, 2 April 1810
2. The Wellands' adventures were recorded by them in a journal, a precis of which was published by *The Times* in September 1930 and republished as Appendix VI in Austen (see Bibliography). I have been unable to trace the original
3. Austen, Appendix VI
4. IOR/G/9/2, Memo from Bertie, 9 June 1810, British Library (APAC)
5. L/MAR/B 184L, log of the *William Pitt*
6. IOR/G/9/2, Report of Capt Meriton, 11 October 1810, British Library (APAC)
7. Kirby, p.225–6
8. IOR/G/9/2, Report of Capt Meriton, 11 October 1810, British Library (APAC)
9. James, p.382
10. IOR/G/9/2, Report of Capt Meriton
11. See L/MAR/B 12A, log of the *Astell*. This was the only Indiaman log to survive the action
12. James, p.386
13. Austen, p.211, Letter of Lieutenant Thomas Pye
14. Austen, p.210
15. All aspects of the Wellands' story are taken from Austen, Appendix VI
16. James, p.406
17. *Le Combat du Grand Port 1810*, thesis by Lieutenant de Vaisseau Roussel, École de Guerre Naval, 1927–8
18. Austen, Appendix VI
19. ADM 1/5411, court martial of Captain Pym, letter from Willoughby to Pym, 20 August 1810
20. Ibid., Pym to Rowley, 20 August 1810. James, p.403, points out that Pym had also claimed personal credit for the occupation by two of his lieutenants of the Ile de la Passe
21. ADM 1/5411, court martial of Captain Willoughby
22. ADM 1/5411, court martial of Captain Pym, evidence of Accused
23. ADM 1/5411, court martial of Captain Willoughby, evidence of Lesby
24. ADM 1/5411, court martial of Captain Pym
25. See the remarks by Mrs Welland in Austen, p.207
26. Austen, p.152
27. Ibid., p.145
28. ADM 1/5411, court martial of Captain Pym
29. *Le Combat du Grand Port 1810*, thesis by Lieutenant de Vaisseau Roussel, École de Guerre Naval, 1927–8
30. James, p.419
31. ADM 1/5411, court martial of Captain Willoughby, evidence of Lieutenant Weiss
32. Ibid.
33. Ibid. Evidence of Willoughby
34. Quoted in Austen, p.152
35. Quoted in Parkinson, *War in the Eastern Seas*, p.392
36. Quoted in Austen, p.153

37. ADM 1/5411, court martial of Captain Willoughby
38. ADM 35/2970, paybook of the *Nereide*
39. Ibid.
40. James, p.421
41. *Le Combat du Grand Port 1810*, thesis by Lieutenant de Vaisseau Roussel, École de Guerre Naval, 1927–8
42. ADM 1/5411, court martial of Captain Pym
43. Ibid., Pym despatch to Rowley
44. ADM 51/2176, log of the *Boadicea*, 27 August 1810
45. James, p.428
46. Quoted in Austen, p.213
47. *The Times*, 3 January, 1811

Chapter 20: 'For shame, hoist the Colours again!'

1. Tapson Journal, 12 September 1810
2. Hall, p.320. The author did not mention Corbet by name but there was no doubt of whom he was writing. It was Hall's study that provoked Jenkin Jones to write his pamphlet
3. Quoted in Nicolson, p.xxii
4. ADD MSS 34920, Nelson letters, Corbet to Nelson, 5 October 1803, British Library
5. The *Africaine*'s log was lost and Tapson and Jones left the only accounts of the action
6. *Le Combat du Grand Port 1810*, thesis by Lieutenant de Vaisseau Roussel, École de Guerre Naval, 1927–8
7. Jones, *Character and Conduct of Captain Corbet Vindicated*
8. Tapson Journal, 12 September 1810
9. ADM 51/2176, log of the *Boadicea*, 12 September 1810
10. Ibid., 13 September 1810
11. Tapson Journal, 13 September 1810
12. Hall, p.321
13. Jones, *Character and Conduct of Captain Corbet Vindicated*
14. Tapson Journal, 13 September 1810
15. Ibid.
16. Ibid.
17. Jones, *Character and Conduct of Captain Corbet Vindicated*
18. Tapson Journal, 13 September 1810
19. Ibid.
20. Ibid., 5 December 1810
21. Ibid.
22. Hall, pp.321–2
23. Tapson Journal, 5 December, 1810

Chapter 21: A close run thing

1. MSS Eur F151/20, Munro papers; a letter from Gahagan to Munro, 1 September 1810,

discloses that Barlow had insufficient ships for the force

2. Ibid., the writer speaks of the great annoyance of the passengers who were going on to Bengal

3. Minto, p.245

4. L/MAR/B 307, log of the *Preston*, 18 September 1810

5. Ibid., 19 September 1810

6. L/MAR/B 175J, log of the *Phoenix*

7. Minto, p.246. It would seem from this letter that Barlow was among those opposed to the expedition

8. ADM 1/5411, the court-martial papers of Captain Pym contain a letter from Rowley to Bertie, 21 September 1810, that describes his thinking

9. James, p.446

10. Ibid., p.444

11. ADM 1/5411, court-martial papers, Rowley to Bertie, 21 September 1810

12. Jones, *Character and Conduct of Captain Corbet Vindicated*

13. ADM 1/63, Bertie to Coker, 13 October 1810

14. ADM 1/5411, court-martial papers, Rowley to Bertie, 21 September 1810

15. L/PS/9/2A, Farquhar to the Earl of Liverpool, 30 August 1810, British Library (APAC)

16. ADM 1/63, Bertie to Coker, 13 October 1810

17. Hall, p.332

18. ADM 1/5411, Rowley to Bertie, 21 September 1810

19. Ibid., Gordon to Bertie, 22 September 1810

20. Ibid., Rowley to Bertie, 21 September 1810

21. ADM 51/2176, log of the *Boadicea*

22. Ibid. The ship's log gives a more detailed account of the action than Rowley's report to Bertie of 21 September

23. Ibid.

24. James, p.442

25. ADM 1/5411, Rowley to Bertie, 21 September 1810

26. L/MAR/B 175J, log of the *Phoenix*, 30 September 1810

27. IOR/G/9/2, Pringle to William Ramsden, 26 September 1810

28. L/PS/9/2A, Farquhar to the Earl of Liverpool, 11 October 1810, British Library (APAC)

29. ADM 1/63, Bertie to Croker, 13 September 1810

30. L/MAR/B, log of the *Preston*

31. Parkinson, *War in the Eastern Seas*, p.399

32. Ibid., quoted on p.402

33. Ibid., p.399

34. L/MAR/B 141Q, log of the *Northumberland*

35. *Le Combat du Grand Port 1810*, thesis by Lieutenant de Vaisseau Roussel, École de Guerre Naval, 1927–8

36. Quoted in Parkinson, *War in the Eastern Seas*, p.407

37. This is an estimate based on the deaths recorded on the Indiamen

38. Quoted in Parkinson, *War in the Eastern Seas*, p.407
39. The terms in full are given in Austen, pp.216–17
40. ADM 1/63, Bertie to Croker, 6 December 1810
41. Mason, pp.70–1
42. Quoted in Austen, p.215
43. The proceedings of all four courts martial are in ADM 1/5411
44. Roger, p.567
45. Flinders Electronic Archive, Letter to Pitot, 1 December 1812
46. Parkinson, *Trade in the Eastern Seas*, p.84

Epilogue

1. Hall, p.337
2. The proceedings of the divorce are contained in MSS Eur F176/36 of the Barlow papers
3. *The Times*, Letters to the Editor, 6 and 12 October, 1830
4. Quote in Parkinson, *Pellew*, p.472
5. Ibid., pp.440–1
6. MSS Eur F176/48, Barlow papers, Pellew to Barlow, 14 January 1820
7. Ibid.

Bibliography

Manuscript Sources

The Asia, Pacific and Africa Collection (APAC), British Library, London: Repository for papers relating to the East India Company including the Marine Department Records. Any study of the East Indiamen will start from Anthony Farrington's *Catalogue of the East India Ships' Journals and Logs, 1600–1834*, and the same author's *Biographical Index of East India Company Maritime Service Officers 1600–1834*. The main collections used in this volume are:

    The L/MAR/B series – logs of the East Indiamen, ledgers and paybooks
    Barlow papers, MSS Eur F176
    Munro papers, MSS Eur F151
    Gwillim/Symonds papers, MSS Eur C240

The National Archives, Kew: Holds all Admiralty papers – ships' logbooks, court-martial papers, paybooks, letters from Commanders-in-Chief, East Indies and Cape

The Mitchell Library at the State Library of New South Wales, Sydney: This archive has provided online the private papers of Captain Matthew Flinders, including his Journal and Letters. See Matthew Flinders Electronic Archive

The William L. Clements Library at the University of Michigan: Contains John Tapson's *Journal 1806–14* for the voyage of the *Africaine*

University of Nottingham, Department of Manuscripts and Special Collections: Holds some of the personal papers of Sir Nesbit Willoughby

Pamphlets and theses

Caird Library, National Maritime Museum: contains a copy of the extremely rare pamphlet of 1839 by Jenkin Jones, *Character and Conduct of the Late Captain Corbet Vindicated*

Bibliothèque centrale du Département Marine à Vincennes. Service Historique de la Défense: *Le Combat du Grand Port 1810*, thesis by Lieutenant de Vaisseau Roussel, École de Guerre Naval, 1927–8

Contemporary published works

Buchan, George, *Practical Illustrations of a Particular Providence: With Observations Applicable to Different Classes of Society*, Edinburgh, 1829

Duncan, Archibald (ed.), *The Mariner's Chronicle*, Vol 1; reprint of early nineteenth-century edition, London, 2004

Eastwick, Robert (ed. Herbert Compton), *A Master Mariner: Being the Life and Adventures of Captain Robert William Eastwick*, London, 1841

Elers, George (ed. Lord Monson and George Leveson Gower), *The Memoirs of George Elers, Captain in 1st Regt of Foot (1777–1842)*, London, 1903

Fay, Eliza, *Original Letters from India, 1779–1815*, London, 1925 (reprint of 1817 edition)

Flinders, Matthew, *A Voyage to Terra Australis*, two volumes, London, 1814

Graham, Maria, *Journal of a Residence in India*, London, 1812

Hall, Captain Basil, *Fragments of Voyages and Travels*, 2nd Series, Vol 3, Edinburgh, 1832

Harris Nicolas, Sir Nicholas (ed.), *The Dispatches and Letters of Vice-Admiral Lord Viscount Nelson*, Vol vi, London, 1846

Hickey, William (ed. Alfred Spencer), *The Memoirs of William Hickey*, four vols, London, 1919

James, William, *The Naval History of Great Britain*, Vol 5, London, 1886

Jones, Captain Jenkin, *Character and Conduct of the Late Captain Corbet Vindicated*, privately published pamphlet, London, 1839

Kaye, John William, *The Life and Correspondence of Maj-Gen Sir John Malcolm*, two vols, London, 1856

Kirby, Major Charles, *The Adventures of an Arcot Rupee*, three vols, London, 1867

Laughton, John Knox (ed.), *The Naval Miscellany*, Vol 1, Navy Records Society, 1902

Macaulay, Thomas, *Essay on Warren Hastings*, London, 1923

Minto, Countess of (ed.), *Lord Minto in India: Life and Letters of Gilbert Elliott 1st Earl of Minto, 1807–14*, London, 1880

Nagle, Jacob (ed. John C. Dann), *The Nagle Journal: A Diary of the Life of Jacob Nagle, Sailor, from 1775 to 1841*, New York, 1988

Owen, Sidney J.(ed.), *A Selection from the Despatches, Treaties and other Papers of the Marquess Wellesley*, Oxford, 1878

Scott, Ernest, *The Life of Matthew Flinders*, Sydney, 1914

Sherwood, Mrs (ed. F. Harvey-Darton), *The Life and Times of Mrs Sherwood 1775–1851*, London, 1910

Wathen, James, *Journal of a Voyage in 1811 and 1812 to Madras and China*, London, 1814

Other works

Addison, John and Hazareesingh, K., *A New History of Mauritius*, London, 1984

Austen, H.C.M., *Fights and Corsairs of the Indian Ocean*, Mauritius, 2001 (reprint of 1935 edition)

Bowen, H.V., Lincoln, M. and Rigy, N. (eds), *The Worlds of the East India Company*, Suffolk, 2002

Brendon, Vyvyen, *Children of the Raj*, London, 2005

Cardew, Sir Alexander, *The White Mutiny: A Forgotten Episode in the History of the Indian Army*, London, 1929

Cordingley, David, *Heroines and Harlots: Women at Sea in the Great Age of Sail*, London, 2002

Cotton, Sir Evan, *East Indiamen: The East India Company's Maritime Service*, London, 1949

Dalrymple, William, *White Mughals: Love and Betrayal in Eighteenth-Century India*, London, 2002

Davison Love, Henry, *Vestiges of Old Madras, 1640–1800*, London, 1913

Dodwell, Henry, *The Nabobs of Madras*, London, 1926

Gardiner, Robert, *Frigates of the Napoleonic Wars*, London, 2006

Gupta, Maya, *Lord William Bentinck in Madras and the Vellore Mutiny, 1803–7*, Delhi, 1986

Harland, John, *Seamanship in the Age of Sail*, London, 1984

Hayter, Alethea, *The Wreck of the* Abergavenny: *The Wordsworths and Catastrophe*, London, 2002

Holmes, Richard, *Sahib: The British Soldier in India*, London, 2005

Hood, Jean, *Marked for Misfortune: An Epic Tale of Shipwreck, Human Endeavour and Survival in the Age of Sail*, London, 2003

Junger, Sebastian, *The Perfect Storm*, London, 1997.

Keay, John, *The Honourable Company: A History of the East India Company*, London, 1993

Keble Chatterton, E., *The Old East Indiamen*, London, 1970 (reprint of 1933 edition)

Kincaid, Dennis, *British Social Life in India, 1608–1937*, London, 1938

King, Dean, *A Sea of Words, a Lexicon and Companion for Patrick O'Brian's Seafaring Tales*, New York, 1995

Lawson, Sir Charles, *Memories of Madras*, London, 1905

Lawson, Philip, *The East India Company: A History*, London, 1993

Longford, Elizabeth, *Wellington: The Years of the Sword*, London, 1969

MacGregor, David R., *Merchant Sailing Ships 1775–1815*, Watford, 1980

Mason, Michael, *Willoughby the Immortal*, Oxford, 1969

Miller, Nathan, *Broadsides: The Age of Fighting Sail*, New York, 2000

Miller, Russell, *The East Indiamen*, Alexandria, Virginia, 1980

Morris, Henry, *The Life of Charles Grant*, London, 1904

Neale, Jonathan, *The Cutlass and the Lash: Mutiny and Discipline in Nelson's Navy*, London, 1985

Nicolson, Adam, *Men of Honour: Trafalgar and the Making of the English Hero*, London, 2005

Padfield, Peter, *Maritime Power and the Struggle for Freedom, 1788–1851*, London, 2003

Parkinson, C., Northcote, *Edward Pellew*, London, 1934

Parkinson, C., Northcote, *Trade in the Eastern Seas, 1793–1813*, London, 1966 (reprint of 1937 edition)

Parkinson, C., Northcote, *War in the Eastern Seas, 1793–1815*, London, 1954

Penny, F.E., *Fort St George Madras*, London, 1900

Penny, F.E., *On the Coromandel Coast*, London, 1908

Philips, C.H., *The East India Company 1784–1834*, Manchester, 1940

Roger, N.A.M., *The Command of the Ocean: A Naval History of Britain, 1649–1815*, London, 2004

Scarr, Deryck, *Slaving and Slavery in the Indian Ocean*, London, 1998

Sutton, Jean, *Lords of the East: The East India Company and its Ships (1600–1874)*, London, 2000

Taylor, Stephen, *The Caliban Shore: The Fate of the Grosvenor Castaways*, London, 2004

Toll, Ian W., *Six Frigates: The Epic History of the Founding of the US Navy*, New York, 2006

Toussaint, Auguste, *Port Louis: A Tropical City*, London, 1973

Venning, Annabel, *Following the Drum: The Lives of Army Wives and Daughters*, London, 2005

Watson, J. Steven, *The Reign of George III, 1760–1815*, Oxford, 1960

Wild, Antony, *The East India Company: Trade and Conquest from 1600*, London, 2000

Wilkinson, Theon, *Two Monsoons: The Life and Death of Europeans in India*, London, 1987

Woodman, Richard, *The Sea Warriors: Fighting Captains and Frigate Warfare in the Age of Nelson*, London, 2001

Woodman, Richard, *A Brief History of Mutiny*, London, 2005

Worden, Nigel, van Heyningen, Elizabeth and Bickford-Smith, Vivian, *Cape Town: The Making of a City*, Cape Town, 1998

Zomoyski, Adam, *1812 – Napoleon's Fatal March on Moscow*, London, 2004

Acknowledgements

I found the seed of this book in William Hickey's four-volume eighteenth-century memoir, over the closing pages in which the old rake, nearing the end of his life, reflected on the loss of many old friends in the Second Fleet. Having just completed a narrative about another Indiaman disaster, I did not immediately pursue the subject, but in wider reading about the Indian Ocean was repeatedly brought back to the hurricanes of 1808/9. Although there was no existing account covering these events and their aftermath, it was clear that the storms had ushered in an era of dramatic change.

While finding myself fascinated by the seafaring world, I must confess to being a novice in a subject in which eagle-eyed experts abound. A seven-day voyage on a vessel of the Sail Training Association is scant preparation for venturing into such tricky waters and, both for simplicity's sake and in order to avoid embarrassment, I have tried to steer clear of sailing terminology that might challenge a reader with similar limitations, and to keep to what I know. I may not always have been successful.

For assistance in navigating my way to crucial documents I must thank Hedley Sutton and the staff of the British Library's Asia, Pacific and Africa Collection, and Bruno Pappalardo at the National Archives in Kew for help with the Admiralty records. Janet Bloom of the William L. Clements Library in Michigan directed me to John Tapson's *Journal*, and valuable research was carried out in France on my behalf by Monique Desthuis-Francis. Anthony Barlow sent me additional information on his ancestor, Sir George Barlow, and the Lord Middleton provided the portrait of Sir

Nesbit Willoughby. Anna Tietze in Cape Town enabled me to trace the portrait of General Hay Macdowall. For advice in their fields I am grateful to Jean Sutton, Jean Hood and Andrea Cordiani.

Julian Loose at Faber & Faber and Starling Lawrence at W.W. Norton are creative as well as stimulating editors whose suggestions have hugely improved this book. My sincere thanks go to them, as well as to Henry Volans and Lucie Ewin at Faber, and Caroline Dawnay, my ever-encouraging agent.

Friends gave generously of their time and knowledge to read the manuscript. Two experienced sailors, Keith Rossiter and Lawrence Balfe, offered insights that saved me from errors. My old friend Tom Fort went through it, twice, with his habitual care and good sense, as did my best friend, my wife Caroline. The person who has always been closest to this book, however, from a ramble on the old Pellew estate at Canonteign to our dizzying time in the yards of a square-rigger and a heart-stopping dawn as we passed over the waters off Cape Trafalgar, who read my work and constantly tested me in getting to the heart of the matter, is my beloved son Wil. This book is for him.

Index